Student Engagement in Higher Education

Student Engagement in Higher Education fills a longstanding void in the higher education and student affairs literature. In the fully revised and updated edition of this important volume, the editors and chapter contributors explore how diverse populations of students experience college differently and encounter group-specific barriers to success. Informed by relevant theories, each chapter focuses on engaging a different student population, including: low-income students, students of color, international students, students with disabilities, LGBT students, religious minority students, student-athletes, homeless students, transfer students, commuter and part-time students, adult learners, student veterans, and graduate students. The forward-thinking, practical strategies offered throughout the book are based on research and the collected professional wisdom of experienced educators and scholars at two-year and four-year institutions of higher education. Current and future faculty, administrators, and student affairs staff will undoubtedly find this book complete with fresh ideas to reverse troubling engagement trends among various college student populations.

Stephen John Quaye is on the faculty in the Student Affairs in Higher Education Program at Miami University.

Shaun R. Harper is on the faculty in the Graduate School of Education and Executive Director of the Center for the Study of Race and Equity in Education at the University of Pennsylvania.

Student Engagement in Higher Education

Theoretical Perspectives and Practical Approaches for Diverse Populations

Second Edition

EDITED BY
STEPHEN JOHN QUAYE AND SHAUN R. HARPER
FOREWORD BY GEORGE D. KUH

Routledge
Taylor & Francis Group

NEW YORK AND LONDON

Second edition published 2015
by Routledge
711 Third Avenue, New York, NY 10017

and by Routledge
2 Park Square, Milton Park, Abingdon, Oxon OX14 4RN

Routledge is an imprint of the Taylor & Francis Group, an informa business

© 2015 Taylor & Francis

First edition published by Routledge 2009.

Library of Congress Cataloging-in-Publication Data

    Student engagement in higher education : theoretical perspectives and practical approaches for diverse populations / edited by Stephen John Quaye, Shaun R. Harper. — Second edition.
      pages cm
    Includes bibliographical references and index.
  1. Student affairs services—United States. 2. Student activities—United States. 3. College students—Services for—United States. 4. Muticultural education—United States/ I. Quaye, Stephen John, 1980– II. Harper, Shaun R., 1975–
LB2342.92.S78   2014
378.1'97—dc23   2013047552

ISBN: 978-0-415-89509-5 (hbk)
ISBN: 978-0-415-89510-1 (pbk)
ISBN: 978-0-203-81016-3 (ebk)

Typeset in Minion
by Apex CoVantage, LLC

We dedicate the second edition of this book to postsecondary educators who take seriously the responsibility of equitably engaging every student at their institutions.

Contents

Foreword

George D. Kuh

Stephen John Quaye, Shaun R. Harper, and the chapter authors have synthesized the best theory and research about today's diverse college students with an eye toward what colleges and universities should do to enhance their success represented by persistence and graduation rates and learning and personal development outcomes. The warrant for examining and understanding the experiences of different groups of historically underrepresented students is research-based. Based on their cogent, massive synthesis of thousands of studies of college student learning and development, Pascarella and Terenzini (2005) concluded that while the impact of college is generally positive for all students, the largest effects are conditional. That is, some groups of students tend to benefit more than their peers from certain collegiate experiences. For example, National Survey of Student Engagement (NSSE) data show that women, full-time enrolled students, those who live on campus, and those who start at and graduate from the same institution tend to be more engaged than their counterparts. Less well documented, and the focus of this book, is what students with various immutable characteristics may need from the institution to take full advantage of their institution's educational resources.

In the opening chapter, Harper and Quaye make it plain that institutional policies, practices, and learning environments can encourage and support, or discourage and hinder students in achieving their educational objectives. A key factor is the institution's philosophy about who is responsible for student learning and success—the individual student or the institution—and how this philosophy is enacted. Through the middle of the 20th century, the dominant approach at the vast majority of colleges and universities was Darwinist; that is, the students who deserved to succeed were those who could figure out on their own how to adjust to and find their way through the institution. In the 1970s, the campus ecology movement emerged, and its apostles (see Strange & Banning, 2001) argued that it was no longer sufficient or educationally sound to think of the institution as a one-size-fits-all shoe into which students must "fit" or squeeze into. Rather, colleges and universities had a moral, ethical, and educational obligation to modify their policies and practices in ways that were academically challenging and socially supportive of students—especially those from historically underrepresented groups.

It is worth emphasizing that such institutional accommodations were not intended to dilute academic rigor and lower performance expectations. Indeed, the goal was the converse; responding to students' needs was essential in order to push *all students* to attain at high levels while at the same time supporting them so that they could attain their educational goals and benefit in desired ways. Today, this proposition is widely (though not universally) espoused and endorsed, but not always enacted as is evident by among other things the disparities in persistence and graduation rates of students from historically underrepresented groups. More than a few students continue to report being alienated and rebuffed as they attempt to navigate campus settings that they perceive privilege some groups over others. To make the proper student-centered adjustments in policies and practices, a school must first understand who its students are, what they are prepared to do academically, and what they expect of the institution and themselves (Kuh, Kinzie, Buckley, Bridges, & Hayek, 2007), which is, of course, the purpose of this volume.

One concrete step a college or university can take is to periodically audit its policies and practices to insure they are working in the mutual interests of all students and the institution, as recommended by Ozaki and Renn in this book (see also Kuh, Schuh, Whitt & Associates, 1991; Kuh, Kinzie, Schuh, Whitt & Associates, 2005a/2010). But it is also essential that faculty, staff, and students be aware of and agree on the intended outcomes (such as persistence or academic achievement) and to monitor intermediate outcomes that are early predictors of success in college, such as satisfaction and course completion rates disaggregated by various student characteristics (Kuh et al., 2007). One of the most important of these early predictors is goal realization or the ability of a student to express in his or her own words what they want to and are getting out of attending college.

Three implications flow from goal realization as a state of mind that are especially important to student success in the early weeks and months of study. The first is that a student be able to explain in plain language in one's own voice "why I am here," not simply repeat what they have been told or heard ("My parents always told me I was going to college and here I am"). Second, the explanation cannot be vacuous ("I don't have any other place to be right now"), but personally relevant and meaningful ("I cannot imagine a better place for me at this time"). Third, goal realization as an early college predictor of success is concrete, to the extent that one can articulate the importance of what they are doing and its value in the present or longer term ("I feel I am doing something worthwhile and learning things that I can use now and other things I am sure will be important to me later").

Goal realization is more than just a facile social science phrase. The inability to articulate and devote effort toward meaningful ends during college explains in part why many students leave school even though they are in good academic standing and financially able to continue (though some students surely point to accumulating debt as problematic, which is exacerbated by seeing little personal benefit by staying in school). Goal realization takes on added importance in the first few academic terms when the majority of students are taking introductory courses that meet general education and other requirements too often delivered via a passive lecture format. It is no surprise that many students—probably the majority—see little connection between their classes and matters of practical relevance to their personal lives.

The connection challenge is further compounded for traditional-age students who are in the dualistic stage of intellectual and cognitive development, which makes it difficult to integrate, synthesize, and apply what they are learning in different courses to other aspects of their lives. The result is that many students who are not involved in a personally meaningful way with some other aspect of the institution—a social or academic organization, athletics, music or drama, student publications, campus employment, and so forth—are less satisfied and struggle to make sense of the experience, all of which makes leaving the institution a more viable option than anything else they can imagine. And when students do not find others like them to connect with—a hospitable, affirming peer affinity group and supportive, encouraging mentors or sponsors—the most attractive option is to return home (Kuh 2007).

An especially promising target of opportunity for promoting goal realization for many students is employment both on and off campus. As I have explained elsewhere (Kuh, 2010a, 2010b), the workplace is a potentially rich venue where students can see how what they are learning in their classes can be used on the job, and vice versa. With a little preparation, as can be seen from the experience at the University of Iowa (Kuh, 2010b), staff and faculty can structure discussions with students that encourage and teach them how to think about their thinking and begin to see college classes that seem abstract and remote can have practical significance in the life outside the classroom. Given that upwards of three-quarters of undergraduates work at some point in the college years, making work more educationally purposeful may well be one of the most effective levers we can pull to enhance student success.

Another noteworthy finding from the engagement research during the last decade is that participating in certain activities appears to be linked to a variety of positive effects, including persistence. These activities, all empirically supported to varying degrees, are called high-impact practices (HIPs) because undergraduate students who do them score much higher than their peers who have not had such experiences on such NSSE engagement measures as academic challenge, active and collaborative learning, student-faculty interaction, and supportive campus environment. This is because HIPs induce students to among other things invest substantial time and energy to educationally purposeful tasks, interact frequently with their teachers and peers, get feedback often, and apply what they are learning (Kuh, 2008). I am also persuaded that doing one of these activities will contribute to goal realization, as mentioned earlier.

In addition, students who have done at least one HIP report more frequent deep learning behaviors and benefit to a greater degree on various self-reported outcomes, such as personal-social development and practical competencies (Kuh, 2008). A review of the literature lends additional support to these promising findings (Brownell & Swaner, 2010), as do results from the ongoing Wabash National Study (Blaich, 2009). More recently, analysis of the college experiences of students from different racial and ethnic backgrounds who participate in one or more HIPs shows that they are more likely to complete a baccalaureate degree. At California State University-Northridge (a Hispanic-serving institution), only about 38% of Latino students who did not do a HIP finished in six years. But almost half (48%) of their peers who did one HIP completed their degree in six years. The completion rate for students who did two HIPs was 65%. CSU Northridge students who are not Latino show a similar positive pattern of effects. These findings have prompted discussions among faculty and staff across the CSU system campuses and at other colleges and universities about how to encourage more students to do one or more of these kinds of activities.

So, as with other engagement practices, all students benefit from HIPs. However, certain groups are less likely to participate in them, including first-generation students, students of color, part-time students, older students, and transfer students. We can speculate why this is, but a clear implication is that those who advise students prior to and after they matriculate must ask students during every contact *when* (not if) they are going to do one of them. Institutional leaders must do their part by insuring that enough of these opportunities are available to meet the demand and are implemented at a level of quality that will, indeed, deliver the positive outcomes mentioned earlier.

Certainly more college experiences can be or are high impact in addition to the ten on the list promulgated by the Association of American Colleges and Universities (2011). Some of the more likely candidates are writing for campus publications, performing in musical or theater productions, participating in intercollegiate athletics, and leading campus organizations. Indeed, there seems to be a small explosion of applying the high impact label to programs and practices in which faculty and staff have a vested interest. Far too few so far have the weight of empirical evidence to bolster such claims. Some programs will meet the evidence test, but in all instances we need to be more circumspect about declaring victory and labeling an activity "high impact" until we have data to support the claim.

So, do we need another book on student engagement? Well, we do not need just any book, but we certainly need this one because finding ways to engage students from historically underrepresented groups must be one of the academy's highest priorities going forward. The contributors to this volume have done a great service by pointing to actions colleges and universities can take consistent with this goal, which is in the national interest as well as that of individual students. We are in their debt for helping us better understand and appreciate the rich diversity of student backgrounds and experiences that characterize college and university campuses today and what institutions can do to promote the success of all their students.

References

Association of American Colleges and Universities. (2011). *The LEAP vision for learning: Outcomes, practices, impact, and employers' views.* Washington, DC: Association of American Colleges and Universities.

Blaich, C. F. (2009, May/June). *High-impact practices and experiences from the Wabash National Study.* Closing plenary address to the AAC&U Institute on General Education and Assessment, Minneapolis, MN.

Brownell, J. E., & Swaner, L. E. (2010). *High-impact educational practices: Do they live up to their name?* Washington, DC: Association of American Colleges and Universities.

Kuh, G. D. (2007). How to help students achieve. *The Chronicle of Higher Education, 53*(41), B12–13.

Kuh, G. D. (2008). *High-impact educational practices: What they are, who has access to them, and why they matter.* Washington, DC: Association of American Colleges and Universities.

Kuh, G. D. (2010a). Foreword: High-impact practices: Retrospective and prospective. In J. E Brownell & L. E. Swaner (Eds.), *High-impact educational practices: Do they live up to their name?* Washington, DC: Association of American Colleges and Universities.

Kuh, G. D. (2010b, November 21). Maybe experience really can be the best teacher. *The Chronicle of Higher Education.* http://chronicle.com/article/Maybe-Experience-Really-Can-Be/125433/?sid=cr&utm_source=cr&utm_medium=en

Kuh, G. D., Schuh, J. H., Whitt, E. J., & Associates (1991). *Involving colleges: Successful approaches to fostering student learning and personal development outside the classroom.* San Francisco, CA: Jossey-Bass.

Kuh, G. D., Kinzie, J., Schuh, J. H., Whitt, E. J., & Associates (2005a/2010). *Student success in college: Creating conditions that matter.* San Francisco, CA: Jossey-Bass.

Kuh, G. D., Kinzie, J., Schuh, J. H., & Whitt, E. J. (2005b). *Assessing conditions to enhance educational effectiveness: The Inventory for Student Engagement and Success.* San Francisco, CA: Jossey-Bass.

Kuh, G. D., Kinzie, J., Buckley, J. A., Bridges, B. K., & Hayek, J. C. (2007). *Piecing together the student success puzzle: Research, propositions, and recommendations.* ASHE Higher Education Report, *32*(5). San Francisco, CA: Jossey-Bass.

Pascarella, E. T., & Terenzini, P. T. (2005). *How college affects students, Volume 2: A third decade of research.* San Francisco, CA: Jossey-Bass.

Strange, C. C., & Banning, J. H. (2001). *Educating by design: Creating campus learning environments that work.* San Francisco, CA: Jossey-Bass.

Acknowledgments

We salute the thoughtful educators and administrators who will use this book to guide bold, imaginative institutional efforts to engage diverse student populations—those who will do the authentic work of aligning espoused values concerning equity, diversity, and inclusiveness with the deliberate actions necessary to actualize those ideals.

A book of this magnitude does not come to fruition without the support of family, friends, and mentors. First, we owe an enormous amount of gratitude to Brenda R. Quaye and Sebastian James Quaye, Stephen's partner and son, respectively, as well as Shawn K. Hill, Shaun's partner, for their unwavering encouragement and love throughout the completion of this book. We also thank Heather Jarrow, an Editor at Routledge, for her guidance, patience, and support throughout working on this book.

We also extend gratitude to the 40 authors in this book for their wisdom, vision, and insights on how to engage diverse populations of students, as well as the Consortium on High Achievement and Success for their commitment to helping students achieve and succeed. Finally, we acknowledge mentors and supporters who have shaped our perspectives about engagement—Marcia Baxter Magolda, Peter M. Magolda, George D. Kuh, Estela Mara Bensimon, Theresa A. Powell, Barbara Henley, Andrew C. Porter, and Kevin Kruger.

Stephen John Quaye
Miami University

Shaun R. Harper
University of Pennsylvania

Chapter 1

Making Engagement Equitable for Students in U.S. Higher Education

Shaun R. Harper and Stephen John Quaye

As American higher education continues to become increasingly diverse, so too will the needs of and challenges faced by our students. It is possible that creating engaging campus environments was easy when the overwhelming majority of students was male, heterosexual, Christian, and economically affluent. That is, at some point in history, responding to the needs of students in the same ways likely produced similar results. Perhaps staff in the student activities office, for example, had it easier when one set of programs was appealing to all students. Or maybe professors were able to plan more efficiently when there were fewer cultural perspectives to consider in readings, curricular development, and class discussions.

A dependency on sameness is no longer appropriate, as contemporary cohorts of students at colleges and universities are different; the ways they experience and respond to their campuses vary. Thus, faculty and student affairs educators must be strategic and intentional about fostering conditions that compel students to make the most of college, both inside and outside the classroom. In their 1991 book, *Involving Colleges: Successful Approaches to Fostering Student Learning and Development Outside the Classroom*, George D. Kuh and colleagues concluded:

> *Involving Colleges* are committed to pluralism in all its forms, and they support the establishment and coexistence of subcommunities that permit students to identify with and receive support from people like themselves, so they can feel comfortable in becoming involved in the larger campus community. (p. 369)

This declaration and subsequent related perspectives guided the conceptualization and writing of the first edition of our book and is the same motivation from which we draw for the second edition. Although we differentiate involvement from engagement later in this chapter, transforming today's campuses into *Involving Colleges* for all students is very much the vision with which this work was undertaken.

In this volume, we amplify the specific challenges faced by diverse populations on college campuses and offer guidance for accepting institutional responsibility for the engagement of students. We trust that readers will be moved to respond with deliberation through conversations, collaborative planning, programs, services, curricular enhancements, and assessment. A cursory scan of the table of contents will confirm that this book is not exclusively about "minority students." Instead, authors focus on a range of populations for whom the published research confirms that engagement, belongingness, and connectivity to the college experience are in various ways problematic. Emphasis is also placed on enhancing outcomes and development among different populations, such as women and men and trans* and veteran students.

The practical implications presented at the end of each chapter are in response to issues noted in the literature, informed by relevant theories, and based on the collective professional wisdom of those who have written. The authors bring to this book several years of full-time work experience in various capacities (faculty, student affairs educators, academic affairs administrators, etc.) at a wide range of two-year and four-year institutions of higher education. Indeed, they are experts in the field who have taken an intricate look at the various populations represented in this book and have devoted a large part of their careers to understanding the needs of these students. Notwithstanding, we neither claim to furnish all the answers or contend that this book contains prescriptive solutions for all engagement problems facing every student population. Instead, experienced educators and scholars have collaborated to produce a resource for the field of higher education and the student affairs profession that will hopefully ignite dialogue, agency, and strategic thinking and action on behalf of undergraduates who are known to typically miss out on the full range of benefits that educationally purposeful engagement affords.

The remainder of this chapter sets the stage for the population-specific chapters that follow. We begin by making clear what we mean by "student engagement" and synthesizing what decades of empirical research contend about the associated gains, educational benefits, and outcomes. Next, the importance of shifting the onus for engagement from students to educators and administrators is discussed as we advocate strategy, intentionality, and reflective action. The role of theory in this book and in engagement practice is then justified. The chapter concludes with a plea for seriousness about aligning espoused values for diversity with institutional actions—we urge an abandonment of empty buzzwords related to multiculturalism on college and university campuses.

Understanding the Nature and Importance of Engagement

Student engagement is simply characterized as participation in educationally effective practices, both inside and outside the classroom, which leads to a range of measurable outcomes. This operational definition is borrowed from Kuh, Kinzie, Buckley, Bridges, and Hayek (2007), who also note:

> Student engagement represents two critical features. The first is the amount of time and effort students put into their studies and other educationally purposeful activities . . . The second component of student engagement is

how the institution deploys its resources and organizes the curriculum, other learning opportunities, and support services to induce students to participate in activities that lead to the experiences and desired outcomes such as persistence, satisfaction, learning, and graduation. (p. 44)

We are persuaded by a large volume of empirical evidence that confirms strategizing ways to increase the engagement of various student populations, especially those for whom engagement is known to be problematic, is a worthwhile endeavor. The gains and outcomes are too robust to leave to chance, and social justice is unlikely to ensue if some students come to enjoy the beneficial byproducts of engagement but others do not.

Engagement and Student Outcomes

"The impact of college is largely determined by individual effort and involvement in the academic, interpersonal, and extracurricular offerings on a campus" (Pascarella & Terenzini, 2005, p. 602). Researchers have found that educationally purposeful engagement leads to the production of gains, benefits, and outcomes in the following domains: cognitive and intellectual skill development (Anaya, 1996; Baxter Magolda, 1992); college adjustment (Cabrera, Nora, Terenzini, Pascarella, & Hagedorn, 1999; Kuh, Palmer, & Kish, 2003); moral and ethical development (Evans, 1987; Rest 1993); practical competence and skills transferability (Kuh, 1993, 1995); the accrual of social capital (Harper, 2008); and psychosocial development, productive racial and gender identity formation, and positive images of self (Evans, Forney, & Guido-DiBrito, 1998; Harper & Quaye, 2007; Torres, Howard-Hamilton, & Cooper, 2003). In addition, Tross, Harper, Osher, and Kneidinger (2001) found that students who devote more time to academic preparation activities outside of class earn higher grade point averages. While all these benefits are important, the nexus between engagement and persistence has garnered the most attention.

Engagement and Persistence

As noted in the first edition of this book (and elsewhere), differences in first-to-second year persistence, as well as in four-year and six-year graduation rates, continually disadvantage many students of color, undergraduate men, lower-income students, first generation college goers, undergraduates who commute to their campuses, and a handful of other student populations. While the reasons for student persistence through degree attainment are multifaceted and not easily attributed to a narrow set of explanatory factors (Braxton, Hirschy, & McClendon, 2004), we know one point for certain: Those who are actively engaged in educationally purposeful activities, both inside and outside the classroom, are more likely to persist through graduation. This assertion has been empirically proven and consistently documented by numerous higher education researchers (e.g., Astin, 1975, 1993; Bean, 1990, 2005; Berger & Milem, 1999; Braxton, Milem, & Sullivan, 2000; Bridges, Cambridge, Kuh, & Leegwater, 2005; Milem & Berger, 1997; Pascarella & Terenzini, 2005; Peltier, Laden, & Matranga, 1999; Stage & Hossler, 2000; Tinto, 1993, 2000, 2005).

Vincent Tinto, the most frequently cited scholar on college student retention, contends that engagement (or "academic and social integration," as he has called it) is positively related to persistence. In fact, his research shows that engagement is the single most significant predictor of persistence (Tinto, 2000). He notes that many students discontinue their undergraduate education because they feel disconnected from peers, professors, and administrators at the institution. "Leavers of this type express a sense of not having made any significant contacts or not feeling membership in the institution" (Tinto, 2000, p. 7). In his 1993 book, *Leaving College: The Causes and Cures of Student Attrition*, Tinto argues that high levels of integration into academic and social communities on campus lead to higher levels of institutional commitment, which in turn compels a student to persist.

Similarly, Bean (1990, 2005) proposes that students leave when they are marginally committed to their institutions. Institutional commitment is strengthened when undergraduates are actively engaged in educationally purposeful endeavors that connect them to the campus and in which they feel some sense of enduring obligation and responsibility (Bean, 2005; Swail, Redd, & Perna, 2003; Tinto, 1993). Those who hold leadership positions in student organizations, for example, assume responsibilities in their groups and know that others depend on them for service, guidance, and follow-through on important initiatives. Thus, they feel committed to their respective organizations and the institution at large, and are less likely to leave than students who are not engaged. The same could be applied to a student who feels like an important contributor to learning and discussions in her or his classes. While the relationships between engagement, student outcomes, and retention are powerful, it is important to acknowledge the conditions under which these are likely to occur.

Distinguishing Educationally Purposeful Engagement

Thirty years ago, Alexander W. Astin defined student involvement as "the amount of physical and psychological energy that the student devotes to the academic experience" (1984, p. 297). Astin's conceptualization of involvement refers to behaviors and what students actually do, instead of what they think, how they feel, and the meanings they make of their experiences. His theory of student involvement is principally concerned with how college students spend their time and how various institutional actors, processes, and opportunities facilitate development. "The extent to which students can achieve particular developmental goals is a direct function of the time and effort they devote to activities designed to produce these gains" (p. 301). This theory is among the most frequently cited in the higher education literature.

While conceptually similar, there is a key qualitative difference between involvement and engagement: it is entirely possible to be involved in something without being engaged. For example, a student who is present and on time for every weekly meeting of an organization but sits passively in the back of the room, never offers an opinion or volunteers for committees, interacts infrequently with the group's advisor or fellow members outside of weekly meetings, and would not dare consider running for an office could still legitimately claim that she is involved in the group. However, few would argue this student is actively engaged, as outcomes accrual is likely to be limited. The same could be said for the student who is involved in a study group for his psychology class, but contributes little and asks few questions when the group meets for study sessions. Action, purpose, and cross-institutional collaboration are requisites for engagement and deep learning (Kinzie & Kuh, 2004; Kuh, Kinzie, Schuh, Whitt, & Associates, 2005; Kuh et al., 2007).

The National Survey of Student Engagement (NSSE), an instrument through which data have now been collected from approximately four million undergraduates at more than 1,500 different four-year colleges and universities since 2000, is constructed around ten engagement indicators and a set of high-impact educational practices:

Academic Challenge—Including Higher-Order Learning, Reflective and Integrative Learning, Quantitative Reasoning, and Learning Strategies.

Learning with Peers—Including Collaborative Learning and Discussions with Diverse Others.

Experiences with Faculty—Including Student–Faculty Interaction and Effective Teaching Practices.

Campus Environment—Including Quality of Interactions and Supportive Environment.

High-Impact Practices—Special undergraduate opportunities such as Service-Learning, Study Abroad, Research with Faculty, and Internships that have substantial positive effects on student learning and retention.

Student engagement in the activities associated with each NSSE indicator is considered educationally purposeful, as it leads to deep levels of learning and the production of enduring and measurable gains and outcomes (Kuh et al., 2005). This focus on student learning and outcomes creates another distinction between involvement and engagement. We offer one additional defining characteristic: the dual responsibility for engagement. In the next section, we argue that students should not be chiefly responsible for engaging themselves (as it has been proven that many do not), but instead faculty and student affairs educators must foster the conditions that enable diverse populations of students to be engaged.

Shifting the Onus for Engagement

Put simply, institutions ought not expect students to engage themselves. Kuh (2001) suggests student engagement is a measure of institutional quality. That is, the more engaged its students are in educationally purposeful activities, the better the institution. Similarly, Pascarella (2001) maintains, "An excellent undergraduate education is most likely to occur at those colleges and universities that maximize good practices and enhance students' academic and social engagement" (p. 22). Given this, we deem it essential for faculty and student affairs educators to view engaging diverse populations as "everyone's responsibility," including their own. And presidents, deans, and other senior administrators must hold themselves and everyone else on campus accountable for ensuring institutional quality in this regard. A clear signal of institutional deficiency is when there are few ramifications for those who either blatantly refuse or unintentionally neglect to enact the practices known to produce rich outcomes for students.

From Negligence to Intentionality

Quaye and Harper (2007) describe the ways in which faculty neglect to incorporate multicultural perspectives into their class discussions and assigned materials. The onus is often placed on students of color to find readings that appeal to their unique cultural interests and to bring up topics related to race in class discussions. There is little accountability for ensuring that professors are thoughtful and strategic about creating classroom experiences that enable students to learn about differences. Interactions with diverse peers inside and outside of class have been positively linked to benefits and outcomes in the following domains: self-concept (intellectual and social), cultural awareness and appreciation, racial understanding, leadership, engagement in citizenship activities, satisfaction with college, high post-baccalaureate degree aspirations, and readiness for participation in a diverse workforce (antonio et al., 2004; Chang, Astin, & Kim, 2004; Chang, Denson, Sáenz, & Misa, 2006; Gurin, Dey, Hurtado, & Gurin, 2002; Harper & antonio, 2008; Hu & Kuh, 2003; Pascarella, Edison, Nora, Hagedorn, & Terenzini, 1996; Villalpando, 2002). "Knowing that students and society could ultimately benefit from new approaches to cross-cultural learning, but failing to take the necessary steps to intentionally create enabling conditions [inside and] outside the classroom is downright irresponsible" (Harper & antonio, 2008, p. 12).

The negligence described here is partially explained by the "magical thinking" that often undergirds practices of student engagement:

> The [magical thinking] rationale provides no guidance for campuses on assembling the appropriate means to create environments conducive to realization of the benefits of diversity or on employing the methods necessary to facilitate the educational process to achieve those benefits. Under this rationale, the benefits will accrue as if by magic. (Chang, Chang, & Ledesma, 2005, pp. 10–11)

Negligence is synonymous with magical thinking; simply providing services for students is not sufficient enough to enrich their educational experiences. Rather, we defend a position of intentionality where faculty and student affairs educators are conscious of every action they undertake and are able to consider the long-range implications of decisions.

Across various campuses, race relations among students are generally poor and campuses are becoming increasingly segregated (Hurtado, Milem, Clayton-Pedersen, & Allen, 1999). Underrepresented students often report there is infrequent interaction between them and their peers in dominant groups, and that there is a lack of attention paid to improving the climate (Ancis, Sedlacek, & Mohr, 2000; Cabrera et al., 1999; Harper & Hurtado, 2007; Hurtado, 1992). When campus climates are hostile and antagonistic toward certain students, disengagement, dropping out, and maladjustment are likely unintended outcomes.

As Chang et al. (2005) and Harper and antonio (2008) note, an erroneous assumption is often made that students will naturally learn about their peers simply by coming into contact with those who share different views, experiences, and identities. For example, simply increasing the numbers of lesbian, gay, bisexual, trans*, and questioning (LGBTQ) students on campus will not automatically create more opportunities for heterosexual students to interact with them. Rather, as authors of chapters throughout this book maintain, educators must facilitate structured opportunities for these dialogues to transpire. Meaningful strategies are necessary that enable institutions to realize the benefits of engaging diverse populations. These solutions must be grounded in students' actual experiences, reflective of their unique backgrounds and interests, and designed with both broad and specific implications in mind.

The insights presented in this book are consistent with Strange and Banning's (2001) design vision for postsecondary institutions. They call for campuses that are "intentionally designed to offer opportunities, incentives, and reinforcements for growth and development" (p. 201). Such a philosophy of engagement responds to the multifaceted and complex needs of diverse populations. When an institution provides reinforcements for students, it means educators have envisioned and enacted the types of learning opportunities that will contribute to student development and engagement. This, of course, requires knowing who students are, understanding their prior knowledge and experiences, the types of educational contexts from which they have come, and what they view as necessary for enabling engagement (Harper, 2007, 2011). Devoting attention to those students who are not as engaged in educationally purposeful activities is an important way to be deliberate in one's practices.

Understanding Before Acting

Creating optimal learning environments in which all students feel connected is difficult, but nonetheless important. Educators must have the requisite skills and expertise to analyze the campus environment and determine where gaps in engagement and achievement exist. More importantly, they must resist the urge to act without considering the effects of potential solutions and instead, spend time understanding the obstacles facing disengaged students. Baxter Magolda and King (2004) suggest educators should participate in self-reflection prior to attempting to develop methods to resolve the issues confronting students. This self-reflection enables the person to contemplate how the limitations and strengths she or he possesses either facilitate or impede student engagement.

Faculty who are interested in providing avenues for students of color to be engaged in predominantly White classroom contexts might decide to incorporate readings that reflect the scholarly contributions of writers of color. On the surface, this practice seems logical and consistent with research that demonstrates the influence of culturally relevant literature on student learning (Ladson-Billings, 1995). However, what this professor might fail to consider is the reactions of White students to these readings. How might the faculty member deal with White students who believe the course is primarily focused on students of color and accuse the instructor of attempting to indoctrinate them with a politically liberal agenda? After thinking about this practice, the faculty member might still decide to proceed in the same manner, but the outcomes will be different as she or he has considered not only the needs of students of color, but also the reactions of and growth opportunities for White students in the course.

Repeatedly emphasized throughout this book is the importance of listening to students in order to understand how to enhance their educational experiences. Since September 11, 2001, several campus environments have become unsafe for and hostile toward Muslim and Arab students. Seeking to improve engagement among these students, institutional leaders might plan campus-wide programs that include cross-cultural dialogues, Arab and Muslim speakers, and panels comprised of religious minority students sharing their experiences on campus. As educators strive to determine why these hateful behaviors persist, they may gradually learn that religious minority students are not only experiencing prejudice from their peers, but also in their courses from professors. The decision to incorporate a wide array of programs aimed at students is often missing in trainings for faculty and student affairs educators on teaching about difference in all its forms. In the current example, if educators failed to ask Arab and Muslim students about their needs and developed interventions to improve their experiences based on assumptions about the issues students face, such efforts would be void of a complex understanding of the challenges confronting these students and would likely be, at best, marginally effective.

This example demonstrates the importance of analyzing problematic trends and outcomes from students' vantage points. One of the most effective ways to improve student engagement is to invite those who are the least engaged to share their knowledge and experiences (Harper, 2007, 2011). As the authors of *Learning Reconsidered* recommend: "All institutions should establish routine ways to hear students' voices, consult with them, explore their opinions, and document the nature and quality of their experience as learners" (ACPA & NASPA, 2004, p. 33). When educators speak with students from diverse backgrounds, they will begin to see patterns in their stories emerge and gain a more nuanced understanding of their needs. In addition, educators can observe the particularities in students' experiences and begin to develop customized services to improve student outcomes.

Barriers to achievement and engagement can result from making decisions without qualitative input from students (Harper, 2011, 2007). Strange and Banning (2001) discuss how a renovation project of a campus building should include insights from multiple people (including students) prior to the construction. Allowing future users of the facilities to comment on its accessibility and openness to multiple groups enables students to feel included in the decision-making process. This sense of ownership can facilitate engagement for various campus members. Some chapters in this book explore the impact of space and campus design on student engagement. For instance, providing opportunities for students with disabilities and students of color to share their opinions about the physical design of a building as well as select potential artwork for the walls, confirms that educators are taking their needs into consideration prior to proceeding. This practice will facilitate the construction of buildings that align with students' needs and interests, thereby, leading to a campus environment that is emblematic of the varied experiences, backgrounds, and perspectives of students.

In an era in which student engagement is receiving increasing attention, providing undergraduates with numerous, sustained opportunities to actively participate in determining the appropriate methods for enriching their academic and social experiences in higher education cannot be overstated. Several scholars (e.g., Baxter Magolda & King, 2004; Harper, 2007, 2011; Harper & antonio, 2008; Kuh et al., 2005, 2007; Strange & Banning, 2001) propose educational practices that are student-centered, well-planned, researched, and guided by student input and assessment data. As Freire (1970) notes, acting without reflecting on why people are oppressed can lead to further oppression. He advises that educators utilize praxis—combining reflection with action. Throughout the book, authors write in this manner and advocate inviting students into dialogues about improving their engagement.

Using Theory to Guide Practice

One of the primary premises of *Student Engagement in Higher Education* is that educators make informed decisions when they utilize relevant theories to guide practice. As such, theories related to identity development, racial/ethnic awareness, stereotypes, deconstructing Whiteness, universal design, and others are tied to the needs of the populations considered in each chapter that follows. "Theory is a framework through which interpretations and understandings are constructed. Theory is used to describe human behavior, to explain, to predict, and to generate new knowledge, [practices], and research" (McEwen, 2003, p. 166). In this book, authors use theories to frame the issues students face and to inform the strategies they propose. In essence, there is interplay between theory and practice, as theory is used to recommend tentative solutions to educational disparities, keeping in mind that those approaches should be continually assessed and revised given the learners and institutional context. Similarly, alternative theories are available as one evaluates the effectiveness of interventions intended to improve engagement.

The use of theoretical frameworks in each chapter is consistent with current student affairs expectations. In *Learning Reconsidered: A Campus-Wide Focus on the Student Experience*, student affairs educators and faculty members sought to redefine student learning in higher education and build a common knowledge base on the most pressing challenges confronting today's college students (ACPA & NASPA, 2004). A new definition of learning that integrates elements of student development and academic learning was proposed. The authors maintain that learning focuses on holism and merging students' classroom knowledge with the co-curricular activities in which they participate. The authors of *Learning Reconsidered* conclude:

> The bottom line is that student affairs preparation must be broad based, inter-disciplinary, grounded in theory, and designed to prepare forward-thinking, confident, and competent educators who will see the big picture and work effectively with other institutional agents to ensure that colleges and universities become learning communities in which students develop the skills they need to enter the rapidly changing world in which we now live. (ACPA & NASPA, 2004, p. 32)

In this statement, readers see elements of theory and practice synergistically bound. For the various populations described in our book to become engaged, they must become the focus of educators across various institutions. Furthermore, those wishing to enrich students' educational experiences must not only devise imaginative ideas for responding to engagement disparities, as the authors in this book do, but also must be informed educators who utilize theories that have received empirical support from researchers—a complementary goal of this book.

For decades, there has existed a superficial separation between faculty and student affairs educators, as the former were thought to be responsible for students' classroom learning, while the latter group focused on students' involvement in co-curricular activities (ACPA, 1994). Even though student affairs educators have sought to challenge and transform this demarcation between students' academic and personal selves, there still continues to be an expectation that professors focus on theory and research, while student affairs educators devote their time toward practice (ACPA & NASPA, 2004; Harper & antonio, 2008). Authors in *Student Engagement in Higher Education* reject this false dichotomy and show how educators in both areas are responsible for facilitating a holistic learning environment. The authors model this by using, for example, psychological, environmental, and student development theories to guide the interventions proposed at the end of each chapter. They share some ideas for how faculty and student affairs educators can build on each other's expertise to improve the educational experiences of students.

An example helps illustrate this point. Some educators endeavor to increase White students' interests and participation in race-related activities and discussions. Yet, there continues to be an overrepresentation of students from minority groups in campus programming aimed at facilitating an appreciation of differences (Saddlemire, 1996). What often happens is that students from dominant groups do not see the connection between these issues and their experiences (Broido, 2000; Jones, 2008). This book contains ideas for using theoretical perspectives pertaining to power and privilege to understand White students' unwillingness to collaborate with their peers of color to improve the campus climate. By understanding different theories, educators can take the necessary time to consider the students at their particular institutions and what research indicates about them. In addition, those who teach in classrooms can work to understand why dominant group members often resist talking about issues of difference. The use of theories can provide a foundation for campus programming and classroom-based dialogues.

We recognize that educators are often busy and must react quickly to crises that occur on campus. Decisions can still be made promptly and effectively if one keeps current with theory and reflectively strives to understand the changing needs and demographics of today's college students. Linking theory with practice is not simple; it requires a willingness to rethink one's assumptions about classroom and out-of-class learning and embrace a holistic approach to education that places students' needs at the forefront. One of the central aims of the book is to offer a wealth of examples where theoretical insights converge with practical solutions.

Beyond Buzzwords: Getting Serious about Engaging Diverse Populations

Diversity, multiculturalism, pluralism, equity and equality, inclusiveness, and social justice are among the many buzzwords used to espouse supposed institutional values. Colleges and universities use these terms liberally in mission statements, on websites, and in recruitment materials. Consequently, various groups of students show up expecting to see evidence of what they have been sold. The most obvious contradiction to these espoused values is the carelessness with which engagement is treated. Students of color and White student participants in Harper and Hurtado's (2007) study expressed extreme disappointment with the institutional rhetoric concerning diversity and inclusiveness. The misalignment of espoused and enacted institutional values must be addressed if students across various groups are to equitably accrue the full range of benefits associated with educationally purposeful engagement—there must be a greater demonstration of institutional seriousness.

"At-risk students" is perhaps one of the most unfair terms used in American education, in P-12 and higher education alike. This suggests that some students are in jeopardy of not succeeding. Our view is that students are placed at risk for dropping out of college when educators are negligent in customizing engagement efforts that connect them to the campus. While some may enter with characteristics and backgrounds that suggest they need customized services and resources, we maintain that student affairs educators and faculty should be proactive in assessing those needs and creating the environmental conditions that would enable such students to thrive. They are placed at risk when engagement is treated the same and population-specific efforts are not enacted. Concerning the engagement of diverse populations of college students, our position is very much consistent with the title of Manning, Kinzie, and Schuh's (2006) book, *One Size Does Not Fit All*. In the chapters that follow, authors advocate moving beyond sameness to customize educational practices and maximize engagement and outcomes for all.

References

American College Personnel Association (ACPA). (1994). *The student learning imperative: Implications for student affairs.* Washington, DC: Author.

American College Personnel Association (ACPA) & National Association of Student Personnel Administrators (NASPA). (2004) *Learning reconsidered: A campus-wide focus on the student experience.* Washington, DC: Authors.

Anaya, G. (1996). College experiences and student learning: The influence of active learning, college environments, and cocurricular activities. *Journal of College Student Development, 37*(6), 611–622.

Ancis, J., Sedlacek, W., & Mohr, J. (2000). Student perceptions of campus cultural climate by race. *Journal of Counseling and Development, 78*(2), 180–185.

antonio, a. l., Chang, M. J., Hakuta, K., Kenny, D. A., Levin, S., & Milem, J. F. (2004). Effects of racial diversity on complex thinking in college students. *Psychological Science, 15*(8), 507–510.

Astin, A. W. (1975). *Preventing students from dropping out.* San Francisco, CA: Jossey-Bass.

Astin, A. W. (1984). Student involvement: A developmental theory for higher education. *Journal of College Student Personnel, 25*(2), 297–308.

Astin, A. W. (1993). *What matters in college? Four critical years revisited.* San Francisco, CA: Jossey-Bass.

Baxter Magolda, M. B. (1992). Cocurricular influences on college students' intellectual development. *Journal of College Student Development, 33*, 203–213.

Baxter Magolda, M. B., & King, P.M. (Eds.). (2004). *Learning Partnerships: Theory and models of practice to educate for self-authorship.* Sterling, VA: Stylus.

Bean, J. P. (1990). Why students leave: Insights from research. In D. Hossler & J. P. Bean (Eds.), *The strategic management of college enrollments* (pp. 147–169). San Francisco, CA: Jossey-Bass.

Bean, J. P. (2005). Nine themes of college student retention. In A. Seidman (Ed.), *College student retention: Formula for student success* (pp. 215–244). Washington, DC: ACE and Praeger.

Berger, J. B., & Milem, J. F. (1999). The role of student involvement and perceptions of integration in a causal model of student persistence. *Research in Higher Education, 40*(6), 641–664.

Braxton, J. M., Hirschy, A. S., & McClendon, S. A. (2004). *Understanding and reducing college student departure. ASHE-ERIC Higher Education Report* (Vol. 30, No. 3). San Francisco, CA: Jossey-Bass.

Braxton, J. M., Milem, J. F., & Sullivan, A. S. (2000). The influence of active learning on the college departure process: Toward a revision of Tinto's theory. *The Journal of Higher Education, 71*(5), 569–590.

Bridges, B. K., Cambridge, B., Kuh, G. D., & Leegwater, L. H. (2005). Student engagement at Minority-Serving Institutions: Emerging lessons from the BEAMS. In G. H. Gaither (Ed.). *What works: Achieving success in minority retention. New Directions for Institutional Research* (no. 125, pp. 25–43). San Francisco, CA: Jossey-Bass.

Broido, E. M. (2000). The development of social justice allies during college: A phenomenological investigation. *Journal of College Student Development, 41*(1), 3–18.

Cabrera, A. F., Nora, A., Terenzini, P. T., Pascarella, E. T., & Hagedorn, L. S. (1999) Campus racial climate and the adjustment of students to college: A comparison between White students and African American students. *The Journal of Higher Education, 70*(2), 134–202.

Chang, M. J., Astin, A. W., & Kim, D. (2004). Cross-racial interaction among undergraduates: Some consequences, causes, and patterns. *Research in Higher Education, 45*(5), 529–553.

Chang, M. J., Chang, J. C., & Ledesma, M. C. (2005). Beyond magical thinking: Doing the real work of diversifying our institutions. *About Campus, 10*(2), 9–16.

Chang, M. J., Denson, N., Sáenz, V., & Misa, K. (2006). The educational benefits of sustaining cross-racial interaction among undergraduates. *The Journal of Higher Education, 77*, 430–455.

Evans, N. J. (1987). A framework for assisting student affairs staff in fostering moral development. *Journal of Counseling and Development, 66*, 191–193.

Evans, N. J., Forney, D. S., & Guido-DiBrito, F. (1998). *Student development in college: Theory, research, and practice.* San Francisco, CA: Jossey-Bass.

Freire, P. (1970). *Pedagogy of the oppressed.* New York, NY: The Continuum International Publishing Group.

Gurin, P., Dey, E. L., Hurtado, S., & Gurin, G. (2002). Diversity and higher education: Theory and impact on educational outcomes. *Harvard Educational Review, 72*, 330–366.

Harper, S.R. (2007). Using qualitative methods to assess student trajectories and college impact. In S.R. Harper & S.D. Museus (Eds.), *Using qualitative methods in institutional assessment*. New Directions for Institutional Research (No. 136, pp. 55–68). San Francisco, CA: Jossey-Bass.

Harper, S.R. (2008). Realizing the intended outcomes of *Brown*: High-achieving African American male undergraduates and social capital. *American Behavioral Scientist, 51*(7), 1–24.

Harper, S.R. (2011). Strategy and intentionality in practice. In J.H. Schuh, S.R. Jones, & S.R. Harper (Eds.), *Student services: A handbook for the profession* (5th ed., pp. 287–302). San Francisco, CA: Jossey-Bass.

Harper, S.R., & antonio, a.l. (2008). Not by accident: Intentionality in diversity, learning, and engagement. In S.R. Harper (Ed.), *Creating inclusive campus environments for cross-cultural learning and student engagement* (pp. 1–18). Washington, DC: NASPA.

Harper, S.R., & Hurtado, S. (2007). Nine themes in campus racial climates and implications for institutional transformation. In S.R. Harper & L.D. Patton (Eds.), *Responding to the realities of race on campus*. New Directions for Student Services (No. 120, pp. 7–24). San Francisco, CA: Jossey-Bass.

Harper, S.R., & Quaye, S.J. (2007). Student organizations as venues for Black identity expression and development among African American male student leaders. *Journal of College Student Development, 48*(2), 133–159.

Hu, S., & Kuh, G.D. (2003). Diversity experiences and college student learning and development. *Journal of College Student Development, 44*(3), 320–334.

Hurtado, S. (1992). The campus racial climate: Contexts for conflict. *Journal of Higher Education, 63*(5), 539–569.

Hurtado, S., Milem, J., Clayton-Pedersen, A., & Allen, W. (1999). *Enacting diverse learning environments: Improving the climate for racial/ethnic diversity in higher education*. ASHE-ERIC Higher Education Report (Vol. 26, No. 8). Washington, DC: The George Washington University, Graduate School of Education and Human Development.

Jones, S.R. (2008). Student resistance to cross-cultural engagement: Annoying distraction or site for transformative learning? In S.R. Harper (Ed.), *Creating inclusive campus environments for cross-cultural learning and student engagement* (pp. 67–85). Washington, DC: NASPA.

Kinzie, J., & Kuh, G.D. (2004). Going deep: Learning from campuses that share responsibility for student success. *About Campus, 9*(5), 2–8.

Kuh, G.D. (1993). In their own words: What students learn outside the classroom. *American Educational Research Journal, 30*(2), 277–304.

Kuh, G.D. (1995). The other curriculum: Out-of-class experiences associated with student learning and personal development. *The Journal of Higher Education, 66*(2), 123–155.

Kuh, G.D. (2001). Assessing what really matters to student learning: Inside the National Survey of Student Engagement. *Change, 33*(3), 10–17.

Kuh, G.D., Kinzie, J., Buckley, J.A., Bridges, B.K., & Hayek, J.C. (2007). *Piecing together the student success puzzle: Research, propositions, and recommendations*. ASHE Higher Education Report (Vol. 32, No. 5). San Francisco, CA: Jossey-Bass.

Kuh, G.D., Kinzie, J., Schuh, J.H., Whitt, E.J., & Associates (2005). *Student success in college: Creating conditions that matter*. San Francisco, CA: Jossey-Bass.

Kuh, G.D., Palmer, M., & Kish, K. (2003). The value of educationally purposeful out-of-class experiences. In T.L. Skipper & R. Argo (Eds.), *Involvement in campus activities and the retention of first-year college students*. The First-Year Experience Monograph Series (No. 36, pp. 19–34). Columbia, SC: University of South Carolina, National Resource Center for the First-Year Experience and Students in Transition.

Kuh, G.D., Schuh, J.H., Whitt, E.J., Andreas, R.E., Lyons, J.W., Strange, C.C., Krehbiel, L.E., & MacKay, K.A. (1991). *Involving colleges: Successful approaches to fostering student learning and development outside the classroom*. San Francisco, CA: Jossey-Bass.

Ladson-Billings, G. (1995). Toward a theory of culturally relevant pedagogy. *American Educational Research Journal, 32*(3), 465–491.

Manning, K., Kinzie, J., & Schuh, J.H. (2006). *One size does not fit all: Traditional and innovative models of student affairs practice*. New York, NY: Routledge.

McEwen, M.K. (2003). The nature and uses of theory. In S.R. Komives & D.B. Woodard (Eds.), *Student services: A handbook for the profession* (4th ed., pp. 147–163). San Francisco, CA: Jossey-Bass.

Milem, J. F., & Berger, J. B. (1997). A modified model of college student persistence: Exploring the relationship between Astin's Theory of Involvement and Tinto's Theory of Student Departure. *Journal of College Student Development, 38*(4), 387–400.

National Survey of Student Engagement (NSSE). (2007). *Experiences that matter: Enhancing student learning and success, annual report 2007.* Bloomington, IN: Indiana University Center for Postsecondary Research.

Pascarella, E. T. (2001). Identifying excellence in undergraduate education: Are we even close? *Change, 33*(3), 19–23.

Pascarella, E. T., & Terenzini, P. T. (2005). *How college affects students, Volume 2: A third decade of research.* San Francisco, CA: Jossey-Bass.

Pascarella, E. T., Edison, M., Nora, A., Hagedorn, L. S., & Terenzini, P. T. (1996). Influence of students' openness to diversity and challenge in the first year of college. *Journal of Higher Education, 67,* 174–195.

Peltier, G. L., Laden, R., & Matranga, M. (1999). Student persistence in college: A review of research. *Journal of College Student Retention, 1*(4), 357–375.

Quaye, S. J., & Harper, S. R. (2007). Faculty accountability for culturally-inclusive pedagogy and curricula. *Liberal Education, 93*(3), 32–39.

Rest, J. R. (1993). Research on moral judgment in college students. In A. Garrod (Ed.), *Approaches to moral development* (pp. 201–213). New York, NY: Teachers College Press.

Saddlemire, J. R. (1996). Qualitative study of White second-semester undergraduates' attitudes toward African American undergraduates at a predominantly White university. *Journal of College Student Development, 37*(6), 684–691.

Stage, F. K., & Hossler, D. (2000). Where is the student? Linking student behaviors, college choice, and college persistence. In J. M. Braxton (Ed.), *Reworking the student departure puzzle* (pp. 170–195). Nashville, TN: Vanderbilt University Press.

Strange, C. C., & Banning, J. H. (2001). *Educating by design: Creating campus learning environments that work.* San Francisco, CA: Jossey-Bass.

Swail, W. S., Redd, K. E., & Perna, L. W. (2003). *Retaining minority students in higher education: A framework for success.* ASHE-ERIC Higher Education Report (Vol. 30, No. 2). San Francisco, CA: Jossey-Bass.

Tinto, V. (1993). *Leaving college: Rethinking the causes and cures of student attrition* (2nd ed.). Chicago, IL: University of Chicago Press.

Tinto, V. (2000). Taking retention seriously: Rethinking the first year of college. *NACADA Journal, 19*(2), 5–10.

Tinto, V. (2005). Moving from theory to action. In A. Seidman (Ed.), *College student retention: Formula for student success* (pp. 371–333). Washington, DC: American Council on Education and Praeger.

Torres, V., Howard-Hamilton, M. F., & Cooper, D. L. (2003). *Identity development of diverse populations: Implications for teaching and administration in higher education. ASHE-ERIC Higher Education Report* (Vol. 29, No. 6). San Francisco, CA: Jossey-Bass.

Tross, S. A., Harper, J. P., Osher, L. W., & Kneidinger, L. M. (2001). Not just the usual cast of characteristics: Using personality to predict college performance and retention. *Journal of College Student Development, 41*(3), 325–336.

Villalpando, O. (2002). The impact of diversity and multiculturalism on all students: Findings from a national study. *NASPA Journal, 40,* 124–144.

Chapter 2
Engaging Students of Color

Stephen John Quaye, Kimberly A. Griffin, and Samuel D. Museus

Although students of color are enrolling in higher education at increasing rates, they still frequently describe their campuses as hostile and antagonistic and perceive their campus environments (e.g., campus climate and culture) differently than their White counterparts (Harper & Hurtado, 2007). In hooks's (1994) *Teaching to Transgress*, she wrote the following:

> Often, if there is a lone person of color in the classroom she or he is objectified by others and forced to assume the role of "native informant." For example, a novel is read by a Korean American author. White students turn to the one student from a Korean background to explain what they do not understand. This places an unfair responsibility onto that student. (p. 43)

This role of "native informant" is all-too-familiar for students of color on predominantly White campuses. Thus, the focus of this chapter is on articulating the challenges faced by students of color, applying theories to make further sense of the challenges, and proposing a set of recommendations for better engaging these students on campus.

The notion that educators have a responsibility to meet the needs of students of color is the premise of this chapter. Far too often, the onus is put on students to assimilate to predominantly White cultural norms and divorce their cultures and identities from learning processes. In this chapter, we advocate for placing the responsibility on educators by shifting their pedagogical practices to match the needs of students of color. In the next section, we describe how curricular and co-curricular environments negatively and positively shape the experiences of students of color. Then, we present two frameworks—campus racial climate and campus racial culture—that help make sense of the positive and negative ways that campus environments shape the experiences of students of color and how college educators can effectively craft environments that foster engagement and ultimately success among these students. Finally, we conclude with several concrete interventions that faculty and student affairs educators can employ to improve the educational experiences and outcomes of these students.

Classroom Environments

To help better understand why and how educators can engage students of color in the classroom, we discuss four factors that influence the experiences of students of color in college classrooms at predominantly White institutions: (1) being one of few students of color, (2) racial stereotypes and stereotype threat, (3) the absence or presence of same-race or same-ethnicity faculty, and (4) Eurocentric and culturally relevant curricular content.

Being One of Few

Students of color often face a profound sense of loneliness, feeling the need to prove their intellectual abilities. Even high-achieving students contend with issues of self-doubt and questions of belonging in higher education (Fries-Britt & Turner, 2001). Continually having to represent their entire race or ethnicity in discussions of diversity and feeling that their actions as a person of color will be generalized to the entire group are two other significant challenges faced by these students in predominantly White classrooms (Tatum, 1992).

The campus racial climate at predominantly White colleges and universities also influences the climate in classrooms (Hurtado & Carter, 1997). In several studies, students of color perceived far more discrimination on their campuses than did White students (Ancis, Sedlacek, & Mohr, 2000; Cabrera & Nora, 1994; Cabrera, Nora, Terenzini, Pascarella, & Hagedorn, 1999; Hurtado, 1992; Smedley, Meyers, & Harrell, 1993). Students of color who perceived less racial tension were more likely to succeed academically (Hurtado, Milem, Clayton-Pedersen, & Allen, 1999). The discrimination these students experienced in comparison to their White counterparts illustrates the dire need for classroom environments to be spaces of comfort and inclusion where students are not questioned on the basis of their racial/ethnic backgrounds.

Racial Stereotypes and Stereotype Threat

The "Proving Process" is a phrase introduced by Fries-Britt and Turner (2001) that calls attention to the struggles of students of color in predominantly White classrooms. Students of color often feel pressure to prove their academic capabilities, and this pressure partially comes from racial stereotypes. Indeed, students of color often report experiencing racial stereotypes that shape their experiences on college campuses in negative ways. For example, negative racial stereotypes that suggest Black and Latino students are academically inferior pose barriers for these students (Fries-Britt & Turner, 2001; Lewis, Chesler, & Forman, 2000), who often encounter questions about their academic capabilities and the right to enroll in higher education through being labeled as "affirmative action" admits (Chang, 1999).

In the classroom, racial stereotypes can negatively affect both engagement in learning activities and academic performance (Museus, 2008b; Steele, 1997). For example, when Black students feel pressure to disprove themselves as academically inferior or Asian American students feel pressure to conform to misconceptions that they are all academically superior, it can lead to them disengaging and diminishing the opportunities to learn and develop. Regarding performance, the aforementioned stereotype-induced pressure can lead to anxiety, which ultimately leads to lower levels of performance on academic tests and tasks (Steele, 1997).

Same-Race and Same-Ethnicity Faculty

Rates of attaining tenure among faculty of color (64%) continue to lag behind those of White faculty (75%) and racial disparities in faculty rank persist, with one investigation finding that faculty of color represent only 12% of the full professorships (Harvey, 2001). This same study found that, in 1997, African American faculty represented only 5% of full-time faculty in higher education, while the percentage for Latino faculty was less than 2%, and Asian Americans made up 5.7% (Harvey, 2001). These data reveal the difficulties for students of color who wish to find same-race and same-ethnicity faculty to serve as mentors and advisors. Additionally, students of color interested in a career in academia might conclude such a feat is unattainable given the underrepresentation of faculty of color across academe as a whole.

Smith (1989) summarizes the influence of faculty of color on students' success in five claims for diversifying campuses. These arguments include the ability of faculty of color to serve as mentors to students of color, their commitment to a more diverse campus climate, their role in creating comfortable and inclusive environments for faculty and staff, their ability to offer diverse perspectives on teaching and learning, and their commitment to a pluralistic view of higher education. For classroom environments to be more inclusive and welcoming for students of color, attention needs to be given to ensuring that faculty members represent a wide array of backgrounds, perspectives, and experiences (Lundberg & Schreiner, 2004; Smith, 1989).

Eurocentric and Culturally Responsive Curricular Content

The cultures of students of color and the problems and issues that exist within their communities are often missing in classroom readings and discussions given the predominant exposure to Western literature (Banks, 1996, 2001). The choices made about instructional content represent a form of power (Delpit, 1988); curricula focused on Western or dominant cultures send the message to students of color that Whiteness is normal and that other practices or beliefs from different cultures are not valued (Delpit, 1988; Schmitz, 1992). Weissman, Bulakowski, and Jumisko (1998) found that stereotypical content in courses created a negative environment for African American students at one community college in Chicago and deepened the racial divide in the classroom. Curricular content can also invalidate the knowledge and experiences of students of color, which are rarely present in any form in higher education settings (Terenzini, Cabrera,

Colbeck, Bjorklund, & Parente, 2001). For most of these students, the marginalization or exclusion of the cultures and communities of students of color begins in K-12 settings, where little, if any, course content reflects the experiences and voices of people of color (Au, 1998; Gallimore & Goldenberg, 2001), and continues through higher education.

In contrast, research shows how curricula that reflect and engage the cultural backgrounds of students of color positively influence their engagement and success (e.g., Kiang, 2002, 2009; Museus, Lam, et al., 2012; Museus, Mueller, & Aquino, 2013). For example, ethnic studies programs can offer curricula that reflect the cultural communities and identities of students of color, thereby permitting those students to identify with the course content while simultaneously building community with faculty and peers of similar racial, ethnic, and cultural backgrounds (Kiang, 2002, 2009; Museus, Lam, et al., 2012).

Co-Curricular Environments

Both higher education scholars and student affairs educators have underscored the importance of engagement in activities outside the classroom. A substantial body of empirical research confirms the relationships that exist between campus involvement and positive educational outcomes (see Gellin, 2003; Kuh, 2009; Moore, Lovelll, Mcgann, & Wyrick, 1998; Pascarella & Terenzini, 2005). Specifically, this body of research connects spending time and investing energy in co-curricular activities to important learning outcomes (e.g., critical thinking and cognitive development), as well as outcomes that promote retention (e.g., sense of belonging and stronger connections to the campus community). Furthermore, engagement in these activities often translates into the development of leadership, collaboration, and time management skills that will serve students well when they enter the workforce (Kezar & Moriarty, 2000; Harper & Quaye, 2007).

While these opportunities may translate into positive student outcomes, studies offer conflicting evidence regarding the extent to which students of color engage in campus activities. Some scholars suggest rates of participation have grown in recent decades and demonstrate how many students of color are engaging and taking leadership in organizations across campuses (Beatty et al., 2010; Desouza & King, 1992; Harper & Quaye, 2007; Lundberg, Schriener, Hovaguimian, & Miller, 2007; Museus, 2008c, 2011b; Sutton & Kimbrough, 2001). However, others suggest that students of color continue to experience challenges as they seek opportunities to engage outside of the classroom (e.g., Allen, 1985, 1992; Guiffrida, 2003; Harper & Hurtado, 2007; Tinto, 1993), as we discuss in the following sections.

Rates of Engagement

The literature has also highlighted the low rates of participation in campus activities among students of color. For example, research shows low rates of engagement among Black students attending predominantly White institutions, often in comparison to the rates of engagement of their peers attending historically Black colleges and universities (HBCUs) (Allen, 1992; Flowers, 2004; Nelson Laird, Bridges, Morelon-Quainoo, & Williams, 2007;

Person & Christensen, 1996). For example, Allen (1985) found that 45% of Black students in his sample felt very little, or not at all, a part of campus life, with only 12% reporting that they felt very much a part of campus activities. While two-thirds of African American students at HBCUs felt they were a part of campus life and 26% reported the highest level of involvement, Black students at predominantly White institutions were less involved. Only 38% of students at PWIs felt that they were a part of campus life, and 8% reported being involved at the highest levels.

Higher education researchers have attributed these students' lower rates of engagement in campus organizations and social activities to negative campus environments (Fleming, 1984; Griffin, Nichols, Perez, & Tuttle, 2008; Harper & Hurtado, 2007; Loo & Rollison, 1986; Museus, 2008b; Person & Christensen, 1996; Tinto, 1993; Turner, 1994). Furthermore, students of color often report that mainstream campus organizations and activities rarely reflect their cultural interests (Davis, 1991; Person & Christensen 1996; Rooney 1985). We discuss these issues in the remainder of this section.

Prejudice and Discrimination
Higher education scholars have studied the impact of chilly (i.e., unwelcoming) racial climates on the experineces and outcmes of students of color (see Harper & Hurtado, 2007). Researchers have documented the relatively high levels of prejudice and discrimination faced by students of color (e.g., Feagin, 1992; Feagin, Vera, & Imani, 1996; Lewis, Chesler, & Forman, 2000). Indeed, scholars have shown how such prejudice and discrimination manifests in racial jokes, racist comments, racial ignorance, and hostility toward students of color because of Affirmative Action. Sometimes prejudice and discrimination escalates into hate crimes, which can have a profound impact on campus environments and students' desires or willingness to engage in them (Hurtado, 1992).

Isolation and Marginalization
In addition, a substantial body of research illuminates the ways that students of color experience isolation and marginalization from the mainstream cultures of PWIs (Allen, 1992; Davis, 1994; Feagin, Vera, & Imani, 1996; Fries-Britt & Turner, 2001; Gonzalez, 2003; Lewis et al., 2000). For example, some studies describe Black students' sense of isolation and alienation from predominantly White activities, noting how slights and insults from peers and assumptions about their backgrounds based on racial background made them less interested in participating in social groups and organizations and furthered their marginalization from the mainstream cultures of campus (Bourke, 2010; Fisher & Hartmann, 1995).

Culturally-Based Campus Organizations
In response to the challenges many students of color face as they seek opportunities to engage in activities outside the classroom, many may seek and participate in culturally-based living options, groups, and organizations to establish a connection to the campus community (Bourke, 2010; Guiffrida, 2003; Museus, 2008c; Patton, 2006). Over the

past decade, researchers have called attention to the critical role that culturally-based co-curricular activities and spaces play in the engagement patterns and outcomes of students of color at predominantly White institutions. Although these organizations are sometimes regarded as evidence of "balkanization" or "self-segregation" on many college campuses, Hurtado and colleagues (1999) suggest culturally-based groups serve as valuable support mechanisms, social outlets for the students, and facilitators for further involvement in campus activities.

Opportunities to Connect and Give Back to Cultural Communities

As mentioned, many students of color report that mainstream campus organizations and activities seldom reflect their cultural identities or interests (Davis, 1991; Person & Christensen 1996; Rooney 1985). This is problematic because there is some evidence indicating that students of color are more likely to become engaged when they can access opportunities to connect with their cultural heritages (Comp, 2008; Guiffrida, 2003; Harper & Quaye, 2007; Museus, 2008b; Museus, Lam, et al., 2012; Rubin, 2004). For example, researchers have written about how students of color engage in study abroad for the purposes of heritage-seeking, in order acquire knowledge related to their community and family histories and cultures (Comp, 2008; Rubin, 2004). Additionally, scholars have written about students who engage in various campus activities so that they can connect with people who have similar cultural backgrounds and give back to their cultural communities (Guiffrida, 2003; Harper & Quaye, 2007; Museus, 2008b).

Safe and Validating Campus Spaces

Subcultures and spaces that reflect the cultural backgrounds of students can function as "safe spaces," instrumental in reducing feelings of isolation, marginality, and alienation among communities of color (Guiffrida, 2003; Kiang, 2002, 2009; Murguia, Padilla, & Pavel, 1991; Museus, 2008b, 2011a; Museus, Lam, et al., 2012; Patton, 2006; Solórzano, Allen & Caroll, 2002; Wang, Sedlacek, & Westbrook, 1992). Work by Person and Christensen (1996), Guiffrida (2003), and Museus (2008c) suggests students experience a sense of mattering and validation in ethnic student organizations, providing a space where students are accepted rather than isolated or alienated. Similarly, Patton (2006) describes the importance of Black cultural centers, noting that, in addition to providing students a place where they can relax, these centers enable students to feel a sense of belonging and family that they were lacking within the larger institution.

Further, cultural organizations and multicultural spaces provide opportunities for students to connect with others they perceive to be "like them," sharing similar backgrounds, experiences, and interests. Museus's (2008c) analysis of interviews conducted with Black and Asian American students suggests they perceive ethnic student organizations as an important means to meet and connect with students who share their cultural background, having similar upbringings and struggles navigating their predominantly

White institution. Through this sense of shared experience and identity, cultural organizations appear to provide avenues for comfort, support, and opportunities to connect with peers in an authentic way (Guiffrida, 2003; McClure, 2006; Museus, 2008c). Cultural organizations also provide students with a sense of cultural connection, allowing them to share in and express their identities through their participation. Participants in Harper and Quaye's (2007) study of Black male leaders noted that they chose to engage in cultural organizations based on their desire to give back to their communities and support other Black students. Similarly, Inkelas (2004) and Museus (2008c) found that students developed a stronger sense of racial and ethnic identity through their participation in ethnic organizations.

Campus Racial Climate and Campus Racial Culture

Sufficiently addressing the distinctive concerns of students of color warrants theories that respond to their racial and ethnic backgrounds and identities. Two theories provide the foundation for the current discussion: campus racial climate and campus racial culture. However, before moving forward with this discussion, it is important to define and distinguish between campus climate and culture. Then, we discuss how the racialized nature of campus climates and cultures shape the engagement and success of undergraduates of color.

Campus climate is an inherently ambiguous concept. Bauer (1998) defined *campus climate* as "the current perceptions, attitudes, and expectations that define the institution and its members" (p. 2). By this definition, climate is a relatively tacit and flexible aspect of the campus environment. The malleable nature of campus climates makes them an easy target for institutional efforts to change environments to get immediate results and improve the experiences of students of color. The drawback of this malleability, however, is that the impact of institutional efforts to improve campus climates can also quickly change or diminish. Thus, efforts to improve campus environments for historically oppressed groups via climate initiatives can sometimes be immediate, short-lived, and may only influence the experiences of a small proportion of students on the college campus in which they are implemented. Thus, it is important for educators focusing on changing their institutional climates to consider both comprehensive and long-term transformation approaches.

In contrast to campus climate, the concept of *campus culture* refers to what Kuh and Whitt (1988) called the deeply embedded

> persistent patterns of norms, values, practices, beliefs, and assumptions that shape the behavior of individuals and groups in a college or university and provide a frame of reference within which to interpret the meaning of events and actions on and off the campus. (pp. 12–13)

Campus culture, therefore, refers the very fabric that permeates all aspects of university life and that shapes and defines the behavior and experiences of individuals within that organization. In the remainder of this section, we discuss the concepts of *campus racial climate* and *campus racial culture*. In doing so, we underscore how race permeates and shapes these two aspects of the environment on college and university campuses.

Campus Racial Climate

Initially proposed by Hurtado et al. (1999), the campus racial climate framework can provide important insights, informing our understanding of the multidimensional nature of climate and how it can influence interest in engagement among students of color. The campus racial climate can be defined as the current attitudes, perceptions, and expectations within an institutional community about issues of race, ethnicity, and diversity (Hurtado et al., 1999). In addition, the campus racial climate framework consists of five factors, including (1) an institution's history and legacy of inclusion or exclusion, (2) compositional diversity, (3) psychological climate, (4) behavioral climate, and (5) organizational/structural diversity (Milem, Chang, & Antonio, 2005). More negative or hostile campus racial climates can negatively influence the interactions of students of color with other members of their campus communities both in and outside the classroom by diminishing the quality, frequency, and potential positive outcomes of their interactions on campus. This, in turn, can inhibit students' patterns of engagement, which ultimately has poor implications for student growth, development, and retention (Cabrera et al., 1999; Hurtado, 1992).

Based on the framework, an institution's campus racial climate is created by internal and external forces, which together shape the climate at each individual campus. The acknowledgement of external forces, namely government policies and the socio-historical contexts of the region, state, or United States, draws attention to how broad societal trends and public policies can influence campus racial climates. For example, legislation and court decisions eliminating affirmative action do not only exist outside of institutions. Rather, they influence campus policies, practices, and attitudes about race and diversity, which may help institutions increase the number of students of color on campuses and the safe spaces that those students construct for themselves, but may also make these students feel less welcome in various campus spaces and less interested in participating in various activities in and outside the classroom.

The dimensions of the campus racial climate framework mentioned above are interconnected. However, each dimension of the framework can be specifically targeted to facilitate institutional transformation. First, an institution's historical legacy of inclusion or exclusion can continue to shape current racial dynamics on college and university campuses (Hurtado et al., 1999). For example, many institutions have a history of perpetuating hostile environments for students of color. Without addressing or acknowledging this history, students of color may feel their campuses are still hostile, unwelcoming places that only enrolled them because of forced desegregation policies.

Compositional diversity is frequently described as the first step that must be taken in developing an environment that fosters positive cross-racial interactions and refers to the actual representation of people of color on campus (Hurtado, et al., 1999; Milem, Chang, & Antonio, 2005). This dimension involves any efforts to increase the physical presence of students, staff, and faculty from underrepresented groups. Despite its importance, the singular act of increasing the number of people of color on campuses will not necessarily create more positive campus racial climates (Cabrera et al., 1999; Chang, 2002; Hurtado et al., 1999; Milem et al., 2005). Rather, the psychological and behavioral dimensions of those racial climates must be addressed. The psychological dimension includes "individuals' views of group relations, institutional responses to diversity, perceptions of discrimination or racial conflict, and attitudes held towards others from different racial/ethnic backgrounds" (Hurtado et al., 1999, p. 25). The behavioral dimension, or quality of interactions and relationships between individuals from diverse backgrounds, reminds readers that they must attend to the nature of interactions between different groups on campus to promote a more hospitable environment. The psychological and behavioral dimensions of racial climates can be perceived as working in tandem, particularly in relation to fostering the engagement of students of color. Negative perceptions of racial climates can make students more reluctant to engage with those from different backgrounds than their own. Similarly, a lack of interactions across difference can lead to negative perceptions of the racial climate and level of inclusion for people of color on campus.

Finally, Milem et al. (2005) added organizational/structural diversity to the original Hurtado et al. (1999) campus racial climate framework. This dimension highlights the important roles that established institutional processes, curricular requirements, and campus decision-making processes play in shaping racial climates. For example, curricular requirements that emphasize Eurocentric principles and disregard work from scholars of color can shape students' interest and engagement in the classroom, just as policies that give student organizations funding and space privilege based on their length of time at their institutions can privilege predominantly White student groups based on the historical demography of their campuses.

Campus Racial Culture

While much of the literature that discusses institutional culture discusses it as a de-racialized phenomenon (e.g., Kuh et al., 2005; Whitt, 1993, 1996), several scholars have highlighted the fact that race shapes the cultures of postsecondary institutions and the experiences of students of color within these cultures (Guiffrida, 2006; Guiffrida, Kiyama, Waterman, & Museus, 2012; Jayakumar, 2012; Jayakumar & Museus, 2012; Kuh & Love, 2000; Museus, 2007, 2008a, 2008c, 2011a, 2011b; Museus & Harris, 2010; Museus & Liverman, 2011; Museus et al., in press; Museus & Quaye, 2009; Museus, Ravello, & Vega, 2012; Quaye & Chang, 2012; Rendón, Jalomo, & Nora, 2000). Building on the work of these scholars, Museus, Ravello, and Vega (2012) defined the *campus racial culture* as

> the collective patterns of tacit values, beliefs, assumptions, and norms that evolve from an institution's history and are manifest in its mission, traditions, language, interactions, artifacts, physical structures, and other symbols, which differentially shape the experiences of various racial and ethnic groups and can function to oppress racial minority populations within a particular institution. (p. 32)

The concept of the campus racial culture is based on the notion that most, if not all, predominantly White institutions are founded on deeply embedded Eurocentric values, beliefs, and assumptions that shape the norms and behaviors of faculty, staff, and students on college campuses (Jayakumar & Museus, 2012; Museus, Ravello, & Vega, 2012). Moreover, the campus racial culture suggests that Eurocentric cultural values, assumptions, and norms that permeate postsecondary institutions can shape the experiences of undergraduates of color in powerful ways. To offer an example of the ways in which the campus racial cultures can significantly affect the experiences of students of color, we highlight the difference between individualistic and collectivist cultural orientations. Because college students of color are more likely to come from cultures with collectivist orientations, evidence suggests that institutions and programs that perpetuate individualistic and competitive values and assumptions might create conditions in which students of color have difficulty engaging, have low levels of satisfaction, and are less likely to succeed (Guiffrida, 2006; Guiffrida et al., 2012). In contrast, institutions and programs that emphasize fostering community and family in academic environments and collaborative learning activities that reflect the values, assumptions, and norms of the racial communities of students of color can increase these students' abilities to connect with the cultures of the campuses and their likelihood of success (Fullilove & Treisman, 1990; Guiffida, 2006; Guiffrida et al., 2012; Museus et al., in press).

There are three other concepts that help better understand the nature of the campus racial culture and how it shapes the experiences of undergraduates of color: cultural (in) congruence, cultural dissonance, and cultural integration (Kuh & Love, 2000; Museus, 2008a, Museus & Quaye, 2009). *Cultural incongruence* refers to the distance between the cultures of students' campuses and the cultures of their home communities (Kuh & Love, 2000; Museus & Quaye, 2009), whereas *cultural dissonance* denotes the tension that students experience as a result of the distance between these campus and home cultures (Museus, 2008a), and excessive cultural dissonance can result in culture shock, or a condition in which students leave cultures with familiar cultural signs and symbols and consequently experience feelings of anxiety, frustration, and helplessness (Oberg, 1960). Scholars have suggested that when students of color encounter Eurocentric cultures on their college campuses that are incongruent with those from their home communities, they are likely to feel increased cultural dissonance, which is inversely related to engagement and success (Museus & Quaye, 2009). Thus, postsecondary educators can increase engagement and success among students of color by decreasing the amount of cultural dissonance these students feel as they navigate predominantly White institutions.

One way that educators can diminish the cultural dissonance that students of color experience as they transition to and navigate their institutions is by utilizing the concept of cultural integration. While the term *integration* has been used for decades to describe students' assimilation into the academic and social subsystems of campus (Tinto, 1987, 1993), the concepts of academic and social integration have been critiqued for being culturally biased and placing an unfair expectation on students of color to assimilate to the dominant cultures of predominantly White institutions (Attinasi, 1989; Tierney,

1992, 1999). To reclaim the term integration and reframe it in a culturally responsive light, higher education researchers have introduced the concept of *cultural integration* to refer to the incorporation of academic and social elements, as well as students' cultural backgrounds and identities, into educational spaces, programs, practices, events, and activities (Museus, 2011b; Museus et al., 2012). They suggest that educators can integrate these academic, social, and cultural elements to bridge the various spheres of students' lives and lead to the creation of stronger connections between students of color and their respective campuses. Empirical evidence indicates that cultural integration can positively influence the engagement and success of students of color because it facilitates students' connections to the academic and social subsystems of campus, while simultaneously strengthening ties to their cultural backgrounds (Museus et al., 2012).

The term cultural integration is based on the underlying assumption that educators can and sometimes do bridge academic and co-curricular divides, as well as the notion that such bridging can have positive effects on engagement and success among students of color. Nevertheless, we recognize that existing literature and many college educators distinguish between the academic (i.e., classroom) and social (i.e., out-of-class) experiences of students in higher education. Thus, in the last section, we discuss strategies for fostering engagement among students of color in these two domains. We acknowledge, however, that many of our recommendations encompass both aspects of campus life.

Student Engagement Strategies

A multipronged method is necessary to engage students of color in predominantly White campus and classroom environments, meaning that using multiple strategies in conjunction is more effective than using one in isolation. Therefore, while we outline several approaches that can be utilized independently in this section, we contend that the strategies are more effective when incorporated into a comprehensive strategic plan that encompasses several of them.

(Re)Examination of the Institutional and Programmatic Missions

Missions are a critical aspect of the cultures that exist within institutions and within specific academic programs. Institutional leaders should make efforts to periodically engage in a critical examination of their respective campus missions, and faculty should engage in periodic reflection on the missions of their programs in order to better understand whether their campuses and programs reflect the diverse communities that they serve. Specifically, such examinations can ensure that institutions and programs aimed at serving racially and ethnically diverse populations promote their recruitment, engagement, and success.

Culturally-Focused Organizations and Spaces

As noted above, the "safe spaces" created in culturally focused campus spaces and organizations, such as culture centers and ethnic student organizations, are critical to the engagement of students of color. In addition to serving as a source of support within a larger environment that is sometimes unwelcoming and less than inclusive, these organizations provide opportunities for students to interact and build connections with peers who share their backgrounds and interests (Guiffrida, 2003; Museus, 2008c, 2011; Museus et al., 2012). They may also offer students of color much-needed opportunities to develop important professional skills and competencies as they take on leadership roles within these groups and serve as an entryway to more broad engagement with faculty and other members of the campus community (Guiffrida, 2003; Harper & Quaye, 2007; Patton, Bridges, & Flowers, 2011). It is important to note that the goals of those who call for the elimination of these groups in order to create more opportunities for engagement across difference and fewer options for self-segregation do not acknowledge the important positive role that these organizations play in the lives of students of color and are therefore misguided. Rather, we must support students as they strive to engage those from racial and ethnic backgrounds different from their own and support racial/ethnic organizations as a key means of support and survival.

Given the positive outcomes stemming from student participation and leadership in culturally-based organizations, institutions must begin or continue to support their goals and efforts. As noted by Patton (2006), cultural centers are often underdeveloped spaces located far from the center of campus activity. Similarly, student organizations focused on addressing the needs of students of color may be allocated fewer resources, be marginalized, or face more stringent disciplinary sanctions than predominantly White organizations (Bourke, 2010). Investing financial resources in culturally based organizations, providing cultural centers with adequate space and staffing, and providing student groups with guidance and mentorship can promote the efficacy of these entities as they aim to engage students.

Climate Assessments and Cultural Audits

It is important for institutions to conduct regular campus racial climate assessments. Such assessments are integral to ensuring that campus administrators, faculty, and staff understand how their students are experiencing their campus racial climates, how various groups experience these climates in disparate ways, and how they can improve these climates for students of color. Student affairs assessment offices play a critical role in helping conduct climate assessments. And, where institutions do not have student affairs assessment offices, campuses can hire consultants to conduct the climate assessments for or with them.

In addition, institutional cultures consist of a complex web of values, beliefs, assumptions, norms, and behaviors (Jayakumar & Museus, 2012; Kuh & Whitt, 1988; Museus, 2007). In fact, some aspects of campus cultures (e.g., cultural assumptions) are so deeply embedded in the organizational fabric of institutions and taken for granted by their members that people within these campuses never reflect on and do not completely understand these cultural elements and how they impact students of color. Jayakumar and Museus, for example, provide several examples of how assumptions that drive the daily behavior of faculty and staff on college campuses can and do negatively affect the experiences and outcomes of students of color. Thus, it is imperative that institutional leaders engage in cultural audits that can uncover these aspects of culture and unpack how they impact students of color (Museus, 2007; Whitt, 1993). However, due to the aforementioned complex and deeply embedded nature of campus cultures, it is important for institutions that seek to engage in cultural audits to involve external assessment specialists who can "make the familiar strange" and prompt institutional members to engage in a critical analysis of their taken-for-granted assumptions (Museus, 2007; Whitt, 1993).

Peer Networks

Educators should provide opportunities for students of color to formulate networks with other peers of color. For instance, periodic forums comprised of students of color provide a space for students to develop and sustain relationships with students across multiple disciplines, where they can candidly discuss the challenges associated with being students of color at predominantly White institutions. These forums can enable students to share their frustrations, positive experiences, and strategies for academically achieving. In addition, third- and fourth-year students can serve as peer mentors for incoming students and provide them with the social networks necessary to succeed during their collegiate tenures. Providing spaces in which students of color can connect with other students enables them to reenergize in the company of others who share similar experiences.

Summer Bridge Programs

Institutions should utilize summer bridge programs, which can enable students of color to develop peer networks and engage in classroom settings prior to the start of the academic year. Students in these programs gather support and confidence from peers involved at the institution while also gaining knowledge and skills that will prepare them for their upcoming academic experience. Summer bridge programs enable students to navigate the campus environment in the company of their peers who are also striving to do the same. Additionally, upper-level students who participated in the program should be invited to mentor students throughout this experience. By involving students who have been actively engaged at the institution, students of color see that they can also achieve in their courses despite their underrepresentation.

Student Advisory Committees

Academic departments should develop student advisory committees. These committees can be comprised of a variety of students who can provide feedback to the academic dean or department chair about deficiencies in academic content, department offerings, and cultural awareness among faculty members. The advisory committee can suggest readings reflective of students' cultural groups and recommend additional syllabi revisions or feedback that faculty can incorporate into their courses. As students are in the best positions to evaluate whether their educational needs are being met, these advisory committees provide students with opportunities to be heard by those who have the power to make changes. Consequently, the dean can filter information to faculty to improve the climate and culture for students of color.

Professional Development for Student Leaders

To engage students of color in a wider range of campus activities and encourage students to more often engage with those from different racial and ethnic backgrounds, we urge institutional leaders to develop trainings and workshops that arm student leaders with tools to promote diversity within and intercultural interactions across their organizations. While the phenomenon of "self-segregation" on college and university campuses has drawn great concern and has been observed by those in various campus communities, students receive little guidance or support in their efforts to engage across difference. Thus, despite students' potential interest in and understanding of the importance of the learning that can take place when they interact with someone from a different racial or ethnic background, they may not engage because of uncertainty, discomfort, or fear and the lack of preparation to deal with these negative emotions (Fisher & Hartmann, 1995; Harper & Hurtado, 2007). This may be a particularly salient concern for White students, considering that they tend to engage across differences outside the classroom at rates lower than students of color (Fisher & Hartmann, 1995; Gurin, Dey, Hurtado, & Gurin, 2002; Hurtado, Griffin, Arellano, & Cuellar, 2008).

Thus, we recommend a series of workshops for student leaders from diverse backgrounds. The workshops would help student leaders develop strategies that would promote inclusion and increase diversity within and diverse interactions across their organizations. For example, campus administrators and student affairs professionals can help students think about how to coordinate programs and activities that provide students with an opportunity to engage in dialogues, across differences. They can also teach students new outreach strategies and how to assess whether or not they have created a comfortable environment within the group for students from a variety of racial and ethnic backgrounds. Furthermore, holding these training sessions with heterogeneous groups creates opportunities for student leaders to engage with each other, building their individual efficacy that is necessary to participate in cross-racial interaction effectively and form a foundation for future collaborations and partnerships between student groups and organizations.

Recruitment and Hiring of Faculty

Institutional leaders should aggressively recruit and hire faculty of color. This obvious strategy is not necessarily innovative; yet, it remains a vital, unmet objective of most colleges and universities (Smith, 2009). Faculty of color are grossly underrepresented across postsecondary institutions as a whole. Like most White students, undergraduates of color pursue fields in which they deem themselves competent and comfortable. For students of color to consider the professoriate, for example, they must identify with same-race or same-ethnicity faculty who can serve as encouraging mentors and role models. Faculty of color can also support students who may feel disconnected and isolated on predominantly White campuses (Fries-Britt & Griffin, 2007; Griffin, 2013). Exposure to faculty of color in multiple disciplines enables students to see that they can also be successful in various careers and, in turn, positively influence the lives of other students of color with whom they work.

Faculty Training and Development

College educators should support faculty training and development. This professional development will include readings, writing reflections, and sharing of culturally relevant learning material and pedagogies, which can become incorporated into the courses of faculty. Each campus may have a unique context and identify faculty leaders to model positive teaching practices differently. In-services or faculty conferences provide forums for modeling to occur through sharing diverse approaches and syllabi from faculty that utilize varied methods of teaching students of color. Faculty who need additional training or are not able to revise their material can receive feedback and help from their colleagues. Institutions should offer support in assisting faculty in reviewing their pedagogy. Faculty who are knowledgeable about inclusive classroom settings can be asked to observe, evaluate, and give feedback to professors who are working toward changing their teaching practices.

Faculty Incentives and Rewards

Institutions should provide incentives and rewards for faculty members who utilize culturally relevant teaching methods. One way to change faculty culture is to reward those who create an enriching and supportive learning environment for students of color. Upper-level administrators should provide incentives and rewards to those who continuously embrace diverse curricular and learning practices and are recognized by students as providing inclusive and culturally relevant learning environments. By giving recognition to faculty who connect with students, positive norms are established at the faculty level that students matter. Other faculty will be more willing to change and incorporate alternative learning approaches into their classroom settings in order to improve their performance and receive recognition.

Diverse Academic Content

Faculty and student affairs educators should utilize a diverse array of academic content to demonstrate the contributions of people of color in various disciplines. As many faculty were not socialized to utilize culturally broad literature during their graduate tenures, they still teach in culturally exclusive ways (Harper & Quaye, 2004). When students of color are exposed to mainly White, Eurocentric perspectives, they come to believe the contributions of their cultural groups are trivial or nonexistent. Furthermore, when undergraduates of color peruse the syllabi on the first day of class, they immediately receive a subtle message concerning the importance (or lack thereof) of their racial or ethnic communities. Faculty who wish to engage students of color must intentionally incorporate readings that pertain to the experiences of these undergraduates and their respective communities. This practice recognizes that students are more likely to be engaged when their professors intentionally integrate culturally diverse perspectives into curricula.

Classroom Discussions on Race and Ethnicity

When race and ethnicity are discussed in the classroom, students of color can feel pressured to be experts and educate White students about these issues, and this pressure can eventually result in fatigue among students of color. Faculty should not expect or rely on students of color to discuss their experiences or insights in order to educate White students every time race and ethnicity emerge in classroom discourse. Instead, inviting White students to discuss their racial and ethnic backgrounds and identities can lessen the pressure placed on students of color to speak as experts on race and ethnicity. Workshops on White privilege should also be conducted so that White students have opportunities to reflect on and ask questions about their Whiteness and how they benefit from systemic privilege and racial oppression. Additionally, educators should not assume that students of color speak using a racial or ethnic lens at all times. They should also recognize that all racial and ethnic groups have multiple, intersecting identities (e.g., socioeconomic, gender, sexual orientation, and political orientation diversity), which influence their experiences with and perspectives on race and ethnicity.

Conclusion

College students of color often encounter campus classrooms and environments that are not attuned to their needs. In this chapter, we highlighted several challenges that face undergraduates of color as they navigate curricular and co-curricular campus environments. Campus racial climates and campus racial cultures were offered as theoretical lenses that can be used to explore how to best engage these students in college. Students of color are not a monolithic group and, as our recommendations illuminate, better engaging these students warrants strategies that are attuned to their backgrounds and needs in both classroom and out-of-class experiences. When used thoughtfully, these strategies respond to the increasing rates of enrollment of students of color within higher education by placing their racial and ethnic identities and cultures at the forefront of the learning process.

References

Allen, W.R. (1985). Black student, White campus: Structural, interpersonal, and psychological correlates of success. *Journal of Negro Education, 54*(2), 134–147.

Allen, W.R. (1992). The color of success: African-American college student outcomes at predominantly White and historically Black public colleges and universities. *Harvard Educational Review, 62*(1), 26–44.

Ancis, J., Sedlacek, W., & Mohr, J. (2000). Student perceptions of campus cultural climate by race. *Journal of Counseling Development, 78*(2), 180–185.

Attinasi, L.C. Jr. (1989) Getting in: Mexican Americans' perceptions of university attendance and the implications for freshman year persistence. *The Journal of Higher Education, 60*(3), 247–277.

Au, K. (1998). Social constructivism and the school literacy learning of students of diverse backgrounds. *Journal of Literacy Research, 30*(2), 297–319.

Banks, J.A. (1996). *Multicultural education, transformative knowledge, and action: Historical and contemporary perspectives.* New York, NY: Teachers College Press.

Banks, J.A. (2001). Multicultural education: Goals, possibilities, and challenges. In C.F. Diaz (Ed.), *Multicultural education in the 21st century* (pp. 11–22). New York, NY: Longman.

Bauer, K.W. (1998). Editor's notes. In K.W. Bauer (Ed.), *New Directions for Institutional Research* (no. 98, 1–5). San Francisco, CA: Jossey-Bass.

Beatty, C.C., Busy, A.A., Erxleben, E.E., Ferguson, T.L., Harrell, A.T., & Sahachartsiri, W.K. (2010). Black student leaders: The influence of social climate in student organizations. *Journal of the Indiana University Student Personnel Association, 2010 Edition*, 48–63.

Bourke, B. (2010). Experiences of Black students in multiple cultural spaces at a predominantly White institution. *Journal of Diversity in Higher Education, 3*(2), 126–135.

Cabrera, A.F., & Nora, A. (1994). College students' perceptions of prejudice and discrimination and their feelings of alienation: A construct validation approach. *The Review of Education, Pedagogy, and Cultural Studies, 16*(3–4), 387–409.

Cabrera, A.F., Nora, A., Terenzini, P.T., Pascarella, E., & Hagedorn, L.S. (1999). Campus racial climate and the adjustment of students: A comparison between White students and African-American students. *The Journal of Higher Education, 70*(2), 134–160.

Chang, M.J. (1999). Does racial diversity matter?: The educational impact of a racially diverse undergraduate population. *Journal of College Student Development, 40*(4), 377–395.

Chang, M.J. (2002). Preservation or transformation: Where's the real educational discourse on diversity. *The Review of Higher Education, 25*(2), 125–140.

Comp, D. (2008). U.S. Heritage-Seeking Students Discover Minority Communities in Western Europe. *Journal of Studies in International Education, 12*(1), 29–37.

Davis, J. E. (1994). College in Black and White: Campus environments and academic achievement of African American males. *Journal of Negro Education, 63*(4), 620–633.

Davis, R. (1991). Social support networks and undergraduate student academic-success-related outcomes: A comparison of Black students on Black and White campuses. In W. R. Allen, E. G. Epps, & N. Z. Haniff (Eds.), *College in Black and White: African American students in predominantly white and in Historically Black Public Universities* (pp. 143–158). Albany, NY: SUNY Press.

Delpit, L. D. (1988). The silenced dialogue: Power and pedagogy in educating other people's children. *Harvard Educational Review, 58*(3), 280–298.

DeSouza, D. J., & King, P. M. (1992). Are White students really more involved in collegiate experiences than Black students? *Journal of College Student Development, 33*(4), 363–369.

Feagin, J. R. (1992). The continuing significance of racism: Discrimination against Black students in White colleges. *Journal of Black Studies, 22*(4), 546–78.

Feagin, J. R., Vera, H., & Imani, N. (1996). *The agony of education: Black students at White colleges and universities.* New York, NY: Routledge.

Fisher, B. J., & Hartmann, D. J. (1995). The impact of race on the social experiences of college students at a predominantly White university. *Journal of Black Studies, 26*(2), 117–133.

Fleming, J. (1984). *Blacks in college.* San Francisco, CA: Jossey-Bass.

Flowers, L. A. (2004). Examining the effects of student involvement on African American college student development. *Journal of College Student Development, 45*(6), 633–654.

Fries-Britt, S., & Griffin, K. A. (2007). The Black box: How high-achieving Blacks resist stereotypes about Black Americans. *Journal of College Student Development, 48*(5), 509–524.

Fries-Britt, S. L., & Turner, B. (2001). Facing stereotypes: A case study of Black students on a White campus. *Journal of College Student Development, 42*(5), 420–429.

Fullilove, R. E., & Treisman, E. M. (1990). Mathematics achievement among African American undergraduates at the University of California, Berkeley: An evaluation of the mathematics workshop program. *Journal of Negro Education, 59*(3), 463–478.

Gallimore, R., & Goldenberg, C. (2001). Analyzing cultural models and settings to connect minority achievement and school improvement research. *Educational Psychologist, 36*(1), 45–46.

Gellin, A. (2003). The effects of undergraduate student involvement on critical thinking: A meta-analysis of the literature 1991–2000. *Journal of College Student Development, 44*(6), 746–762.

Gonzalez, K. P. (2003*).* Campus culture and the experiences of Chicano students in a predominantly White university. *Urban Education, 37*(2), 193–218.

Griffin, K. A. (2013). Voices of the "Othermothers": Reconsidering Black professors' relationships with Black students as a form of social exchange. *Journal of Negro Education, 82*(2), 169–183.

Griffin, K. A., Nichols, A. H., Perez, D. I., & Tuttle, K. D. (2008). Making campus activities and student organization inclusive for racial/ethnic minority students. In S. R. Harper (Ed.), *Creating inclusive campus environments for cross-cultural learning and student engagement* (pp. 121–138). Washington, DC: NASPA.

Guiffrida, D. A. (2003). African American student organizations as agents of social integration. *Journal of College Student Development, 44*(3), 304–319.

Guiffrida, D. A. (2006). Toward a cultural advancement of Tinto's theory. *The Review of Higher Education, 29*(4), 451–472.

Guiffrida, D. A., Kiyama, J. M., Waterman, S., & Museus, S. D. (2012). Moving from individual to collective cultures to serve students of color. In S. D. Museus & U. M. Jayakumar (Eds.). *Creating campus cultures: Fostering success among racially diverse student populations* (pp. 68–87). New York, NY: Routledge.

Gurin, P., Dey, E., Hurtado, S., & Gurin, G. (2002). Diversity and higher education: Theory and impact on educational outcomes. *Harvard Educational Review, 72*(3), 330–366.

Harper, S. R., & Hurtado, S. (2007). Nine themes in campus racial climates. In S. R. Harper & L. D. Patton (Eds.), Responding to the realities of race on campus. *New Directions for Student Services* (pp. 7–24). San Francisco, CA: Jossey-Bass.

Harper, S. R., & Quaye, S. J. (2004). Taking seriously the evidence regarding the effects of diversity on student learning in the college classroom: A call for faculty accountability. *UrbanEd, 2*(2), 43–47.

Harper, S., & Quaye, S.J. (2007). Student organizations as venues for Black identity expression and development among African American male student leaders. *Journal of College Student Development, 48*(2), 127–144.

Harvey, W. (2001). *Minorities in Higher Education, 2000–01*. Washington, DC: American Council on Education.

hooks, b. (1994). *Teaching to transgress: Education as the practice of freedom*. New York, NY: Routledge.

Hurtado, S. (1992). The campus racial climate: Contexts of conflict. *The Journal of Higher Education, 63*(5), 539–569.

Hurtado, S., & Carter, D. (1997). Effects of college transition and perceptions of the campus racial climate on Latino college students' sense of belonging. *Sociology of Education, 70* (4), 324–345.

Hurtado, S., Griffin, K.A., Arellano, L., & Cuellar, M. (2008). Assessing the value of climate assessments: Progress and future directions. *Journal of Diversity in Higher Education, 1*(4), 204–221.

Hurtado, S., Milem, J., Clayton-Pedersen, A., & Allen, W. (1999). *Enacting diverse learning environments: improving the climate for racial/ethnic diversity in higher education. ASHE-ERIC Higher Education Report Volume 26*(8). Washington, DC: The George Washington University, Graduate School of Education and Human Development.

Inkelas, K.K. (2004). Does participation in ethnic cocurricular activities facilitate a sense of ethnic awareness and understanding? A study of Asian Pacific American undergraduates. *Journal of College Student Development, 45*(3), 285–302.

Jayakumar, U.M. (2012). Social praxis in shaping supportive cultures and traditionally White institutions. In S.D. Museus & U.M. Jayakumar (Eds.). *Creating campus cultures: Fostering success among racially diverse student populations* (pp. 130–149). New York, NY: Routledge.

Jayakumar, U.M., & Museus, S.D. (2012). Mapping the intersection of campus cultures and equitable outcomes among racially diverse student populations. In S.D. Museus & U.M. Jayakumar (Eds.). *Creating campus cultures: Fostering success among racially diverse student populations* (pp. 1–27). New York, NY: Routledge.

Kezar, A., & Moriarty, D. (2000). Expanding our understanding of student leadership development: A study exploring gender and ethnic identity. *Journal of College Student Development, 41*(1), 55–69.

Kiang, P.N. (2002). Stories and structures of persistence: Ethnographic learning through research and practice in Asian American Studies. In Y. Zou & H.T. Trueba (Eds.), *Advances in Ethnographic Research: From Our Theoretical and Methodological Roots to Post-Modern Critical Ethnography* (pp. 223–255). Lanham, MD: Rowman & Littlefield.

Kiang, P.N. (2009). A thematic analysis of persistence and long-term educational engagement with Southeast Asian American college students. In L. Zhan (Ed.), *Asian American Voices: Engaging, Empowering, Enabling* (pp. 21–58). New York, NY: NLN Press.

Kuh, G.D. (2009). What student affairs professionals need to know about student engagement. *Journal of College Student Development, 50*(6), 683–706.

Kuh, G.D., Kinzie, J., Schuh, J.H., Whitt, E.J., & Associates (2005). *Student success in college: Creating conditions that matter*. San Francisco, CA: Jossey-Bass.

Kuh, G.D., & Love, P.G. (2000). A cultural perspective on student departure. In J.M. Braxton (Ed.), *Reworking the student departure puzzle* (pp. 196–212). Nashville, TN: Vanderbilt University Press.

Kuh, G.D., & Whitt, E.J. (1988). The invisible tapestry: Culture in American colleges and universities: *ASHE-ERIC Higher Education Report, 17*(1). Washington, DC: Association for the Study of Higher Education.

Lewis, A.E., Chesler, M., & Forman, T.A. (2000). The impact of "colorblind" ideologies on students of color: Intergroup relations at a predominantly White university. *The Journal of Negro Education, 69*(1/2), 74–91.

Loo, C.M., & Rollison, G. (1986). Alienation of ethnic minority students at a predominantly White university. *The Journal of Higher Education, 57*(1), 58–77.

Lundberg, C.A., & Schreiner, L.A. (2004). Quality and frequency of faculty-student interaction as predictors of learning: An analysis by student race/ethnicity. *Journal of College Student Development, 45*(5), 549–565.

Lundberg, C.A., Schriener, L.A., Hovaguimian, K.D., & Miller, S.S. (2007). First-generation status and student race/ethnicity as distinct predictors of student involvement and learning. *NASPA Journal, 44*(1), 57–83.

McClure, S. M. (2006). Voluntary association membership: Black greek men on a predominantly white campus. *Journal of Higher Education, 77*(6), 1036–1057.

Milem, J., Chang, M. J., & Antonio, A. L. (2005). *Making diversity work on campus: A research-based perspective*. Washington, DC: Association of American Colleges and Universities.

Murguia, E., Padilla, R. V., & Pavel, M. (1991). Ethnicity and the concept of social integration in Tinto's model of institutional departure. *Journal of College Student Development, 32*(5), 433–439.

Museus, S. D. (2007). Using qualitative methods to assess diverse campus cultures. In S. R. Harper & S. D. Museus (Eds.), *Using qualitative methods in institutional assessment: New Directions for Institutional Research* (no. 136, 29–40). San Francisco, CA: Jossey-Bass.

Museus, S. D. (2008a). Focusing on institutional fabric: Using campus culture assessments to enhance cross-cultural engagement. In S. R. Harper (Ed.), *Creating inclusive environments for cross-cultural learning and engagement in higher education* (pp. 205–234). Washington, DC: National Association of Student Personnel Administrators.

Museus, S. D. (2008b). The model minority and inferior minority myths: Stereotypes and their implications for student learning. *About Campus, 13*(3), 2–8.

Museus, S. D. (2008c). The role of ethnic student organizations in fostering African American and Asian American students' cultural adjustment and membership at predominantly White institutions. *Journal of College Student Development, 49*(6), 568–586.

Museus, S. D. (2011a). Generating Ethnic Minority Success (GEMS): A collective-cross case analysis of high-performing colleges. *Journal of Diversity in Higher Education, 4*(3), 147–162.

Museus, S. D. (2011b). Using cultural perspectives to understand the role of ethnic student organizations in Black students' progress to the end of the pipeline. In D. E. Evensen & C. D. Pratt (Eds.), *The end of the pipeline: A journey of recognition for African Americans entering the legal profession* (pp. 162–172). Durham, NC: Carolina Academic Press.

Museus, S. D., & Harris, F. (2010). The elements of institutional culture and minority college student success. In T. E. Dancy II (Ed.), *Managing diversity: (Re)visioning equity on college campuses* (pp. 25–44). New York, NY: Peter Lang.

Museus, S. D., Lam, S., Huang, C., Kem, P., & Tan, K. (2012). Cultural integration in campus subcultures: Where the cultural, academic, and social spheres of college life collide. In S. D. Museus & U. M. Jayakumar (Eds.). *Creating campus cultures: Fostering success among racially diverse student populations* (pp. 106–129). New York, NY: Routledge.

Museus, S. D., & Liverman, D. (2011). Analyzing high-performing institutions: Implications for studying minority students in STEM. In S. R. Harper, C. Newman, & S. Gary (Eds.), *Students of color in STEM: Engineering a new research agenda: New Directions for Institutional Research* (no. 148, pp. 17–27). San Francisco, CA: Jossey-Bass.

Museus, S. D., Mueller, M. K., & Aquino, K. (2013). Engaging Asian American and Pacific Islander culture and identity in graduate education. In S. D. Museus, D.C. Maramba, & R. T. Teranishi (Eds.), *The misrepresented minority: New insights on Asian Americans and Pacific Islanders, and the implications for higher education* (pp. 106–123). Sterling, VA: Stylus.

Museus, S. D., & Quaye, S. J. (2009). Toward an intercultural perspective of racial and ethnic minority college student persistence. *The Review of Higher Education, 33*(1), 67–94.

Museus, S. D., Ravello, J. N., & Vega, B. E. (2012). The campus racial culture: A critical race counterstory. In S. D. Museus & U. M. Jayakumar (Eds.). *Creating campus cultures: Fostering success among racially diverse student populations* (pp. 28–45). New York, NY: Routledge.

Nelson Laird, T. F., Bridges, B. K., Morelon-Quainoo, C. L., & Williams, J. M. (2007). African American and Hispanic student engagement at minority serving and predominantly White institutions. *Journal of College Student Development, 48*(1), 39–56.

Oberg, K. (1960). Culture shock: Adjustment to new cultural environments. *Practical Anthropology, 7,* 177–182.

Patton, L. D. (2006). The voice of reason: A qualitative examination of Black student perceptions of their Black culture center. *Journal of College Student Development, 47*(6), 628–646.

Patton, L.D., Bridges, B.K., & Flowers, L.A. (2011). The effects of greek affiliation on African American students' engagement. *College Student Affairs Journal, 29*(2), 113–123.

Person, D.R., & Christensen, M.C. (1996). Understanding Black student culture and Black student retention. *NASPA Journal, 34*(Fall 1996), 47–56.

Quaye, S.J., & Chang, S.H. (2012). Creating a culture of inclusion in the classroom: From marginality to mattering. In S.D. Museus & U.M. Jayakumar (Eds.), *Creating campus cultures: Fostering success among racially diverse student populations* (pp. 88–105). New York, NY: Routledge.

Rendón, L.I., Jalomo, R.E., & Nora, A. (2000). Theoretical considerations in the study of minority student retention in higher education. In J. Braxton (Ed.), *Reworking the student departure puzzle* (pp. 127–156). Nashville, TN: Vanderbilt University Press.

Rooney, G.D. (1985). Minority students' involvement in minority student organizations: An exploratory study. *Journal of College Student Personnel, 26*(5), 450–456.

Rubin, K. (2004). Going To Study. *International Educator, 13,* 26–33.

Schmitz, B. (1992). *Core curriculum and cultural pluralism: A guide for campus planners.* Washington, DC: Association of American Colleges.

Smedley, B., Meyers, H., & Harrell, S. (1993). Minority-status stresses and the collegeadjustment of ethnic minority freshmen. *The Journal of Higher Education, 64*(4), 434–452.

Smith, D. (1989). The *challenge of diversity: Involvement or alienation in the academy?* ASHE-ERIC Higher Education Report No. 5. Washington, DC: The George Washington University, Graduate School of Education and Human Development.

Smith, D.G. (2009). *Diversity's promise for higher education: Making it work.* Baltimore, MD: The Johns Hopkins University Press.

Solórzano, D.G., Allen, W.R., & Carroll, G. (2002). Keeping race in place: Racial microaggressions and campus racial climate at the University of California Berkeley. *Chicano Latino Law Review, 23*(Spring), 15–112.

Steele, C.M. (1997). A threat in the air: How stereotypes shape intellectual identity and performance. *American Psychologist, 52*(6), 613–629.

Tatum, B.D. (1992). Talking about race, learning about racism: The application of racial identity development theory in the classroom. *Harvard Educational Review, 62*(1), 1–24.

Terenzini, P.T., Cabrera, A.F., Colbeck, C.L., Bjorklund, S.A., & Parente, J.M. (2001). Racial and ethnic diversity in the classroom: Does it promote student learning? *The Journal of Higher Education, 72*(5), 509–531.

Tierney, W.G. (1992). An anthropological analysis of student participation in college. *Journal of Higher Education, 63*(6), 603–618.

Tierney, W.G. (1999). Models of minority college-going and retention: Cultural integrity versus cultural suicide. *The Journal of Negro Education, 68*(1), 80–91.

Tinto, V. (1987). *Leaving college: Rethinking the causes and cures of student attrition.* Chicago, IL: University of Chicago Press.

Tinto, V. (1993). *Leaving college: Rethinking the causes and cures of student attrition* (2nd ed.). Chicago, IL: University of Chicago Press.

Turner, C.S.V. (1994). Guests in someone else's house: Students of color. *The Review of Higher Education, 17*(4), 355–370.

Wang, Y., Sedlacek, W.E., & Westbrook, F.D. (1992). Asian Americans and student organizations: Attitudes and participation. *Journal of College Student Development, 33,* 214–221.

Weissman, J., Bulakowski, C., & Jumisko, M. (1998). A study of White, Black and Hispanic students' transition to a community college. *Community College Review, 26,* 19–38.

Whitt, E.J. (1993). Making the familiar strange. In G.D. Kuh (Ed.), *Cultural perspectives in student affairs work* (pp. 81–94). Lanham, MD: University Press of America and American College Personnel Association.

Whitt, E.J. (1996). Assessing student cultures. In M.L. Upcraft & J.H. Schuh (Eds.), *Assessment in student affairs: A guide for practitioners* (pp. 186–216). San Francisco, CA: Jossey-Bass.

Chapter 3
Engaging Undergraduate Women of Color

Lori D. Patton, Jessica C. Harris, Jessica Ranero-Ramirez, Isabella Villacampa, and Joyce Lui

All women, including Black, Latina, and Asian American women are outpacing their male counterparts in college enrollment and degree attainment (Buchmann & DiPrete, 2006; Hayes, 2012). At face value, the fact that women earn more degrees than men is something to celebrate. Buchman and DiPrete (2006) call this phenomenon a gender gap reversal and insist there is a "growing female advantage in college completion" (p. 515). The female advantage, numerically speaking, means that as more women earn degrees at rates higher than the men within their respective groups, we can anticipate changes in the labor market and in family structures that may favor all women. While the gender advantage in degree attainment among college men and women may signal major changes in society, it also generates concern among university administrators who see the continued increase in women as a contributor to an emergent gender gap that disadvantages men. Institutional leaders are also considering how affirmative action related programs might serve male students in terms of increasing their representation (Buchman & DiPrete, 2006).

In this chapter, we argue that despite a greater representation of all women on campus, issues rooted in racial and gender discrimination continue to disproportionately affect the collegiate experiences of women of color. In other words, a "female advantage" has not been realized by women of color. The lack of an advantage has important implications for how women of color are engaged during college. Moreover, how women of color experience college is complicated when considering the oppressive structures that exist beyond but heavily influence the campus environment. While the literature on student engagement is plentiful, more research is needed to help college and university leaders create meaningful opportunities to thoughtfully engage women of color.

To write this chapter, we combed the literature to identify key articles that could collectively represent women of color and evidence of campus engagement. Rather than finding a robust set of materials from which to pull, we consistently found gaps in the literature, indicating the dire need for more scholarship that raises important questions about women of color and contributes to institutional policies, programs, and practices to support these populations. Perhaps the most difficult aspect in writing a chapter of this nature is gaining a sense of who qualifies as a woman of color and what circumstances led to the use of this terminology.

Deconstructing "Women of Color"

The term "women of color" grew out of a movement of resistance and a need for liberation among women who were oppressed due to racism and gender discrimination (Roshanravan, 2010). The term itself was politically charged and used to express solidarity amongst and for groups of racially minoritized women in the United States. More recently this term has been used to reference these same groups of women biologically, but not politically. The biological perspective is problematic because it reduces women of color to a monolithic racial group whose members share the same experiences due to their gender (women) and race (non-White). An essentialized view such as this renders invisible the process of differential racialization, through which all groups of color have been and continue to be racialized to serve dominant White interests (Delgado & Stefancic, 2001). When essentialism is used as a framework to understand women of color their individual experiences are automatically discounted. The term may also fail to account for additional experiences that women encounter due to other marginalized identities, such as the homophobic campus environment an Asian American lesbian must traverse or the ageism a non-traditional age Native American woman might encounter in the classroom.

While the phrase "women of color" was meant to bring together a group of individuals, exactly who qualifies for membership in this group is widely debated. For instance, the inclusion of Asian American women within "women of color" is often contested because of the model-minority stereotype, an "identity that reinforces public perceptions of Asian peoples as unlikely victims of racism or as suspicious comrades in coalitional struggle against racial injustice" (Roshanravan, 2010, p. 3). An Asian woman's presumed inability to fully grasp the intersections of patriarchal and racial oppression revokes her membership and access to "women of color." This example illustrates that the definition of women of color does not always default to all non-White American women. With this in mind, we ask with what groups do Jewish or Muslim women students of European descent align themselves? Additionally, do international students who physically appear as women of color in an American context but whose bodies and minds have not yet been racialized in a U.S. context fit into this "women of color" term? "Women of color" was meant to bridge the gaps between differently raced women who also faced gender subordination. However, the term's exclusion of some racial groups has created chasms in this community that prevent "cross-racial coalition movement against white capitalist institutions" (Roshanravan, 2010, p. 3).

Finally, while this term may build a bridge between racially minoritized women, it also constructs an image in opposition to non-racialized, or White, women. In other words, the term "women of color" suggests that White women are the normative, foundational group of American women. We do not say "women of Whiteness" when referring to White women as a group, but when referring to all "others" we say "women of color." For those who fall into the "women of color" category, the term marks us as non-White and connotes a negative difference, a malady.

The purpose of the above deconstruction is not to argue for a discontinuation of the use of "women of color." Indeed we embrace its use throughout this chapter. However, we offer this history and critique of the term so that readers may remain cognizant of the full weight of what it means to be "women of color" when reading about the complexity of their racialized and gendered experiences with engagement on the college campus.

In this chapter, we make references to women of color broadly speaking but also offer examples and literature that focus on Latina, Black, and Asian American/Pacific Islander women. Our decision to present the chapter in this way was based on a desire to consider women of color collectively and individually, while also clearly acknowledging that such a task is difficult at best. We also acknowledge the absence of literature on a range of populations that are considered to be collegiate women of color. Our omission is not simply due to page constraints, but is also symptomatic of the larger literature base that provides very little information on diverse groups of racially minoritized women represented in this chapter, and even less or nonexistent literature on populations not represented in this chapter. In the sections below, we identify four cross-cutting themes that reveal the issues faced by women of color in college, offer rich frameworks for examining their experiences, and propose recommendations for engaging them on campus.

Barriers that Undermine Substantive Engagement among Women of Color

Equating Representation with Engagement

Recent literature on racially minoritized students has been consistent in reporting that women have higher graduation rates than their male counterparts. For example, Latina/os are the most rapidly growing population in the United States (Fry & Gonzales, 2008; Fry & Passel, 2009). Latina women account for almost half of the U.S. Latino population and by 2050 Latinas will make up 25% of women of all ages in the United States (Maes, 2010). Moreover, Latinas are enrolling and graduating at higher rates than their male counterparts (Saenz & Ponjuan, 2009). Yet, very little is known about how Latinas are engaged in collegiate settings. Some scholars suggest that Latinas are still encountering many barriers and challenges as they navigate through college (Espinoza, 2010; Gloria & Castellanos, 2012; Hernandez-Truyol, 2003). However, the mere fact that they have a greater representation than men, signals to institutional leaders and administrators that these women do not need resources or attention. As a result, a dominant discourse has emerged, suggesting that Latinas are engaged; if they were not, fewer would be attending college and graduating.

Similarly, the literature related to Asian American and Pacific Islander (AAPI) students—men and women alike—has glaring gaps. AAPI students have a presence in higher education; a presence some would argue is too much. According to Chen and Hune (2011), the presence of AAPI students in higher education, "has been met with praise, as well as concerns with overrepresentation" (p. 165). Due to the model minority myth AAPI students have been viewed as academically gifted and treated as "honorary Whites." The large numeric representation of AAPI women is enough to support any assertion that these students are already engaged. Stereotypes rooted in the model minority myth prohibit opportunities for engagement in any meaningful or culturally relevant way.

To understand the representation of AAPI women in relation to engagement, it is necessary to explore how they have been differentially racialized in comparison to other women of color. For example, Sue, Bucceri, Lin, Nadal, and Torino (2007) conducted a study on racial microaggressions experienced by Asian Americans. Microaggressions include the "everyday verbal, nonverbal, and environmental slights, snubs, or insults, whether intentional or unintentional, that communicate hostile, derogatory, or negative messages" (Sue, 2010, p. 3). The ten participants, nine who were women, commented that in their daily interactions, they were presumed to be intelligent by teachers and fellow students. Furthermore, their academic prowess was relegated to math and science subjects. These microaggressions, made participants feel "trapped" and pressured to live up to these stereotypes. One female participant in the study lamented a major consequence was that while she was viewed as smart, "other people of color were perceived as less intelligent [creating] tensions between her and other Black and Latino coworkers" (p. 94). The failure of institutions to fully engage AAPI women has a great deal to do with the existence of a Black/White binary (Delgado, 1998). This binary not only pits racially minoritized groups against one another, but also ensures that issues pertaining to African Americans are deemed more important than other groups. Consequently, AAPI groups are dismissed from conversations about race and racism.

Differential racialization of AAPI women as a model minority group also leads to the perception that they are either oblivious to racial discrimination or simply do not experience racism. The maintenance of a belief that AAPI women lack racial consciousness and awareness of racism, trivializes their experiences with racial discrimination, dismisses the inequities that some AAPI women face and positions them as having experiences that more closely align with White people (Sue et al., 2009). Hune (1998) shared that due to the perceptions that AAPI women lack racial (and gender) salience, they may be unwelcome in coalitions among women of color and made to feel invisible in spaces occupied by a majority of White women. Thus, AAPI women may miss out on opportunities to gain more leadership skills and have cross-cultural relations with other women on campus. Unsurprisingly, the scholarship in higher education is continually attempting to capture the layered experiences of AAPI women. However, much of this research does not disaggregate the experiences of AAPI women from AAPI men. As a result very little remains known about their college experiences.

A final example of the (dis)connect between representation and engagement is in the statistical representation of Black women in college versus their male counterparts. U.S. Department of Education statistics indicate that in 2008–09 Black women earned 66% of the bachelor's degrees conferred to Black students, suggesting that Black women earned nearly twice as many degrees as their male counterparts. Despite their numerical presence Black women represent an interesting anomaly. While they historically and currently maintain a presence in the academy, their experiences linger largely invisible and unacknowledged. In other words, they along with other racially minoritized women, do attend and graduate from college, most often at rates higher than their male counterparts. Unfortunately, the reigning discourse insinuates a subtle, yet direct link between their representation and engagement on campus.

Women of color may very well be engaged within their college environments, potentially leading to their high representation on the college campus and degree attainment. It is important to keep in mind that the statistics are within group comparisons. For example, Latina women outnumber Latino men, but not White students who represent the majority of higher education. A great deal of academic and social programming caters to racially dominant groups. While women of color may outnumber their male counterparts, this representation does not mean women of color are significantly engaged. To the contrary, deeply embedded structures of racism and patriarchy that exist on every college campus can be prohibitive in efforts of engagement. Therefore, we argue that many women of color make it through college in spite of, not because of their levels of engagement. We also contend that engagement for women of color is difficult due to a range of issues that mere structural diversity cannot address.

Exoticization and Perpetuation of Stereotypes

Where their bodies are concerned, women of color occupy a very interesting space in higher education. The space is liminal in that these women have a strong physical presence on campus yet their physicality is simultaneously devalued. Scholars have written about how women of color face a range of microaggressions rooted in the exoticization of their bodies. In Renn's (2004) in depth study, multiracial women raised issues of exoticization. She explains, "Issues of exotification have been really central to me and to my development, in the way that I've been accepted and the way that people have dealt with me . . ." (p. 172). This participant's quote speaks volumes about the subtleties with which women's bodies are used to determine social relations on campus and implications of educational outcomes. The social relations for women of color become increasingly complex based upon how particular groups are constructed through controlling images. Hill Collins (2000) describes controlling images as creations, "designed to make racism, sexism, poverty, and other forms of social injustice appear to be natural, normal, and inevitable parts of everyday life" (p. 69). Through controlling images, privileged groups create the parameters through which oppressed groups are defined. These parameters are used to not only reaffirm the power and normativity of the dominant group, but also to relegate all others to a space of inferiority (Pyke & Johnson, 2003).

Women of color in college are not immune to controlling images. Certain images are particularly harmful in that they contribute to the process of exoticization. For AAPI women, assumptions about being sexually submissive, having particular physical traits (smooth skin and shiny black hair), and pleasing White men sexually, reduces them to passive inferiors (Sue et al., 2007) who must confront hypersexualized and subservient identities, while facing sexual harassment by superiors and peers in higher education (Cho, 1997).

The phenomenon of subordination through exoticization also plays out for Black women in particular ways on the college campus. Black women are hypersexualized on one hand and deemed sexually unappealing on the other. Historically, Black women's bodies have been situated as polar opposites to White women's bodies indicating less desirable women on one end and highly desirable women on the other. For example, Patton and Winkle-Wagner (2012) explained:

> White women are represented as the epitome of beauty in magazines, the dutiful mother and wife on television sitcoms, or the object of affection and attraction for men (of any race) in feature films . . . they are valued and desired above all other women, and in this case Black women, who in many instances have neither been deemed as beautiful nor desirable. (p. 182–183)

This social construction has stood the test of time, ensuring that Black women's bodies are debased. On the college campus, this devaluation results in few Black cheerleaders, homecoming queens, and any other role where European standards of beauty are the norm. Conversely, the presence of Black women's bodies in the media, via hip-hop videos and reality television shows, creates an image of Black women as sexually desirable only, but not appealing for serious relationships or friendships where these women might be holistically appreciated (Railton & Watson, 2005).

Regardless of racial standing, these examples illustrate a clear distinction regarding how the bodies of women of color are positioned as less than and not deserving of respect. Many women of color traverse the college campus having the construction of these stereotypes placed upon them by peers, administrators, and professors. These constructs grow increasingly hard to navigate for women of color and eventually seep into their collegiate experiences, which influences outcomes such as engagement and identity development. Unfortunately, no major research has examined the relationship between the exoticization of women of color and their collegiate experiences. As a result, women of color must negotiate a societal and academic culture rooted in the minimization of their experiences. They have to face ideologies of exoticization along with a desire to achieve their college education. A participant in Jackson's (1998) study succinctly summarizes this juggling act:

> It means having to deal with a lot of negative stereotypes in particular. And I think it's just images people get and then they really don't understand. So, it's totally become a matter of me trying to, I don't know, trying to straighten

out, trying to reconstruct some of the notions people have in their heads and trying to set them straight about it. (p. 367)

While engaging in such reconstruction may be validating and reaffirming for female students of color, the process can also contribute to great frustration and detract greatly from campus engagement. It is imperative that educational leaders address these pre-existing stereotypes and misunderstandings with other students, staff, and faculty so that straightening out and reconstruction do not become the sole responsibility of female students of color.

Balancing Incongruence between Family and the Academy

Another area of study that lends itself to better understanding strategies for engaging women of color on campus is the examination of family and academics. Despite the existence of more progressive thinking, women are still expected to be the key caretakers within their families. Responsibilities associated with taking care of family and oneself can be a major driving force for why some women of color come to college and graduate, but perhaps may be less engaged. For example, the challenges that many Latina students encounter throughout their collegiate experiences are often rooted in the incongruence that exists between their cultural values and the values of higher education (Espinoza, 2010; Gloria & Castellanos, 2012). The culture of academia expects students to be solely devoted to their academic pursuits. Espinoza (2010) explained that "This normative expectation is problematic for graduate women whose identity and sense of belonging is tied to close family connections" (p. 318). The close tie to family is rooted in the philosophy of *familismo* (Espinoza, 2010; Sy & Romero, 2008). Familismo places great value on family, both nuclear and extended and emphasizes cooperation and interdependence. Familismo is often used to explain why Latina/o students feel a sense of obligation to their families. Obligations can include language translation, care of siblings, financial contributions, spending time with family, and staying close to home (Espinoza, 2010; Montoya, 2003; Sy & Romero, 2008).

For Latinas, their identity is not only tied to the value of familismo, but is also influenced by the value of *marianismo* (Delgado Bernal, Elenes, Godinez, & Villenas, 2006; Espinoza, 2010; Sy & Romero, 2008). Marianismo is modeled on the Catholic Virgin Madonna and has traits of dependence, subordination, and selfless devotion to family. Both familismo and marianismo create tension for some Latinas in higher education because time in school competes with time with family (Espinoza, 2010). It is important to note that although obligation to family has often been represented as a barrier or challenge to Latino student success, research has also shown that family is the most significant source of support for Latinos in higher education (González, Jovel, & Stoner, 2004; Rios-Aguilar & Deil-Amen, 2012; Sy & Romero, 2008; Villalpando, 2003; Zell, 2010).

Some of the connections to family and expectations among women in AAPI families are evident in the work of Maramba (2008). She found that Filipinas felt pressure to do well in school while simultaneously maintaining their roles at home, which included chores and helping their parents. One study participant shared how she balanced her immigrant parents' expectations regarding women, which were very different from cultural norms in the United States. The women in this study also indicated that their parents were more strict with respect to their schooling and social life. At home, disagreeing with parents or challenging them was disrespectful, but in educational contexts, challenging ideas was promoted as a strategy for developing critical thinking skills. At school, the participants were taught to disagree and discuss, yet culturally these strategies were frowned upon.

In an earlier study, Cambodian and Hmong American women discussed how education was incredibly important because they wanted to get a higher paying job to help with family finances (Kiang, 1996). However, they had concerns because too much education could potentially serve as a hindrance to finding a husband and could delay childbearing (Lee, 1997). Thus Hmong American women oscillated between the need to succeed in school and the fear of having "too much" academic success, which could ultimately limit their personal goals.

The discourse surrounding education as a hindrance to marriage and family also has relevance for Black women. The limited literature indicates that familial relationships are important and critical to Black women's success in college. A study conducted by Barnett (2004), focused on family support for Black students at an Ivy League university. While she focused on the aggregate of Black students in the study, she also discussed specific experiences for Black college women. The women participants in her study had very close relationships with their mothers and saw them as "best friends" (p. 63). They sought the support and advice of their mothers, oftentimes, before speaking to their fathers or any other trusted supporter.

While family played a critical role in how women of color navigated the college terrain, cultural conflicts that also affected their experiences and life circumstances emerged. For example, Black women deal with societal and cultural rules that push them towards marriage and family; ideals that may come into conflict with education. Black women, for example, have cultural influences through which they are socialized to believe that educational success is closely tied to whether or not they will marry. However, the communication they receive also contains messages of the importance of them maintaining their independence (Berkowitz & Padavic, 1999). Mass media has issued similar edicts for Black women. National and local news headlines have placed Black women in the forefront of discourse linking education and marriage. For instance, these recent headlines and their corresponding news stories suggest that the more education Black women receive, the less likely they are to marry and have children: "Black, Female, and Single" (Stanley, 2011), "Marriage, Family on the decline for highly educated black women" (Baker, 2009), and "Marriage eludes high-achieving black women" (Alexander, 2009).

When examining the role of family and its link to education across the spectrum for women of color, it seems that many of these women are driven to pursue a college education, but are most successful when they have familial support. Additionally, much of the reason that women of color choose to attend college is because their family pushed them towards it or they hope to graduate and return home to their community to give back. However, as mentioned above, many Latina, Black, and Asian American women feel that their familial influences can be as much a push factor as it can be a pull. In other words, the same familial support that pushes students towards educational endeavors may be rooted in cultural expectations and norms that conflict with higher education, such as marrying and raising a family while young, i.e., college going age. This push and pull experienced by women of color from family, both actively and passively, contributes greatly to their ability to engage fully in the campus community.

Invisibility, Help-Seeking, and Pushing Through

The last crosscutting theme represented in the literature focuses on the convergence of invisibility, help seeking, and pushing through barriers. It is more difficult to discuss this convergence individually because each aspect yields implications for the next. However, the racialization of our society creates particular circumstances that construct how silence becomes situated for women of color. The silencing of women of color can potentially prohibit them from seeking assistance on campus and subsequently feeling compelled to be independent and handle matters with little support. Undoubtedly, women of color get things done, but the process by which they do so can be isolating, time-consuming, and overwhelming. Proceeding through college without adequate support and engagement could be a choice; but could also result from being overlooked and ignored.

For instance, AAPI women often face conflicting cultural norms and the pressure of excelling in college, while simultaneously being overlooked or hypervisible. Particularly at predominantly White institutions, Hune (1998) highlighted how AAPI women often felt isolated and alone. They felt they were either being overlooked or were receiving extraordinary attention. On one hand, they were ignored due to physical attributes such as being petite or looking too young for their age to be attending college. During other moments, they garnered too much attention, which included, people stopping them to ask how to pronounce their name or to say something in another language. This phenomenon of invisibility emerged as a finding in Sue et al.'s (2009) study in which participants felt disregarded when racial discussions emerged and were presumed to be immigrants as opposed to U.S. citizens. In such instances and in numerous other experiences, the bottom line is that feeling invisible creates a condition in which AAPI women feel as if no one genuinely cares about them. This can inhibit any efforts they might pursue toward seeking help, leaving them to push through college alone.

For some Latinas, invisibility, help seeking, and managing barriers has a great deal to do with the cultural incongruity that they experience in higher education. However, the manner in which they navigate college might best be understood through a Chicana feminist lens that creates a space for the multiple dimensions and fluidity that is engrained in Latina identity (Anzaldua, 2007; Delgado Bernal et al., 2006; Moraga & Anzaldua, 1983). For Latina women, cultural conflict is normalized and suggests that Latinas live in a borderland between the academy, which promotes invisibility, and their communities of origin. Anzaldua (2007) introduced the concept of mestiza identity, which is developed through the process of constantly navigating two cultures. The mestiza identity, characterized by resiliency, learns to live with ambiguity and contradiction (Anzaldua, 2007; Espinoza, 2010; Moraga & Anzaldua, 1983). In this third space that exists between two opposing cultures, mestiza identity is characterized by Latinas who learn two ways of thinking and speaking (Anzaldua, 2007; Espinoza, 2010). As explained by Espinoza (2010), Chicana feminist theories "elucidate the borders Chicana/Latina women are forced to cross on a daily basis, constantly shifting in and out of different social contexts with diverse gender expectations to which they adjust" (p. 321). Latinas' abilities to navigate multiple identities are one of several strengths that they possess. Other traits such as self-efficacy, sense of purpose, and ability to continuously strategize also contribute to the success of Latinas in higher education (Zell, 2010). Many Latinas find strength and a desire to persevere from their sense of responsibility to future generations of Latina/os in higher education (Segura, 2003).

Issues of invisibility, help seeking, and navigating barriers are continual challenges encountered by Black women in college. Benjamin (1997) noted that Black women remain "marginalized, misnamed, maligned, and made invisible in the academy" (p. 2). This invisibility has persisted through time and has given credence to a faulty myth of 100% success. Rosales and Person (2003) stated, "The myth that black women have achieved high levels of educational . . . attainment over the past twenty years may contribute to the lack of attention by colleges and universities" (p. 53). In other words, the more statistics reflect an increase in educational attainment among Black women, the greater the likelihood that their needs and presence in the academy are ignored. Thomas et al. (2009) suggested that despite facing a range of barriers, including invisibility, Black women continued to enroll in college and exhibited self-efficacious behaviors, where they drew from intrinsic and extrinsic motivators.

In addition, spirituality is considered to be a significant factor in the perseverance of Black college women. Spirituality, according to Patton and McClure (2009), contributed significantly to their participants' ability to confront adversity with a belief that things would ultimately work out in their favor. Despite their efforts to succeed in college, it is important to note that there are also physical and psychological costs for Black women depending on how they handle challenges in college. In their study on perceived racial discrimination and its connection to depression in Black women students, West, Donovan, and Roemer (2009) learned that 83% of their participants had experienced subtle forms of racism. In addition, participants who engaged in the use of active coping strategies experienced fewer symptoms of depression and could "buffer the effects of racial discrimination," while those who used denial and avoidance strategies, had increased symptoms of depression (p. 343). The literature clearly suggests that Black women can persevere, but this perseverance can have negative health consequences and perpetuate a stereotypical image of the Black matriarch. Fleming (1983) defines this stereotype as one in which Black women are imagined to be independent, strong, and domineering. Stereotypes such as these, which may be perpetuated by others and by Black women, could have an impact on the extent to which they are exposed to opportunities for campus engagement if they are perceived as not needing any services or support in college.

Given the hegemonic, gender-driven society in which we live, all women have historically and systemically been treated in ways that silence their voices. This silence robs women of their ability to communicate and strips them of their ability to advocate for themselves, and for one another. In order to strive some women of color find a voice, by living and learning in-between marginalized spaces. While some may find comfort in this borderland, others may fall between this space, remaining invisible, silenced, disengaged, and even more troubling, unnoticed.

Theories and Concepts

Intersectionality

Intersectionality originated in the works of Kimberlé Crenshaw (1991), who focused on the intersections of race and gender for Black women. Crenshaw argued that when identities are treated as isolated and mutually exclusive entities, individuals who possess multiple marginalized identities often get "theoretically erased" (p. 139). The scholarship on intersectionality explains how an intersectional approach to understanding identities engages the complexities of self and argues that a more holistic understanding of identity may be exposed when individuals examine intersecting multiple identities (Anzaldúa, 1987). The scholarship also draws attention to the interconnectedness of identities, and the reality that individuals "have layered identities and can simultaneously experience oppression and privilege" (Dill, McLaughlin, & Nieves, 2007, p. 629). Rather than an additive approach that ranks identity, an intersectional approach engages the complexities of identity and argues that a more holistic understanding of identity might be garnered when identities are examined at their intersections.

Within the context of higher education, an intersectional approach to the engagement experiences of women color allows for a more nuanced understanding of their needs, which in turn offers scholars and practitioners better tools to address these needs. More specifically, applying an intersectional framework to women of color in higher education exposes both the patriarchy and racism that intersect to influence these students' experiences in the college environment. For instance, an Asian female student may disengage from a course after her White male professor tokenizes her because of her (gender and racial) identity. To understand this woman's experience through a gendered lens only, is limiting the possibility of developing a more complex understanding of what role racism and stereotypes play, as well as any number of confounded factors that allow scenarios like this one to emerge. Additionally, the power and privilege held by the White male professor and its role in shaping the classroom experience must be examined through a larger framework that acknowledges how systems of oppression are deeply rooted and interconnected. With an intersectional framework, the layered interactions women of color experience daily on college campuses may be exposed, problematized, and addressed.

While Crenshaw (1989, 1991) first wrote about the intersections of race and gender in the context of women of color and their experiences with employment and later with violence, intersectionality theory can, and does, account for other marginalized identities among women students of color such as sexuality, class, and religion. Therefore, an intersectional approach allows for a student's multiple identities to be validated. It also allows for a more holistic approach to their engagement and development.

Marginality and Mattering

Another theoretical perspective that can be used to understand the positioning of women of color in college, as well as shape efforts to fully engage them, is Schlossberg's concepts of marginality and mattering. Marginality refers to students who feel and are relegated to the margins of campus environments and their culture. Feelings of marginality can lead students to express depression, anger, or sadness. The accumulation of these feelings can affect the extent to which students feel as if they matter and has implications for whether a student chooses to remain at an institution or leave. According to Schlossberg (1989), for some, living in the margins is a permanent condition in which individuals necessarily must navigate two worlds; this is particularly true for women of racially minoritized groups. Mattering, on the other hand, is comprised of five components that when implemented, can serve as a framework that disrupts marginality. The five components include: attention, or feeling noticed; importance or feeling a sense of care; ego extension, or feeling that someone will be proud of successes or sympathetic with failures; dependence, or feeling needed, and appreciation, or feeling as if one's contributions are valued.

Given the experiences that women of color face in higher education, namely invisibility, along with devaluation of their personhood and contributions, the concepts of marginality and mattering can be easily applied. Schlossberg (1989) emphasized that colleges and universities need to make students feel as if they matter and that they have support on campus. While women of color are certainly making strides in higher education, a supportive campus that is committed to making these women feel as if they matter and engages these women in ways that actually matter can likely make a huge difference in the connections that they feel to the campus and enhance their engagement both inside and beyond the classroom.

Student Engagement Strategies

A range of programs and services can be implemented to provide opportunities for engagement among diverse groups of women of color. In this section, we offer several strategies that center the experiential knowledge that women of color possess, disrupt institutional cultures that maintain systems of invisibility and marginality, and provide them with resources and support as they pursue higher education.

Women of Color Peer Mentoring Programs

Peer mentoring programs can be very effective in providing women of color with sources of support and friendships in college. A range of patterns could be used to develop a peer-mentoring program. For example, the program could pair first year women with those who are juniors and seniors. Or, pairings could be based upon race/ethnicity. Women of color who have been heavily involved in campus activities and leadership might be paired with others who are interested in learning more about how they can become engaged on campus. Regardless of the program's design, peer mentoring will be most effective when informal and formal opportunities are in place to create and strengthen ties between women. The mentor could serve as a resource of personal support to the mentee by providing individual attention and exposure to new ideas as she navigates college and her multiple identities. Additionally, accountability to the mentee can serve as motivation for the mentor to reapply concepts to her own life and continually develop in her own personal growth.

Leadership Retreats

A retreat for women of color is one way to provide them with opportunities for leadership development. The retreat can serve as a vehicle to not only develop leadership skills, but also to explore how their presence on campus as a leader can have a significant impact on the larger campus. Activities might include personality and strengths assessments, learning about leadership styles, development of communication skills, and guided reflection on what it means to be a woman of color in a campus leadership role. The training materials should be created using a critical lens that helps the retreat participants understand how race and gender factor into how individuals lead and engage in important decision making, as well as how they work with others. For women of color who may feel invisible or silenced, an off-campus setting with trusted facilitators would be an opportunity to gain confidence in a supportive and empowering environment. The learning that occurs during the retreat can be transferred to the campus setting. A retreat environment is particularly beneficial because the participating women have a chance to develop meaningful relationships in a focused setting. After the retreat, the women bring their enhanced leadership capabilities back to campus and continue those relationships by supporting each other in long-lasting affinity spaces.

Undergraduate Courses

The creation of undergraduate courses focusing on women of color would be an excellent way to situate their experiences in the curriculum and build a partnership between Women's Studies and Ethnic Studies departments and programs. A curriculum that includes studies on women of color demonstrates an institutional commitment to diversifying the curriculum and valuing the significant contributions of women of color to society. Acknowledging women of color through the curriculum can foster classroom spaces where all students can come to gain more knowledge and understanding about women of color. These courses can create spaces for valuable discussions on political, educational, and social topics related to women of color that are less likely to be found in general academic programs. Course topics can include examination of invisibility or being silenced, occupying multiple marginalities, and self-image and identity. Furthermore, these courses can be used as an activist training ground to encourage all students to advocate for the improvement of educational environments for all people, but particularly for women of color.

WOC-Themed Community in Residence Hall

Residence hall learning communities can serve as a bridge to connect women of color with individuals who share a common passion or interest. A themed community on women of color can serve as a platform for bringing together diverse populations of women and providing a space for coalition building through frequent interaction. Women in the themed community should have ample opportunities to collaboratively live in, work in, and contribute to their own vision of community. Residence Life programming models generally address topics of interpersonal skills, academics, and life management. In addition, Residence Life staff can implement specialized programming to create unique opportunities for exploration and development. In a woman of color themed community, these programs can be further tailored to meet specific needs and interests of the women who participate in the community. Activities can include book clubs, movie night watch and discussion parties (particularly movies that positively represent women of color in featured roles), service related projects in communities that the residents represent, etc.

Quality Advisory Support

Many women of color choose to join campus organizations and sororities that serve as a support network and promote their engagement on campus. However, these groups sometimes find it difficult to secure committed advisors. University administrators should be more attentive to the needs of multicultural organizations and sororities by providing quality advising, guidance, or mentorship. Advisors should demonstrate a genuine investment in the betterment of these multicultural organizations and sororities and should also be aware of happenings across campus and encourage student leaders in the organizations to pursue a wide variety of opportunities beyond their respective groups. This can include intentional involvement in campus-wide activities or showcases and participation in events that do not typically have a felt presence from women of color students. Advisors should actively guide multicultural organizations and sororities to ensure their activities are consistent with the goal of uplift and positivity. Beyond supporting general social events, advisors can help multicultural organizations and sororities to create events that strengthen the women of color networks on campus.

Women of Color Campus Organizations

Another strategy for engaging women of color is forming an organization that includes women of color undergraduate students, graduate students, staff, and faculty members. This type of organization can serve as a space that allows women of color to explore the intersections of race and gender as well as their preconceived notions about one another. In forming an organization where women of color are central, it is critically important to consider the mentoring relationships that can be fostered as a result of the interactions between undergraduate students, graduate students, staff, and faculty members. When women of color come together, the main goal should be community building. Women of color do not magically develop solidarity; it requires relationship building. Thus, the organizers of this group should lead with knowledge regarding the diversity among women of color.

Parental and Family Involvement

Parents and families are critical sources of support for women of color. Colleges and universities must understand that parent outreach and involvement can demonstrate the institution's commitment to embracing student's families. Simply inviting parents to attend a family weekend is not enough because many women of color have parents and family members who have never been on a college campus, may not feel welcomed, or do not understand the purpose of family weekends. Families may feel that they do not need the college or university to designate a weekend for families because family is important not only during one weekend a year, but every weekend and every day. In fact, many parents may prefer for their children to come home and spend time with them instead of spending another weekend away. This does not mean that culturally inclusive methods of bringing family to campus cannot be practiced. Campus administrators, in collaboration with orientation program, family outreach programs, culture centers, and student organizations can host a family appreciation dinner on campus where students can honor their parents for the support given to them as they pursue their education. This program could prove beneficial by incorporating the value of family support, while allowing the family members to witness first-hand the benefit of their student's participation in college. Furthermore, inviting parents to campus can increase their comfort level and trust of their student's institution because they are able to see and experience the college or university for themselves.

Hiring More Women of Color Faculty and Administrators

Women of color are rarely located in key administrative positions on campus or within the faculty ranks. However, the presence of these individuals can send a powerful message to students that they too can be leaders while in college and post-graduation. Women of color who hold administrative positions and/or serve in tenure-track faculty posts can be a resource for students who need role models and advocacy. Women of color students can serve as search committee members and liaisons to faculty and administrators by giving them information about the pulse and climate of the campus. Through these relationships, faculty may gain ideas for future research, which could involve having an undergraduate research team comprised of women of color. Undergraduate women of color might also provide ideas for where women of color administrators can direct their attention as far as policy and programming. Conversely, women of color professionals can serve as active advisors to WOC organizations and mentors to individual students.

Conclusion

Many women of color come to campus with the capacity to juggle multiple identities and expectations. Moreover, they are resilient in their efforts to obtain a college education. Women of color have drive and motivation, a sense of purpose, a willingness to be collaborative, and a desire to achieve further education. Thus any strategy college and university administrators employ should be committed to providing spaces and outlets where the qualities that women of color bring are viewed as assets and contributions to the campus environment. These engagement strategies should also be geared toward disrupting negative stereotypes about various women of color and empowering these students to succeed. Culturally relevant spaces and programs that move away from deficit depictions of women of color are key in engaging these women. Given the literature presented and accompanying frameworks, engaging women of color clearly requires the implementation of affirming, holistic, strengths-based strategies. Such strategies should be designed to promote inclusion, recognize the intersections of identity and disrupt the oppressive structures within higher education that women of color regularly face.

References

Alexander, B. (2009, August 13). Marriage eludes high-achieving Black women. *MSNBC*. Retrieved from www.nbcnews.com/id/32379727/ns/health-sexual_health/t/marriage-eludes-high-achieving-black-women/#.UtmGeZH0CMI

Anzaldúa, G. (1987). *Borderlands: La frontera; the New Mestiza*. San Francisco, CA: Aunt Lute Press.

Anzaldua, G. (2007). *Borderlands: The new mestiza = La frontera* (3rd ed.). San Francisco, CA: Aunt Lute Books.

Baker, D. (2009, August 8). Marriage, Family on the decline for highly educated Black women. *Yale News*. Retrieved from http://news.yale.edu/2009/08/08/marriage-family-decline-highly-educated-black-women

Barnett, M.A. (2004). A qualitative analysis of family support an interaction among Black college students at an Ivy League university. *Journal of Negro Education, 73*(1), 53–68.

Benjamin, L. (Ed.). (1997). *Black women in the academy: Promises and perils*. Gainesville, FL: University Press of Florida.

Berkowitz, A., & Padavic, I. (1999). Getting a man or getting ahead: A comparison of White and Black sororities. *Journal of Contemporary Ethnography, 27*(4), 530–557.

Buchmann, C., & DiPrete, T.A. (2006). The growing female advantage in college completions: The role of family background and academic achievement. *American Sociological Review, 71*(4), 515–541.

Chen, E.W., & Hune, S. (2011). Asian American Pacific islander women from Ph.D. to campus president: Gains and leaks in the pipeline. In G. Jeane-Marie & B. Lloyd-Jones (Eds.), *Women of color in higher education: Changing directions and new perspectives* (pp. 163–190). Bingley, England: Emerald.

Cho, S.K. (1997). Converging stereotypes in racialized sexual harassment: Where the model minority meets Suzie Wong. *The Journal of Gender, Race, & Justice, 1*, 177–211.

Crenshaw, K.W. (1989). Demarginalizing the intersection of race and sex: A Black feminist critique of anti-discrimination doctrine, feminist theory and antiracist politics. *The University of Chicago Legal Forum, 1989*, 139–167.

Crenshaw, K. (1991). Mapping the margins: Intersectionality, identity politics and violence against women of color. *Stanford Law Review, 43*(6), 1241–1299.

Delgado, R. (1998). The Black/White binary: How does it work? In R. Delgado & J. Stefancic (Eds.), *The Latino condition: A critical reader* (pp. 369–375). New York, NY: New York University Press.

Delgado, R. & Stefancic, J. (2001). *Critical race theory: An introduction.* New York, NY: New York University Press.

Delgado Bernal, D., Elenes, C.A., Godinez, F.E., & Villenas, S. (Eds.). (2006). *Chicana/Latina education in everyday life: Feminista perspectives on pedagogy and epistemology.* Albany, NY: State University of New York Press.

Dill, B.T., McLaughlin, A.E., & Nieves, A.D. (2007). Future directions of feminist research: Intersectionality. In S.N. Hessee-Biber (Ed.), *Handbook of feminist research: Theory and praxis* (pp. 629–637). Thousand Oaks, CA: Sage.

Espinoza, R. (2010). The good daughter dilemma: Latinas managing family and school demands. *Journal of Hispanic Higher Education, 9*(4), 317–330.

Fleming, J. (1983). Black women in Black and White college environments: The making of a matriarch. *Journal of Social Issues, 39*(3), 41–54.

Fry, R., & Gonzales, F. (2008). *One-in-five and growing fast: A profile of Hispanic public school students.* Washington, DC: Pew Hispanic Center.

Fry, R., & Passel, J.S. (2009). *Latino children: A majority are U.S. born offspring of immigrants.* Washington, DC: Pew Hispanic Center.

Gloria, A.M., & Castellanos, J. (2012). Desafíos y bendiciones: A multiperspective examination of the educational experiences and coping responses of first-generation college Latina students. *Journal of Hispanic Higher Education, 11*(1), 82–99.

González, K.P., Jovel, J.E., & Stoner, C. (2004). Latinas: The new Latino majority in college. In A.M. Ortiz (Ed.), *Addressing the unique needs of Latino American students.* New Directions for Student Services (no. 105, pp. 17–27). San Francisco, CA: Jossey-Bass.

Hayes, D. (October 12, 2012). Despite outpacing men in educational attainment women's pay still lagging. *Diverse Issues in Higher Education* [online]. Retrieved from http://diverseeducation.com/article/48716

Hernandez-Truyol, B.E. (2003). Latinas-everywhere alien: Culture, gender, and sex. In A.K. Wing (Ed.), *Critical Race Feminism: A Reader* (2nd ed., pp. 57–69). New York, NY: New York University Press.

Hill Collins, P. (2000). *Black feminist thought: Knowledge, consciousness and the politics of empowerment.* New York, NY: Routledge.

Hune, S. (1998). *Asian Pacific American women in higher education: Claiming visibility and voice.* Washington, DC: Association of American Colleges and Universities.

Jackson, L.R. (1998). The experience of both race and gender on the experiences of African American college women. *The Review of Higher Education, 21*(4), 359–375.

Kiang, P.N. (1996). Persistance stories and survival strategies of Cambodian Americans in college. *Journal of Narrative and Life History, 6*(1), 39–64.

Lee, S.J. (1997). The road to college: Hmong women's pursuit of higher education. *Harvard Educational Review, 67*(4), 803–827.

Maes, J. (2010). *Latinas and the educational pipeline.* Mayor's Office for Education and Children, Denver, CO.

Maramba, D.C. (2008). Immigrant families and the college experience: Perspectives of Filipina Americans. *Journal of College Student Development, 49*(4), 336–350.

Montoya, M.E. (2003). Mascaras, Trenzas, y Grenas: Un/masking the self while un/braiding Latina stories and legal discourse. In A.K. Wing (Ed.), *Critical Race Feminsm: A Reader* (2nd ed., pp. 70–77). New York, NY: New York University Press.

Moraga, C., & Anzaldua, G. (Eds.). (1983). *This bridge called my back: Writings by radical women of color* (2nd ed.). New York, NY: Kitchen Table, Women of Color Press.

Patton, L.D., & McClure, M. (2009). Strength in the spirit: African American college women and spiritual coping mechanisms. *Journal of Negro Education, 78*(1), 42–54.

Patton, L.D., & Winkle-Wagner, R. (2012). Race at first sight: The funding of racial scripts between Black and White women. In K. Dace (Ed.), *Unlikely allies in the academy: Women of color and White women in conversation* (pp. 181–191). New York, NY: Routledge.

Pyke, K.D., & Johnson, D.L. (2003). Asian American women and racialized femininities: "Doing" gender across cultural worlds. *Gender and Society, 17*(1), 33–53.

Railton, D., & Watson, P. (2005). Naughty girls and red blooded women: Representations of female heterosexuality in music video. *Feminist Media Studies, 5*(1), 51–63.

Renn, K.A. (2000). Patterns of situational identity among biracial and multiracial college students. *Review of Higher Education, 23*(4), 399–420.

Rios-Aguilar, C., & Deil-Amen, R. (2012). Beyond getting in and fitting in: An examination of social networks and professionally relevant social capital among Latina/o university students. *Journal of Hispanic Higher Education, 11*(2), 179–196.

Rosales, A.M., & Person, D.R. (2003, Winter). Programming needs and student services for African American women. In M.F. Howard-Hamilton (Ed.), *Meeting the needs of African American women.* New Directions for Student Services (no. 104, pp. 53–66). San Francisco, CA: Jossey-Bass.

Roshanravan, S.M. (2010). Passing-as-if: Model-minority subjectivity and women of color identification. *Meridians: Feminism, Race, Transnationalisms, 10*(1), 1–31.

Saenz, V.B., & Ponjuan, L. (2009). The vanishing Latino male in higher education. *Journal of Hispanic Higher Education, 8*(1), 54–89.

Schlossberg, N.K. (1989). Mattering and marginality: Key issues in building community. In D.C. Roberts (Ed.), *Designing campus activities to foster a sense of community.* New Directions for Student Services (no. 48, pp. 5–15). San Francisco, CA: Jossey-Bass.

Segura, D.A. (2003). Navigating between two worlds: The labyrinth of Chicana intellectual production in the academy. *Journal of Black Studies, 34*(1), 28–51.

Stanley, A. (2011, December 10). Black, female, and single. *The New York Times.* Retrieved from www.nytimes.com/2011/12/11/opinion/sunday/black-and-female-the-marriage-question.html?pagewanted=all&_r=0

Sue, D.W. (2010). Microaggressions, marginality, and oppression: An introduction. In D.W. Sue (Ed.), *Microaggressions and marginality: Manifestation, dynamics, and impact* (pp. 3–22). Hoboken, NJ: Wiley.

Sue, D.W., Bucceri, J., Lin, A.I., Nadal, K.L., & Torino, G.C. (2007). Racial microaggressions and the Asian American experience. *Asian American Journal of Psychology, S*(1), 88–101.

Sy, S.R., & Romero, J. (2008). Family responsibilities among Latina college students from immigrant families. *Journal of Hispanic Higher Education, 7*(3), 212–227.

Thomas, D.M., Love, K.M., Roan-Belle, C., Tyler, K.M., Brown, C.L., & Garriott, P.O. (2009). Self-efficacy, motivatiosn, and academic adjustment among African American women attending institutiosn of higher education. *Journal of Negro Education, 78*(2), 159–171.

Villalpando, O. (2003). Self-segregation or self-preservation? A critical race theory and Latina/o critical theory analysis of a study of Chicana/o college students. *International Journal of Qualitative Studies in Education, 16*(5), 619–646.

West, L.M., Donovan, R.A., & Roemer, L. (2009). Coping with racism: What works and doesn't work for Black women? *Journal of Black Psychology, 36*(3), 331–349.

Zell, M.C. (2010). Achieving a college education: The psychological experiences of Latina/o community college students. *Journal of Hispanic Higher Education, 9*(2), 167–186.

Chapter 4
Engaging College Men of Color

Shaun R. Harper, Jonathan Berhanu,
Charles H.F. Davis III, and
Keon M. McGuire

Much attention has been devoted in recent years to the status and experiences of college men of color, particularly Black and Latino male undergraduates. Perhaps Harper (2013a) offers the most succinct description of what scholars have recently documented about these populations:

> They are outnumbered at most colleges and universities, their grade point averages are among the lowest of all undergraduate students, their engagement in classrooms and enriching out-of-class experiences is alarmingly low, and their attrition rates are comparatively higher than those of White students in U.S. higher education . . . Encounters with racism, racial stereotypes, microaggressions, and low expectations from professors and others undermine their academic outcomes, sense of belonging, and willingness to seek help and utilize campus resources. (p. 3)

These problems help partially explain racialized sex gaps in postsecondary degree attainment (see Figure 4.1) and other phenomena related to college completion—for example, fewer than one-third of Black undergraduate men who start baccalaureate degree programs graduate within six years, which is the lowest college completion rate among both sexes and all racial groups. Educators, institutional leaders, higher education researchers, and policymakers have become increasingly concerned about the disproportionate occurrences and effects of these issues on undergraduate men of color.

While some scholarship on Latino undergraduate men has been published in the higher education literature over the past 15 years (e.g., González, 2002; Guardia & Evans, 2008; Morales, 2009; Saez, Casado, & Wade, 2009; Sáenz & Ponjuan, 2009, 2011; Schwartz, Donovan, & Guido-DiBrito, 2009; Villalpando, 2006), far greater emphasis has been placed on researching and documenting trends concerning Black men in higher education (Harris & Wood, 2013). Presented in Tables 4.1 and 4.2 are examples of books, reports, and peer-reviewed journal articles published about Black undergraduate men between 1997 and

2013. Black male students have also been the focus of several articles published in *The Chronicle of Higher Education*, *Diverse Issues in Higher Education*, *Inside Higher Ed*, and several other news outlets; the outcomes and experiences of Asian American, Latino, and Native American men have not received much media coverage.

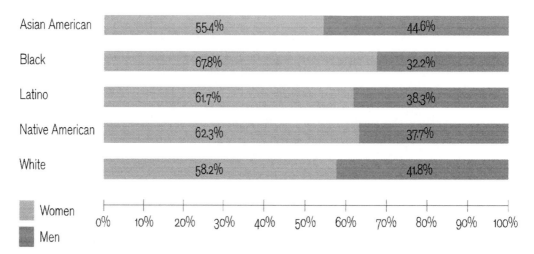

FIGURE 4.1. Sex Differences in Postsecondary Degree Attainment, All Levels
Source: Harper and Harris (2012). Reprinted with permission from the University of Pennsylvania, Center for the Study of Race and Equity in Education

TABLE 4.1. Books and Reports on Black Undergraduate Men, 1997–2012

Publication Type	Author(s)/Editor(s)
Books	Bonner II (2010)
	Byrne (2006)
	Cuyjet (1997)
	Cuyjet (2006)
	Dancy II (2012)
	Frierson, Pearson, & Wyche (2009)
	Frierson, Wyche, & Pearson (2009)
	Hilton, Wood, & Lewis (2012)
	Jones (2004)
	Palmer & Wood (2012)
	Ross (1998)
Reports	Harper (2006a)
	Harper (2012)
	Harper & Harris (2012)
	Harper & Porter (2012)
	Harper, Williams, & Blackman (2013)

TABLE 4.2. Select Peer-Reviewed Journal Articles on Black Undergraduate Men, by Subgroup/Sector, 1998–2013

Subgroup/Sector	Author(s)
Achievers and Student Leaders	Bonner II (2003)
	Harper (2013b)
	Harper & Quaye (2007)
	Harper et al. (2011)
	Warde (2008)
Community Colleges	Bush & Bush (2010)
	Glenn (2004)
	Hagedorn, Maxwell, & Hampton (2002)
	Strayhorn (2012)
	Wood (2012)
	Wood, Hilton, & Lewis (2011)
	Wood & Turner (2011)
Fraternity Members	McClure (2006a)
	McClure (2006b)
	Ray (2012)
Gay/Bisexual Men	Goode-Cross & Good (2009)
	Goode-Cross & Tager (2011)
	Harris (2003)
	Patton (2011)
	Strayhorn, Blakewood, & DeVita (2008)
	Strayhorn & Mullins (2012)
Historically Black Colleges and Universities	Harper & Gasman (2008)
	Palmer, Davis, and Hilton (2009)
	Riggins, McNeal, & Herndon (2008)
	Washington, Wang, & Browne (2009)
Student-Athletes	Beamon & Bell (2006)
	Benson (2000)
	Martin, Harrison, & Bukstein (2010)
	Oseguera (2010)
	Singer (2005)

Conversations at national conferences and elsewhere tend to be centered around the following questions: why are there so few men of color in college, why do they perform so poorly in their academics, why do they drop out in such high numbers, and why are they so disengaged inside and outside of college classrooms (Harper, 2013a). In this chapter, we problematize the engagement question in two ways. First, we use literature on Black undergraduate men to show the one-sided, deficit-oriented way engagement has been framed. Second, we critique the misplacement of the onus for engagement. Consistent with other parts of this book, we advocate for greater institutional responsibility in engaging students. Hence, the theories we use herein focus on shifting frames and understanding campus environments as organizational contexts that either encourage or undermine the engagement of undergraduate men of color. The chapter concludes with some conditions and strategies we believe are necessary to better engage Asian American, Black, Latino, and Native American men in enriching educational experiences.

Disengagement Trends

As noted previously, there is lopsidedness in the published research on college men of color. More has been published in the past decade and a half on Black undergraduate men than all of the three other racial groups combined. This is especially true in the engagement literature. With the exception of a handful of publications that include two or more racial groups (e.g., Harper, 2013a; Harper & Associates, 2014; Harper, Williams, Pérez, & Morgan, 2012; Harris & Wood, 2013; Lee & Ransom, 2011; Strayhorn, 2010), everything else focuses on a single race, almost always Blacks. Given this, the literature we review in this section is very much reflective of what has been written. Although our synthesis focuses entirely on Black undergraduate men, anecdotes from educators and administrators at national conferences suggest similar disengagement trends are also prevalent among Native American, Latino, and some Asian American male subgroups (e.g., Hmong and Laotian students).

Engagement-related gender disparities among Black collegians are not a new phenomenon, but trends have reversed. Previous researchers (Allen, 1986; Fleming, 1984; Gurin & Epps, 1975) found that Black men were considerably more engaged than were Black women in the 1970s and 1980s. Reportedly, Black men gained more, were more actively engaged in the classroom, interacted more frequently with faculty, and developed more positive identities and educational and career aspirations during that era. More recent evidence confirms the engagement pendulum has swung in the other direction, as Black women now report significantly higher levels of engagement.

In their study of gender differences in engagement, Harper, Carini, Bridges, and Hayek found: "women no longer lag behind men in their academic and social engagement experiences. Overall, the engagement picture for women appears to be considerably less grim . . . women have overcome the engagement odds and social passivity of years past" (2004, pp. 277, 279). This claim is substantiated by other empirical research studies published in recent years. Gender shifts in engagement have occurred across a range of institutional types, including two-year and community colleges. In comparison to their same-race male peers, Black female respondents to the Community College Survey of Student Engagement were more likely to:

- **Discuss ideas from readings or classes** with others outside of class "often" or "very often" (57% women vs. 45% men).

- **Use the Internet** to work on an assignment "often" or "very often" (60% women vs. 52% men).
- Report that their college encouraged them to **spend significant time studying** (80% of women vs. 73% of men reported "quite a bit" or "very much").
- **Have plans to continue their studies** (31% of men vs. 24% of women had no plan or were uncertain about their intent to continue college). (CCSSE, 2005, pp. 7–8)

Cuyjet's (1997) analysis of data from the College Student Experiences Questionnaire also captured many alarming gender disparities, but at four-year institutions. His study was based on data from 6,765 Black student respondents to the national survey who attended a wide range of colleges and universities across the country. Cuyjet found that Black men devoted less time to studying, took notes in class less often, spent significantly less time writing and revising papers, and participated less often in class-related collaborative experiences than did Black female respondents to the survey. Furthermore, Black women in comparison to their same-race male peers were more engaged in campus activities, looked more frequently in their campus newspapers for notices about upcoming events and engagement opportunities, attended more meetings and programs, served on more campus committees, and held more leadership positions at their institutions. Playing recreational sports and exercising in campus fitness facilities were the only areas on the survey where Black men reported higher levels of engagement.

Black male student leaders in Harper's (2006b) study indicated that while Black women were reaping the benefits of leadership and engagement, the overwhelming majority of their male counterparts were spending their time doing nothing, pursuing romantic endeavors with female students, playing basketball and working out in the campus fitness center, video gaming, and working jobs to earn money for familial responsibilities and material possessions (clothes, shoes, cars, etc.). Participants overwhelmingly indicated their Black male peers invested minimal out-of-class time to academic endeavors. These claims are supported by findings in Harper et al.'s (2004) study. In their analysis of data collected from 1,167 Black undergraduates at 12 Historically Black Colleges and Universities (HBCUs) that participated in the National Survey of Student Engagement, the researchers found significant differences between men and women on the *Level of Academic Challenge* benchmark of the survey. As mentioned in Chapter 1, activities in this area include studying, reading, rehearsing, preparing for class, writing long papers, applying theories and course concepts to practical situations, and working hard to meet professors' expectations. Black male HBCU students were less engaged than were their female counterparts in this domain.

Also regarding out-of-class engagement trends at HBCUs, the general consensus among the Black male student leaders in Kimbrough and Harper's (2006) qualitative study is that Black men are grossly disengaged. Data were collected from Student Government Association presidents, fraternity chapter leaders, and resident assistants (RAs) at nine different HBCUs. Among the numerous engagement-related gender disparities cited, Kimbrough and Harper note that only seven of 49 student government members at two different HBCUs were men. In sum, the student leaders confirmed that purposeful engagement, especially outside the classroom, is extremely unpopular among Black men at HBCUs (as is the case throughout most of higher education). At HBCUs and PWIs (predominantly White institutions) alike, Sutton and Kimbrough (2001) report sororities and fraternities are among the most popular venues for out-of-class engagement among Black undergraduates. However, Harper and Harris (2006) contend these groups have declined in popularity among men, as chapters on many campuses have fewer than 10 members.

Participants in Kimbrough and Harper's (2006) study offered five explanations for these Black male disengagement trends: (1) Men deem sports, physical activity, and athleticism more socially acceptable and "cooler" than campus leadership and purposeful engagement; (2) male students typically encounter difficulty working together, which is often required in student organizations; (3) many Black men come to college having already been socialized to devalue purposeful engagement; (4) there is a shortage of Black male role models and mentors on campus who actively and strategically promote purposeful engagement; and (5) many Black men are unable to meet the minimum 2.5 grade point average requirement for membership in one of the five historically Black fraternities. Harper (2006b) contends that gender disparities in Black student enrollments have contributed to a decline in male leadership on most campuses. Since they do not see many others who are highly engaged on campus, many Black men conclude that engagement is socially inexpedient and perhaps even feminine—definitely not normative (Harper, 2004).

While all are most likely true and some have been empirically proven, the problem with these explanatory factors is that they almost exclusively attribute disengagement to students' attitudes and behaviors, not the institutions they attend. Educators and administrators are in many ways complicit in the cyclical reproduction of these trends. Negligence in fostering the necessary conditions for engagement and the infrequency of collective efforts to study and craft strategic responses to factors that compel Black men's detachment from the educational experience have been inadequately considered. Perhaps institutions, especially predominantly White colleges and universities, have not fully recognized the value in engaging, retaining, and graduating Black male students and other undergraduate men of color. Furthermore, deficit views of them usually compel institutional fascination with the undercurrents of disengagement instead of learning from highly engaged and successful students within these populations.

Theories and Concepts

As mentioned earlier, we advocate approaching the treatment of engagement differently by shifting the responsibility from undergraduate men of color to educators and administrators. To this end, we have decided against placing disengagement issues in an explanatory framework comprised of developmental, psychosocial, and student-centered theories. Instead, we have chosen theories and concepts that help make sense of college and university campuses as organizations for learning and environments that can be changed. Moreover, we make use of theories pertaining to the racial implications of engendering care for undergraduate men of color at PWIs and possibilities associated with anti-deficit views of student achievement.

Organizational Learning Theory

According to Argyris and Schön (1996), learning occurs when organizations "adapt to changing environments, draw lessons from past successes and failures, and detect and correct errors of the past, anticipate and respond to impending threats, engage in continuous innovation, and build and realize images of a desirable future" (p. xvii). Organizational learning extends beyond individuals, but instead is collective (Kezar, 2005). Concerning engagement disparities that persistently disadvantage undergraduate men of color, educators and administrators on the campus could tap available data sources and engage in dialogues that help illuminate the undercurrents of inequities, make clear what is needed to foster an environment for success, and come to understand the complexity of factors that require mediation for the actualization of institutional goals. Theories suggest that organizational stakeholders would share this knowledge and make sense of it collectively.

Despite the focus on collaboration, individuals play an important role in the learning process. For example, Bensimon (2005) describes three key concepts related to the role of individuals in organizational learning:

(1) Learning is done by individuals who are members of an organizational entity such as a college or university, an administrative division, an academic department, or a research team; (2) individuals inquire into a problem collectively, on behalf of an organizational entity; and (3) organizational culture and structures can promote or inhibit individual learning. (p. 101)

Moreover, Kezar (2005) contends that trust between individual collaborators, the establishment of new information systems, rewards and incentives, knowledge sharing and open communication, collaborative inquiry teams, and staff development are all necessary features of organizational learning.

Argyris and Schön (1996) describe two types of learning in organizations: single-loop and double-loop. The former places emphasis on external factors for problems in organizations (e.g., "these Asian American males do so poorly because they are insufficiently prepared for college"). This version of learning leads to incremental change, as organization members fail to recognize their own role in the stifling of desired outcomes (Kezar, 2005). In short, problems are narrowly examined, attribution is almost always external, and organizational toxins often remain unexamined. Bensimon (2005) posits that equity requires double-loop learning, which "focuses attention on the root causes of a problem and the changes that need to be made in the attitudes, values, beliefs, and practices of individuals" (p. 104). This version of organizational learning would require, for example, an inward examination of why a Latino male student sits passively and performs poorly in courses where he is constantly stereotyped by the professor and classmates, exposed to culturally-irrelevant perspectives in assigned readings, and only expected to be engaged when an opportunity arises for him to be the token spokesperson for all Latino persons. Double-loop learning would also oblige teams of educators to gather qualitative insights into how Latino males view the campus as a normative space for engagement—what they learn should guide future efforts to make necessary environmental adjustments.

Theoretical Perspectives on Environmental Press

Environmental press refers to the norms of a campus environment that can be described as distinctive to the institution by students, faculty, and staff, as well as visitors (Pace & Stern, 1958; Stern, 1970; Strange, 2003). Presses are characteristic of what is generally acceptable and normative within the campus environment (Pace, 1969). As such, they shape the behaviors students display and the degrees to which they buy into perceived consensus on a campus. If the majority of male students of color are disengaged, then most will conclude that engagement is not the "thing to do." Strange and Banning (2001) explained that certain environmental presses can inhibit student growth, particularly when there is significant distance between what the student needs and the prevailing press of the campus. For example, Native American male students need to be engaged to acquire the political acumen required for the cultivation of meaningful relationships with administrators, but if the normative press of the campus is disengagement among this particular population, then few are likely to act in ways counter to it.

Baird (1988) noted the following: "Presses are of two types, first as they exist in reality or an objective inquiry discloses them to be (alpha press), and second as they are perceived or interpreted by the individual (beta press)" (p. 3). Baird also presents two versions of beta presses, *private* and *consensual*. The first is related to the unique view a student has about her or his experience, whereas the latter pertains to estimations of commonalities in experiences and outcomes. At the end of a three-day visit that included observations and several focus groups, a consultant could conclude that undergraduate men of color are largely disengaged, and it is primarily the institution's fault. The real indicators of disengagement would be the alpha press. An individual Cambodian male sophomore could attribute his disengagement to the insufficient provision of clubs and activities that appeal to his unique cultural interests (private beta press), but might also believe most of his same-race male peers are disengaged due to the overwhelming Whiteness of social offerings on the campus (consensual beta press).

Were the current problems concerning achievement among undergraduate men of color strategically addressed, then the consensual beta press could become that most within these populations are actively engaged . . . it is normal. Likewise, the alpha press that a Black male prospective student would encounter might lead him to the following conclusion: "Wow, should I choose to enroll at this university, there is going to be a serious expectation that I become as actively engaged as all the other Black dudes here." We believe presses can be changed, but only if educators willingly accept responsibility for undertaking the complex work of cultural change. But why would they? What is in it for them?

Critical Race Theory and Interest-Convergence

Based on scholarly perspectives from law, sociology, history, ethnic studies, and women's studies, Critical Race Theory (CRT) illuminates the inequitable distribution of power and privilege as well as racism and racial disadvantages within organizations (Bell, 1987; Delgado & Stefancic, 2001). CRT also challenges misconceptions regarding colorblindness, merit, and racial equity; critiques claims of liberalism; and ignites consciousness that leads to social justice and advances for people of color (Crenshaw, Gotanda, Peller, & Thomas, 1995). One of the tenets of CRT is interest-convergence, which, according to Delgado (1995), "encourage racial advances for Blacks only when they also promote white self-interests" (p. xiv). It is used in this theoretical framework to help answer a question like, "why would an institution whose faculty and staff is almost exclusively White engage in double-loop learning and take on the challenge of creating a normative culture of engagement for Black males and other undergraduate men of color?"

Interest-convergence helps explain the motivating factors that might compel majority advocacy on minority issues—essentially, there has to be something in it for Whites and they must see value in their efforts. Critical Race Theorists argue that White persons rarely act on behalf of minority groups "out of the goodness of their hearts." Consequently, Delgado and Stefancic (2001) contend that efforts to eradicate racism have produced minimal results due to the insufficient convergence of interests. That is, people of color have long hoped for racial justice, equity, and fairness, but those interests have not converged effectively with the goals of the powerful persons from whom those things have been sought. Students of color often want more faculty of color, but in most instances it is not until protests ensue, media attention is garnered, and the institution is embarrassed by the public exposure of its structural problems with race that administrators move in any serious way to hire cohorts of minority faculty.

"We cannot ignore and should learn from and try to recognize situations when there is a convergence of interests" (Bell, 2000, p. 9). Making clear how retaining undergraduate men of color will ultimately increase the overall retention rates for a predominantly White college is one example. Another is pointing out the outcomes that will accrue for White student leaders via their interactions with Asian American, Black, Latino, and Native American men (e.g., developing cross-cultural communication skills that will be employable in future settings, which will make the institution look like it graduates progressive people who are not ignorant racists). And a third example is that changing the environmental press of the campus could garner for the institution a better reputation which will ultimately stimulate increased financial contributions from alumni of color. Donnor (2005) offers an example of when interests do not converge effectively between Black male student-athletes and universities with major sports programs:

> Critical race theory offers a means to better recognize and more fully understand the forces that have constructed a system in which African American athletes are cheered on the field by wealthy alumni and powerful fans while at the same time denied opportunities to earn the degree that could lead to wealth and power of their own. (p. 63)

A college president is quite powerful and could steer most agendas she or he deem worthwhile. But agenda movement often comes at a cost, hence White presidents and other senior administrators must see the value of expending their political capital in support of equity and engagement for male students of color. Surely, there will be resistance from faculty and others if the ways in which the White majority will benefit are not made clear.

Harper's Anti-Deficit Achievement Framework

Harper (2012) introduced a framework that researchers, educators, and administrators can use to better understand Black male student success in college. The framework was used in his National Black Male College Achievement Study, a qualitative research project that included individual interviews with 219 Black undergraduate men attending 42 colleges and universities in 20 states across the United States. The framework (see Figure 4.2) is informed by three decades of literature on Black men in education and society, as well as theories from sociology, psychology, gender studies, and education. It inverts questions that are commonly asked about educational disadvantage, underrepresentation, insufficient preparation, academic underperformance, disengagement, and Black male student attrition. Harper's framework counters the *orientation* (focus on stereotypical characteristics associated with the culture of disadvantage and poverty), *discourse* (lack of preparation, motivation, study skills, blaming students and/or their backgrounds), and *strategies* (compensatory educational programs, remedial courses, special programs, all focused on fixing the student) associated with the *Deficit Cognitive Frame* that Bensimon (2005, p. 103) describes.

Harper (2012) noted this framework is not intended to be an exhaustive or prescriptive register of research topics; instead, it includes examples of the anti-deficit questioning employed in his national study. The framework is also adaptable for the study of achievement among Asian American, Latino, and Native American male undergraduates. It includes *some* questions that educators and researchers *could* explore to better understand how Black undergraduate men successfully navigate their way to and through higher education and onward to rewarding post-college options. Insights into questions such as those listed in Figure 4.2 shed light on three pipeline points (pre-college socialization and readiness, college achievement, and post-college success) as well as eight researchable dimensions of achievement (familial factors, K-12 school forces, out-of-school college prep resources, classroom experiences, out-of-class engagement, enriching educational experiences, graduate school enrollment, and career readiness). Each dimension includes 2–4 *sample* questions. Given what the literature says about the significant impact of peers and faculty on college student development and success (see Pascarella & Terenzini, 2005), particular attention should be devoted to understanding their role in the undergraduate experiences of male students of color who are highly engaged and academically successful.

PRE-COLLEGE SOCIALIZATION AND READINESS

FAMILIAL FACTORS

How do family members nurture and sustain Black male students' interest in school?

How do parents help shape Black men's college aspirations?

K-12 SCHOOL FORCES

What do teachers and other school agents do to assist Black men in getting to college?

How do Black male students negotiate academic achievement alongside peer acceptance?

OUT-OF-SCHOOL COLLEGE PREP RESOURCES

How do low-income and first generation Black male students acquire knowledge about college?

Which programs and experiences enhance Black men's college readiness?

COLLEGE ACHIEVEMENT

CLASSROOM EXPERIENCES

Which instructional practices best engage Black male collegians?

How do Black men craft productive responses to stereotypes encountered in classrooms?

What compels one to speak and participate actively in courses in which he is the only Black student?

How do Black undergraduate men earn GPAs above 3.0 in majors for which they were academically underprepared?

FACULTY

PERSISTENCE

PEERS

ENRICHING EDUCATIONAL EXPERIENCES

What developmental gains do Black male achievers attribute to studying abroad?

How do Black men cultivate value-added relationships with faculty and administrators?

What do Black male students find appealing about doing research with professors?

OUT-OF-CLASS ENGAGEMENT

What compels Black men to take advantage of campus resources and engagement opportunities?

What unique educational benefits and outcomes are conferred to Black male student leaders?

How do achievers foster mutually supportive relationships with their lower-performing same-race male peers?

POST-COLLEGE SUCCESS

GRADUATE SCHOOL ENROLLMENT

What happened in college to develop and support Black male students' interest in pursuing degrees beyond the baccalaureate?

How do Black undergraduate men who experience racism at predominantly White universities maintain their commitment to pursuing graduate and professional degrees at similar types of institutions?

CAREER READINESS

Which college experiences enable Black men to compete successfully for careers in their fields?

What prepares Black male achievers for the racial politics they will encounter in post-college workplace settings?

How do faculty and other institutional agents enhance Black men's career development and readiness?

Figure 4.2. Harper's (2007) Anti-Deficit Achievement Framework

Source: Harper (2012). Reprinted with permission from the University of Pennsylvania, Center for the Study of Race and Equity in Education

Before presenting a set of strategies, we first describe some conditions we believe are necessary before an institution can claim seriousness about improving engagement among undergraduate men of color. First, campus leaders must make this a high institutional priority. Recognizing there are countless issues that merit the attention of senior administrators, the decision to focus on this particular population should be data-driven. At many colleges and universities, analyses of engagement and retention data could easily justify the need to devote immediate attention to this particular population. These findings should stimulate a cross-campus campaign that is aggressive and conveyed with urgency. Institutional leaders also must have goals for the gains, outcomes, and levels of engagement they hope to see among Asian American, Black, Latino, and Native American male undergraduates; resources must be invested toward these efforts in order to confirm that creating a culture of engagement is indeed a priority. These goals should be documented, widely disseminated, and frequently discussed across the campus. An assistant professor in the English department, for example, should not accidentally discover the university has goals for addressing many of the same engagement issues that plague male students of color in her courses—it would be better if she and others across the campus received a communiqué articulating the institution's objectives for improving engagement and outcomes for these specific student populations.

Institutional leaders must also have high expectations for men of color and those who are positioned to engage them, both inside and outside the classroom. Clarity in the articulation of these expectations is critical. Strategic planning by administrators and other stakeholders is also essential. Strategy must permeate the campus at large as well as specific aspects of the institution (the student affairs division, the mathematics department, classes that emphasize writing, etc.). Given that undergraduate men in general and male students of color in particular graduate at rates lower than their female peers (Harper & Harris, 2012), it seems appropriate to suggest that presidents hire an outside strategist to advise senior administrators on how to best reverse this trend. Accountability is another necessary condition. Faculty, staff, and administrators should be held accountable for advancing the institution's agenda for male student success. For example, if improving Black male student-athlete retention rates and increasing student-athlete engagement in activities outside the athletics department have been identified as institutional goals, the athletic director must be willing to hold coaches and others within the department accountable for implementing new approaches, documenting efforts, and demonstrating effectiveness in this regard. Also, the person to whom the athletic director reports (usually the president) must hold her or him accountable for contributing to the institution's goals by making engagement a proven priority in the athletics department.

Lastly, collaboration among various institutional stakeholders—from food service workers to the Director of Residence Life to the Dean of Engineering and students themselves—is also a requisite indicator of seriousness. Stakeholders from across the campus must be brought together to help actualize the institution's goals and develop ways to reinforce expectations for student achievement and engagement. Simply convening faculty and staff once in a gymnasium to listen to a speaker and expecting them to be compelled to partner is exactly opposite of what we are recommending here. Instead, specific approaches to fostering collaborative partnerships must be written into the aforementioned strategic plans. In sum, high priority, goals, high expectations, strategy, accountability, and collaboration are all necessary indicators of institutional seriousness. To be clear, we are asserting that institutional stagnation will ensue and disengagement will remain normative among undergraduate men of color in the absence of these important conditions. Notice that everything we have written in this section requires leadership, specifically presidential action. What we are proposing in this chapter is likely to become a serious campus-wide priority if the president is involved.

Student Engagement Strategies

As indicated in the previous section, evidence of collaborative effort across the campus is one way to determine if an institution is serious about improving engagement among male students of color. In this section we present possible ways that faculty, staff, and administrators can partner to reverse problematic trends and outcomes. This is not to diminish the worth of individual action and one-on-one work with students. But no lone academic advisor, faculty member, or administrator in multicultural affairs (or anywhere else) can single-handedly create a campus-wide culture of engagement. Caring and committed individuals are important, but it is usually the case that a small cohort of such persons is treated as the default source of advocacy for students of color (and this group is often primarily comprised of staff of color). Student engagement must be everyone's responsibility at the institution, especially if the status of male students of color is ever to be improved. To this end, below are four ideas for collaborative partnerships.

- The Equity Scorecard process developed by Professor Estela Mara Bensimon and a team of researchers in the Center for Urban Education (CUE) at the University of Southern California is perhaps the best available model of collaboration and organizational learning (see Bauman, 2005; Bauman, Bustillos, Bensimon, Brown, & Bartee, 2005; Bensimon, 2004; Harris & Bensimon, 2007; Peña, Bensimon, & Colyar, 2006)—it is one we highly recommend for institutions that are serious about closing racialized and gendered gaps that disadvantage undergraduate men of color. This process brings together faculty, staff, administrators, and institutional researchers who work in teams to examine unique data sources that could provide some insights into inequities that would otherwise remain hidden. Ideally, there should be alignment between a group's representation in the student body and its members' engagement in various experiences or acquisition of certain outcomes. For example, an analysis of students listed on the dean's list might reveal that Latino males comprise 4.3% of the student population on campus, but 0.3% of achievers on the dean's list. The team not only makes this discovery, but also partners to investigate the origins of and explanatory factors for this gap. In the process, team members are engaged in thinking about how their own practices contribute to the inequities they have uncovered, and they learn much about the organization in which these disparities are continually reproduced. This enables them to approach planning and institutional transformation efforts with greater enthusiasm, purpose, and focus. What we have offered here is a simplified summary of the process; thus, readers are encouraged to retrieve the published work we cited above. Any institution looking to take on the enormous task of engaging undergraduate men of color should consider consulting CUE to help facilitate the Equity Scorecard process. The ways in which it can guide institutional action and facilitate organizational learning have not been overstated here.

- A second collaborative strategy is the formation of engagement teams for male students of color. These teams can be comprised of academic advisors, faculty, and professionals in athletics, student activities, residence life, ethnic culture centers, and first-year student program offices. Members of this team can work to create with students individual engagement plans that guide the expenditure of their time outside of class, provide a set of strategies for managing engagement in different types of classroom environments (being engaged in an Intro to Asian American History class may be more challenging for some than a Physics course). The team can work together to establish protocol and common approaches to engagement planning; meet at least twice per semester or quarter with each of the men whose engagement plans they supervise; and meet with each other periodically to assess effectiveness, share approaches that have worked for them individually, and learn from each other strategies for reaching resistant students whose engagement plans have not quite taken shape.

- A committee on improving the academic status of male students of color is a third collaborative partnership idea. Deans and department chairs, administrators from student affairs and multicultural affairs, basketball and football coaches, faculty, and students can work together to envision, implement, and assess a systematic set of initiatives to improve grades, transfer trends (at community colleges), and retention and graduation rates among male undergraduates. An equally important function of this committee should be ensuring that undergraduate men of color are introduced to the rich harvest of learning opportunities that are available on and external to the campus (e.g., study abroad programs, internships, and summer research programs with faculty). The committee should rely on data from the Equity Scorecard team, as well as qualitative interviews with men who have persisted, performed well, and benefited from participation in enriching educational experiences. In addition, the team should coordinate an initiative that is data-driven and imaginative. Its work will not prosper, however, if committee members hold low expectations for their work or deficit views of men of color on campus.

- Staff from the counseling office, male graduate students of color, faculty, and student affairs educators, to name a few, can partner to offer advisory support to ethnic student organizations. Harper and Quaye (2007), Harper (2013b), as well as several contributors to Cuyjet's (2006) edited volume amplify the important role such groups play on predominantly White campuses. Accordingly, they provide an outlet for men of color to gather and be themselves; learn from the diversity within the group and challenge stereotypes they have about each other; discuss ideas and problems that pertain directly to them without fear of judgment from White onlookers and women; and share resources and navigational insights that could help improve their individual and collective existence on campus. While these groups are enormously powerful, they would benefit greatly from a strong web of supporters who collaboratively offer advisement. These advisors should work with student leaders in these groups to create an agenda that addresses many of the strengths and weaknesses men bring to the college setting; having a counselor (preferably a man of color) on the team would be especially helpful.

These partnership ideas are not meant to be prescriptive—meaning, it was not our intent to offer four ideas that will solve every engagement problem plaguing male students of color on all college and university campuses. Instead, it is the essence, seriousness, and coordinated nature of these ideas that we are hoping will inspire readers. Again, all efforts should be data-driven and context specific—the problems with and possibilities for male student engagement at the University of Arizona are surely different from those at the University of Wisconsin and the University of Pennsylvania. Thus, thoughtful and well-informed implementation by collaborators is essential.

Conclusion

We hope we have made clear in this chapter that the formation of active collaborative teams that involve stakeholders from across the campus who start with assessment and then act in aggressive and strategic ways is the ultimate demonstration of institutional seriousness concerning success for undergraduate men of color. But an institution must be ready to take on this challenge—presidents and other senior leaders must convey with enthusiasm the high priority, goals, and expectations the institution has for reversing troublesome engagement trends; they must be actively involved in the formation of strategy; and they must hold themselves and everyone else employed by the institution accountable. To make this work, the ways in which White faculty, staff, and students at PWIs will ultimately benefit must be made clear.

The problems and possibilities of engagement for male students of color are too critical to bring in a speaker for a three-hour professional development workshop. Such an approach is neither enduring nor likely to compel audience members to immediately act in the collaborative ways described in this chapter. Serious issues (e.g., men of color dropping out of college at rates higher than other groups) require serious partnerships and planning. Institutional leaders must be involved, and efforts cannot be isolated to a certain segment of the campus (e.g., student affairs or multicultural affairs). Resources should not be wasted flying in speakers for professional development workshops if the institution does not mean what it says about equity and diversity in its mission statement, on its website, and in public speeches made by its president. We remain optimistic that readers of this chapter will be inspired to treat Asian American, Black, Latino, and Native American male student engagement and achievement with greater seriousness and higher levels of institutional responsibility and accountability.

References

Allen, W.R. (1986). *Gender and campus differences in Black student academic performance, racial attitudes, and college satisfaction.* Atlanta, GA: Southern Education Foundation.

Argyris, C., & Schön, D.A. (1996). *Organizational learning II: Theory, method, and practice.* Reading, MA: Addison-Wesley.

Baird, L.L. (1988). The college environment revisited: A review of research and theory. In J.C. Smart (Ed.), *Higher education: Handbook of theory and research* (Vol. 4, pp. 1–52). New York, NY: Agathon.

Bauman, G.L. (2005). Promoting organizational learning in higher education to achieve equity in educational outcomes. In A.J. Kezar (Ed.), *Organizational learning in higher education.* New Directions for Higher Education (No. 131, pp. 23–35). San Francisco, CA: Jossey-Bass.

Bauman, G.L., Bustillos, L.T., Bensimon, E.M., Brown, M.C., & Bartee, R.D. (2005). *Achieving equitable educational outcomes with all students: The institution's roles and responsibilities.* Washington, DC: Association for American Colleges and Universities.

Beamon, K.K., & Bell, P.A. (2006). Academics versus athletics: An examination of the effects of background and socialization on African American male student athletes. *Social Science Journal, 43*(3), 393–403.

Benson, K.F. (2000). Constructing academic inadequacy: African American athletes' stories of schooling. *The Journal of Higher Education, 71*(2), 223–246.

Bell, D.A. (1987). *And we are not saved: The elusive quest for racial justice.* New York, NY: Basic Books.

Bell, D.A. (2000). *Brown vs. Board of Education:* Forty-five years after the fact. *Ohio Northern Law Review, 26*, 1–171.

Bensimon, E.M. (2004). The diversity scorecard: A learning approach to institutional change. *Change, 36*(1), 45–52.

Bensimon, E.M. (2005). Closing the achievement gap in higher education: An organizational learning perspective. In A.J. Kezar (Ed.), *Organizational learning in higher education.* New Directions for Higher Education (No. 131, pp. 99–111). San Francisco, CA: Jossey-Bass.

Bonner II, F.A. (2003). To be young, gifted, African American, and male. *Gifted Child Today, 26*(2), 26–34.

Bonner II, F.A. (2010). *Academically gifted African American male college students.* Santa Barbara, CA: Praeger.

Byrne, D. (Ed.). (2006). *Models of success: Supporting achievement and the retention of Black males at HBCUs*. New York, NY: Thurgood Marshall College Fund.

Bush, E. C., & Bush, V. L. (2010). Calling out the elephant: An examination of African American male achievement in community colleges. *Journal of African American Males in Education, 1*(1), 41–62.

Community College Survey of Student Engagement (CCSSE). (2005). *Engaging students, challenging the odds: 2005 Findings*. Austin, TX: University of Texas.

Crenshaw, K., Gotanda, N., Peller, G., & Thomas, K. (Eds.). (1995). *Critical race theory: The key writings that formed the movement*. New York, NY: New Press.

Cuyjet, M. J. (Ed.). (1997). *Helping African American men succeed in college*. New Directions for Student Services (No. 80). San Francisco, CA: Jossey-Bass.

Cuyjet, M. J. (Ed.). (2006). *African American men in college*. San Francisco, CA: Jossey-Bass.

Dancy II, T. E. (2012). *The brother code: Manhood and masculinity among African American males in college*. Charlotte, NC: Information Age.

Delgado, R. (1995). *Critical race theory: The cutting edge*. Philadelphia, PA: Temple University Press.

Delgado, R., & Stefancic, J. (2001). *Critical race theory: An introduction*. New York, NY: New York University Press.

Donnor, J. K. (2005). Towards an interest-convergence in the education of African American football student-athletes in major college sports. *Race Ethnicity and Education, 8*(1), 45–67.

Fleming, J. (1984). *Blacks in college: A comparative study of students' success in Black and in White institutions*. San Francisco, CA: Jossey-Bass.

Frierson, H. F., Pearson, W., & Wyche, J. H. (Eds.). (2009). *Black American males in higher education: Diminishing proportions*. Bingley, England: Emerald.

Frierson, H. F., Wyche, J. H., & Pearson, W. (Eds.). (2009). *Black males and higher education: Research, programs and academe*. Bingley, England: Emerald.

Glenn, F. S. (2004). The retention of Black male students in Texas public community colleges. *Journal of College Student Retention, 5*(2), 115–133.

González, K. P. (2002). Campus culture and the experiences of Chicano students in a predominantly White university. *Urban Education, 37*(2), 193–218.

Goode-Cross, D. T., & Good, G. E. (2009). Managing multiple-minority identities: African American men who have sex with men at predominately White universities. *Journal of Diversity in Higher Education, 2*(2), 103–112.

Goode-Cross, D. T., & Tager, D. (2011). Negotiating multiple identities: How African American gay and bisexual men persist at a predominantly White institution. *Journal of Homosexuality, 58*(9), 1235–1254.

Guardia, J. R., & Evans, N. J. (2008). Factors influencing the ethnic identity development of Latino fraternity members at a Hispanic serving institution. *Journal of College Student Development, 49*(3), 163–181.

Gurin, P., & Epps, E. G. (1975). *Black consciousness, identity and achievement: A study of students in historically Black colleges*. New York, NY: Wiley.

Hagedorn, L. S., Maxwell, W., & Hampton, P. (2002). Correlates of retention for African American males in community colleges. *Journal of College Student Retention, 3*(3), 243–263.

Harper, S. R. (2004). The measure of a man: Conceptualizations of masculinity among high-achieving African American male college students. *Berkeley Journal of Sociology, 48*(1), 89–107.

Harper, S. R. (2006a). *Black male students at public universities in the U.S.: Status, trends and implications for policy and practice*. Washington, DC: Joint Center for Political and Economic Studies.

Harper, S. R. (2006b). Enhancing African American male student outcomes through leadership and active involvement. In M. J. Cuyjet (Ed.), *African American men in college* (pp. 68–94). San Francisco, CA: Jossey-Bass.

Harper, S. R. (2012). *Black male student success in higher education: A report from the national Black male college achievement study*. Philadelphia, PA: University of Pennsylvania, Center for the Study of Race and Equity in Education.

Harper, S. R. (2013a). *Five things student affairs administrators can do to improve success among college men of color*. Washington, DC: National Association of Student Personnel Administrators.

Harper, S. R. (2013b). Am I my brother's teacher? Black undergraduates, peer pedagogies, and racial socialization in predominantly White postsecondary contexts. *Review of Research in Education, 37*(1), 183–211.

Harper, S.R., & Associates. (2014). *Succeeding in the city: A report from the New York City Black and Latino Male High School Achievement Study*. Philadelphia, PA: University of Pennsylvania, Center for the Study of Race and Equity in Education.

Harper, S.R., Carini, R. M, Bridges, B.K., & Hayek, J. (2004). Gender differences in student engagement among African American undergraduates at historically Black colleges and universities. *Journal of College Student Development, 45*(3), 271–284.

Harper, S.R., Davis, R.J., Jones, D.E., McGowan, B.L., Ingram, T.N., & Platt, C.S. (2011). Race and racism in the experiences of Black male resident assistants at predominantly White universities. *Journal of College Student Development, 52*(2), 180–200.

Harper, S.R., & Gasman, M. (2008). Consequences of conservatism: Black male students and the politics of historically Black colleges and universities. *Journal of Negro Education, 77*(4), 336–351.

Harper, S.R., & Harris III, F. (2006). The impact of fraternity membership on African American college men. In M.J. Cuyjet (Ed.), *African American men in college* (pp. 128–153). San Francisco, CA: Jossey-Bass.

Harper, S.R., & Harris III, F. (2012). *A role for policymakers in improving the status of Black male students in U.S. higher education*. Washington, DC: Institute for Higher Education Policy.

Harper, S.R., & Porter, A.C. (2012). *Attracting Black male students to research careers in education*. Philadelphia, PA: University of Pennsylvania, Center for the Study of Race and Equity in Education.

Harper, S.R., & Quaye, S.J. (2007). Student organizations as venues for Black identity expression and development among African American male student leaders. *Journal of College Student Development, 48*(2), 133–159.

Harper, S.R., Williams Jr., C.D., & Blackman, H.W. (2013). *Black male student-athletes and racial inequities in NCAA Division I college sports*. Philadelphia, PA: University of Pennsylvania, Center for the Study of Race and Equity in Education.

Harper, S.R., Williams, C.D., Pérez II, D., & Morgan, D.L. (2012). His experience: Toward a phenomenological understanding of academic capital formation among Black and Latino male students. *Readings on Equal Education, 26*(1), 65–87.

Harris III, F., & Bensimon, E.M. (2007). The equity scorecard: A collaborative approach to assess and respond to racial/ethnic disparities in student outcomes. In S.R. Harper & L.D. Patton (Eds.), *Responding to the realities of race on campus*. New Directions for Student Services (No. 120, pp. 77–84). San Francisco, CA: Jossey-Bass.

Harris III, F., & Wood, J.L. (2013). Student success for men of color in community colleges: A review of published literature and research, 1998–2012. *Journal of Diversity in Higher Education, 6*(3), 174–185.

Harris, W.G. (2003). African American homosexual males on predominantly White college and university campuses. *Journal of African American Studies, 7*(1), 47–56.

Hilton, A.A., Wood, J.L., & Lewis, C.W. (Eds). (2012). *Black males in postsecondary education: Examining their experiences in diverse institutional contexts*. Charlotte, NC: Information Age.

Jones, R.L. (2004). *Black haze: Violence, sacrifice, and manhood in black Greek-letter fraternities*. Albany, NY: State University of New York Press.

Kezar, A.J. (2005). What campuses need to know about organizational learning and the learning organization. In A.J. Kezar (Ed.), *Organizational learning in higher education*. New Directions for Higher Education (No. 131, pp. 7–22). San Francisco, CA: Jossey-Bass.

Kimbrough, W.M., & Harper, S.R. (2006). African American men at historically Black colleges and universities: Different environments, similar challenges. In M.J. Cuyjet (Ed.), *African American men in college* (pp. 189–209). San Francisco, CA: Jossey-Bass.

Lee, J.M., & Ransom, T. (2011). *The educational experiences of young men of color: A review of research, pathways, and progress*. New York, NY: The College Board.

Martin, B.E., Harrison, C.K., & Bukstein, S. (2010). "It takes a village" for African American male scholar-athletes: Mentorship by parents, faculty, and coaches. *Journal for the Study of Sports and Athletes in Education, 4*(3), 277–295.

McClure, S.M. (2006a). Voluntary association membership: Black Greek men on a predominantly White campus. *The Journal of Higher Education, 77*(6), 1036–1057.

McClure, S.M. (2006b). Improvising masculinity: African American fraternity membership in the construction of a Black masculinity. *Journal of African American Studies, 10*(1), 57–73.

Morales, E.K. (2009). Legitimizing hope: An exploration of effective mentoring for Dominican American male college students. *Journal of College Student Retention, 11*(3), 385–406.

Oseguera, L. (2010). Success despite the image: How African American male student-athletes endure their academic journey amidst negative characterizations. *Journal for the Study of Sports and Athletes in Education, 4*(3), 297–324.

Pace, C.R. (1969). *College and university environment scales*. Princeton, NJ: Institutional Research Program for Higher Education, Educational Testing Service.

Pace, C.R., & Stern, G.G. (1958). An approach to the measurement of psychological characteristics of college environments. *Journal of Educational Psychology, 49*, 269–277.

Palmer, R.T., Davis, R.J., & Hilton, A.A. (2009). Exploring challenges that threaten to impede the academic success of academically underprepared Black males at an HBCU. *Journal of College Student Development, 50*(4), 429–445.

Palmer, R.T., & Wood, J.L. (Eds.). (2012). *Black men in college: Implications for HBCUs and beyond*. New York, NY: Routledge.

Pascarella, E.T., & Terenzini, P.T. (2005). *How college affects students, Volume 2: A third decade of research*. San Francisco, CA: Jossey-Bass.

Patton, L.D. (2011). Perspectives on identity, disclosure, and the campus environment among African American gay and bisexual men at one Historically Black College. *Journal of College Student Development, 52*(1), 77–100.

Peña, E.V., Bensimon, E.M., & Colyar, J.C. (2006). Contextual problem defining: Learning to think and act from the standpoint of equity. *Liberal Education, 92*(2), 48–55.

Ray, R. (2012). Sophisticated practitioners: Black fraternity men's treatment of women. *Journal of African American Studies, 16*(4), 638–657.

Riggins, R.K., McNeal, C., & Herndon, M.K. (2008). The role of spirituality among African American college males attending a Historically Black University. *College Student Journal, 42*(1), 70–81.

Ross, M.J. (1998). *Success factors of young African American males at a historically Black college*. New York, NY: Praeger.

Saez, P.A., Casado, A., & Wade, J.C. (2009). Factors influencing masculinity ideology among Latino men. *Journal of Men's Studies, 17*(2), 116–128.

Sáenz, V.B., & Ponjuan, L. (2009). The vanishing Latino male in higher education. *Journal of Hispanic Higher Education, 8*(1), 54–89.

Sáenz, V.B., & Ponjuan, L. (2011). *Ensuring the academic success of Latino males in higher education*. Washington, DC: Institute for Higher Education Policy.

Schwartz, J.L., Donovan, J., & Guido-DiBrito, F. (2009). Stories of social class: Self-identified Mexican American male college students crack the silence. *Journal of College Student Development, 50*(1), 50–66.

Singer, J.N. (2005). Understanding racism through the eyes of African American male student-athletes. *Race Ethnicity and Education, 8*(4), 365–386.

Stern, R.A. (1970). *People in context: Measuring person-environment congruence in education and industry*. New York, NY: Wiley.

Strange, C.C. (2003). Dynamics of campus environments. In S.R. Komives & D.B. Woodard (Eds.), *Student services: A Handbook for the profession* (4th ed., pp. 297–316). San Francisco, CA: Jossey-Bass.

Strange, C.C., & Banning, J.H. (2001). *Educating by design: Creating campus learning environments that work*. San Francisco, CA: Jossey-Bass.

Strayhorn, T.L. (2010). When race and gender collide: Social and cultural capital's influence on the academic achievement of African American and Latino males. *The Review of Higher Education, 33*(3), 307–332.

Strayhorn, T.L. (2012). Satisfaction and retention among African American men at two-year community colleges. *Community College Journal of Research and Practice, 36*(5), 358–375.

Strayhorn, T.L., Blakewood, A.M., & DeVita, J.M. (2008). Factors affecting the college choice of African American gay male undergraduates: Implications for retention. *National Association of Student Affairs Professionals Journal, 11*(1), 88–108.

Strayhorn, T. L., & Mullins, T. G. (2012). Investigating Black gay male undergraduates' experiences in campus residence halls. *Journal of College and University Student Housing, 39*(1), 141–160.

Sutton, E. M., & Kimbrough, W. M. (2001). Trends in Black student involvement. *NASPA Journal, 39*(1), 30–40.

Villalpando, O. (2006). *Conditions that affect the participation and success of Latino males in college.* Washington, DC: Joint Center for Political and Economic Studies.

Warde, B. (2008). Staying the course: Narratives of African American males who have completed a baccalaureate degree. *Journal of African American Studies, 12*(1), 59–72.

Washington, T. A., Wang, Y., & Browne, D. (2009). Difference in condom use among sexually active males at Historically Black Colleges and Universities. *Journal of American College Health, 57*(4), 411–418.

Wood, J. L. (2012). Leaving the 2-year college: Predictors of Black male collegian departure. *Journal of Black Studies, 43*(3), 303–326.

Wood, J. L., Hilton, A. A., & Lewis, C. W. (2011). Black male collegians in public two-year colleges: Student perspectives on the effect of employment on academic success. *National Association of Student Affairs Professionals Journal, 14*(1), 97–110.

Wood, J. L., & Turner, C. S. (2011). Black males and the community college: Student perspectives on faculty and academic success. *Community College Journal of Research and Practice, 35*(1), 135–151.

Chapter 5
Engaging White Students on Multicultural Campuses

Robert D. Reason

In the original volume of this book, Sallee, Logan, Sims, and Harrington (2009) framed the discussion of engaging White students using an all-too-familiar occurrence on college campuses. These authors began their chapter with a discussion of a White student's letter to a campus newspaper claiming "reverse discrimination" (p. 200) because of the lack of a White Student Union. The scenario presented a range of reactions from students and campus professionals from various racial backgrounds and worldviews. The scenario relayed a challenge to student affairs and higher education professionals that could just as easily happen today as when the chapter was originally published. It provides an appropriate framework to open this chapter as well.

Challenges Faced by White Students

I would add a complementary, equally common, but perhaps more pernicious, scenario to frame the discussion of engaging White students on multicultural campuses. Students beginning college after the turn of the millennium are understood to be the most diverse group of students to ever enroll (Broido, 2004). Along with efforts to introduce multicultural education at all levels of schooling, beginning in early elementary school, increasing exposure to diverse others means that White college students are likely to come to college having explored issues of difference and *believing* they learned all they need to know about racial differences (Giroux, 1997b).

White students under this latter scenario are likely to come to campus with the belief that they "get it." They arrive on college campuses believing they are open, accepting, and willing to embrace racial differences among their peer groups. This might even be true for some. White students whose high school experiences involved racially diverse peers and intentionally-designed diversity interventions are likely to have thought more about their own racial identity and feel more comfortable with racially diverse others than other White students (Perry, 2002).

Unfortunately, neither the structure of most American high schools nor the cognitive/ developmental abilities of most high school students allow these benefits to be widespread. We can assume that many, if not most, of the White students entering colleges and universities need some more focused attention on their own racial identities and the skills necessary to successfully engage in a multicultural community. The belief that they already get it poses yet another obstacle to White students' engagement on diverse college campuses.

The challenge facing student affairs professionals under both scenarios described above is one of the intersection of racial identity development and cognitive complexity of traditionally-aged college students. Under both scenarios, White students must be challenged to think on two levels: the systemic and the individual. White students must concurrently make sense of the role of racial identity groups, groups that do not play salient roles in most White students' racial development, and their own personal experiences. These students, by virtue of their racial identities, are part of a system that reinforces oppression, even as some may try to push against individual racist actions. This creates great, potentially stifling, dissonance for many White students. In order to overcome this dissonance and encourage racial identity development and engagement of White students on multicultural college campuses, White students must be challenged and supported in both cognitive development and racial identity development.

The development of racial attitudes involves cognitive processes (King & Shuford, 1996); therefore, an understanding of cognitive development must inform attempts to engage White students on multicultural campuses. Most cognitive development theorists agree that individuals move from dualistic, egocentric worldviews toward more complex, relativistic, and socio-centric views (Evans, Forney, Guido, Patton, & Renn, 2010). King and Shuford and King and Howard-Hamilton (2003) concluded that multicultural competence requires higher-order, cognitively complex reasoning skills that are more closely associated with upper-division students, not entering first-year students. Many cognitive skills necessary for White students to develop as racial justice allies—reflection, perspective-taking, empathy—are similarly higher-order cognitive skills (King & Baxter Magolda, 2005; Reason, Roosa Millar, & Scales, 2005). "Those [students] further along in the educational process are more likely to be able to make reasoned judgments about controversial issues" (King & Shuford, p. 163), like racial justice attitudes and race-conscious policies.

The development of complex cognitive processes must be accompanied by a concurrent development of racial identity (King & Baxter Magolda, 2005). King and Baxter Magolda use Baxter Magolda's three dimensions of self-authorship—cognitive, interpersonal, and intrapersonal—to describe a model for understanding intercultural maturity among college students. This model is multidimensional and includes a sense of self, a sensitively to diverse others, and an understanding of the role one's own identity plays in engagement across racial differences. In this model, a strong sense of identity provides the foundation upon which one's unexamined beliefs can be challenged and true engagement can occur. According to data from Baxter Magolda's longitudinal study of the development of self-authorship, students who were low in intercultural maturity, with a less developed sense of self, understood that making and building diverse friendships was based on minimizing differences. Assuming this colorblind perspective often allowed White students to minimize the cognitive dissonance created when engaging with diverse others. On the other hand, students with more developed intercultural maturity were able to recognize the existence of multiple perspectives related to issues of diversity. The recognition of diverse perspectives and the resulting interrogation of racial attitudes and experiences were less likely to threaten these students' racial identities or discourage engagement across differences.

The ability for White students to effectively engage on multicultural college campuses, therefore, requires these students to have a developed sense of White racial identity, which is best understood as a complex interaction of psychosocial and cognitive development (King & Baxter Magolda, 2005). The remainder of this section builds on this assumption, presenting first three key studies that demonstrate how White students respond to the challenges that face them by developing their White racial identities in order to engage effectively on multicultural campuses. In the subsequent section, I present theories of White racial identity, ultimately arguing that a cognitively complex understanding of Whiteness is the best foundation upon which to encourage White students to engage on multicultural college campuses. This discussion is followed by the presentation of several tangible suggestions for not only engaging White students but also for encouraging White students to build those cognitive skills upon which a positive White racial identity can be established and positive engagement across differences can be built.

Very few studies have addressed the issues of Whiteness empirically (Eichstedt, 2001). The theoretical frameworks discussed in the next section comprise the majority of writing on this topic. Empirical research is needed into how White students' racial identities are affected by college experiences and how the resulting changes to racial understanding affect students' engagement. In this section, I present the findings from three research-based studies of Whiteness to exemplify how White students can respond to the challenge of engagement on multicultural campuses. Although only one is directly related to college students, all can inform the work of higher education professionals who hope to encourage engagement among White students.

Perry's Work in High Schools

Perry (2002) completed ethnographic studies of two distinct California high schools: one predominantly White, the other racially and ethnically heterogeneous, revealing the importance of peer culture and structural diversity in formulating a sense of Whiteness for the students in these two high schools. The racial make-up of the two high schools allowed for very different experiences related to race for the White students at each school, which resulted in different understandings of Whiteness for each group of students. For students in the racially-homogenous high school, Whiteness was understood as "normal" (p. 181). These students were not challenged to explore race in any meaningful way and were left with a shallow understanding of their own racial identities.

On the other hand, the White students in the racially heterogeneous high school demonstrated a much more reflective understanding of race and Whiteness (Perry, 2002). Akin to what critical race theorists posited, these students constructed a discursive, problematic racial understanding. Their school environment made race much more salient, and often more contentious. School officials in this particular school encouraged exploration of racial differences through intentionally designed interventions both inside and outside the classroom, which pushed students of all races to confront and work through racialized situations. The White students demonstrated a more thoughtful understanding of a White culture, a more nuanced sense of White people as multicultural beings, and greater skills at interacting across racial and ethnic differences.

Eichstedt's Problematic White Identities

While Perry (2002) explored White racial development as it occurred in high school students, Eichstedt's (2001) study examined how 16 White racial justice activists constructed their sense of Whiteness. Although her sample was all White, all 16 of her respondents were either gay or lesbian and half were Jewish. Eichstedt, therefore, cautioned against direct application of her findings to other White people, although her study does inform understanding of how race is constructed by White racial justice allies.

Unlike the clean linear process of building racial identity suggested by early theorists, respondents to Eichstedt's (2001) study discussed a messy understanding of Whiteness. These racial justice allies struggled with and questioned the role of Whiteness in their lives. Respondents discussed the importance of incorporating an understanding of racial privilege into their White identities. The antiracism activist identity of her respondents was, at least partially according to Eichstedt, a way to both overcome guilt and enact a sense of responsibility. Eichstedt's conclusions reinforce the importance of rearticulating Whiteness in a manner that encourages action. She noted:

> [White people] must be able to narrate their own racialized history, identify themselves as white, catalog the unearned advantages they accrue because they are white, and demonstrate their willingness to claim themselves as racist . . . However, to remain antiracism activists they must find a way to balance this negative identity with some positive constructions of self—or they will not be able to continue the work. (p. 465)

Whiteness, according to Eichstedt's respondents, was a balance between a sense of identity (negative and positive), a cognitive understanding of power and privilege, and a desire for action in support of social justice.

Reason's Complicated Whiteness

Between 2004 and 2005, I engaged in a series of interviews with 15 White college students who were identified because of their vigorous racial justice actions on campus. This research was part of a larger study of how college experiences affect the development of racial justice attitudes and actions in White college students (Reason et al., 2005).

Interestingly, respondents articulated their struggle with Whiteness not as a process of deconstruction, but as a process of re-articulation similar to Giroux's ideas (1997b), seeking a sense of Whiteness that was "not defined with dominant White, masculinist definitions of racial, economic, and cultural democracy" (Giroux, 1997b, p. 386). Respondents to this study discussed a multi-layered process, with parts that could be considered both intrapersonal and interpersonal. Respondents struggled to understand Whiteness and how it informed their senses of self. They also went through a process that included an exploration of the role race played in their interpersonal relationships and how it informed their worldviews (Reason, 2008).

Like the activists in Eichstedt's (2001) study, the students in my study landed on an understanding of Whiteness that was dynamic and fluid, situational and relational. Students in this study understood their Whiteness as part of a coherent whole, a dimension of their identities that intersected and overlapped with other dimensions, like gender, sexuality, and social class. Many students discussed the privilege of being able to "ignore" their race in most situations at this predominantly White campus but talked of attempting to make race more salient. Students' increased racial salience resulted in their willingness to question and explore issues of race in their daily lives, articulating a nuanced understanding of how their racial identities fit within the larger society within which Whiteness is dominant and oppressive.

Students in this study also examined their relationships and opinions about social policy through a lens that included an understanding of power and privilege. For these students, their racial identity, which included an understanding of power and privilege, was a salient part of their relationships with other White students and students of color. The students demonstrated active reflection on race and racialized experiences, were able to articulate the role of race at the individual level and systemic level, and had practiced skills necessary for engaging across differences.

White Racial Identity, White Racial Consciousness, and Whiteness: Theoretical Perspectives

Research related to White racial identity tends to take two forms: traditional developmental theories and critical race theory (CRT) perspectives. Higher education researchers often ground their studies in developmental theories, with two theories forming the foundation for most of our understanding: Helms's White racial identity model (Helms, 1984, 1990, 1995) or the White racial consciousness model (Rowe, Behrens, & Leach, 1995). While empirically useful and heuristic, these models pose both psychometric and theoretical problems primarily related to disagreements about what constituted identity. In contrast, critical race theorists tend to utilize a concept of "Whiteness," meant to encompass the way White people understand their own racial situations (Giroux, 1997a), without making any developmental assumptions. This section juxtaposes and critiques the traditional White racial models and writings about Whiteness.

Traditional White Racial Identity Models

Helms's theory of White racial identity development (1990, 1995) and the more recent White racial consciousness approach (LaFleur, Rowe, & Leach, 2002; Leach, Behrens, & LaFleur, 2002) share several characteristics. Both approaches have gained wide acceptance in the higher education literature. Although underlying assumptions about development differ, both approaches focus on the attitudes that White people hold about people of color, relying on quantitative measures to assess racial attitudes held by White people (Rowe et al., 1995).

Helms's Theory of White Racial Identity

On the vanguard of research investigating White racial identity (WRI), Helms's theory (1990, 1995) forms the foundation for much of the thinking about White racial identity development. In the most recent iteration, Helms (1995) posited that White people proceed through a series of developmental statuses, beginning with a need to abandon inherent racism and moving toward a positive sense of racial identity that includes antiracist attitudes. This journey of White racial identity development, according to Helms (1995), includes six status levels: contact, disintegration, reintegration, pseudo-independent, immersion/emersion, and autonomy.

Helms's statuses are often understood to describe the behaviors and feelings of White people toward people of color, although Helms included both a set of racial attitudes and a set of information process strategies associated with White people in each status group (Leach et al., 2002). These more cognitive characteristics of Helms's statuses are often overlooked or ignored. Statuses, according to Leach and his colleagues, are "constructs referring to dynamic cognitive-affective information-processing strategies that people use to deal with racial information" (p. 68). As with similar cognitive-based developmental models, growth occurs as individuals make sense of information that challenges previously held beliefs (Evans et al., 2010).

White Racial Consciousness

The White racial consciousness (WRC) approach examines the attitudes of White people toward people of color and social justice movements (LaFleur et al., 2002; Leach et al., 2002). Proponents of WRC proposed that racial attitudes cluster, which allows researchers to view them from a typological perspective. Attitudes are considered *achieved* when an individual demonstrates both personal exploration of, and commitment to, a set of attitudes regarding race. Conversely, attitudes not based on personal exploration or commitment are considered *unachieved*. An individual's cluster of racial attitudes at a given time will be the best predictor of observable behaviors related to racial justice.

Although similar in some aspects to Helms's (1995) WRI theory, a White racial consciousness perspective has several advantages according to proponents (LaFleur et al., 2002; Leach et al., 2002). In general, WRI describes a trajectory of progressive "levels of sensitivity to other racial/ethnic groups but little about a White identity" (Leach et al., 2002, p. 68). The WRC approach attempts to capture White people's attitudes toward people of color. This approach purposefully "eschews larger personality abstractions, such as identity or any developmental sequence, and merely proposes that there are various clusters or types of racial attitudes held by White people" (Leach et al., 2002, p. 69). Therefore, proponents believe the WRC approach is more parsimonious and avoids assumptions of linear identity development inherent in WRI theories.

Critiques of Traditional Approaches

Researchers using either traditional approach to White identity focus almost exclusively on attitudes about *racialized others*, to the exclusion of an internal sense of *self* (Gallagher, 2000). Any sense of personal racial identity for White people is largely ignored in the research literature based on these theoretical approaches. Although attitudes about racialized others must be part of our understanding of White racial identity, it is overly constricting to construct an identity based solely on those external attitudes. Unfortunately, traditional White racial identity models do not allow Whiteness to be "understood in ways other than being in opposition to nonwhites" (Gallagher, p. 83).

Further, the assumed endpoint, or ideal, racial status in each of these traditional approaches is problematic. The implicit assumption by most readers of these theories is an idealized endpoint, a self-actualization (Thompson, 2003). The focus on achieving self-actualization reinforces idealized assumptions about White people, particularly "good" Whites, as pure and moral. Although most appropriately a critique of Helms's (1995) stage theory, this critique is also applicable to the WRC approach (LaFleur et al., 2002) that, while not subscribing to stage-like developmental assumptions, nonetheless uses terms like "unachieved" and "achieved" to describe different types of White racial consciousness.

Finally, Thompson (1999) critiqued these traditional approaches based on the a-historical nature of the stages; the artificial separation of race from other subjectivities an individual holds; and the tendency for theorists to base White identity solely on attitudes relating to African Americans, ignoring other people of color. The a-historical nature of White racial identity development stages de-contextualizes our understanding of Whiteness. According to Thompson, racial identities are most appropriately understood in light of the social justice movements of the time, which influence how individuals experience and make sense of race during a specific era. We similarly receive only a partial understanding when race is viewed as separate and distinct from other positions, specifically, gender, sexuality, and socioeconomic class. Finally, according to Thompson, the duality of Black–White comparisons upon which most traditional theories are built, is no longer appropriate in our multicultural and multiracial society.

Traditional understanding of White racial identity development, therefore, leads to an essentialized, albeit incomplete, understanding of Whiteness that prioritizes making White people feel good about themselves (Thompson, 2003). These assumptions break down our understanding of Whiteness into attitudes and behaviors that one *must* possess in order to be achieved or autonomous, defining the core essence of Whiteness distinct from other positions an individual holds. These perspectives also encourage White people to value a positive sense of self over political action, working through guilt to some form of self-actualization.

Critical Race Theory and Whiteness

In response to concerns over stage-like and essentialist understandings of White racial identity development, critical race theorists have assumed a more discursive framework to conceptualize Whiteness. Discussion among critical race theorists tends to focus on deconstructing Whiteness (Bailey, 1998) or rearticulating Whiteness (Frankenberg, 1993; Giroux, 1997a). Regardless of the approach, critical race theorists attempt to problematize—to make messy—our understanding of Whiteness.

Deconstruct or Rearticulate?

Whiteness is often conflated with White racism, which is the foundation of the push to deconstruct Whiteness (Giroux, 1997a). As Roediger (1994) concluded, "It is not merely that 'whiteness' is oppressive and false; it is that 'whiteness' is *nothing but* oppressive and false" (p. 13). For Roediger and others (e.g., Bailey, 1998), Whiteness is inseparable from domination, oppression, exploitation, and privilege enjoyed by White people (Giroux, 1997b). From this vantage point, Whiteness must be abolished or deconstructed.

Another group of theorists fear this stance may cause backlash from White people, particularly those who might be inclined toward racial justice attitudes and actions (Frankenberg, 1993; Giroux, 1997a; Tatum, 2003). This second set of critical race theorists prefers a reexamination of what it means to be White in a racist society. Giroux called for a "rearticulation of Whiteness" (p. 293) in such a way that would allow White people to move beyond the assumption that "the only role they could play in the struggle against racism was either to renounce their Whiteness and adopt the modalities of the subordinated group or to suffer the charge that any claim to White identity was tantamount to racism" (p. 294). Without rearticulating Whiteness, White people, particularly those who identify as antiracist, are left to define themselves by what they are against (*anti*-racism) or by what they are not (*non*-racist) (Thompson, 1996).

According to Thompson (1996), White people must give up the desire to define themselves unproblematically if they are to begin rearticulating race. Articulating a problematic sense of Whiteness begins by accepting that Whiteness is influenced by other of identity such as class, sexuality, gender, and age (Frankenberg, 1993). Identifying multiple dimensions of identity also allows White people to begin to recognize situations where they may be "outsiders" (Thompson, 1996, p. 106), while still recognizing their insider status based upon race. A sense of Whiteness built upon these assumptions is likely to be nuanced, complicated, and dynamic (Giroux, 1997b). Despite the more nuanced approach to Whiteness offered by critical race theorists, their approaches are still somewhat new to many higher education and student affairs scholars and practitioners; therefore, the practical applications of this theory are not as evident.

Common Understandings among Theorists

The theorists discussed above assume race as a social and political construction that has no reality outside of the socio-historical context in which we live (Reed, 1996). Accepting race as a social and political construction, however, must not imply that race does not exist. Racial categorization brings with it social, political, and economic consequences that are quite real. Race, as an assumed definitive system of categorization, has been used to sort people into groups, often to maintain and extend existing power differentials between groups of people (Spickard, 1992).

Similarly, traditional theorists and CRT theorists both assume that Whiteness is a position that carries with it political and social power (Frankenberg, 1993). Recognition of power and privilege afforded to White people based solely upon their perceived race is a necessary, but insufficient, step in any racial identity process. Frankenberg quoted a respondent in her study as saying Whiteness is "a privilege enjoyed but not acknowledged, a reality lived in but unknown" (p. 51). Whiteness, then, is a position of structural advantage, a standpoint from which to look at oneself, others, and society, and a set of cultural practices assumed/labeled "American" or "normal."

Student Engagement Strategies

The literature reviewed thus far leads to several themes that can inform high-quality practices on college campuses. These themes also support the notion that in order to engage White students on multicultural campuses, faculty and student affairs educators must focus on encouraging students to develop a sense of racial identity as well as the cognitive complexity. Interventions meant to engage White students on multicultural campuses not only must combine cognitive and affective components (King & Baxter Magolda, 2005), but the theories and research reviewed in the previous sections suggest that interventions should explicitly invite White students to engage (Reason et al., 2005), offer opportunities for facilitated engagement across differences (Eichstedt, 2001; Perry, 2002), provide opportunities for sustained reflection on issues of race and culture that challenge and support White students' development of a racial identity (Eichstedt, 2001; Reason et al., 2005), and encourage an action-oriented agenda that provides White students with concrete opportunities to apply their learning (Eichstedt, 2003; Reason et al., 2005). The following interventions were chosen as examples that combine these essential elements.

Intergroup Dialogues

Intergroup dialogues take many forms. When implemented as designed, however, intergroup dialogues incorporate each of the elements identified from the aforementioned literature review. An intergroup dialogue can be defined as a "face-to-face facilitated learning experience that brings together students from different social identity groups over a sustained period of time to understand their commonalities and differences, examine the nature and impact of societal inequalities, and explore ways to work together toward greater equality and justice" (Zúñiga, Nagda,

Chesler, & Cytron-Walker, 2007, p. 2). According to Zúñiga and her colleagues, intergroup dialogues help to raise participants' consciousness of difficult issues, develop participants' awareness of their own and others' personal and social identities, and develop participants' knowledge of social systems that sustain oppression and privilege. Further, because these dialogue groups build relationships across differences, they foster the development of communication skills and promote the development of empathy.

For White students in particular, Roosa Millar (2006) found that intergroup dialogues can provide a reflective space to explore previously unexamined racial biases. Further, she found that for many White students in the intergroup dialogues she studied, the "authentic dialogue often leads to action" (p. 168), an empirical finding supporting the theory undergirding intergroup dialogues (Schoem, 2003; Schoem & Hurtado, 2001). Research on the outcomes of participation in intergroup dialogues suggests that students, particularly White students, begin to think more systemically about racial inequalities (Zúñiga et al., 2007). Once students recognize and make sense of the systems of racial oppression, they begin to recommend systemic actions to address racial injustice and move away from feeling individually threatened by difficult conversations. These findings suggest a likely outcome of participation in intergroup dialogues for White students is a greater engagement in multicultural environments.

Much planning and preparation are required for authentic intergroup dialogues; student affairs educators cannot simply pull together a diverse group of students and assume positive outcomes will result. In fact, without skilled facilitation and a pedagogical plan, engagement in diverse groups might be deleterious for students (Allport, 1954; Zúñiga et al., 2007). Intentionally selected and well-trained facilitators play a key role in successful intergroup dialogues. Zúñiga and her colleagues also suggest a four-stage developmental approach to the curriculum of these groups: (1) focus on building relationships between participants; (2) explore differences and similarities between participants; (3) discuss controversial or hot topics; and (4) develop an action plan to move the group toward engagement. Training sessions and a pre-developed curriculum are available through the National Intergroup Dialogue Institute (www.igr.umich.edu/about/institute).

Coursework related to Race Relations and Whiteness

Courses related to race relations and the exploration of Whiteness can serve many of the same functions as intergroup dialogue groups (Reason et al., 2005; Roosa Millar, 2006). Roosa Millar, for example, described a two-course sequence during which students engage in the study of societal racism and racial inequality in a larger lecture-format course followed by in-depth discussion and analysis in a seminar-formatted course. Such a course sequence can be designed to nurture both cognitive understanding (e.g., the structural nature of racism and inequality) and affective development (e.g., exploration of how race and racial identities affect students' daily experiences on campus). Sallee and her colleagues (2009) suggested that these courses should be "designed to facilitate White students' questioning and analyzing of racial identity development within a framework that positions White identity development alongside a consideration of other racial/ ethnic identities" (p. 214). These authors suggested grounding this exploration in the theories of White racial identity development, discussed earlier in this chapter, as well as readings related to privilege and oppression (e.g., Adams et al., 2000). The literature reviewed earlier also suggests that such courses should assume an action-oriented pedagogy, focusing on actively engaging students in the struggle for racial justice.

Workshop Series

Although a single diversity workshop has been shown to encourage attitude and behavioral change in college students (Pascarella & Terenzini, 2005), the theories and empirical research presented in this chapter suggest that a sustained series of workshops may influence White students' development more powerfully. One particularly powerful framework in which to think about a workshop series is Pedersen's (1988) awareness, knowledge, and skills framework. Although originally created as a framework to train multiculturally-competent mental health counselors, this framework has been widely cited and used by student affairs educators as a developmental approach to encouraging the development of multicultural competence in students and student affairs educators (Pope & Reynolds, 1997; Pope, Reynolds, & Mueller, 2004).

A well-designed workshop series using Pedersen's framework (1988) would begin by addressing White students' awareness of self (as a racial being) and racially-diverse others. Awareness workshops, either early in the academic year or early in a student's academic career, would address "those values, attitudes, and assumptions essential to working with students who are culturally different" than the student (Pope et al., 2004, p. 14). These workshops would focus on self-awareness as a White person, as well as self-evaluation of existing assumptions and beliefs that may be inaccurate or inappropriate on a multicultural campus.

Building upon students' awareness of difference, the second phase of such a workshop series would focus on increasing students' knowledge of cultural groups. Basic multicultural knowledge workshops would explore the history, traditions, and values of various cultures. These workshops, as students become more knowledgeable about other cultures, should move toward explorations of the role of systemic power and institutional oppression in maintaining or obstructing cultural groups' positions within societal power structures (Pope et al., 2004). This section of the workshop series should culminate in the exploration of histories of social justice movements.

The final stage of Pedersen's (1988) framework includes teaching students the practical skills necessary to engage effectively and comfortably across differences. White students need opportunities to "effectively apply the multicultural awareness and knowledge [they] have internalized . . . to communicate across cultures and understand how cultural influences the content as well as the verbal and nonverbal aspects of communication" (Pope et al., 2004, p. 15). Essential in this time of practice is the need for White students to reflect on, critically evaluate, and improve these communication skills.

Developmental Programming through
Multicultural Student Affairs Offices

Although multicultural student affairs offices at PWIs must focus primarily on supporting students of color in often hostile environments, these offices have long histories of educating White students (Washington, 2011). For multicultural student affairs educators, educating White students often involves focusing on ally development. Although developing racial justice allies is an essential end goal, the theory and literature discussed earlier suggests that a developmental approach is necessary, beginning with introduction and awareness activities and culminating in ally development undertakings and actions.

Although similar to suggestions above for a workshop series, a developmental approach to programming situated within a multicultural student affairs office has several benefits. Washington (2011) suggests that engaging White students in multicultural student affairs programming invites these students into a space that they likely perceived as "not for them" (p. 246). This experience, in and of itself, may be difficult for White students who likely have never previously felt racially out-of-place. Building upon this initial sense of racial salience through reflection or conversation may very well serve as a catalyst for further exploration for many White students, but those of us in student affairs must first recognize and engage the educational potential of this simple experience; to do this, we must invite White students into these spaces. Of course, the true educational benefit of multicultural programming in multicultural spaces comes from sustained reflection and engagement. Finding ways, like a developmental workshop series, to engage White students beyond this initial discomfort is essential for learning to occur.

Inviting White students into multicultural student spaces is not without costs (Washington, 2011). Washington provides an in-depth discussion of the possible costs of such a decision, but he also discusses the likely benefits to students of color and White students. Throwing open the doors of a multicultural student services space to White students should not be done without much thought and discussion, but doing so can potentially engage White students in very meaningful ways. Done intentionally, and with a theoretical foundation, the end product of a developmental approach to engaging White students in multicultural student spaces will likely be the development of racial justice allies (Reason et al., 2005; Washington, 2011).

Living-Learning/Learning Communities

Sallee and her colleagues (2009) suggested that student affairs educators establish living-learning environments "dedicated to fostering multicultural understanding" (p. 217). Such living-learning environments can take many forms and can incorporate academic coursework with intentional co-curricular learning activities (Barefoot, 2005). Regardless of the specific form this environment takes, these communities should include intentional and widely understood learning objectives; provide opportunities for extended engagement about issues of difference; and incorporate training on how to reflect upon the lessons learned through this engagement.

Living-learning communities remain a powerful educational tool in higher education (Barefoot, 2005). Duah-Agyeman (2004), writing about Syracuse University's Multicultural Living-Learning Community, provided an example of the transformative power of such living-learning communities. The Syracuse model included the characteristics described above, but Duah-Agyeman's discussion also highlighted the importance of a multi-layered support structure needed to facilitate such an environment, including the importance of meaningful collaboration between student affairs and academic affairs units across campus.

Conclusion

In this chapter, I reviewed both theoretical and empirical literature related to White identity and Whiteness and their relationship to engaging White students on multicultural campuses. The synthesis of the existing literature revealed the necessity of encouraging White students to explore their racial identities, identities comprised of interpersonal, intrapersonal, and cognitive components. Given our current understanding of how identities develop over time, and the ways in which higher education and student affairs professionals can assist in that development, I provided a comprehensive (but not exhaustive) list of possible interventions. These interventions, and any interventions, meant to increase White students' engagement on a multicultural college campus should explicitly invite White students to participate, include trained facilitators to encourage positive engagement, require sustained reflection on issues of race and racism, and promote racial justice action. These four characteristics were supported by both the theoretical and empirical research as essential components of good practice in engaging White students on multicultural campuses.

References

Adams, M., Blumenfeld, W. J., Castaneda, R., Hackman, H. W., Peters, M. L., & Zúñiga, X. (2000). (Eds.), *Readings for diversity and social justice: An anthology on racism, anti-Semitism, sexism, heterosexism, ableism, and classism.* New York, NY: Routledge.

Allport, G. (1954). *The nature of prejudice.* Reading, MA: Addison-Wesley.

Bailey, A. (1998). Locating traitorous identities: Toward a view of privilege-cognizant White character. *Hypatia, 13*(3), 27–42.

Barefoot, B. O. (2005). Current institutional practice in the first college year. In M. L. Upcraft, J. N. Gardner, B. O. Barefoot & Associates (Eds.), *Challenging and supporting the first-year student: A handbook for improving the first year of college* (pp. 47–63). San Francisco, CA: Jossey-Bass.

Broido, E. M. (2004). Understanding diversity in Mellennial students. In M. D. Coomes & R. DeBard (Eds.), *Serving the Millennial generation (New Directions for Student Services*, no. 106) (pp. 73–86). San Francisco, CA: Jossey-Bass.

Duah-Agyeman, J. (2004). Multicultural living/learning community: By the students, for the students. In S. N. Hurd & R. Federman Stein (Eds.), *Building and sustaining learning communities: The Syracuse University experience* (pp. 120–138). Bolton, MA: Anker.

Eichstedt, J. L. (2001). Problematic White identities and a search for racial justice. *Sociological Forum, 16*, 445–470.

Evans, N. J., Forney, D. S., & Guido, F., Patton, L. D., & Renn, K. A. (2010). *Student development in college: Theory, research, and practice* (2nd ed.). San Francisco, CA: Jossey-Bass.

Frankenberg, R. (1993). Growing up White: Feminism, racism and the social geography of childhood. *Feminist Review, 45*, 51–84.

Gallagher, C. A. (2000). White like me? Methods, meaning, and manipulation in the field of White studies. In F. Winddance-Twine, & J. W. Warren (Eds.), *Racing research, researching race: Methodological dilemmas in critical race studies* (pp. 67–92). New York, NY: New York University Press.

Giroux, H. A. (1997a). Rewriting the discourse of racial identity: Towards a pedagogy and politics of Whiteness. *Harvard Educational Review, 67*(2), 285–320.

Giroux, H. A. (1997b). White squall: Resistance and the pedagogy of Whiteness. *Cultural Studies, 11*(3), 376–389.

Helms, J. (1984). Toward a theoretical explanation of the effects of race on counseling: A Black and White model. *Counseling Psychologist, 12*, 153–165.

Helms, J. (1990). Toward a model of White racial identity development. In J. Helms (Ed.), *Black and White racial identity: Theory, research, and practice* (pp. 49–66). Westport, CT: Greenwood.

Helms, J. (1995). An update of Helms's White and People of Color Racial Identity Models. In J. C. J. Ponterotto, L. Suzuki, & C. Alexander (Eds.), *Handbook of multicultural counseling* (pp. 181–198). Thousand Oaks, CA.: Sage.

King, P. M., & Baxter Magolda, M. B. (2005). A developmental model of intercultural maturity. *Journal of College Student Development, 46*, 571–592.

King, P. M., & Howard-Hamilton, M. (2003). An assessment of multicultural competence. *NASPA Journal, 40*, 119–133.

King, P. M., & Shuford, B. C. (1996). A multicultural view is a more cognitively complex view: Cognitive development and multicultural education. *American Behavioral Scientist, 40*, 153–164.

LaFleur, N. K., Rowe, W., & Leach, M. M. (2002). Reconceputalizing White racial consciousness. *Journal of Multicultural Counseling and Development, 30*, 148–152.

Leach, M. M., Behrens, J. T., & LaFleur, N. K. (2002). White racial identity and White racial consciousness: Similarities, differences and recommendations. *Journal of Multicultural Counseling and Development, 30*, 66–80.

Pascarella, E. T., & Terenzini, P. T. (2005). *How college affects students: A third decade of research.* San Francisco, CA: Jossey-Bass.

Pedersen, P. (1988). *A handbook for developing multicultural awareness.* Alexandria, VA: American Association for Counseling and Development.

Perry, P. (2002). *Shades of White: White kids and racial identities in high school.* Durham, NC: Duke University Press.

Pope, R. L., & Reynolds, A. L. (1997). Student affairs core competencies: Integrating multicultural awareness, knowledge, and skills. *Journal of College Student Development, 38,* 266–277.

Pope, R. L., & Reynolds, A. L. & Mueller, J. A. (2004). *Multicultural competence in student affairs.* San Francisco, CA: Jossey-Bass.

Reason, R. D. (2008). Rearticulating whiteness: A precursor to difficult dialogues on race. *College Student Affairs Journal, 26,* 127–135.

Reason, R. D., Roosa Millar, E. A., & Scales, T. C. (2005). Toward a model of racial justice ally development in college. *Journal of College Student Development, 46,* 530–546.

Reed, A. (1996, September 24). Skin deep. *Village Voice,* p. 22.

Roediger, D. A. (1994). *Toward the abolition of whiteness: Essays on race, politics, and working class history.* New York, NY: Verso.

Roosa Millar, E. A. (2006). *Reflection to action: A grounded case study of an intentionally designed racial justice curriculum* (Unpublished dissertation). Pennsylvania State University, University Park, PA.

Rowe, W., Behrens, J. T., & Leach, M. M. (1995). Racial/ethnic identity and racial consciousness: Looking back and looking forward. In J. C. J. Ponterotto, L. Suzuki, & S. C. Alexander (Eds.), *Handbook of multicultural counseling* (pp. 218–235). Thousand Oaks, CA: Sage.

Sallee, M. W., Logan, M. E., Sims, S., & Harrington, W. P. (2009). Engaging White students on a multicultural campus: Developmental needs and institutional challenges. In S. R. Harper & S. J. Quaye (Eds.), *Student engagement in higher education: Theoretical perspectinves and practial approaches for diverse populations* (pp. 199–221). New York, NY: Routledge.

Schoem, D. (2003). Intergroup dialogue for a just and diverse democracy. *Sociological Inquiry, 73,* 212–227.

Schoem, D., & Hurtado, S. (2001). *Intergroup dialogue: Deliberative democracy in school, college, community, and workplace.* Ann Arbor, MI: University of Michigan Press.

Spickard, P. R. (1992). The illogic of American racial categories. In M. P. P. Root (Ed.), *Racially mixed people in America* (pp. 12–23). Newbury Park, CA: Sage.

Tatum, B. D. (2003). *Why are all the Black kids sitting together in the cafeteria? And other conversations about race.* New York, NY: Basic Books.

Thompson, A. (2003). Tiffany, friend of people of color: White investments in antiracism. *International Journal of Qualitative Studies in Education, 16*(1), 7–29.

Thompson, B. (1996). Time traveling and border crossing: Reflections on White identity. In B. Thompson & S. Tyagi (Ed.), *Names we call home: Path on racial identity* (pp. 93–110). New York, NY: Routledge.

Thompson, B. (1999). Subverting racism from within: Linking White identity to activism. In C. Clark & J. O'Donnell (Ed.), *Becoming and unbecoming White: Owning and disowning a racial identity* (pp. 64–77). Westport, CT: Bergin & Garvey.

Washington, J. (2011). Working with majority students. In D. Lazarus Stewart (Ed.), *Multicultural student services on campus: Building bridges, re-visioning community* (pp. 245–253). Sterling, VA: Stylus.

Zúñiga, X, Nagda, B. A., Chesler, M., & Cytron-Walker, A. (2007). *Intergroup dialogue in higher education: Meaningful learning about social justice* (ASHE Higher Education Report, v. 32, no. 4). San Francisco, CA: Jossey-Bass.

Chapter 6
Engaging Multiracial College Students

C. Casey Ozaki and Kristen A. Renn

Leila stood at the top of the stairs that led to the administration building's courtyard. She often passed through the building and courtyard on her way back to her residence hall after class; most students passed through this part of campus sometime during their day. Today, as Leila was watching students walk by, it occurred to her that they all seemed to look alike and that she didn't really look like any of them. Coming from the outskirts of Chicago, she'd always been surrounded by all kinds of people. Her friends represented a spectrum of races and cultures. When Leila decided to attend Bowden College, she knew she was going to a predominantly White, small college and that she would look different from most of the other students, but she was unprepared for how different she would feel. One semester into her first year, Leila was realizing that college meant more than getting good grades and making new friends; it was also challenging her to figure out who she was—especially when she didn't necessarily see a space for the person she was envisioning.

Before she even stepped on campus, Leila was reminded of how she didn't quite fit into the racial categories that exist. Leila identified as half Filipino and half White. Some of the many surveys and information-gathering forms she completed when she applied and was admitted allowed her to select more than one racial option, but most forced her to choose one race or gave her an "Other" option. She often felt uneasy, given that her options seemed to be to either deny one of her parent's heritage or to identify herself as an "other"—an alien of sorts.

While Leila really liked her suitemates and enjoyed the friends she was making, she missed having friends with whom she could laugh about the idiosyncrasies of having an Asian family or that she could lament with over missing home-cooked meals. She visited the Asian Pacific Islander student group on campus, but when multiple students acted surprised that she was Filipino, teasing her about being a "watered-down" Asian, Leila decided not to return. She understood they were just teasing and did not mean to offend, but it made her doubt whether or not she belonged in the group even more. All of these experiences were prompting Leila to examine her racial and ethnic identity even more and left her wondering if there were any other "mixed" students on campus experiencing the same thing.

Leila loved being in college and was enjoying Bowden College, but these experiences left her feeling isolated at times and without peers with whom she could process and discuss these kinds of issues. The majority students had each other, and the students of color who identified as monoracial had their groups, but where were the "mixed" students supposed to go? For that matter, were there any other "mixed" students on campus?

Leila's story is one example of the challenges multiracial students—those with parents from more than one racial or ethnic heritage—may face when they enter the college campus environment. One of the developmental undertakings often faced by traditional-aged college students is the task of establishing an identity; race and ethnicity are often particularly relevant to determining an answer to the question "Who am I?" (Chickering & Reisser, 1993). As college students engage in this task, they not only consider their own feelings and thoughts in the process of identity development, but are also influenced by family, friends, peers, social groups, and organizational structure and policies (Evans, Forney, Guido, Patton, & Renn, 2010). When the cultural and structural norms across these influences are focused on the monoracial student experience and identity, multiracial students may struggle to find social and physical places of belonging (King, 2011; Renn, 2004).

In this chapter, we begin by describing the issues multiracial students encounter within higher education. We include consideration of the current societal context, campus policies and campus culture, in addition to interpersonal interactions among students individually and within student organizations. Next, we demonstrate how Ecological and Intersectional theoretical approaches frame and enlighten a discussion of multiracial students' needs and challenges. Finally, based on these needs and challenges, we recommend strategies for administrators, staff, and faculty to enhance services to multiracial students in college campus environments.

Needs and Challenges of Multiracial Students

Societal and Higher Education Context

Prior to the 1990s, there was little attention given to biracial and multiracial individuals' experiences in general and specifically in higher education (Renn, 2008). As the theoretical literature grew and investigation into the identity development of multiracial people emerged (Renn, 2000, 2004; Root, 1990; Wijeyesinghe, 2001), recognition of this often invisible population grew. During this time, the U.S. Office of Management and Budget (OMB) issued Statistical Directive 15 (in 1995, with a revised version in 1997). This directive expanded to five racial categories[1] available to individuals when identifying their demographic information to federal agencies and required such agencies to allow individuals to choose more than one racial category, taking effect on the 2000 U.S.

Census. This change in U.S. policy allowed Americans for the first time to respond with the full range of racial categories with which they identify. Furthermore, such attention was recently enhanced as the United States scrutinized President Barack Obama's presentation and treatment of his mixed heritage (Literté, 2010).

In addition to the events that contributed to an increase in awareness of the multiracial population among the American social consciousness, data from the 2010 U.S. Census indicate that a significant proportion of them have yet to go to college. Humes, Jones, and Ramirez (2011) found that 9 million people reported more than one race; this group comprises 2.9% of the total population and is a 32% increase over the number reporting more than one race in 2000 (the overall population growth rate was 9.7%). Frey (2011) estimated that 5% of children born in 2010 were more than one race, whereas less than 1% of the population 35 years and older is more than one race. Furthermore, Nasser and Overberg (2011) indicated that 5.6% of individuals under 18 identified as more than one race, while only 2.6% of individuals older than 18 similarly identified. Based on these figures, we predict an increasing number of college students who are likely to identify as multiracial in the coming years. How educators fully serve, support, and engage this growing collegiate population has yet to be widely established.

"Which Box(es) Do I Check?"

As multiracial students anticipate their transition from secondary to higher education, they are often confronted with challenges even before arriving on campus. As 98% of racial data is collected at application (Renn, 2009), the reporting of demographic information is often one of the first interactions with a college that students encounter. The revisions to Directive 15 were implemented in higher education in 2010–2011, so institutions must at some point provide students with the opportunity to report race using more than one category. This change is important because multiracial students and their families have repeatedly expressed feelings of discomfort, resentment, and exclusion at being limited to checking one racial category when identifying themselves (Renn, 2004; Shih & Sanchez, 2005; Townsend, Markus, & Bergseiker, 2009). Contrary to these negative outcomes, being able to have and claim their multiracial identity in private and public (e.g., demographic forms) contexts is psychologically beneficial to mixed heritage people (Binning, Unzueta, Huo, & Molina, 2009; Shih & Sanchez, 2005; Townsend et al., 2009). During a developmental period in which students are actively constructing who they want to be, privately and publically (Chickering & Reisser, 1993), encountering institutional contexts in which those identifications are limited can not only be psychologically distressing, but also influence the social construction of those identities (Renn & Lunceford, 2004; Townsend et al., 2009).

"What Are You?"

As students enter the college setting, they are not only engaged with developing their identities, but are also challenged to do this while establishing peer groups and friendships and developing a sense of belonging (Evans et al., 2010). Navigating the complex physical and social environment of college is challenging for most students, but for multiracial students, there is the additional task of managing and responding to perceptions about their race and ethnicity (Renn, 2004; Talbot, 2008). Students live and learn in complex ecologies where race is a central organizing concept of student culture and life.

Race and ethnicity are among the characteristics that we in the United States draw upon in an effort to understand and categorize people around us. When multiracial individuals do not fit into the pre-determined categories of race and ethnicity into which we are conditioned to organize people, a common question asked is, "What are you?" Such a question infers that the person being questioned does not fit or belong within the expected five standard monoracial categories. The presumption that a person should look or act in particular ways or have specific cultural knowledge associated with monoracial categories often has the consequence of asking the multiracial person to legitimize his or her racial and ethnic identity (King, 2008, 2011; Renn, 2004; Talbot, 2008). Another repercussion of the predominantly monoracial construction of race in the U.S. consciousness is the invisibility of multiraciality. As others have difficulty identifying and placing the multiracial student into known categories, assumptions are made about what his or her race and ethnicity are or should be depending on physical appearance. These assumptions lead to miscategorization and invisibility of multiraciality as a valid racial option and require the student to explain, legitimize, and educate about their identities to peers and friends on campus in ways that are not required by students who identify, personally and phenotypically, with the predominant monoracial categories (King, 2008, 2011; Miville, Constantine, Baysden, & So-Lloyd, 2004; Renn, 2004; Talbot, 2008).

Furthermore, the physical appearance of multiracial students may contribute to how others choose to accept or reject them as a part of a monoracial group. A student's skin color, hair color and texture, or eye shape may lead others to make assumptions about the groups to which he or she belongs. Further, for example, a multiracial Black and White student may be "too" dark or light skinned, leading him or her to feel pressured to identify as Black without identifying other heritage(s) or to be rejected by other Black students (Renn, 2004; Rockquemore, 2002; Talbot, 2008).

The experience of having to negotiate the "in" and "out" groups of racial politics on college campuses proves particularly tricky for multiracial students. While they are attempting to explore and develop their racial and ethnic identities, they are also asked to publically identify, legitimate, and educate about their racial identities to others, potentially causing additional stress and confusion. Deciding which boxes to check and answering "What are you?" questions draw attention to racial identity in ways that it may not for students from monoracial groups.

Navigating Racially- and Ethnically-Focused Student Services

One arena where the negotiation of race and identity for multiracial students often plays out in the college environment is among race- and ethnicity-based student services and organizations. Race- and ethnicity-based student organizations were originally established to support students of color in meeting others from similar racial and ethnic backgrounds and have a space to identify and share relevant issues (Patton, 2010). These groups also serve to organize and advocate on behalf of students from underrepresented groups (Young & Hannon, 2002).

For the multiracial student looking for a place to meet others, explore issues of identity, and find a sense of belonging within the greater college campus, negotiating participation and belonging among race-based student organizations can be challenging and confusing. Monoracial student organizations can create communities that multi-racial students perceive as exclusionary, whether due to the organization's actions or students' perceptions of belonging based on their physical features and cultural/language knowledge (King, 2011; Literté, 2010; Ozaki & Johnston, 2008; Renn, 2000, 2004). Literté (2010) found that because monoracial student organizations exist to

> institutionalize and legitimate the identities of "Black," "Latino/a," and "Asian Ameri-can," they also implicitly deny the existence and veracity of biracial identity and per-sons. Hence, many biracial students view ROSS (race-oriented student services) with discomfort, because they seemingly inhibit students' ability to develop "true self con-sciousness" and secure institutional validation. (p. 126)

As a result, multiracial student organizations have developed on many campuses (Ozaki & Johnston, 2008; Taniguchi & Heidenreich, 2005), but many institutions lack the resources, leadership, or number of multiracial students needed in order to support and sustain such organizations. Therefore, students on campuses without multiracial student organizations are often required to negotiate the ROSS terrain in environments that are often ambivalent toward multiraciality at best.

Theoretical Approaches

To provide a theoretical background for understanding multiracial students' experiences, success, and impediments to success in college, we describe two theoretical approaches: ecology and intersectionality. These theories are the foundation for the engagement strategies we present in the next section.

Campus Ecology

Ecological approaches to student development emerged from multiple areas of study, including human ecology, developmental ecology, and campus ecology (Evans et al., 2010; Renn & Patton, 2010). The underlying premise of this family of theories is that individuals exist in dynamic contexts of mutual influence. A person interacts with his or her environment, and those interactions influence both the person and the environment. Akin to biological conceptions of ecology, an individual's characteristics make him or her well-suited to some environments; but when there is a mismatch, the person must adapt the environment or adapt to the environment in order to thrive.

In translating the ecological concept to student development, scholars (e.g., Dennis, Phinney, & Chuateco, 2005; King, 2011; Renn, 2003; Seggie & Austin, 2010) have relied heavily on the work of developmental psychologist Urie Bronfenbrenner (1979, 1993) for his model that integrates personal characteristics with developmental contexts and processes over time. Key to this approach is understanding how people invite varied responses from the context and react differentially to them according to personal traits; thus, two people from the same background may experience an environment very differently and two people from very different backgrounds may have similar experiences in the environment.

Kristen Renn (2003, 2004) and Charmaine Wijeyesinghe (2001, 2012) are scholars of bi- and multiracial college student identities and experiences. Whereas Renn's approach was explicitly ecological, Wijeyesinghe's approach is consistent with the principles of a person–environment ecological stance without explicitly stating so. Both Renn and Wijeyesinghe refer to the work of Maria P. P. Root (1990, 1998, 1999), who was an early integrator of ecological frameworks into studies of bi- and multiracial youth.

Based on a multi-campus qualitative study of mixed race students, Renn (2000, 2003, 2004) proposed five patterns of bi- and multiracial identity among college students. The five patterns are:

1. **Monoracial identity**, in which students claim a single, monoracial identity from among their heritage groups.
2. **Multiple monoracial identities**, in which students alternate between/among heritage group identities. Alternation may be over an extended period of time ("Last year I generally hung out with my Asian friends, but this year I'm more with my Latina group") or may be more frequent ("I'll be going to Black Gospel Choir practice tonight after I have dinner with my mostly White housemates in the Vegan Co-op").
3. **Multiracial identity**, in which students claim a biracial, multiracial, mixed race, or other named identity that represents more than one heritage at the same time. For example, students might call themselves Hapa (Asian and White), Blaxican (Black and Mexican), or use some other term.
4. **Extraracial identity**, in which students "opt out" of racial categorization or denounce/deconstruct the system of racial classification in the United States. For no student in Renn's study was this the *only* identity, but about one-quarter of participants fit this pattern some of the time.
5. **Situational identity**, in which students shift identity based on circumstances. A highly ecological concept, this pattern is based on how interactions between person and environment shape the individual's racial identity over time and in differing conditions.

In every pattern, Renn (2000, 2003, 2004) located mutual influences between person and environment, the hallmarks of an ecological approach to understanding identity and development. Peers, academic settings, family, faculty, friendship groups, and extracurricular activities were forces acting on and with multiracial students to send messages about racial identities. Key factors included students' appearance, their knowledge of culture (e.g., language, traditions, food, holidays) related to their various heritage groups, and academic exposure to material about their heritage groups and about the concept of race itself. Another factor in students' ability to move among multiracial identity patterns was the campus ethos regarding membership in different student communities. On campuses where they could move easily among social groups (such as a sports team, the choir, and the progressive student activists), students reported more ease in identifying situationally than did their multiracial peers on campus where the boundaries between student sub-cultures were less permeable.

In another (implicitly) ecological approach, Wijeyesinghe (2001, 2012) proposed an eight-factor model of multiracial identity, positing that each factor influenced choice of racial identity. Her Factor Model included:

1. Racial ancestry
2. Early experience and socialization
3. Physical appearance
4. Other social identities (e.g., gender, sexuality, ability)
5. Religion
6. Cultural attachment
7. Political awareness and orientation, and
8. Social and historical context.

The Factor Model includes elements of Renn's (2000, 2003, 2004) and Root's (1998, 1999) ecological approaches but combines person and environment within some factors. For example, "physical appearance" includes a student's skin color, hair color and texture, and so forth, but also includes the ways that other people react to the student in response to observing this appearance. Religion is largely missing from other models of multiracial identity and represents both an internal experience and an environmental context that supports some choices of racial identity and may suppress others.

Wijeyesinghe (2001, 2012) depicts the factors as eight arrows pointing inward to the multiracial individual. In this way, the model would seem to rely more on the environmental press on the person than on the mutual interactions, but in discussing the model, Wijeyesinghe makes clear that the influences go both ways in some areas and the person–environment connection cannot be severed. If not a purely ecological model, certainly the Factor Model adds substantially to understanding the factors that influence bi- and multiracial student identities and experiences on campus.

It is important to note here that neither Renn nor Wijeyesinghe proposed anything like a stage model of multiracial identity. Indeed, they joined Root in eschewing this approach. Renn and Wijeyesinghe offer models for understanding the processes of and influences on multiracial identity. These areas—particularly as articulated clearly by Wijeyesinghe—offer guidance for higher education programs, policies, and practices as we describe at the end of this chapter.

Intersectionality

In addition to ecological models, the emerging area of intersectionality has much to offer the understanding of multiracial students' identities and experiences. Even from a non-theoretical, commonsense interpretation of the concept of intersections, bi- and multiracial students would seem to be included in this idea. They exist, after all, at the biological intersections of heritage groups that for hundreds of years in the United States were legally barred from marriage or sexual union (Courtroom History, n.d.). But intersectionality as a theoretical perspective takes that commonsense interpretation farther, lending important nuances to understanding multiracial students in higher education.

Intersectionality is a theoretical approach that is gaining ground in student development research as a way to understand how race, gender, sexual orientation, social class, and a host of other felt and ascribed identities interact. After decades of, first, studying all students as though they were the same and, second, breaking down components of identity into separate domains (e.g., race, sexuality, gender), intersectionality offers a way to put the pieces back together through understanding how the domains are mutually constitutive (Abes, Jones, & McEwen, 2007; Jones, 2009). Being a gay Black man is different from being a gay White man or a straight Black man.

In the case of multiraciality, scholars have identified gender, sexuality, and different racial heritage combinations as intersecting identities. Rockquemore (2002) reported that Black/White biracial women experienced particular gender effects in their experiences; some women found themselves courted by White men because they were seen as "exotic" (but not too threatening), whereas Black men sought them out because they were typically lighter-skinned than monoracially-identified Black women on campus. These same students reported that Black women often treated biracial Black/White peers with some contempt, accusing them of being arrogant or standoffish because biracial women had lighter skin and "good" hair. Reactions from Black and White men and from Black women led Rockquemore's participants to have a heightened sense of both racial and gender identities.

Intersections of multiracial identity and sexual orientation among students have received some attention. King (2011) studied female college students who identified as "multiracial/biracial–bisexual/pansexual" (p. 440). This combination led participants to "try on" different identities (p. 446) and to "negotiate self" understandings (p. 447), while struggling to find a place to fit on campus. Renn (2004) identified intersections of multiracial identity and lesbian/gay/bisexual (LGB) identities among some of her participants, one of whom noted that already knowing that she was biracial helped her to understand herself as "outside the box" in terms of sexuality. Different from the students in King's study, this student found that understanding race as socially constructed facilitated her understanding of sexuality as socially constructed.

In considering multiracial students and engagement through an intersectional lens, we urge attention to the ways that college environments sometimes press students to make choices among identities. For example, Renn (2004) found that multiracial students in a pre-orientation session for students of color at one university were asked to choose one racial group with which to affiliate during the three-day program. King (2011) reported that some participants felt that they had to choose to affiliate with LGB students or with students of color. As noted earlier, Rockquemore (2002) learned that biracial Black/White women experienced particular pressure on campus related to student dating and social patterns.

Intersectionality and ecology are compatible frameworks through which to understand multiracial student identities and experiences. Both depend on complex, mutual influences of person and environment, and both hold racial and other identities as social constructions that may vary within an individual, across contexts, and across the lifespan. Intersectionality and ecology also account for multiple levels of identity-based empowerment and oppression that operate to affect an individual's opportunities in education and elsewhere. For these reasons, we find them to be robust frameworks from which to understand multiracial student identities and experiences.

Student Engagement Strategies

Thus far, we have laid the groundwork for understanding the needs and challenges of multiracial students within higher education and presented theoretical frameworks intended to provide helpful lenses for understanding multiracial students' experiences in relation to their contexts and other identities. With this foundation, we suggest the following approaches and strategies for administrators, faculty, and staff working with these students.

Conduct an Audit of Campus Policies and Procedures

Conduct an audit of campus policies and procedures with an eye toward identifying those that require or imply that individual students, faculty, and staff identify in only one monoracial category. As of 2010, all institutions were required to collect and report data on student race and ethnicity using the same "check all that apply" format used by the U.S. Census and other federal agencies. Many institutions were already ahead of that requirement, but many others waited to change their admissions forms and data systems (see Renn, 2009). Beyond admissions forms—which is where 98% of institutions collect federally required data on student race and ethnicity (Renn, 2009)—a myriad of institutional systems were not required to conform to this standard. Students continue to report instances where they are asked to identify themselves in a single racial category once they arrive on campus. They also report that such inquiries violate their rights to self-identification in more than one category, as multiracial, outside categories, or situationally. These violations lead to a sense of invisibility and not belonging. Conversely, the opportunity to "check all that apply" and to see themselves represented in institutional data provides support.

Recruit, Hire, and Support Multiracial Staff and Faculty and Promote Student Connections

Having multiracial staff and faculty on campus who are available to support and interact with multiracial students is important in order to foster a connection on campus with people with similar experiences. Being able to connect with multiracial students, staff, and faculty is critical for developing a sense of belonging and identity construction (Renn, 2004). Having visible multiracial staff and faculty available to multiracial students may demonstrate the institution's commitment to people "like them."

Provide Multiracially-Inclusive Diversity Trainings

Work with student affairs educators who conduct workshops and training sessions to help them understand that not all students identify in one racial group. A popular "diversity training" exercise divides students into groups by race (typically, Black, White, Asian, Latino, and Native American). Bi- and multiracial students, if compelled to choose one of these groups, may not feel comfortable or may receive clear verbal and non-verbal feedback from peers that they are not welcome in the group they have chosen. Similarly, talking about student diversity without naming multiraciality excludes this group and continues to keep students invisible in the campus milieu.

Establish Multiracial Student Organizations

If there is no organization for multiracial students on campus, take steps to introduce programming that addresses their interests. Collaborate with monoracial groups of students of color (e.g., Black Student Union, Asian Pacific Islander Association, La Raza) to sponsor speakers, programs, and events that highlight the contributions of multiracial people. Work with academic departments who are bringing speakers to campus. The MAVIN Foundation (www.mavinfoundation.org), among other non-profit organizations, offers a number of resources for campus programming ideas. The foundation sponsors a leadership retreat for mixed race youth and college students as well.

Treat Student Organizations Equally

If there is a multiracial student organization on campus, make sure that it is treated similarly to other identity-based student organizations. Whether as "jumping off points" for leadership in other organizations or as "an oasis from the monoracial world" (Renn, 2004), these groups can provide support, social outlets, and educational programs that create a more supportive campus climate for multiracial students. Particularly on campuses that have well-established race- and ethnicity-based student organizations, competition for resources can exist when adding a similar organization (Ozaki & Johnston, 2008); therefore, policies that equalize the student organization playing field can help to preserve the goals and efforts of such organizations while promoting cooperation.

Foster and Support Strong Student Leadership

For campuses where multiracial student organizations do not currently exist or are new, the process of organizing, gathering, and advocating for multiracial student needs can be a significant task. As described previously in this chapter, accurately identifying multiracial students who do not self-identify, but may be interested in starting or participating in a student organization is a challenge given the phenotypic ambiguity that often accompanies multiracial people. Furthermore, at times, information about student organizations and activities that might be of particular interest to students of color is provided to students based on their demographic information collected at application. For institutions that do not provide the option to indicate more than one racial category or do not store data in this format, sharing information about potentially supportive opportunities on campus would be difficult. Therefore, to form formal and informal networks and student organizations, the student, staff, and faculty leadership must be strong and well supported (Ozaki & Johnston, 2008; Wong & Buckner, 2008).

Include Multiracial Issues in the Curriculum

Faculty must take care to include a multiracial perspective in their courses and curriculum. As issues of diversity and equity have established their necessity in general education curricula, information about multiracial issues have yet to be as interwoven. Not only would inclusion in more curricula and courses educate students about multiracial issues, but it would also serve to legitimize multiracial identity while creating a more inclusive environment (Renn, 2003; Williams, Nakashima, Kich, & Daniel, 1996). Furthermore, Renn (2004) found that exposing students to postmodern conceptions of race in the classroom helped provide students with the language and cognitive skill required to understand their experiences.

Create a Campus Culture of Boundary-Crossing

A campus culture that promotes boundary-crossing will inherently acknowledge and legitimize the experiences and identities of multiracial students. Not only will recognizing the cross-racial/ethnic experiences of students promote inclusion of multiracial students in predominantly monoracial environments, but it will also provide greater space for students to explore experiences and meaning across felt and ascribed identities. By encouraging students and groups to interact across different backgrounds and identities, they will not only be exposed to differences but also be exposed to a culture in which differences are valued. One way to stimulate boundary-crossing is to encourage student groups and organizations to interact and program together. Furthermore, providing additional resources, such as funding, to programs that promote boundary-crossing would likely serve as an incentive. In addition, faculty and student affairs educators can encourage dialogues across monoracial and multiracial groups, in addition to promoting discussions and understanding of intersectionality across all identity-based organizations.

Conclusion

In the vignette at the beginning of this chapter, Leila struggled with many of the needs and issues faced by multiracial students across institutions of higher education in the early 21st century. She faced feelings of isolation and invisibility and questions about the legitimacy of her racial identity and belonging. While Leila recognized that the intention of her peers and campus environment was not to make her feel this way, the lack of connection with similar peers and a sense that the campus was not designed to include students who did not fall into a designated racial category had the unfortunate consequence of exclusion.

Although Leila was a fictional character, her experience is reminiscent of the needs, issues, and challenges told by multiracial college students anecdotally and through research. Staff, faculty, and administrators can expect multiracial students to come to college in increasing numbers. They must, therefore, critically examine how their institutions are structured and designed. What messages are sent to multiracial college students when they do not have a "box to check" that reflects their identity or when they see other students on campus who have physical and psychological spaces in which to examine and develop their racial and ethnic identities, but none exists for them? The engagement strategies we propose are designed to help educators responsible for creating campus environments consider how they can be intentionally inclusive of multiracial students at structural, group, and individual levels.

Note

1. Black or African American, American Indian or Alaska Native, Asian, Native Hawaiian or Other Pacific Islander, White; ethnicity is defined as "Hispanic or Latino" or "Not Hispanic or Latino."

References

Abes, E. S., Jones, S. R., & McEwen, M. K. (2007). Reconceptualizing the model of multiple dimensions of identity: The role of meaning-making capacity in the construction of multiple identities. *Journal of College Student Development, 48*(1), 1–22.

Binning, K. R., Unzueta, M. M., Huo, Y. J., & Molina, L. E. (2009). The interpretation of multiracial status and its relation to social engagement and psychological well-being. *Journal of Social Issues, 65*(1), 35–50.

Bronfenbrenner, U. (1979). *The ecology of human development: Experiments by nature and design.* Cambridge, MA: Harvard University Press.

Bronfenbrenner, U. (1993). The ecology of cognitive development: Research models and fugitive findings. In R. H. Wozniak & K. W. Fischer (Eds.), *Development in context: Acting and thinking in specific environments* (pp. 3–44). Hillsdale, NJ: Erlbaum.

Chickering, A. W., & Reisser, L. (1993). *Education and identity* (2nd ed.). San Francisco, CA: Jossey-Bass.

Courtroom History. (n.d.). Retrieved November 6, 2011, from http://lovingday.org/courtroom-history

Dennis, J. M., Phinney, J. S., & Chuateco, L. I. (2005). The role of motivation, parental support, and peer support in the academic success of ethnic minority first-generation college students. *Journal of College Student Development, 46*(3), 223–236.

Evans, N. J., Forney, D. S., Guido, F., Patton, L., & Renn, K. A. (2010). *Student development in college: Theory, research, and practice* (2nd ed.). San Francisco, CA: Jossey-Bass.

Frey, W. H. (2011, August 26). America reaches its demographic tipping point. Blogpost. Washington, DC: The Brookings Institution. Retrieved November 16, 2011, from www.brookings.edu/opinions/2011/0826_census_race_frey.aspx

Humes, K. R., Jones, N. A., & Ramirez, R. R. (2011). *Overview of race and Hispanic origin: 2010.* 2010 Census Briefs. Washington, DC: US Department of Commerce, Economics and Statistics Administration, US Census Bureau.

Jones, S. R. (2009). Constructing identities at the intersections: An autoethnographic exploration of multiple dimensions of identity. *Journal of College Student Development, 50*(3), 287–304.

King, A. R. (2008). Student perspectives on multiracial identity. In K. A. Renn & P. Shang (Eds.), Biracial and multiracial college students: Theory, research, and best practices in student affairs. *New Directions for Student Services* (pp. 33–42). San Francisco, CA: Jossey-Bass.

King, A. R. (2011). Environmental influences on the development of female college students who identify as multiracial/biracial-bisexual/pansexual. *Journal of College Student Development, 52*(4), 440–455.

Literté, P. E. (2010). Revising race: How biracial students are changing and challenging student services. *Journal of College Student Development, 51*(2), 115–134.

Miville, M., Constantine, M., Baysden, M., & So-Lloyd, G. (2005). Chameleon changes: An exploration of racial identity themes of multiracial people. *Journal of Counseling Psychology, 52*, 507–516.

Nasser H. E., & Overberg, P. (2011, August 9). How America changed. *USA Today.* Retrieved November 16, 2011, from www.usatoday.com/NEWS/usaedition/2011-08-10-1Acensusturningpoints-CV-_CV_U.htm

Ozaki, C. C., & Johnston, M. P. (2008). The space in between: Issues for multiracial student organizations and advising. In K. A. Renn & P. Shang (Eds.), Biracial and multiracial college students: Theory, research, and best practices in student affairs. *New Directions for Student Services* (pp. 53–62). San Francisco, CA: Jossey-Bass.

Patton, L. D. (Ed.). (2010). *Culture centers in higher education: Perspectives on identity, theory, and practice.* Sterling, VA: Stylus.

Renn, K. A. (2000). Patterns of situational identity among biracial and multiracial college students. *The Review of Higher Education, 23*(4), 399–420.

Renn, K. A. (2003). Understanding the identities of mixed race college students through a developmental ecology lens. *Journal of College Student Development, 44*, 383–403.

Renn, K. A. (2004). *Mixed race college students: The ecology of race, identity, and community.* Albany, NY: State University of New York Press.

Renn, K. A. (2008). Research on bi- and multiracial identity development: Overview and synthesis. In K. A. Renn & P. Shang (Eds.), Biracial and multiracial college students: Theory, research, and best practices in student affairs. *New Directions for Student Services* (pp. 13–21). San Francisco, CA: Jossey-Bass.

Renn, K. A. (2009). Education policy, politics, and mixed heritage students in the United States. *Journal of Social Issues, 65*(1), 165–183.

Renn, K. A., & Lunceford, C. J. (2004). Because the numbers matter: Transforming racial and ethnic data in postsecondary education to meet the challenges of a changing nation. *Educational Policy, 18*, 752–783.

Renn, K. A., & Patton, L. D. (2010). Campus ecology and environments. In J. D. Schuh, S. R. Jones, & S. L. Harper (Eds.), *Student services: A handbook for the profession* (5th ed., pp. 242–256). San Francisco, CA: Jossey-Bass.

Rockquemore, K.A. (2002). Negotiating the color line: The gendered process of racial identity construction among Black/White biracial women. *Gender & Society, 16*(4), 485–503.

Root, M.P.P. (1990). Resolving 'Other' status: Identity development of biracial individuals. *Women and Therapy, 9*(1/2), 185–205.

Root, M.P.P. (1998). Experiences and processes affecting racial identity development: Preliminary results from the Biracial Sibling Project. *Cultural Diversity and Mental Health, 4*(3), 237–247.

Root, M.P.P. (1999). The biracial baby boom: Understanding the ecological constructions of racial identity in the 21st century. In R.H. Sheets & E.R. Hollins (Eds.), *Racial and ethnic identity in school practices: Aspects of human development* (pp. 67–90). Mahwah, NJ: Erlbaum.

Seggie, F.N., & Austin, A.E. (2010). Impact of the headscarf ban policy on the identity development of part-time unveilers in Turkish higher education. *Journal of College Student Development, 51*(5), 564–583.

Shih, M., & Sanchez, D.T. (2005). Perspectives and research on the positive and negative implications of having multiple racial identities. *Psychological Bulletin, 131*, 569–591.

Talbot, D.M. (2008). Exploring the experiences and self-labeling of mixed-race individuals with two minority parents. In K.A. Renn & P. Shang (Eds.), *Biracial and multiracial college students: Theory, research, and best practices in student affairs.* New Directions for Student Services (pp. 23–32). San Francisco, CA: Jossey-Bass.

Taniguchi, A.S., & Heidenreich, L. (2005, Fall). Re-Mix: Rethinking the use of "Hapa" in mixed-race Asian/Pacific Islander American community organizing. *WSU McNair Journal*, 135–146.

Townsend, S.S.M., Markus, H.R., & Bergseiker, H.B. (2009). My choice, your categories: The denial of multiracial identities. *Journal of Social Issues, 65*(1), 183–202.

Wijeyesinghe, C.L. (2001). Racial identity in multiracial people: An alternative paradigm. In C.L. Wijeyesinghe & B.W. Jackson, III (Eds.), *New perspectives on racial identity development: A theoretical and practical anthology* (pp. 129–152). New York, NY: New York University Press.

Wijeyesinghe, C.L. (2012). Racial identity in multiracial people: An alternative paradigm. In C.L. Wijeyesinghe & B.W. Jackson, III (Eds.), *New perspectives on racial identity development: Integrating emerging frameworks* (2nd ed., pp. 129–152). New York, NY: New York University Press.

Williams, T.K., Nakashima, C.L., Kich, G.K., & Daniel, G.R. (1996). Being different together in the university classroom: Multiracial identity as transgressive education. In M.P.P. Root (Ed.), *The multiracial student experience: Racial borders as the new frontier* (pp. 359–379). Thousand Oaks, CA: Sage.

Wong, M.P.A., & Buckner, J. (2008). Multiracial student services come of age: The state of multiracial student services in higher education in the United States. In K.A. Renn & P. Shang (Eds.), *Biracial and multiracial college students: Theory, research, and best practices in student affairs.* New Directions for Student Services (pp. 43–52). San Francisco, CA: Jossey-Bass.

Young, L.W. & Hannon, M.D. (2002, February). The staying power of Black cultural centers. *Black Issues in Higher Education, 18*(26), 104. Retrieved from http://iibp.chadwyck.com/iibp/full_rec?ACTION=byid&ID=00056814

Chapter 7
Engaging International Students

Jenny J. Lee

International students constitute a significant and growing student population in many colleges and universities around the world. The latest accounts showed that almost 4.3 million students were enrolled in institutions outside their country of citizenship in 2011, an increase of about 10% from the previous year (Organisation for Economic Cooperation and Development [OECD], 2013), suggesting that international education will remain and likely increase in global demand in the years to come. As people are traveling abroad with increased accessibility to greater modes of transportation and routes, crossing national borders specifically for educational purposes has become more commonplace than ever before.

Study abroad destinations tend to be in the United States and Western European countries. In fact, the top five receivers of international students, the United States, the United Kingdom, Australia, Germany, and France, attract about half of all international students combined (OECD, 2013). The United States continues to be the leading destination for cross-border study, hosting over 800,000 international students (Institute of International Education [IIE], 2013). The main driver has been the prestige associated with studying at a U.S. university, especially given the country's high concentration of the world's most highly-ranked universities (e.g., Academic Ranking of World Universities compiled by the Shanghai Jiao Tong University). As such, there has been an enrollment rise of approximately 7% in the past year (IIE, 2013), and in a recent survey of 380 U.S. campuses, over 70% observed an increase at their institution (IIE, 2013). Despite this continuous flow, the growing trend is not guaranteed. While the absolute number of international students has been rising steadily, the United States experienced a major decline in the global proportion of international students over the past decade, from 23% of the world's share in 2000 to about 17% in 2011 (OECD, 2013). Meanwhile, Australia and New Zealand, for example, have observed a 2% increase in their share of international students, and the Russian Federation has become a new competitor in the international student market (OECD, 2011). With the increase and diversity of individuals studying outside their home countries and the greater range of international education opportunities than ever before, the global market is tipping away from the United States and Western Europe and toward Oceania and Asia.

In order to fully appreciate the significance of such global trends, it helps to understand the benefits that overseas students offer to the countries that educate them. Among the most apparent motivations for attracting international students are their financial contributions. With declining public investments in higher education around the world, international tuition and fees, which are typically much higher than what colleges and universities charge their in-state students, can potentially subsidize university operations. In Australia, for example, international education is the country's third largest export, with international student fees replacing its public contributions at a growing rate. Although international students constitute only 3.9% of all students in the United States, their financial contributions are still notable (IIE, 2011). In 2012, these students and their dependents contributed approximately $25 billion to the U.S. economy, with over 70% coming from sources outside the United States, including personal, family, home governments and sending universities (IIE, 2013).

Many international students, particularly graduate students and postdocs, have become vital to the United States in maintaining its competitive edge in areas of science, technology, engineering, and mathematics (STEM; Cantwell & Lee, 2010; Haddal, 2006). Data from the National Science Foundation (NSF) Survey of Earned Doctorates indicated that non-U.S. citizens (permanent residents and temporary visa holders) accounted for over 40% of science and engineering doctorates between 2002–2006, with an increase of 44% compared to U.S. citizens over that same time period (NSF, 2007). Furthermore, non-U.S. citizens comprised more than half of all doctorate recipients in the engineering and computer science fields (64.8%), mathematics (57.2%), and physics (58.0%) (NSF, 2007). Among undergraduates, international students comprised 36.4% of all students in the STEM fields. Given domestic skill shortages in the STEM areas, colleges and universities have had to rely increasingly on international students and graduates as researchers to maintain their scientific knowledge production (Cantwell & Lee, 2010). These students work in scientific labs, assist in grant-writing, lead major research projects, serve as teaching assistants or instructors, and comprise a significant portion students of and graduates from STEM departments, thereby raising the prestige of many elite universities.

Beyond their monetary and scientific contributions, international students provide a wealth of cultural knowledge and diverse perspectives that are vital in preparing future students to compete successfully in the global economy. A narrow U.S.-centric education is no longer sufficient in the current era of globalization. As countries are becoming increasingly interdependent, knowledge about and experiences in diverse cultures, economies, politics, social issues, and languages outside the United States are being recognized as valuable forms of capital. Moreover, past higher education research has empirically demonstrated the many positive learning outcomes associated with interacting with diverse students, such as heightened critical thinking, self-awareness, motivation, leadership skills, intellectual and civic development, educational aspirations, and cultural awareness (e.g., antonio, 2001; Chang, 1999; Chang, Astin, & Kim, 2004; Gurin, Dey, Hurtado, & Gurin, 2002). In addition to the learning and associated outcomes that international students offer, they also provide helpful social networks, linking individuals and groups across borders. Given that international students are often among the most privileged members in their home countries, they may provide valuable connections to influential individuals and organizations throughout the world. For example, international students have also been found to be vital bridges for faculty and students in cross-border scholarly research, thereby linking institutions globally (Maldonado-Maldonado & Cantwell, 2007).

Although international students offer countless benefits to U.S. colleges and universities, they are perhaps also the most misunderstood. For some, being marginalized and invisible on campuses is evident as they are often mistaken for or categorized with domestic students of color. Despite any physical resemblance, international students' past educational experiences, worldviews, and cultural knowledge can be quite different compared to that of a domestic student who shares the same racial background. Among the limited studies that have compared domestic and international students, "international students were more likely than local students to experience problems and to a greater degree" (Mullins, Quintrell, & Hancock, 1995, p. 210), such as in finding part-time work, fear of failure, workload, and nervousness/tension, to name a few. Although such dissimilarities between international and domestic students are vast and hardly disputed, scant resources tend to be devoted to a single isolated international affairs office that is somehow responsible for catering to the many complex immigration issues as well as academic and social needs for the often thousands of students from all over the world in a single campus. Even the category of "international students" imply a homogeneous group that combines together all non-U.S. students despite them having more differences between them than any commonalities, with the exception of a shared purpose in choosing to study outside their home countries. Their motivations for studying in the United States, their past experiences, and future goals are as varied as the countries from which they originate and even within a single sending country, there can be as many diverse backgrounds are as represented in the United States.

Challenges for International Students

Despite the great variety of cultures that international students represent, the challenges that international students face tend to be relatively similar in initially entering any foreign environment with varying degrees of difficulty. Early entry issues regarding mastering the local language, cultural norms, food tastes, as well as the social "shock" of being away from family and friends back home can be expected, especially for students traveling to countries with very different cultures and that are on opposite ends of the globe. Countless studies have illuminated such anticipated concerns (e.g., Li & Kaye,

1998; Pritchard & Skinner, 2002; Wilton & Constantine, 2003) and without adequate attention and support, their problems can sometimes manifest to extreme stress and depression (Chen, 1999; Constantine, Okazaki, & Utsey, 2004).

For readers less familiar with the specific challenges of studying in another country, some common issues are reported in the following sections.

Second Language and Learning

International students whose first language is not English have the obvious challenge of learning academic content in their non-native language. Understanding lectures, including professors and teaching assistants speaking too quickly and with unfamiliar jargon, was reported as being especially challenging (Ramsay, Barker, & Jones, 1999). Faculty office hours and even study groups can be quite daunting as simply being able to converse freely and ask questions cannot be taken for granted. Without the ability to confidently ask and understand class discussions, silence may be mistaken for disengagement. When faculty were asked what they believe to be international students' greatest detriment to success, the vast majority indicated that international students do not fully participate in class discussions (Tompson & Tompson, 1996). Even a proficient English-speaker can experience hurdles in comprehending regional and foreign-based accents. Beyond understanding literary English, an inability to understand idioms and slang can also create some discomfort, even among students whose first language is English but who were not raised in the United States. Meanwhile, troubles in being able to freely converse in the host language may not only lead to challenges in daily functions but also result in a considerable stress and a negative self-concept (Chen, 1999).

Social Isolation

What tends to follow language barriers are social isolation and loneliness, particularly outside the classroom. When asked to rank their greatest concerns, international students indicated developing social networks as their primary challenge (Bartram 2007; Tompson & Tompson, 1996), reporting "loneliness and fear of not fitting in kept them mentally preoccupied" (Tompson & Tompson, 1996, p. 55). Based on extensive interviews with over 200 international students in Australia, Sawir, Marginson, Deumert, Nyland, and Ramia (2008) identified three forms of loneliness: personal, social, and cultural. While personal loneliness (loss of familial contact) and social loneliness (loss of social networks) are commonly understood and anticipated, they also recognized cultural loneliness, based on an absence of their familiar cultural and/or linguistic environment. They further uncovered a strong corresponding relationship between loneliness and problems developing cross-cultural relationships.

Though many students may find social support in international student clubs and organizations, other universities may not have adequate representation from particular countries, and those students from less populous nations may feel especially alone. Even among groups where there is a large representation of international students from particular countries, there might still be cultural isolation. Such racial balkanization is worrisome as misinformation may be passed around and never corrected. Further, they may isolate themselves in self-imposed campus enclaves. Schmitt, Spears, and Branscombe (2003) found that part of the reason that international students gravitate toward each other is due to a shared identity of rejection. That is, "identification with international students increased in response to perceiving prejudice and suppressed the costs of perceiving oneself as excluded from the host community" (p. 1), and "identification with other international students is not based on similar intragroup traits, but is constructed in context based on their common treatment from the majority" (p. 5). Moreover, perceived discrimination was more positively related to identification with other international students than to identification with one's home country. These findings are especially insightful because they challenge the assumption that international students congregate due to any preexisting group identities and history of devaluation but rather form alliances based on their shared common challenges. The researchers also found that while perceived discrimination might lead to a decrease in self-esteem, they also found that identifying with other international students mediated a positive relationship between perceived discrimination and self-esteem. In other words, a shared group international student identity could lead to a healthier and more positive sense of self, helping to overcome experiences of mistreatment. Yet, despite tendencies to withdraw into culturally similar or internationally based social networks and their potential benefits, international students nevertheless desire to interact and befriend local members of the host community (Mullins et al., 1995).

Positive relationships are vital, not only in fostering a healthy identity but also in learning. Previous research indicated that Asian students from Confucius backgrounds tend be more collectivist in their approach to learning, relying more on group interaction in their studies (Ramburuth & McCormick, 2001), and, without adequate social learning environments, they may especially be at academic risk. These findings are most applicable for international students from other collectivist cultures. Collaboration may be a preferred style of learning for many international students, but forced group work does not automatically lead to an ideal learning environment where everyone benefits. Without communication and group work based on mutual respect and trust, some international students may feel further isolated in a small group setting.

Cultural Norms

Understanding the host cultural norms can also be difficult for international students. Ways of interacting with professors, such as how to address them and whether to make eye contact, can be considerably different from what might be expected in the home country. For instance, avoiding eye contact can be perceived as a signal of respect and reverence in one culture but the same gesture might also be perceived as being untrustworthy in another (Lee & Opio, 2011). Classroom interactions may also widely differ by culture, especially among countries that uphold greater formality between teachers and students as compared to the United States (Ninnes, Aitchison, & Kalos, 1999). While Asian cultures might frown upon openly questioning authority, criticism and debate tend to be highly valued in the United States. Such forms of learning and interacting may be very unusual, sometimes even culturally unacceptable, and thus challenging for many overseas students. There may be internal conflicts in whether to speak out in class and appear disrespectful. Even honoring a professor's allowance of being called by his or her first name or eating and drinking during class could be a source of tension for some international students. Faculty and student peers might confuse an international student's humility and modesty, two highly valued traits outside the United States, as ignorance and incompetence. Further, cross-cultural miscommunication might also arise, such as different perceptions of gender roles and opposite-sex relationships (Lacina, 2002). Physical touch and socializing with members of the opposite sex could be interpreted differently based on one's culture. What might be intended as a harmless and innocent embrace in one culture could be mistaken as a personal violation in another.

Despite such cultural challenges, international students tend to keep their problems to themselves rather than seeking institutional support (Constantine, Anderson, Berkel, Caldwell, & Utsey, 2005; Lee & Rice, 2007). Research on international college students are mostly found within the counseling literature, indicating the psychological "problems" that this student sector tends to face related to their "adjustment." In their examination of Asian students, Heggins and Jackson (2003) suggested that they tend to underutilize counseling and other support services due to cultural differences and stigmas associated with psychological concerns. These students instead seek out existing social networks for support. Similar findings were reported for African students, who indicated they would not seek out support due to unfamiliarity with counseling services and possible distrust (Constantine et al., 2005). With such preceding studies in mind, it is helpful to keep in mind that among the international students who experience major psychological distress, many may not seek out professional support due to unfamiliarity or fear of being stigmatized. As a result, there may be serious consequences if such problems are left unaddressed, such as depression (Constantine et al., 2004; Mori, 2000) and lowered career aspirations (Reynolds & Constantine, 2007).

Costs and Visa Procedures

Several studies have also noted the financial burden of studying abroad is a major concern and stressor among overseas students (Chen, 1999; Mori, 2000; Ramburuth & McCormick, 2001). In the Institution for International Education's (IIE) global survey of over 9,000 prospective students, cost was cited as the primary obstacle to studying in the United States; 60% perceived U.S. tuition to be the most expensive among all host countries and second in the cost of living, following the U.K. (Chow, 2011). Changes in the cost of living, particularly for students from developing countries, can have a major toll on the mental and physical energy required in seeking supplemental income while being required to maintain their full-time student status. Without readily accessible resources from family in their home countries, these students are often left on their own to cover their basic living and educational necessities. Some students may have experienced additional financial setbacks with a depreciating home currency while living abroad, resulting in even less monetary support from home (Chen, 1999). Their financial troubles tend to be considerably greater than local students given that they have very little or no access to loans and scholarships and must pay out-of-state tuition (Lin & Yi, 1997).

In the same IIE survey (Chow, 2011), almost half of the respondents indicated that the United States had difficult or complex student visa procedures and the highest requirements of any host destination in the world (Chow, 2011). The U.S. visa procedures are notoriously cumbersome and delays in processing can create a host of problems in preparing for relocation, ranging from travel arrangements, securing university housing, signing up for classes, and other time-sensitive tasks. Further, the Student Exchange Visitor Information System (SEVIS), a mandatory program that requires all higher education institutions to screen and track international students and scholars, was implemented in 2001. This surveillance program was introduced given that several of those directly involved in the attacks on the World Trade Center on September 11, 2001, arrived to the United States on student visas. However, SEVIS has been scrutinized as both costly and inefficient in its intended purpose to identify potential terrorists (Urias & Yeakey, 2009). Hosting universities have protested that the program is extremely burdensome and that the Department of Homeland Security has provided little training in its implementation (Haddal, 2006). Given the difficulties of attaining visas as well as problems with national security, some international students have questioned whether studying in the United States is worth facing these challenges (Haddal, 2006).

Discrimination

There have been numerous reports of discrimination and hostile acts against international students, in the U.S. and globally, particularly following the attacks on September 11, 2001 (Constantine et al., 2005; Lane, 2002; Lee & Rice, 2007; MacWilliams, 2004; McMurtie, 2001; Perry, 2010). Among the more recent incidents, nine Chinese students were attacked and robbed in the U.K., leading university administrators at Sussex Downs College to educate their 400 international students on how to protect themselves (BBC, 2011). In an even more grave example, an Indian student from Punjab was stabbed to death in Melbourne, Australia. This incident was not an isolated case. There had been a series of racial attacks in Melbourne against Indian students, resulting in violent protests the previous year, a strain in bilateral ties between the two countries, and a 20% drop in Indian student enrollment in Australian universities (Perry, 2010). Based on a survey of international students in Southern Australia, more than half of the respondents indicated prejudice and racism to be a problem both on and off campus and were more likely to rate "fair treatment of international students as poor" compared to local students (Mullins et al., 1995). In New Zealand, three Korean students were attacked, leading the headmaster of Nelson College to admit, "Racism towards people from Asian backgrounds was a national issue" and then state, "It was hard for most schools to operate without income from international students" (*Nelson Mail*, 2009). Such financial consequences were of similar concern for college administrators in the U.K. (BBC, 2011) and Australia (Perry, 2010). In their study of African students in the United States, Constantine and her colleagues (2005) identified several acts of mistreatment, including verbal assaults from teaching staff and perceptions of intellectual inferiority and of being uncivilized. Negative stereotypes manifested in social challenges, including finding roommates and developing friendships. Lee and Rice (2007) also identified cases of sexual harassment, verbal assaults, and physical attacks against international students in the United States.

Theoretical Frameworks

Despite such accounts, the overriding literature on international students frame their challenges as a form of "maladjustment" (Chen, 1999, p. 49), placing the burden on international students to adapt and overcome any challenges that are set up by their hosts. Among the most common theoretical frameworks in conceptualizing the issues that arise among international students are adaptation (Anderson, 1994; Zhou, Jindal-Snape, Topping, & Todman, 2008), adjustment (Mori, 2000; Ramsay et al., 1999; Reynolds & Constantine, 2007), acculturation (Chen, 1999; Constantine et al., 2004; Heggins & Jackson, 2003), and intercultural competence (Wilton & Constantine, 2003), all of which assume international students' incorporation of the host culture's values, beliefs, and behaviors. The fundamental problem with such viewpoints is that they not only place the responsibility on the newcomer to adjust, but they also discount the cultural value that international students offer in bettering the host environment. The acculturation framework, for instance, assumes cultural superiority and devalues what newcomers may offer; that is, that there is a "better way" to be and live, namely from the position of the host society in comparison to the environment of origin. As an example, Ninnes, Aitchison, and Kalos (1999) pointed out how Indians in Australia were perceived as being culturally deficient in their culture and previous educational experiences as compared to local students. A common strategy in helping international students cope with "culture shock" and then "acculturation" has been "the development of stress-coping strategies and culturally relevant social skills . . . and should result in psychological adjustment and sociocultural adaptation" (Zhou et al., 2008, p. 69).

In her discourse analysis of media regarding international students in Australia, Devos (2003) uncovered ways that these students are perceptually being marginalized as "foreign and 'the other'" (p. 164). They are highly valued for their economic contributions as "fee paying students" (p. 160) but they are also targeted as responsible for lowering academic standards with "corrupt[ion]," "malaise," and metaphors of "disease" and an "epidemic" (p. 162). She elaborated, "international students are simultaneously a source of contempt (for their inadequate English language skills), resentment (that we have to accept them at all) and paradoxically, anxiety ('will they like us?')" (p. 164). Meanwhile, the media constructed local Australian academics as victims of poorly prepared and inferior international students who are overrunning the Australian higher education system (Devos, 2003).

A second major limitation to the existing literature is that most research on international students examined this population as a homogenous group, often in comparison to local students, although some studies have sought to differentiate student experiences by their region or country of origin. The top three sending countries to U.S. higher education (i.e., China, India, and South Korea) comprise nearly half (46%) of the total international enrollments (IIE, 2011). These three Asian countries similarly account for over half (52%) of all students studying abroad worldwide (OECD, 2011). Despite the dominance of Asians among international students, there have been limited attempts to differentiate between them or compare them to students from other regions. Among the few studies, Wilton and Constantine (2003) reported that Latin American international students experienced greater psychological distress than Asian students. But in another comparison survey of international students from seven regions of the world, Hanassab and Tidwell (2002) found that Africans faced the greatest discriminatory challenges, and that Asian students reported the highest psychological distress. The authors also reported minimal difficulties among Canadians and Western Europeans, who reported being more socially involved with U.S. nationals and reported fewer troubles. In a similar vein, African students related "lower self-efficacy, acculturative stress, and depression compared to other international students" (Constantine et al., 2004, p. 237), suggesting that the reasons might have to do with "African students may face a larger gap between their culture of origin and American culture" (p. 238), and that racism might also be present. Despite a lack of research that systematically differentiates students' experiences by their countries of origin (see Chow, 2011, as an exception), the studies that have included Anglo students have consistently found that these students (i.e., Canadians, Australians, and Western Europeans) studying in the United States and Australia experienced far less social isolation and related challenges compared to students from Asian and developing countries (Chow, 2011; Hanassab & Tidwell, 2002; Lee & Rice, 2007; Lee & Opio, 2011).

Neo-Racism

Past studies have demonstrated that many international students have had innumerable negative encounters and experiences with their university hosts, particularly those from non-Western and developing nations. Negative views about the lack of openness to outside cultures held by those in the United States are pervasive. In the IIE survey previously discussed, 30% of the over 9,000 respondents indicated that the United States does not welcome international students (Chow, 2011).

The guiding framework for this chapter, neo-racism, is based on the premise that international students are being discriminated against, not simply based on the color of their skin, but also based on negative assumptions about their home country. The experiences of international students from China, for example, may be exceedingly more difficult than the experiences of U.S.-born Chinese Americans. The concept of neo-racism has its roots in France as immigrants from the Arab regions were being mistreated under the justification of preserving the "French race" (Balibar, 2005, p. 170) and "legitimate polices of exclusion" (Balibar, 2007, p. 81). Balibar (2007) elaborated:

> The new racism is a racism of the era of "decolonization," of the reversal of population movements between the old colonies and the old metropolises,

and the division of humanity within a single political space . . . It is a racism whose dominant theme is not about biological heredity but the insurmountability of cultural differences, a racism which, at first sight, does not postulate the superiority of certain groups or peoples in relation to others but "only" the harmfulness of abolishing frontiers, the incompatibility of life-styles and traditions. (p. 84)

Balibar (2005) goes on to explain that even in France, there is no true ethnic basis. He wrote:

No nation, that is, no national state, has an ethnic basis, which means that nationalism can not be defined as an ethnocentrism except that precisely in the sense of the product of fictive ethnicity. To reason any other way would be to say that "peoples" do not exist naturally any more than "races" do, either by virtue of their ancestry, a community of culture or preexisting interests. (p. 166)

Since then, Lee and Rice (2007) and Lee and Opio (2011) have applied this concept of neo-racism to explain the many documented cases of discrimination against international students, particularly post-September 11, 2001. They argued that institutions should consider the value that international students offer to their host institutions but also critically examine ways that faculty, staff, students, and the local community might be in some ways responsible for creating an unwelcome, and sometimes hostile, environment for their international guests. They also found that students from developing and non-Western countries experienced the greatest challenges compared to their international White counterparts. Thus, not all international students face the same difficulties, nor are international students' issues akin to those of students of color. For example, research has indicated that Africans encountered prejudicial treatment from African Americans (Constantine et al., 2005; Lee & Opio, 2011).

Student Engagement Strategies

While higher education institutions may have limited influence in preventing all assaults and hostile acts of discrimination, they nevertheless play a very influential role in bettering the experiences of international students and promoting their success. Their experiences can directly impact the flow of future students to the institution as international student choices often are determined by the recommendation of friends, family, and other contacts back home (Lee, 2010; Pimpa, 2003). Faculty, staff, and students are, thus, responsible for creating a welcoming environment to international guests.

All too often, recommendations for supporting the international student population have been as broad-based as "choose the right kind of classes," "develop good personal practices," and "study with friends" (Abel, 2002, p. 16). These suggestions vastly underestimate their academic and personal competencies and ignore the fundamental cultural problems that might underlie an international student's difficulties in navigating a new environment and foreign and complex system of obtaining academic and social support. Even what might be a seemingly helpful suggestion, such as "Preparing for the culture shock of a very different experience by auditing classes beforehand, visiting campus organizations, and speaking with American students about what to expect should prove helpful" is simply unrealistic for an international student without the necessary funds and domestic contacts to follow such advice. Such suggestions that are typically provided for domestic students simply do not apply. As a further example, consider the following goals for "good time management" that were specifically prepared for international students:

- Plan two hours of study for each hour of class time.
- Plan to study during the day. Research shows that sixty minutes of study during the day is equivalent to ninety minutes of study at night.
- Plan blocks of study time. Studying in one-hour blocks is usually best.

Such well-intended suggestions do not take into account that at least a third of all international students do not speak English as their first language; far more hours are needed to simply comprehend class material. Furthermore, a Western conception and emphasis on time is highly presumed, not taking into account the many different approaches to studying, such as simply until one masters the material, rather than being dictated by the clock.

With the preceding review of the major challenges facing international students in mind, it is important for anyone who interacts with international students to have what I call "international consciousness," global awareness, appreciation, and understanding of the cultural diversity that extends beyond our national borders. Some might find it helpful to place themselves in the position of someone who has not lived in the United States and is traveling here for the first time and perceiving and interacting within the environment with new eyes. Given the wide breadth of cultures and viewpoints that are represented in this population, it is important for faculty, staff, and students to embody an international consciousness, including openness to learning from these students as individuals. Thus, below are some suggestions in supporting international students.

Forming Connections with International Students

Get to personally know international students. Given the challenges in identifying the specific needs of overseas students from every country or region without overgeneralizing, getting to know these students is crucial step in best supporting these students. As the literature review demonstrated, negative stereotypes and assumptions about students from "foreign" countries have a dangerous effect on their experiences abroad. The best and most effective way in dismantling any prejudices would be to get to know international students as individuals with rich cultural backgrounds and new perspectives to offer. Most of these students enter the United States with very few networks, if any, and are prone to isolation and loneliness. Matching them with domestic student "buddies" and arranging occasional social gatherings are certainly helpful, but they can also appear quite forced and artificial. Less task-oriented attempts, such as kind gestures, a listening ear, and frequent contact, may especially help these students feel welcome and at ease. International student organizations play vital roles in creating a system of social support but it is also important to not isolate these students to their cultural groups, as they desire to befriend local students as well.

Providing Financial Support

While some international students come from wealthy backgrounds, many other international students experience considerable stress, particularly in regards to their finances. Without much access to scholarships, financial aid, and with a cap on working on campus part-time, many struggle to make ends meet. Devalued currencies abroad and limited governmental assistance, if any, are additional economic challenges. When part-time job opportunities become available, international students apply but are sometimes turned away, due to limited English proficiency and foreign accents. With limited opportunities for many students whose language is not English to converse with native English speakers in their home country, their ability to read and write are often much stronger than their oral communication skills. However, international students also tend to be highly motivated and determined as they already made the commitment to learn outside the comforts of their home country.

Thinking Practically

For anyone who has travelled abroad, it is easy to consider that even the basic tasks, such as finding and understanding public transportation or opening a bank account, can be taken for granted. When befriending international students, one will soon discover their many practical concerns that are hardly raised by their U.S. counterparts. Chief among them are being met at the airport or arranging transportation from the airport and to help then find adequate housing. In some cases, students arrive in the United States alone and for the first time, without any knowledge on how to get to the campus or where to live. There are some students who live in hotels for the first several weeks of the school term until they find adequate and affordable housing. Helping students with these basic arrangements can save them considerable stress and anxiety. Further, workshops and/or reading materials on the U.S. culture, particularly on the norms regarding the local area where the university is located, can also be valuable. As there might be negative stereotypes about some students' home country, they may also have negative stereotypes about the United States or the particular region of the country.

Providing Advocacy

Quite often, attempts to welcome and support international students tend to be restricted to their initial orientation to the university. Sometimes the greatest challenges occur after they have settled into their regular schedule and routine. Unexpected and unanticipated maltreatment might occur, whether it is a degrading remark from a professor, sexual harassment from a supervisor, or social isolation from classmates. Though such examples might appear anecdotal and infrequent, previous research has demonstrated that such acts do occur but are often not reported. International students may fear deportation or retribution for causing trouble and may instead suffer silently. Although international affairs offices on campus are the primary source of international student support, they tend to be overburdened with complex immigration procedures, including SEVIS, and a myriad of international student administrative concerns. Other campus offices may be less familiar with the needs and struggles of overseas students. Thus, faculty, students, as well as administrators across the university should be sensitive to the different circumstances of international students compared to their domestic peers and serve them accordingly. Moreover, creating a welcoming atmosphere is foundational in building trust in case problems arise.

Outreach among Student Affairs Educators

Considerable costs and staffing resources are often used to recruit full-fee paying students from overseas. But there is far less attention on maintaining their expectations and satisfaction upon their arrival. There are countless student support services that international students may not be aware of, particularly because such services may not exist in the universities in their home countries. The student affairs profession is relatively new and may be unfamiliar to those outside the United States. Beyond providing a written directory of support programs, student affairs staff should reach out to international students, educating them on ways that students can seek out support and encouraging them to take advantage of what these programs offer and how to participate. Related to this recommendation, student affairs staff should be sensitive to the needs and issues for overseas students and try to avoid a one-size-fits-all program that focuses solely on domestic assumptions. International student support training is essential for any office that works with students, not just international student affairs offices.

Internationalizing Campuses

"Internationalization" is a hot buzzword in promoting the prestige of U.S. colleges and universities. The way internationalization is most often implemented and observed, however, is in the international composition of its students and sometimes faculty. Though a high proportion of international students is indeed a marker of internationalization, merely accounting for international enrollment numbers could simply be nothing more than a financial ploy to attract and bring in as many full fee-paying students as possible. Internationalization should incorporate international perspectives, views, values, and cultures into campus life both in and outside the classroom. Cultural centers are one obvious area where diversity is central and celebrated. However, these centers tend to focus on the needs of Americans of color, and as such international students may not feel welcome. For example, previous research has documented ways that African American students might discriminate against African students (Constantine et al., 2005; Lee & Opio, 2011). Thus, it is important to expand the roles of cultural centers to serve students beyond our domestic borders and possibly bridge understandings between U.S. students of color and their international student counterparts. In the classroom, faculty and students should be especially attentive to what international students might offer by way of new viewpoints and interpretations of class materials.

Conclusion

International students represent a large component of many colleges and universities. Given increased demands for globalization and postsecondary missions that reflect internationalization, it is critical to understand the unique challenges and needs of this growing population. In this chapter, I discussed ways to better understand international students and utilized different theories to make further sense of their needs. These recommendations noted above are not an exhaustive list of the ways to increase the engagement of international students on campus. They reflect international consciousness as faculty, student affairs educators, and students step beyond their comfort zones to educate themselves about international students and employ practices that are attuned to these students' various needs.

References

Abel, C. F. (2002). Academic success and the international student: Research and recommendations. *New Directions for Higher Education, 117,* 13–20.

Anderson, L. E. (1994). A new look at an old construct: Cross-cultural adaptation. *International Journal of Intercultural Relations, 18,* 293–328.

antonio, a. l. (2001). The role of interracial interaction in the development of leadership skills and cultural knowledge and understanding. *Research in Higher Education, 42,* 593–617.

Balibar, E. (2005). Racism and nationalism. In P. Spencer & H. Wollman (Eds.), *Nations and nationalism: A reader* (pp. 163–172). Piscataway, NJ: Rutgers University Press.

Balibar, E. (2007) *Is there a neo-racism?* In T. Das Gupta, (Ed.), *Race and racialization: Essential readings* (pp. 83–88). Toronto: Canadian Scholars Press.

Bartram, B. (2007). The Sociocultural Needs of International Students in Higher Education: A Comparison of Staff and Student Views. *Journal of Studies in International Education, 11*, 205–214.

BBC (2011, November 18). BBC News—Alert after foreign students attacked in Lewes. BBC. Retrieved from www.bbc.co.uk/news/uk-england-sussex-15787553

Cantwell, B., & Lee, J.J. (2010). Unseen workers in the academic factory: Perceptions of neo-racism among international postdocs in the US and UK. *Harvard Education Review, 80*(4), 490–517.

Chang, M.J. (1999). Does racial diversity matter? The educational impact of a racially diverse undergraduate population. *Journal of College Student Development, 40,* 377–395.

Chang, M.J., Astin, A.W., & Kim, D. (2004). Cross-racial interaction among undergraduates: Some causes and consequences. *Research in Higher Education, 45,* 527–551.

Chen, C.P. (1999). Common stressors among international college students: Research and counseling implications. *Journal of College Counseling, 2,* 49–65.

Chow, P. (2011). *What international students think about US higher education: Attitudes and perceptions of prospective students in Africa, Asia, Europe and Latin America.* New York, NY: Institute for International Education.

Constantine, M.G., Anderson, G.M., Berkel, L.A., Caldwell, L.D., & Utsey, S.O. (2005). Examining the cultural adjustment experiences of African international college students: A qualitative analysis. *Journal of Counseling Psychology, 52*, 57–66.

Constantine, M.G., Okazaki, S., & Utsey, S.O. (2004). Self concealment, social self efficacy, acculturative stress, and depression in African, Asian, and Latin American international college students. *American Journal of Orthopsychiatry, 74*, 230–241.

Devos, A. (2003). Academic standards, internationalisation, and the discursive construction of "the international student." *Higher Education Research & Development, 22*, 155–166.

Gurin, P., Dey, E., Hurtado, S., & Gurin, G. (2002). Diversity and higher education: Theory and impact on educational outcomes. *Harvard Educational Review, 72,* 330–366.

Haddal, C.C. (2006). *Foreign students in the United States: Policies and legislation* (CRS Report for Congress). Congressional Research Service, Order Code RL31146, The Library of Congress.

Hanassab, S., & Tidwell, R. (2002). International students in higher education: Identification of needs and implications for policy and practice. *Journal of Studies in International Education, 6,* 305–322.

Heggins, W.J., & Jackson, J.F. (2003). Understanding the collegiate experience for Asian international students at a Midwestern research university. *College Student Journal, 37,* 379–392.

Institute of International Education (IIE). (2010). *Fall 2010 International student enrollment survey.* Retrieved from www.iie.org/en/Research&/Fall_2010_Survey_Report.ashx

Institute of International Education (IIE). (2011). *Open doors report on international educational exchange.* Retrieved from www.iie.org/opendoors

Institute of International Education (IIE). (2013). *Open doors report on international educational exchange.* Retrieved from www.iie.org/opendoors

Lacina, J.G. (2002). *Preparing international students for a successful social experience in higher education* (New Directions for Higher Education, No. 117, pp. 21–28). Retrieved from www.eric.ed.gov/ERICWebPortal/detail?accno=EJ647399

Lane, K. (2002, June 6) "So where are you from?" *Community College Week, 14,* 2.

Lee, J.J. (2010). International students' experiences and attitudes at a US host institution: Self-reports and future recommendations. *Journal of Research in International Education, 9*, 66–84.

Lee, J.J. & Opio, T. (2011). Coming to America: Challenges and difficulties faced by African international student athletes. *Sport, Education and Society, 16*, 629–644.

Lee, J.J., & Rice, C. (2007). Welcome to America? International student perceptions of discrimination and neo-racism. *Higher Education, 53,* 381–409.

Li, R.Y., & Kaye, M. (1998). Understanding overseas students' concerns and problems. *Journal of Higher Education Policy and Management, 20,* 41–50.

Lin, J. G., & Yi, J. K. (1997). Asian international students' adjustment: Issues and program suggestions. *College Student Journal, 31*, 473–479.

MacWilliams, B. (2004). Foreign students attacked in Ukraine. *The Chronicle of Higher Education, 50*(36), A45.

Maldonado-Maldonado, A., & Cantwell, B. (2007, April). *Rethinking the role of international students in North America: A borderland case study in understanding university collaboration.* Paper presented at the annual meeting of the Consortium on North American Higher Education Collaboration, Montreal, Québec.

McMurtie, B. (2001, October 5) Arab students in US head home, citing growing hostility. *The Chronicle of Higher Education.* Retrieved from http://chronicle.com/prm/weekly/v48/i06/06a04201.htm

Mori, S. (2000). Addressing the mental health concerns of international students. *Journal of Counseling and Development, 78*, 137–144.

Mullins, G., Quintrell, N., & Hancock, L. (1995). The experiences of international and local students at three Australian universities. *Higher Education Research and Development, 14*, 201–231.

National Science Foundation (NSF). (2007). *U.S. doctoral awards in science and engineering continue upward trend in 2006.* Arlington, VA: Division of Science Resources Statistics (NSF 08–301).

Nelson Mail. (2009, January 1). Overseas enrolments set to drop. Retrieved from www.stuff.co.nz/nelson-mail/news/128664

Ninnes, P., Aitchison, C., & Kalos, S. (1999). Challenges to Stereotypes of International Students' Prior Educational Experience: Undergraduate Education in India. *Higher Education Research and Development, 18*, 323–342.

Organisation for Economic Cooperation and Development (OECD). (2011). Education at a glance 2011: OECD indicators. *Organisation for Economic Cooperation and Development.* Retrieved from www.oecd.org/dataoecd/61/2/48631582.pdf

Organisation for Economic Cooperation and Development (OECD). (2013). Education at a glance 2013: OECD indicators. *Organisation for Economic Cooperation and Development.* Retrieved from www.oecd.org/dataoecd/61/2/48631582.pdf

Perry, M. (2010, January 4). Australia condemns Indian student death. *Reuters.* Retrieved from http://ca.reuters.com/article/topNews/idCATRE60309T20100104

Pimpa, N. (2003). The influence of peers and student recruitment agencies on Thai students' choices of international education. *Higher Education 7*, 178–192.

Pritchard, R. M. O., & Skinner, B. (2002). Cross-cultural partnerships between home and international students. *Journal of Studies in International Education, 6*, 323–354.

Ramburuth, P., & McCormick, J. (2001). Learning diversity in higher education: A comparative study of Asian international and Australian students. *Higher Education, 42*, 333–350.

Ramsay, S., Barker, M., & Jones, E. (1999). Academic adjustment and learning processes: A comparison of international and local students in first-year university. *Higher Education Research and Development, 18*, 129–144.

Reynolds, A. L., & Constantine, M. G. (2007). Cultural adjustment difficulties and career development of international college students. *Journal of Career Assessment, 15*, 338–350.

Sawir, E., Marginson, S., Deumert, A., Nyland, C., & Ramia, G. (2008). Loneliness and international students: An Australian study. *Journal of Studies in International Education, 12*, 148–180.

Schmitt, M. T., Spears, R., & Branscombe, N. R. (2003). Constructing a minority group identity out of shared rejection: The case of international students. *European Journal of Social Psychology, 33*, 1–12.

Tompson, H. B., & Tompson, G. H. (1996). Confronting diversity issues in the classroom with strategies to improve satisfaction and retention of international students. *Journal of Education for Business, 72*, 53–57.

Urias, D., & Yeakey, C. C. (2009). Analysis of the U.S. student visa system: Misperceptions, barriers, and consequences. *Journal of Studies in International Education, 13*, 72–109.

Wilton, L., & Constantine, M. G. (2003). Length of residence, cultural adjustment difficulties, and psychological distress symptoms in Asian and Latin American international students. *Journal of College Counseling, 6*, 177–186.

Zhou, Y., Jindal-Snape, D., Topping, K., & Todman, J. (2008). Theoretical models of culture shock and adaptation in international students in higher education. *Studies in Higher Education, 33*, 63–75.

Chapter 8
Engaging Lesbian, Gay, and Bisexual Students on College Campuses

Dafina-Lazarus Stewart and
Mary F. Howard-Hamilton

Students enter college with a range of sexualities (Cawthon & Guthrie, 2011; Strayhorn, Blakewood, & DeVita, 2008), and some develop non-heterosexual identities during their undergraduate years. Lesbian, gay, and bisexual (LGB) students in college represent an aspect of diversity that has been subject to oppression and marginalization in society at large, as well as in higher education. Notwithstanding, much remains to be understood about their experiences and the educational practices and conditions that promote their development, sense of belonging, and respectability on college campuses. We review literature in the next section that reveals multiple issues that affect LGB undergraduate students and then use human rights, intersectionality, and queer theory frameworks to understand these issues and the implications of each for informing campus policies and practices relative to LGB students. The chapter concludes with recommendations for educators to transform college and university campuses into safe and affirming environments that encourage the engagement of LGB undergraduates.

Issues Affecting LGB Undergraduates

Six major themes capture, at least in part, some challenges pertaining to LGB students in college (Cawthon & Guthrie, 2011; Rankin, 2003). These issues are interlocking and reflect the heterosexism and homophobia that limit and define the lives of non-heterosexual people. We found the following themes to be particular manifestations of this in the college environment: claiming identity and language; navigating disclosure of one's sexual orientation; negotiating heteronormative campus environments; reframing and redefining significant relationships and life events; intersections with other aspects of identity; and finding and developing mentoring relationships with relevant campus role models.

Identity and Language

The first theme in the literature on LGB undergraduates concerns identity and language (Rankin, 2003). Although people who defy normative gender roles and relationships have existed for centuries and across cultures, it is an artifact of contemporary societies that those people have constructed a social group identity. As Young (1990) has defined social groups, they share common experiences of relating to other groups, may develop communal ways of being in the world, and signals of belonging to the group. Lesbian, gay, and bisexual people have formed communities of meaning, in the parlance of Mohanty (2010), which help group members to make meaning of their experiences and find support and affirmation. Yet, LGB people are not a monolithic group and the impact of other systems of oppression (racism, sexism, ageism, classism, etc.) has prompted the development of communities within communities.

Consequently, different ways of naming the self and social customs and norms have also arisen that are not shared across groups. Moreover, the need to affirm an LGB identity in defiance of heterosexual cultural norms, means that many young people are redefining their own sexuality at the same time as they are seeking out accepting communities and deciding how to present themselves to others, both within and outside LGB communities. Services and programming aimed at supporting LGB students may not be sought by students who are questioning their sexuality but are not developmentally ready (Cass, 1990; Cawthon & Guthrie, 2011; D'Augelli, 1996; McCarn & Fassinger, 1996) to be associated with an LGB campus community.

Further, the language used to name and represent non-heterosexual identities are not shared across groups (Rankin, 2003). *Lesbian* and *gay* may be common and familiar terms and are part of the dominant terminology used in social advocacy circles; however, for some, particularly among Black same-gender loving communities, these are racialized terms, reflecting predominantly White, middle-class men and women. The racism and classism within the predominantly White lesbian and gay community has spurred the creation of new terms to name and claim a space within and apart from the mainstream group. Therefore, while some students may readily respond to and claim an identity as lesbian, gay, or bisexual, other students may prefer instead to be referred to as same-gender loving (SGL), queer, "people-loving," and pansexual, or by their gender expression as femme, stud, aggressive, queen, or butch. Language use also varies by geographic region and institutional culture, so while *queer* may be the preferred term used at one campus for anyone who defies normative sexual relationships, students at another campus may prefer using an acronym. The right to name oneself and claim identity should be retained by the members of the community, not imposed by others, especially for a group whose name and identity have been so maligned by experts and authorities. This is in part the rationale for the growing list of letters used to name campus offices serving non-heterosexual students, to be as inclusive as possible of the varying ways that individuals connect to community.

Navigating the Disclosure of Sexual Orientation

Second, sexual identity is often referred to as a "hidden" identity, as people who are lesbian, gay, or bisexual are not identifiable through their physical features. Consequently, unless someone who is non-heterosexual self-identifies as such, heterosexist assumptions will mark anyone in the community as heterosexual. Earlier models of lesbian and gay identity development characterized coming out, the process of disclosing one's lesbian or gay identity to others as a fundamental component of establishing a healthy and mature sexual identity (Cass, 1990; D'Augelli, 1996). However, more recent work has found that this is not necessary (Fassinger, 1998; McCarn & Fassinger, 1996). In fact, Fassinger's (1998) model of lesbian, gay, and bisexual identity development described two parallel developmental processes, one which follows the internal development of identity and the other which traces identification with a community, which does include disclosing one's sexual orientation. Other researchers have also noted that coming out is a continual and evolving process and is often strategically navigated by lesbian, gay, and bisexual individuals (Cawthon & Guthrie, 2011; Evans, Forney, Guido, Patton, & Renn, 2010; Strayhorn & Mullins, 2012). Moreover, people may be out to selective circles of relationship, from more intimate relationships outward to families of origin, work places, and other social spheres (Croteau & Talbot, 2000; Payne Gold & Stewart, 2011).

On campus, this may mean that lesbian, gay, and bisexual students may also strategically navigate disclosing their sexual identity. Some students may be out on campus to peers and administrators, but not out at home to parents and other relatives. Other students may be out in one student organization, but not in another; out in their residence hall, but not in the classroom; or for part-time students, out in class, but not at their full-time employment. Moreover, there may be students who are open about their sexual identity, but who do not choose to participate in student organizations for LGB students and allies. It is important to not presume any of these students are stunted in their sexual identity development or that they do not have a healthy self-concept as an LGB person. Rather, as Fassinger's (1998) research illustrated, coming out is a deeply personal decision and one that must be considered continuously throughout an LGB person's life due to societal homophobia and heterosexism.

Negotiating Campus Environments

Third, LGB students negotiate multiple, overlapping but sometimes disparate, campus environments. The campus environment includes the macro environment, as well as the micro environments of residence halls, classes, student organizations, and campus events. Campus climates are shaped by multiple factors and each must be considered when assessing the ways in which LGB students experience college. Writing about the campus racial climate, Chang, Milem, and antonio (2011), building on the work of Hurtado, Milem, Clayton-Pedersen, and Allen (1998), described five elements of the campus climate: institutional legacy, compositional diversity, perceptions of climate, intergroup and intragroup relations, and organizational structure. Increasing numbers of institutions have revised non-discrimination statements and policies, added domestic partner benefits for faculty and staff, developed living communities for non-heterosexual students and allies, and some even have sought ways to affirmatively recruit and admit LGB-identifying students. As these changes have been implemented, the institutional legacy and organizational structure of macro campus climates are becoming more and more inclusive and welcoming for its LGB members. However, it is in the micro cultures formed in residence halls, student organizations, and classrooms where the climate is experienced most tangibly through the environment's compositional diversity, perceived climate, and intergroup relations.

Although the numbers of LGB-identifying students may increase, due to the two themes raised above, students may not know that there are LGB students in their class, on their hall, or in their student organization. Moreover, without a critical mass of LGB students on campus, there will still be spaces where an LGB student may feel isolated and where dominant cultural norms of heteronormativity work to marginalize the perspectives, experiences, and needs of LGB students. Uneven and ineffective training of faculty and staff may leave LGB students vulnerable to bullying, ostracism, and marginalization in classroom and co-curricular environments that are not safe spaces for LGB students. In addition, fraternity and sorority life and athletics teams are often highly heteronormative environments (Cawthon & Guthrie, 2011; Evans et al. 2010; Patton, Kortegast, & Javier, 2011) that marginalize and exclude LGB students. Yet, fraternities, sororities, and athletics are also among some of the co-curricular experiences that are highly correlated to positive student learning and development outcomes (Pascarella & Terenzini, 2005). The daily experience of "microaggressions" (Delgado & Stefancic, 2001; Yosso & Lopez, 2010) or "triggers" (Obear, 2007) can result in intellectual, emotional, and physical fatigue (Smith, 2004) which results in a lack of access to powerful learning and development experiences, and other negative college outcomes, such as attrition and lowered academic achievement.

Reframing and Redefining Relationships and Life Events

The fourth theme in the literature on LGB undergraduates is the need to reframe and redefine significant relationships and life events in defiance of heterosexual norms and traditions. These events or rites of passage include relationships with family and significant others; deciding a major and career aspirations; and, body image and personal expression. As D'Augelli (1996) found in his research, participants identified the need to "become LGB offspring," redefining with parents their expectations for familial roles, intimate relationships, and potential grandchildren. Parental rejection, whether emotional or financial, may also necessitate LGB students in college to independently navigate mature adult responsibilities (e.g., paying tuition bills, filing taxes, and maintaining a residence) earlier than their peers.

D'Augelli (1996) also found that lesbians and gay men needed to write new scripts for romantic relationships that did not rely on heteronormative traditions and values. The culturally recognized or acknowledged holidays, ceremonies, and celebrations exclude persons who are same gender loving and allies who are supportive of nontraditional relationships. There are very few Valentine cards in stores for gay and lesbian couples and a note recognizing a marriage or birth or adoption of a child may require a different message for LGB persons celebrating these experiences. The change in scripts can be daunting and exhausting for students who need to be empowered yet experience push-back from an environment that is not sensitive to their needs.

Questions about selecting a major and future career aspirations are inescapable elements of the college experience. In order to answer these questions, however, LGB students must consider additional factors that heterosexual students need not. For instance, LGB students need knowledge of non-discrimination statutes in the states and localities where they are job searching, information about whether a potential employer offers domestic partnership benefits, and whether the local area hosts an attractive social scene for dating, activism, and other involvements. LGB undergraduates may find their experience with campus activism on issues of sexual orientation and gender identity to be so powerful that they seek to build careers as activists, social workers, or in other helping professions.

Finally, as noted by Chickering and Reisser (1993), the college experience has a significant impact on establishing identity especially for traditional age undergraduates, including body image and personal expression through clothes, mannerisms, tastes, and habits. For LGB undergraduates, this may include the need to become comfortable with and affirm their gender expression. Within the LGB community, individuals exhibit gender expressions that may either defy the normative expectations for their biological sex or that may defy the external society's and the LGBT community's expectations for people who identify as lesbian, gay, or bisexual. For example, masculine-identified lesbian women encounter stereotypes and discrimination because their gender expression does not match society's expectations for women to be feminine. On the other hand, feminine-identified lesbian women often have their sexuality dismissed, denied, or challenged because they do not fit the expectations of what a lesbian "should look like" that are held by both heterosexuals and some members of the LGB community. Gay men also experience these challenges across the continuum of gender expression (Strayhorn & Mullins, 2012). In the midst of both these examples, bisexual men and women continually have either their same-gender attraction challenged because they "look straight" or have their opposite-gender attraction denied because they "look gay." In order to deal with these externally imposed pressures, LGB undergraduates must come to terms with their sexuality and gender expression, affirm that expression, and locate sources of support and affirmation.

Identity Intersections

The recent work of Abes and Kasch (2007), Jones and McEwen (2000), Abes, Jones, and McEwen (2007), and Stewart (2009, 2010) has brought to light the need to consider the multiple dimensions of individual's identities in student development as well as how they intersect in shaping identity and are experienced across systems of oppression. Our society is becoming exponentially more diverse through people's integration of multiple social identity facets into their identities and persona, such as socioeconomic status, race, gender, convictional belief, and sexual orientation to name only a few. The recognition and integration of multiple identities into one's persona may be called intersectionality and "it takes into account the simultaneous experience of self as belonging to multiple social groups and the ways that one's identity and experiences are influenced by the cultures and expectations of these multiple groups" (Renn & Bilodeau, 2011, p. 60).

The particular intersections of race, gender, and sexuality have received attention recently in the literature. Patton (2011) articulated the experiences of six gay or bisexual Black men grappling with the intersection of race and identity on a historically Black college campus. Patton's findings affirmed that the environment has a tremendous impact on student behavior and culture. Moreover, she found the Black college environment steeped in traditions with the additional invisible baggage of racial cultural norms and beliefs instilled by the Black community. The Black community can be a homophobic space for LGB people (Ferguson & Howard-Hamilton, 2000), unless there are family members, mentors, and allies willing to assist in navigating the terrain and providing a voice for LGB students of color. Patton (2011) noted that the men in her study resonated with their sexual identity as well as with other identity aspects, such as religion, major, culture, and being Black men. "Approaching identity in this way also seemed to be more intrinsically rewarding because they could see themselves beyond their attraction to men" (Patton, 2011, p. 93). The intersectionality of these Black gay men's identities provided them with the ability to find a safe space with persons from the same race, religion, or gender beyond those in their gay or lesbian community. Relatedly, Patton and Simmons (2008) described the challenges that lesbians of color in their study faced. For these women, the "triple consciousness" of race, gender, and sexuality identified them as "sisters" and members of the Black community, but also as outside the community because lesbian sexuality is outside the accepted gender roles for Black women.

Abes and Jones (2004) found that social class also manifested as a salient identity and oppressive system that influenced lesbian women's understanding and expression of their sexual identity. Moreover, as discussed by Hutchings (2003), class identities are imbued with gendered and sexualized notions of appropriate behavior. For instance, working-class notions of gender are often steeped in hegemonic masculinity. The signals of legitimacy that inform social class groups may work to complicate the acceptance and affirmation of same-gender sexual attraction and identification.

Separate, but often intertwined with race, ethnicity, and class, is the intersection of sexuality and convictional belief systems. As found by Love, Bock, Jannarone, and Richardson (2005), LGB undergraduates often struggle to reconcile their sexual identities with their religious upbringings. Findings by Payne Gold and Stewart (2011) confirmed these data and also revealed that some LGB undergraduates have found ways to develop their own spirituality and have joined faith communities that affirm their sexuality. Nevertheless, as noted by Astin, Astin, and Lindholm (2010), young adults in college are desperately seeking avenues to explore issues of spirituality, faith, religion, and meaning. LGB undergraduates are no different (Love et al., 2005) and need places to explore these issues, understand and challenge the dominant models of religion that exclude LGB people, and practice a faith and spirituality that is meaningful to them. These issues may be heightened for LGB and questioning undergraduates attending religiously affiliated colleges. Students in such settings may have no place to turn for spiritual guidance where they can openly discuss their sexuality without fear of disciplinary action, up to and including expulsion, or being subjected to a deliverance and counseling model that demonizes same-gender attraction and relationships.

Mentors and Role Models

Finding positive mentors and role models on campus is a challenge for most marginalized groups. This is no less true for LGB undergraduates. Out and engaged LGB faculty and staff may be few in number and, in some institutional contexts (e.g., religious institutions), may be prohibited from employment due to religious policies that prohibit non-heterosexual identities and same-gender relationships. Those that are present may be difficult to identify by students due to the issues already discussed above and in the absence of a programmatic or other organizational unit that can effectively bring LGB faculty, staff, alumni, and current students into community with each other.

From navigating identity and language to strategically disclosing one's identity and doing so in the midst of working through challenges that all undergraduates face, declaring a major and developing mature relationships with parents, partners, and friends, LGB undergraduates shoulder a heavy burden. Although these issues do complicate the experiences of LGB undergraduates, dealing with these issues does not always lead to attrition and dissatisfaction. LGB undergraduates are finding ways to be successful in spite of these challenges and the realities of their lives as sexually minoritized group members. Moreover, many of these issues are shared by trans* students, both by virtue of the similar structure of cisgender oppression and their own possible sexual identity as lesbian, gay, or bisexual. Sexual identity and gender identity are not to be conflated, and it is important to remember that trans* individuals also have a sexual identity that may fall anywhere on the continuum of sexual fluidity. In the next section, we consider theoretical frameworks that have been visibly active in shaping campus policy and practice concerning LGB undergraduates. The issues discussed above become operationalized through the theories and concepts discussed below.

Theories and Concepts

The six themes discussed above do not dictate particular courses of action or meaning-making frames to understand the experiences of LGB undergraduates. Rather, the implications of these issues for policy and practice depend on how one views sexuality and diversity issues on campus. We offer three possible theoretical frameworks that could be used to inform policy and practice regarding LGB undergraduates. After summarizing each framework's key ideas and approaches, we suggest the strengths and challenges of each.

Human Rights

The first theoretical framework is one we are calling *human rights*. Sharing characteristics of Judith Palmer's (1989) paradigm "Right the Wrongs" and Manning's (2009) philosophy of anti-oppression, the human rights framework primarily seeks to end discrimination and injustice toward LGB populations on campus. Adherents of this framework devote their energy to identifying discriminatory policies and practices that adversely affect LGB students and revising or changing them. As a consequence of this work some universities have changed their non-discrimination policies to include sexual orientation, domestic partnership benefits have been extended to faculty and staff, and student organizations have been prevented from excluding LGB students from leadership and membership on the basis of their sexuality. Great strides have been made for LGB equality as a result of this framework in action. However, missing from this framework, similar to the social justice perspective in the disability rights movement (Evans, 2008), is attention to how individuals make meaning of and frame their identities as LGB persons and undergraduates. Although LGB students may be empowered to assume roles as campus and community activists, their needs as developing adults whose first role is to be students may not be nurtured.

Intersectionality

Arising from feminist theory and critical race theory through the work of Black women such as Audre Lorde (1984), Patricia Hill Collins (1998), and Kimberlé Crenshaw (1991), intersectionality has found its way into higher education and student development scholarship (Harper, Wardell, & McGuire, 2011; Jones, 2009; Patton & Simmons, 2009; Stewart, 2010). Intersectionality is grounded in the understanding that identities are not additive and unitary, but multiple and intersubjectively constituted (Bowleg, 2008); that identity categories are not inherent but are strategically useful for discussing systematic oppression (McCall, 2005); and that multiple identity locations across oppression and privilege differentially shape the experiences of people otherwise similarly occupying singular identity categories (Crenshaw, 1991). Applying an intersectional framework to the issues faced by LGB undergraduates results in a different set of priorities. Although sharing the advocacy agenda of the human rights paradigm, policies and practices informed by intersectionality might seek to document and address the experiences of LGB students whose sexual identities overlap with other minoritized identities, such as race, (trans) gender, social class, and other hierarchies of privilege. Student organizations and programming that directly seek to support, affirm, and educate about queer people of color, queer lives in rural areas, and international LGB people may be developed. However, using an intersectional approach may be criticized for its impracticality. Intersectionality-driven practices and programs may be challenged by budget constraints and calls for greater efficiencies in the use of human, fiscal, and supportive resources. The strengths of this approach are that it is driven by empowering students' identities and can illuminate crucibles of privilege within the LGB community as well as the larger campus.

Queer Theory

Queer theory is informed by and evolved from lesbian and gay studies, critical race theory, as well as feminist and poststructural theorizing (Talburt, 2011). According to Talburt (2011), "queer theory is less a systematic method or framework than a collection of approaches to questioning normative assumptions about sex, gender, and sexuality" (p. 86) and it views sexuality, gender, and gender expression as fluid rather than fixed. This framework also takes into account that one's sexuality is an identity and that gender is bonded, but not synonymous, with sexuality (Talburt, 2011). These theorists also question the attachment of sexuality to identity. In other words, "by positioning *queer* not as a noun but as a verb—an ongoing process of identification with or against others—queer theory seeks to open up alternatives to processes of normalization" (Talburt, 2011, p. 89). Through this framework, identity labels are de-emphasized and even discarded, while seeking to disrupt and challenge presumptions of normality and unitary identities (Duggan, 1995; Talburt, 2011). Like intersectionality, queer theory has an activist orientation intended to transform institutions and social systems. By exploding binary categories of sexuality and gender, queer theorists believe such transformation can occur (Dilley, 1999; Talburt, 2011). However, this emphasis on the fluidity of identities and rejection of identity categories has been critiqued for its inability to effectively respond to oppression based on identity categories and the individual agency of identity politics (Gamson, 2000).

Overall, queer theory is not a developmental framework like many of our student affairs models and concepts (Patton & Chang, 2011). Queer theory challenges our prescribed internalized beliefs about social construction of sexual identity and provides perspectives that could restructure notions of gender identity. Connecting theoretical concepts that allow individuals to be free to construct their identity irrespective of traditional strictures is liberating for the students and those around them.

Student Engagement Strategies

Given the strengths brought by each of the above frameworks, we advocate for blending all three. Our recommendations for practice to improve and empower the engagement of LGB undergraduates reflect the influence of the human rights, intersectionality, and queer theory frameworks. We believe this is necessary to address the issues raised in the literature and in our own lived experiences and practice with LGB undergraduates.

Informed by the human rights framework, one implication of this discussion is universities must work to combat heteronormativity across campus. This includes continuing the progress achieved in expanding institutional non-discrimination statements, domestic partner benefits, and reforming student health centers to more effectively serve the unique medical and counseling needs of LGB students. Beyond these policy gains, further work is needed to reform practices, so that campus traditions like homecoming, holiday sales promotions in college bookstores, and marketing campaigns demonstrate awareness and respect for the diversity brought by LGB faculty, staff, and students and are inclusive and reflective of LGB people on campus.

Understanding and effectively addressing the multiple and intersecting identities of LGB students, as advocated by the intersectionality framework, compels multiple spheres of action for college and university educators. One implication of this framework is to explicitly acknowledge the heterogeneity that exists within the LGB community related to sex, gender, race, social class, ability, and convictional beliefs through programming and student groups. For example, programs and speakers should reflect multiple cross-sections of the LGB community and varied perspectives on LGB lives and advocacy. Students who occupy the crossroads of multiple marginalized identities should have the opportunity to engage those issues in community conversations across campus. Also, student advocacy to create organizational spaces that reflect the intersections of sexual identity with other aspects of self should be encouraged and supported (Russell, 2012).

In common with critical race theory (Delgado & Stefancic, 2001), queer theorists have also advocated for the creation and use of counter-stories or counter-narratives (Tierney & Dilley, 1998) as tools to dismantle hegemonic systems. We advocate for college educators to create safe spaces for LGB students to congregate and discuss their lives and experiences, casting doubt on the myths created and held by the majority—thereby producing their own counter-narratives. College campuses should provide areas that are comfortable (i.e., cultural center or lounge) and can be a resource center to educate all students about the lesbian and gay communities. Similar to racial and ethnic cultural centers discussed by Patton (2010), such spaces would also render important education to the campus community as a whole.

Intersectional and queer theory frameworks both prioritize individual meaning-making and naming. In response to this, LGB and queer students should be explicitly encouraged to engage in the process of naming and identifying their spaces on campus. The language used in naming and labeling resource centers, student organizations, and programming should reflect what has meaning for the queer community on a campus at a particular time. As Edelman (1995) asserted, "Every name only gives those desires—conflictual, contradictory, inconsistent, undefined—a fictive border" (p. 345). Identity labels are neither fixed nor stable;

university bureaucracies must become nimble enough to accommodate the inevitable shifts in identity and meaning reflected through the evolution of language. Labels and organized identities should be evaluated on a periodic basis to keep pace with evolving understandings of self and community among LGB students across time. Inviting students to participate in these dialogues is a useful educational and reflective tool in itself, helping to promote more complex and sophisticated meaning-making systems, as well as intra- and inter-community dialogue.

Implications for the academic curriculum informed by queer theory also exist. There should be some formal pedagogical process to educating all students about gender, sexuality, heterosexism, and heteronormativity. It is quite rare to find queer studies academic units on college campuses; however, LGB identity could be included as an educational component in first-year seminar courses. Queer theory began in curricular areas such as sociology, history, politics, women studies, and cultural studies, hence there could be an infusion of new queer pedagogical approaches in compatible academic areas. Patton (2011) encouraged professional organizations as well as graduate preparation programs to train individuals to meet the needs of millennial LGB college students. Students are disclosing their sexualities at an earlier age because of the proliferation of information available in cyberspace and the media (Rankin, 2003). Moreover, it is easier to find LGB communities on-line and in the local community that may or may not be safe for adolescents beginning their gender or sexual journey. Providing seminars, workshops, internships, assistantships, and teaching opportunities for individuals who need the cultural competency skills for working with LGB students should be an integral component of teaching and training programs.

Overall, institutional support and individual support are the significant areas LGB students need to find on campus in order to matriculate successfully as fully functioning and developmentally whole individuals (Cawthon & Guthrie, 2011). Providing intentionally rich and empowering institutional environments throughout the campus as well as role models, teachers, and mentors for cognitive and psychosocial support could be the keys to lifelong developmental confidence for LGB students.

Conclusion

Lesbian, gay, and bisexual undergraduates are a growing population in higher education but they are not a monolithic one. As sexually minoritized individuals and communities continue to navigate issues of identity and language and our society grows up into the promise of "liberty and justice for all," higher education has a unique opportunity. Colleges and universities are poised to become places where all students, including

LGB undergraduates, can learn, develop, and grow as empowered citizens and engaged members of our campus communities. Higher education can also develop its capacity to realize "education as the practice of freedom" (hooks, 1994) through changing the debate about the status and role of LGB people in the U.S. and throughout the world. Doing so will take dedicated leaders and a committed corps of educators equipped with the awareness, knowledge, and skills to effectively address the issues faced by LGB undergraduates in U.S. higher education.

References

Abes, E.S., & Jones, S.R. (2004). Meaning-making capacity and the dynamics of lesbian college students' multiple dimensions of identity. *Journal of College Student Development, 45*(6), 612–632.

Abes, E.S., Jones, S.R., & McEwen, M.K. (2007). Reconceptualizing the model of multiple dimensions of identity: The role of meaning-making capacity in the construction of multiple identities. *Journal of College Student Development, 48*, 1–22.

Abes, E.S., & Kasch, D. (2007). Using queer theory to explore lesbian college students' multiple dimensions of identity. *Journal of College Student Development, 48*(6), 619–636.

Astin, A.W., Astin, H.S., & Lindholm, J.A. (2010). *Cultivating the spirit: How college can enhance students' inner lives.* San Francisco, CA: Jossey-Bass.

Bowleg, L. (2008). When Black + lesbian + woman ≠ Black lesbian woman: The methodological challenges of qualitative and quantitative intersectionality research. *Sex Roles, 59*(5/6), 312–325.

Cass, V. (1990). The implications of homosexual identity formation for the Kinsey model and scale of sexual preference. In D.P. McWhirter, S.A. Sanders, & J.M. Reinisch (Eds.), *Homosexuality/heterosexuality: Concepts of sexual orientation* (pp. 239–266). New York, NY: Oxford University Press.

Cawthon, T., & Guthrie, V. (2011). Lesbian, gay, bisexual, and transgender college students. In M.J. Cuyjet, M.F. Howard-Hamilton, & D.L. Cooper (Eds.), *Multiculturalism on campus: Theory, models, and practices for understanding diversity and creating inclusion* (pp. 291–326). Sterling, VA: Stylus.

Chang, M.J., Milem, J.F., & antonio, a. l. (2011). Campus climate and diversity. In J.H. Schuh, S.R. Jones, S.R. Harper, & Associates (Eds.), *Student services: A handbook for the profession* (5th ed., pp. 43–58). San Francisco, CA: Jossey-Bass.

Chickering, A.W., & Reisser, L. (1993). *Education and identity* (2nd ed.). San Francisco, CA: Jossey-Bass.

Collins, P.H. (1998). It's all in the family: Intersections of gender, race, and nation. *Hypatia, 13*(3), 62–82.

Crenshaw, K. (1991). Mapping the margins: Intersectionality, identity politics, and violence against women of color. *Stanford Law Review, 43*(5), 1241–1299.

Croteau, J.M., & Talbot, D.M. (2000). Understanding the landscape: An empirical view of lesbian, gay, and bisexual issues in the student affairs profession. In N. Evans & V. Wall (Eds.), *Toward acceptance: Sexual orientation and today's college campus* (pp. 3–28). Washington, DC: American College Personnel Association.

D'Augelli, A.R. (1996). Enhancing the development of lesbian, gay, and bisexual youths. In E.D. Rothblum & L.A. Bond (Eds.), *Preventing heterosexism and homophobia* (pp. 124–150). Thousand Oaks, CA: Sage.

Delgado, R., & Stefancic, J. (2001). *Critical race theory: An introduction.* New York, NY: New York University Press.

Dilley, P. (1999). Queer theory: Under construction. *International Journal of Qualitative Studies in Education, 12*(5), 457–472.

Duggan, L. (1995). The discipline problem: Queer theory meets lesbian and gay history. *GLQ: A Journal of Gay & Lesbian Studies, 2*, 179–191.

Edelman, L. (1995). Queer theory: Unstating desire. *GLQ: A Journal of Lesbian & Gay Studies, 2*, 343–346.

Evans, N.J. (2008). Theoretical foundations of Universal Instructional Design. In J.L. Higbee & E. Goff (Eds.), *Pedagogy and student services for institutional transformation: Implementing Universal Design in higher education* (pp. 11–23). Minneapolis, MN: University of Minnesota Press.

Evans, N.J., Forney, D.S., Guido, F.M., Patton, L.D., & Renn, K.A. (2010). *Student development in college: Theory, research, and practice* (2nd ed.). San Francisco, CA: Jossey-Bass.

Fassinger, R.E. (1998). Lesbian, gay, and bisexual identity and student development theory. In R.L. Sanlo (Ed.), *Working with lesbian, gay, bisexual, and transgender college students: A handbook for faculty and administrators* (pp. 13–22). Westport, CT: Greenwood Press.

Ferguson, A.D., & Howard-Hamilton, M.F. (2000). Addressing issues of multiple identities for women of color on college campuses. In V.A. Wall & N.J. Evans (Eds.), *Toward acceptance: Sexual orientation issues on campus* (pp. 283–297). Lanham, MD: University Press of America.

Gamson, J. (2000). Sexualities, queer theory, and qualitative research. In N. Denzin & Y. Lincoln (Eds.), *Handbook of qualitative research* (2nd ed., pp. 347–365). Thousand Oaks, CA: Sage.

Harper, S.R., Wardell, C.C., & McGuire, K.M. (2011). Man of multiple identities: Complex individuality and identity intersectionality among college men. In J.A. Laker & T. Davis (Eds.), *Masculinities in higher education: Theoretical and practical considerations* (pp. 81–96). New York, NY: Routledge.

hooks, b. (1994). *Teaching to transgress: Education as the practice of freedom*. New York, NY: Routledge.

Hurtado, S., Milem, J.F., Clayton-Pedersen, A.R., & Allen, W.R. (1998). Enhancing campus climates for racial/ethnic diversity: Educational policy and practice. *The Review of Higher Education, 21*, 279–302.

Hutchings, M. (2003). Information, advice, and cultural discourses of higher education. In L. Archer, M. Hutchings, & A. Ross (Eds.), *Higher education and social class: Issues of exclusion and inclusion* (pp. 97–118). New York, NY: Routledge Falmer.

Jones, S.R. (2009). Constructing identities at the intersections: An autoethnographic exploration of multiple dimensions of identity. *Journal of College Student Development, 50*(3), 287–304.

Jones, S.R., & McEwen, M.K. (2000). A conceptual model of multiple dimensions of identity. *Journal of College Student Development, 41*(4), 405–414.

Lorde, A. (1984). *Sister outsider: Essays and speeches*. Berkeley, CA: Crossing Press.

Love, P.G., Bock, M., Jannarone, A., & Richardson, P. (2005). Identity interaction: Exploring the spiritual experiences of lesbian and gay college students. *Journal of College Student Development, 46*(2), 193–209.

Manning, K. (2009). Philosophical underpinnings of student affairs work on difference. *About Campus, 14*(2), 11–17.

McCall, L. (2005). The complexities of intersectionality. *Signs, 30*(3), 1771–1800.

McCarn, S.R., & Fassinger, R.E. (1996). Revisioning sexual minority identity formation: A new model of lesbian identity and its implications for counseling and research. *The Counseling Psychologist, 24*(3), 508–534.

Mohanty, S.P. (2010, June 1). Diversity's next challenges. *Inside Higher Ed*. Retrieved June 18, 2010, from www.insidehighered.com/layout/set/print/views/2010/06/01/mohanty

Obear, K. (2007). Navigating triggering events: Critical skills for facilitating difficult dialogues. *Generational Diversity, 15*(3), 23–29.

Palmer, J. (1989). Three paradigms for diversity change leaders. *OD Practitioner: Journal of the Organization Development Network, 21*(1), 15–18.

Pascarella, E.T., & Terenzini, P.T. (2005). *How college affects students: A third decade of research, Vol. 2*. San Francisco, CA: Jossey-Bass.

Patton, L.D. (2010). On solid ground: An examination of the successful strategies and positive student outcomes of two Black culture centers. In L.D. Patton (Ed.), *Culture centers in higher education: Perspectives on identity, theory, and practice* (pp. 63–79). Sterling, VA: Stylus.

Patton, L.D. (2011). Perspectives on identity, disclosure, and the campus environment among African American gay and bisexual men at one historically Black college. *Journal of College Student Development, 52*(1), 77–100.

Patton, L.D., & Chang, S. (2011). Identity makeover millennial edition: Using contemporary theoretical frameworks to explore identity intersections among LGBTQ millennial populations. In F.A. Bonner II, A.F. Marbley, & M.F. Howard-Hamilton (Eds.), *Diverse millennial students in college: Implications for faculty and student affairs* (pp. 193–209). Sterling, VA: Stylus.

Patton, L.D., Kortegast, C., & Javier, G. (2011). LGBTQ millennials in college. In F.A. Bonner II, A.F. Marbley, & M.F. Howard-Hamilton (Eds.), *Diverse millennial students in college: Implications for faculty and student affairs* (pp. 175–192). Sterling, VA: Stylus.

Patton, L.D., & Simmons, S.L. (2008). Exploring complexities of multiple identities of lesbians in a Black college environment. *The Negro Educational Review, 59*(3), 197–215.

Payne Gold, S., & Stewart, D.L. (2011). Lesbian, gay, and bisexual students coming out at the intersection of spirituality and sexual identity. *Journal of LGBT Issues in Counseling, 5*(3–4), 237–258.

Rankin, S. (2003). *Campus climate for gay, lesbian, bisexual, and transgender people: A national perspective.* New York, NY: National Gay and Lesbian Task Force Policy Institute.

Renn, K.A., & Bilodeau, B.L. (2011). Lesbian, gay, bisexual, and transgender identity development theories. In B.J. Bank (Ed.), *Gender and higher education* (pp. 55–62). Baltimore, MD: The Johns Hopkins University Press.

Russell, E.A.I. (2012). *Voices unheard: Using intersectionality to understand identity among sexually marginalized undergraduate college students of color* (Unpublished doctoral dissertation). Bowling Green State University, Bowling Green, OH.

Smith, W.A. (2004). Black faculty coping with racial battle fatigue: The campus racial climate in a post-civil rights era. In D. Cleveland (Ed.), *A long way to go: Conversations about race by African American faculty and graduate students* (pp. 171–190). New York, NY: Peter Lang.

Stewart, D.L. (2009). Perceptions of multiple identities among Black college students. *Journal of College Student Development, 50*(3), 253–270.

Stewart, D.L. (2010). Researcher as instrument: Understanding "shifting" findings in constructivist research. *Journal of Student Affairs Research and Practice, 47*(3), 291–306.

Strayhorn, T.L., Blakewood, A.M., & DeVita, J.M. (2008). Factors affecting the college choice of African American gay male undergraduates: Implications for retention. *National Association of Student Affairs Professionals Journal, 11*(1), 88–108.

Strayhorn, T.L., & Mullins, T.G. (2012). Investigating Black gay male undergraduates' experiences in campus residence halls. *Journal of College and University Student Housing, 39*(1), 141–160.

Talburt, S. (2011). Queer theory. In B.J. Bank (Ed.), *Gender and higher education* (pp. 86–93). Baltimore, MD: Johns Hopkins University Press.

Tierney, W.G., & Dilley, P. (1998). Constructing knowledge: Educational research and gay and lesbian studies. In W.F. Pinar (Ed.), *Queer theory in education* (pp. 40–60). Mahwah, NJ: Erlbaum.

Yosso, T.J., & Lopez, C.B. (2010). Counterspaces in a hostile place: A critical race theory analysis of campus culture centers. In L.D. Patton (Ed.), *Culture centers in higher education: Perspectives on identity, theory, and practice* (pp. 83–104). Sterling, VA: Stylus.

Young, I.M. (1990). Five faces of oppression. In I.M. Young (Ed.), *Justice and the politics of difference* (pp. 39–65). Princeton, NJ: Princeton University Press.

Chapter 9
Engaging Trans* Students on College and University Campuses

Susan B. Marine and
D. Chase J. Catalano

The recently issued *State of Higher Education for Lesbian, Gay, Bisexual, and Trans* People* reported on the experiences of over 5,000 students, faculty members, staff members, and administrators who identify as lesbian, gay, bisexual, trans*, queer and questioning (LGBTQQ), and documented the numerous challenges that typify trans identities and experiences on campus (Rankin, Weber, Blumenfeld, & Frazer, 2010). The report "revealed the perception that, while heterosexism may at times surface in some subtle ways on campus, trans* oppression is often manifested in overt and blatant ways" (Rankin et al., 2010, p. 12). Harassment, violence, marginalization, tokenization, and exploitation are the core of how trans* oppression is manifesting on our college and university campuses, which are microcosms of the broader societal culture. The evidence suggests that we must attend to the lives of trans* people in order to create sustainable inclusion and engagement in higher education.

In this chapter, we will define terms, provide a framework of needs and challenges, and offer detailed recommendations for educators and administrators working with trans* student populations. We use the terms "trans*" and "trans" interchangeably throughout this chapter intentionally, acknowledging that neither term will fit perfectly or universally identify student populations as diverse and understudied as trans populations.

Defining Terms

Much of the difficulty with understanding or generating any agreement on terminology regarding trans identities is rooted in our interchangeable colloquial uses of terms such as "gender" and "sex" (Fausto-Sterling, 2000; Hubbard, 1998; Kessler, 1998; Kessler & McKenna, 1978). Our current understanding of gender roles and gender expression (masculine and feminine) has become intrinsically linked with biological sex (male and female) (Connell, 2002; Feinberg, 1998). Stryker (2008) points out that gender is historical, temporal, geographical, cultural, contingent, and contextual, whereas sex is considered scientifically immutable and fixed. Precisely because the basis of understanding gender is rooted in the faulty assumption of only two sexes, a binary of gender is an unstable construct. Trans, as both an identity category and set of experiences, disrupts the presumed sexual and gender binaries. Additionally, the superficially constructed walls of the binary of gender hold up the roof of the sexual identity binary ("male" and "female"). Trans identities signal instability in both the walls and the roof, and introduce the potential for the whole structure to collapse in on itself. To remove the potential of trans identities from causing ripples in the dominant binaries that construct normative gender and sexuality, trans identities are often pathologized as a psychological disorder, are stigmatized, and therefore banished from the realm of "normal" categories of understanding. Trans identities reflect changes between, subverting of, and/or obscuring of gender binary identities and expressions. Our focus on trans identities encourages transness to be relevant to our everyday conversations on gender, and understood in the scope of possibilities of gender expressions and identities, as well as sexualities.

Given these complexities, it is helpful to understand the term *trans** to encompass a wide range of identities, appearances, and behaviors that blur or cross gender lines. Within this trans* umbrella are transsexuals, who live some or all of the time in a sex different from their biological sex; cross-dressers (formerly called transvestites), who wear clothes typically associated with the "opposite" gender; drag kings and drag queens, who cross-dress within a specific performance context; and gender radicals (Gagne & Tewksbury, 1999) and genderqueers, who identify outside of binary gender or sex systems altogether (Lombardi & Davis, 2006). Although we are mindful of the contestation of these terms, we use trans and trans* as umbrella terms because of their current recognition in broader literature. It is important to remember that just as within the breadth and depth of trans communities in our society, college student populations will reflect the multiplicity of trans identities and may create new terms to define their gender.

There are many examples of how all gender identities, but especially trans identities, are "under-construction" (Stryker, 2008, p.1), especially through a perusal of literature on trans identities. In this chapter we will use the term "trans*" or "trans" alternately in an effort to be inclusive, to resist intergroup or imposed hierarchy (Martin & Yorkin, 2006; Schilt & Waskiewicz, 2006), and to reflect the broadest possibilities for self-identification. Therefore, "trans*" includes those who subvert the gender binary (Bornstein, 1998) and/or "whose gender identity conflicts with their sex assigned at birth" (Bilodeau, 2005, p. 30). Definitional distinctions are important, but just as important is that we make space for all individuals to "describe and label their own gender identities in whatever ways feel most appropriate to them" (Catalano, McCarthy, & Shlasko, 2007, p. 219).

What significantly adds to the confusion around trans* identities, beyond our cultural expectations of gender normativity and sexual orientation binarism (heterosexual and homosexual), is the consistent condensing of lesbian, gay, and bisexual identities with trans* identities (often seen via the moniker: LGBT). Thus, trans identity is often mistaken as a sexual orientation, when in fact it is a gender identity and/or a form of gender expression. There is a complex history to the connection between trans identities and marginalized sexual orientations, which is beyond the scope of this chapter (for in-depth discussions on the historical linkages and tensions between trans identities and sexual orientations see Minter, 2006; Stryker, 2008).

Throughout this chapter, we will also use the term *cisgender* in reference to those who are not trans identified. "'Cis' is the Latin prefix for 'on the same side,' and indicates an identity for those who experience a match between the gender they were assigned at birth, their bodies, and their personal identity" (Schilt & Westbrook, 2009, p. 461). While there is an underlying tension in trans communities about how "the same side as" reinforces the privilege of non-trans people, the term is useful in eliminating distinctions of "real" or "biological" woman/man when making comparative statements. Additionally useful terms include "genderism" and "trans* oppression." Genderism is the practice of strict adherence to a binary gender system that, by definition, oppresses those who fall outside of it (Bilodeau, 2005; Hill, 2002; Hill & Willoughby, 2005; Wilchins, 2002). Trans* oppression is the "system of oppression that targets and marginalizes people who are trans* in the broadest sense" (Catalano & Shlasko, 2010, p. 425). Research indicates that genderism and trans* oppression are common experiences of college students who identify as trans (Beemyn, 2005; Bilodeau, 2005; Rankin et al., 2010).

Trans Students on College Campuses

Current student affairs literature that specifically addresses trans students fits within three categories: the experiences of trans students, theoretical and developmental approaches (some of which are reviewed later in this chapter), and targeted institutional suggestions to increase trans inclusion and accessibility on campuses. There are a very limited number of empirical studies on trans students' experiences and those available have a small sample size (Bilodeau, 2005; McKinney, 2005; Pusch, 2005). There have emerged a number of anthologies of trans and genderqueer voices, but none are specifically focused on college and university experiences. The literatures on theoretical models of identity development are also limited in their participant size, and typically include the life experiences of trans individuals across the age spectrum. Much of the literature to date focuses on programmatic interventions and strategies for improved inclusion of trans students (Beemyn, 2005; Beemyn, Curtis, Davis, & Tubbs, 2005; McKinney, 2005; Sanlo, 1998; Sanlo, Rankin, & Schoenberg, 2002). One study published to date explores the perceptions of student affairs professionals in a specific institutional context as they encounter, and make meaning of their work with, trans students (Marine, 2011a).

While there may be few empirical studies on trans* students, we are able to glean important knowledge from what is available. Pusch (2005), who observed the communications of trans students in Internet relay chat rooms, identified how the trans participants in his study "who came out to others dealt not only with their own selves and bodies in transition, but with how other people responded to these changes. They experienced both support and resistance from family and friends, which, in turn, affected how they came to understand their identities" (p. 48). Trans students are dealing with their trans identities on multiple levels; not only are they having internal conversations about who they are and how they want to express their gender, but they are also dealing with inter-personal relationships (friends and families), institutional navigation (college/university offices and organizations, and the medical industrial complex for transition related treat-ments), and cultural practices related to gender, family, and sexuality.

Pusch's (2005) study also indicates that issues of individual agency and voice become subsumed through the power of the medical community. One participant recounted how a doctor confirming his gender identity was "helpful" because it validated what he had been telling his parents. The medical community becomes the voice of authority when trans people who are considered too young to make such decisions about self-identification, and Pusch noted that "trans* people typically see therapists and doctors to confirm their identities and to gain access to hormones and sex reassignment surgeries" (p. 51). Gender compliance and gender conformity are cultural messages that can push trans identified students towards transition, often as a means to find acceptance within the broader culture, and especially within families who are often main sources of emotional and financial support.

The on-campus experiences of trans students force them to deal with a host of issues they must navigate if they identify as trans. McKinney (2005), in a national survey of trans students, noted the following themes from his data on their experiences in col-lege: lack of faculty and staff education about trans issues, lack of programming for the community, lack of campus resources, inadequate counseling services, and health care that fails to meet the needs of trans students. He also noted that graduate students had similar issues, but their means to address those issues were different, possibly attributed to age. In conclusion, this study addresses the fact that student affairs as a profession is supposed to support and advance college students' development, and reminds us "it is our responsibility to offer trans* students meaningful, humane, and knowledgeable sup-port" (McKinney, 2005, p. 74).

Much of the writing on trans students to date seeks to improve inclusion and access for them. The major areas of higher education that have been identified for this effort are: training and support, educational programming, adjustment of procedures for college records and documentation, counseling and health services, provision of gen-der inclusive bathrooms and locker rooms and campus housing, and other support services (Beemyn, 2005; Beemyn, Curtis et al., 2005; Beemyn, Domingue, Pettitt, & Smith, 2005; Lees, 1998; Marine, 2011b). There are numerous roadblocks limit-ing trans students' connections to campus communities and that impact their ability to engage with student life more broadly. Often, institutions wait until trans stu-dents are on campus to address issues of housing and identification, at which point trans students may have already been subjected to a number of experiences termed "microaggressions" (Sue, 2010; Sue et al., 2007). Microaggressions are intentional and unintentional, verbal, behavioral, or environmental, brief everyday exchanges that send negative messages to people of marginalized identities (see e.g., Nadal, Rivera, & Corpus, 2010; Solorzano, Ceja, & Yosso, 2000; Sue, 2010). Even when trans inclusion has been addressed prior to students' arrival, there are typically no policies in place, but rather, practices to address trans students on a case-by-case basis, which force students to find the "right" person who will understand their issues and support them through negotiating institutional obstacles (Beemyn & Pettit, 2006).

As noted earlier, trans and genderqueer students may or may not seek to undergo bio-medical transition-related options such as hormones or surgeries. It is critical to be cautious in our understanding of trans identities to avoid assuming transition is an ultimate or expected outcome, lest we begin to apply forces that many trans and gen- derqueer people are seeking to resist (Spade, 2003). There are many choices available to students who identify as trans, and many of those choices are not related to transition (such as choosing one's name, preferred pronouns, and degree of "outness" to school officials, friends, and family). In this sense, it is important to address the multiplicity of trans identities, understanding that they are not all on the path of transitioning. Some trans people are committed to resisting the binary, others want to discreetly move across it, other want to muddle and confound it, and others imagine genders that are beyond a construction of bodies.

In conversations with trans students, student affairs practitioners should be inten- tionally open to allow them to disclose whether they are seeking transition services. We respectfully disagree with Nakamura (1998) that transition is a public event, that trans issues should be considered on a case-by-case basis, that workshops meant to teach oth- ers about trans identities and concerns can be effectively modeled after lesbian and gay issues due to similarity, and that trans* students feel ashamed of their status. While the literature supports the position that there may be a tenuous period during initial com- ing out and beginning transitions, promoting the notion that being trans is synonymous with experiencing shame is colluding with oppression. However, we do concur with her assertion that "in no circumstances should a university require students to have surgical sex reassignment in order to change the gender on their student records" (Nakamura, 1998, p. 185). Students may feel an urgency to seek out bio-medical transition services because of alienation related to an unreadable gender expression or gender identity, resistance or rejection from parents about trans identity, or from a desire for transition. We advocate that for those who are interested in supporting and including trans students that they understand the complexities and components of transitioning, knowing that there are those who will and those who will not seek to transition and others who cannot afford to do so, even if it is their wish.

Theories and Concepts

For most of its history, the field of developmental psychology has viewed trans* indi- viduals in concert with those who are lesbian, gay, and bisexual. Many who identify as LGB also express non-normative gender identities, for example, as an effeminate man or a butch (masculine) woman. Collapsing gender identity and sexual orientation into one community has some problematic consequences. For instance, the movement to secure rights for persons who identify as lesbian, bisexual, or gay has been led throughout history by people who claim and express a wide variety of trans* identities, but this fact is seldom acknowledged (Carter, 2004; Feinberg, 1997; Minter, 2006; Stryker, 2008).

Unfortunately, this practice has not served trans students well, nor has it advanced higher education's work with and support of them. It is crucial, therefore, to consider trans students' development in their own right, resisting the tendency to lump them in with those of minoritized sexual orientations. As Forshee (2008) has noted, "unless trans* individuals identify as such, trans*-specific topics should not be synthesized with data on lesbian, gay, and bisexual populations. The conflation of sexual orientation and gender identity confuses research on each population's unique needs and perspectives" (p. 232). Gender and sexuality are often intertwined, but they are far from synonymous. Some who identify as trans began their gender identity journeys as part of a LGB community because of society's conflation of gender expression and sexual orientation, and thus there appear to be parallels of experience. However, we caution that this connection may be due to several factors that are unrelated to the unique needs of trans people. The conventional use of LGBT has come to connote that resources for trans people are linked with LGBQ communities, even when they are lacking (Valentine, 2007). Some LGBQ communities are more accepting of gender transgression, providing an initial geography of opportunity for exploration. Citations in trans related literature are often LGB focused articles that exclude trans populations experiences and do not disaggregate L, G, or B from T (e.g., using heterosexism to refer the experiences of LGBT populations does not address issues of trans* oppression as distinct and different), and researchers sometimes utilize LGBTQ listservs and organizations to recruit participants for trans studies, which are not representative of the full array of trans identities. The developmental literature on trans* adults is relatively nascent, and begs further definition. Yet there are two theories that offer important guideposts for supporting this student population effectively.

Devor's Model of Transsexual Identity Development

Aaron Devor's 14-stage model (2004) of transsexual identity development, created from insights gleaned from two decades of clinical work, suggests that the path toward a stable and solid sense of gender identity for trans individuals is one that is significantly informed by the process of self-discovery, mediated by the reactions of others, both trans and cisgender, in the individual's life. The process begins with a persistent state of anxiety about one's gender identity, which gives way to confusion about one's originally assigned gender and sex. The trans person begins to experience a sense of disconnect between what they are told about themselves and their inner, felt sense of gender; this can happen from early childhood, as evidence suggests that children as young as 3 experience dissonance between their assigned and felt gender (Vanderburgh, 2009).

As individuals begin attempting to reconcile their assigned gender with that of their internal sense, they look around to those they know, searching out models of a more coherent gender identity for themselves, or what Devor calls "identity comparison" (2004, p. 49). Eventually, such comparisons lead to a *discovery of transgenderism*—in reading, in observing pop culture, in exploring the vast array of gender identities in one's own LGBT/queer community, and in searching on the Internet, a new sense of gendered possibilities emerge. Initial identity confusion about one's own trans* status, reconciled through exposure and comparison with an existing group of trans*-identified others, enables tolerance and eventual acceptance of one's trans* identity. Trans individuals may claim and express numerous iterations of their gender, and while some prefer to remain in this in-between space for their adult lives, many will opt for some form of *transition*— from one gender to another, from one stable gender to a mix of genders, or simply from cisgender to trans. Through formation of community with others, and with time to heal from the process of having to constantly negotiate their gender and sex with others in their lives, Devor suggests that trans individuals will first work to accept, then integrate, their original, suppressed gender identity with their previous sense of self, arriving at a coherent and comfortable gender identity. This process culminates in taking action to further the visibility of trans identities through expression of *pride*.

While Devor's (2004) model is a positive conceptualization of how trans individuals come to understand who they are, the extent to which the more advanced stages can be reached depend less on the determination of the individual than on the extent to which they face serious and persistent obstacles in a culture hostile to their authentic expression. What ultimately appears to be universally necessary for the development of trans identity is what Devor calls "witnessing and mirroring"—access to trans individuals and cultural images of trans-positivity, followed by a decision to enact one's own trans identity in community with others. Given that Devor's work captured narratives of trans individuals across the age spectrum, it is reasonable to be cautious in assuming it accurately applies to late adolescents attending college.

Bilodeau's Framework for Trans College Student Identity Development

To date, there is only one published article that offers a specific frame for the trans college student identity development. Brent Bilodeau (2005) considered the developmental trajectories of two trans students at a midwestern college, and theorized the milestones of their development based loosely on D'Augelli's (1994) framework of lesbian, gay, and bisexual identity development. Bilodeau called these milestones "processes," noting the interplay of these processes in the students' successful transition away from their original cisgender identities. Analyzing their narratives of discovery, Bilodeau observed a first process of *exiting a traditionally gendered identity*—noting dissonance between available options of "male" and "female," and taking the next step to discern one's true gender. Having opened the door to exploration, students in this study *developed a trans* identity,* often by parsing options with select others and deliberating on comfort and fit with various terms and expressions. As noted by one of the students in this study, in reference to another trans friend, "Alix and I shaped our gender identities together. We spent so much time talking and debating" (p. 35). Communing with others in person and online led students to *develop a trans* social identity*, including seeking a home in the campus LGBT organization. This often required advocacy on the part of the newly-identified trans students, as these groups were not always fully inclusive in practice. Attending conferences and seeking out faculty as mentors was an additional aspect of creating a social identity for one's self.

The confidence afforded by connection to others ushered in the next process—*becoming a trans* offspring*. This process was complicated for one student by a preexisting distance in the family as a result of sexual abuse, a vivid reminder that one rarely enters into a family disclosure process unfettered by past dynamics. *Developing a trans* intimacy status* followed, as the students began to negotiate their newly emerging identity with potential and actual partners. While it is safe to assume this could be a complex undertaking, both students in this study reported success in this arena, which they attributed to the openness of their current partners. Finally, the students took steps to *enter a trans* community*, making connections with trans-identified others, creating social change through community activism and the artistic performance.

These theories are helpful for expanding our understanding of the hurdles faced by trans* students in their quest to live as the gender they experience, but theories of identity development not centered in late adolescence can obscure the particularities of arriving at one's identity while in college, particularly for the 63% of college students who are between the ages of 18 and 25 (U.S. Census Bureau, 2009). We then must extrapolate from these later adult reflections on transition, despite the fact that the initial exploration of gender identity is a common experience for trans* youth upon matriculating in college (Beemyn, 2005; Pusch, 2005). In addition to our limited understanding of how they develop and what developmentally instigative characteristics (Evans et al., 2010) look like for this population, we have a very limited sense of what college means for them, during as well as after their years on campus. More research that enables their voices to be heard and understood in the context of the college experience is thus an imperative.

Student Engagement Strategies

Given what we know, to date, about the experiences of trans students on college campuses, the following recommendations can be undertaken by student affairs professionals and other educators to improve their status, and to reduce the social and psychological cost of trans oppression.

Educators Doing Gender-Reflection

One of the benefits of doing gender-reflection work is that it allows cisgender and trans* people to communicate about shared experiences of gender socialization and resistance. The utility of doing gender-reflection work for both trans and cisgender people is to avoid communication of unintentional microaggressions, verbally or non-verbally, to trans people (Nadal et al., 2011). Our work as educators means that we must continuously unpack our socialization, in an attempt to understand how we came to view the world as we do, and how we may change our perceptions towards building a more inclusive community. Educators can begin with a resource, *My Gender Workbook: How to Become a Real Man, a Real Woman, the Real You, or Something Else Entirely* authored by Kate Bornstein (1998). This book includes numerous exercises and activities for reflection on one's own personal gender journey, including ways to identify significant events in one's life that solidified gender identity and strategies to meaningfully challenge the dominant culture's restrictive definitions of gender. Another resource for facilitation and teaching on trans issues can be found in the chapter on Trans* Oppression in *Teachings for Diversity and Social Justice* (*2nd edition;* Catalano et al., 2007).

Listening to Trans Students

While reading this chapter is an important step on the journey to working meaningfully with trans students, it offers an overview, and not a complete picture of the experiences of this diverse student population. The next step in understanding the challenges and supports inherent for any minority group is to take the time to seek out, and remain open to, the perspectives of the affected population, without presuming we already know what they need. To that end, student affairs educators can best understand areas of needed change through a concerted effort to obtain first-person perspectives from trans students in their community. Assurance of confidentiality and safety in these conversations is paramount; students should never have to feel they are "on display" for the learning benefit of others. Putting out the word through related student communities (i.e., women's and gender study programs, LGBT centers, and LGBT student organizations) that educators and professionals on campus are open and interested in learning more about trans student experiences is a good first step. As noted by Hanson (2010), this effort should only be undertaken if the institution is ready to begin acting on the information that is offered. It is important to avoid tokenizing trans students, asking them to from their own experiences, but not on behalf of all trans communities.

Engaging in Self-Education on Trans Politics, Identities, Interests, and Concerns

Student experiences and narratives are important for context, and educators should do their own reading and content learning on broader issues of trans identity. Institutions can support this effort through professional development for staff and faculty. We must seek beyond the students we work with day-to-day to educate ourselves about trans student experiences, and to begin that work with conversations about how gender functions in our own lives and in our institutions. A noted increase in the number of trans and genderqueer students on our campuses (Beemyn et al., 2005) means a continual need to educate ourselves on their experiences and needs. Hart and Lester (2011) noted that when college communities attempt to engage in conversations on trans issues, there are often superficial responses marked by the power of an institutionally enforced silence, which reveals absences of discourse, policy, and practice changes. Whether our silences are born out of lack of knowledge, assumptions that we have already addressed these issues, or an attempt to wait until we are certain we have trans students at our institution, our silence has an impact of making trans students invisible and ultimately, underserved.

Addressing the Material Realities and Necessities for Change

A common refrain when considering how colleges can change the campus to be more trans inclusive is, "Well, how many trans students are there, anyway?" Rarely in our work as educators do we consider whether the relatively small number of trans students present on our campuses is a function of imposed invisibility and marginality. As noted in the literature review, there are a number of areas where institutions can focus their attention to address trans inclusion: college records and documentation, counseling and health services, bathrooms and locker rooms, campus housing, and support services. Working to include gender identity and expression into the institution's non-discrimination policy sets an important stage for addressing trans students visibility. However, this is a short-term fix of a larger issue, especially if the statement is not followed by intentional policy and practice shifts (Beemyn & Pettit, 2006).

Colleges can best address trans* students' needs through creation of a standing task force or committee that works to address the system-wide adjustments needed to make campuses more inclusive of trans students. The work begins with assessment of current practices and areas for improvement. A thoughtful, diverse group of faculty, staff, and students, committed to the practice of collaborative transformation (Marine, 2011b) of the campus, can then work together to identify areas needing improvement and marshal the human and other resources required to make change. We suggest utilizing the articles by Beemyn (2005) and Beemyn et. al., (2005) to use as a guide to set an agenda for working groups on institutional trans inclusion.

Improving Trans Inclusion Practices of LGBT Centers and Reducing Institutional Marginalization

Currently, approximately 153 U.S. colleges and universities, representing less than 3% of all institutions, have a professional staff member (working at least 50% time) or graduate assistant (solely dedicated to LGBT services) to support, advocate, and educate on LGBT student needs (Consortium of Higher Education LGBT Resource

Professionals, 2011). Given such limited numbers, any attempt to be inclusive of all sexualities and genders, is an unfair burden for those in these roles to be expected to meet all needs of LGBT students, let alone specifically trans students. While centers were designed to pull marginalized identities into visibility, we have instead developed centers on the periphery, typically solely responsible for LGBTQ support and advocacy. Broader campus collaborations and investments must occur to avoid the idea that all trans related issues be filtered through one office, and in some cases, one staff person. Even when there is a center at a given institution, it does not mean that trans students will go there for advice or support. Trans students may not seek out an LGBT center for a variety of reasons; it is reasonable (and likely) that a trans student with a financial aid problem may go to the Financial Aid Office, and that a trans student struggling with balancing their identity development process and their coursework may seek out an academic adviser instead of the staff of the LGBT center. As legal issues related to trans students begin to play out in the courts and on campus, the staff of the Financial Aid Office need to be knowledgeable about topics such as the ways that the federal financial aid system might trigger an investigation into a student's record when their assigned and declared gender do not match (Burns, 2011).

For information on a current list of colleges and universities that have gender identity and expression policies (including non-discrimination policies) refer to the Trans* Law and Policy Institute's website (www.transgenderlaw.org/college/index.htm).

Conclusion

Trans activist Leslie Feinberg (1998) wrote, "gender is the poetry each of us makes out of the language we are taught" (p.10). Arguably, there is no richer time in a person's life than the college years to create that poetry, and no environment more fertile than the contemporary college campus to explore, define, and redefine one's sense of self as a gendered being in the world. As educators, we have the responsibility—and the privilege—to bear witness to, and support, the poetry making of our students, and to be honest and thoughtful about our own process of gender identification. Knowing and understanding the lives of trans* students, and constructing environments that affirm all students regardless of gender, is what we are called to do. We must know, care, and act to create change to signal that in higher education, all genders are welcome.

References

Beemyn, B.G. (2005). "Trans on campus: Measuring and improving the climate for transgender students." *On Campus with Women* 34(3): retrieved on (date/) from www.aacu.org/ocww/volume34_33/feature.cfm?section=32

Beemyn, B., Curtis, B., Davis, M., & Tubbs, N.J. (2005). Transgender issues on college campuses. Gender identity and sexual orientation: Research, policy, and personal perspectives. In R.L. Sanlo (Ed.), *Gender identity and sexual orientation: Research, policy, and personal perspectives: New directions for student services* (pp. 49 –60). San Francisco, CA: Jossey-Bass.

Beemyn, B.G., Domingue, A., Pettitt, J., & Smith, T. (2005). "Suggested steps to make campuses more trans-inclusive." *Journal of Gay & Lesbian Issues in Education, 3*(1), 89–94.

Beemyn, B.G., & Pettit, J. (2006). How have trans-inclusive non-discrimination policies changed institutions? *GLBT Campus Matters, 3*(1), 6–7.

Bilodeau, B. (2005). Beyond the gender binary: A case study of two transgender students at a midwestern research university. *Journal of Gay and Lesbian Issues in Education, 3*(1), 29–44.

Bornstein, K. (1998). *My gender workbook: How to become a real man, a real woman, the real you, or something else entirely.* New York, NY: Routledge.

Burns, C. (2011). Unequal aid discriminatory treatment of gay and transgender applicants and families headed by same-sex couples in the higher education financial aid process. Report for Center for American Progress. Retrieved on October 15, 2011, from www.americanprogress.org/issues/2011/08/pdf/lgbt_higher_ed.pdf

Carter, D. (2004). *Stonewall: The riots that sparked the gay revolution.* New York, NY: St. Martin's Press.

Catalano, D.C., McCarthy, L. & Shlasko, D. (2007). Transgender oppression. In M. Adams, L.A. Bell, & P. Griffin (Eds.), *Teaching for diversity and social justice* (2nd ed., pp. 219–245). New York, NY: Routledge.

Catalano, D.C., & Shlasko, D. (2010). Transgender oppression. In M. Adams W. Blumenfeld, C. Castañeda, H.W. Hackman, M.L. Peters, & X. Zúñiga (Eds.), *Readings for diversity and social justice* (2nd ed., pp. 423–456). New York, NY: Routledge.

Connell, R.W. (2002). *Gender.* Cambridge, UK: Polity.

Consortium of Higher Education Resource Professionals (2011). Listing of LGBT resource centers and staff. Retrieved on October 13, 2011, from www.lgbtcampus.org/directory/3

D'Augelli, A. (1994). Lesbian and gay male development: Steps toward an analysis of lesbians' and gay men's lives. In B. Greene & G.M. Herek (Eds.), *Lesbian and gay psychology: Theory, research, and clinical applications* (pp. 118–132). Newbury Park, CA: Sage.

Devor, A.H. (2004). Witnessing and mirroring: A fourteen stage model of transsexual identity formation. *Journal of Gay and Lesbian Psychotherapy, 8*(1/2), 41–67.

Evans, N.J., Forney, D.S., Guido, F.M., Patton, L.D., & Renn, K.S. (2010). *Student development in college: Theory, research and practice* (2nd ed.). San Francisco, CA: Jossey Bass.

Fausto-Sterling, A. (2000). *Sexing the body: Gender politics and the construction of sexuality.* New York, NY: Basic Books.

Feinberg, L. (1997). *Transgender warriors: Making history from Joan of Arc to Dennis Rodman.* Boston, MA: Beacon.

Feinberg, L. (1998). *Trans liberation: Beyond pink or blue.* Boston, MA: Beacon Press.

Forshee, A.S. (2008). Transgender men: A demographic snapshot. *Journal of Gay & Lesbian Social Services, 20*(3), 221–236.

Gagne, P., & Tewksbury, R. (1999). Knowledge and power, body, and self: An analysis of knowledge systems and the transgendered self. *Sociological Quarterly, 40*(1), 59–83.

Hanson, D.E. (2010, November 10). Institutions can launch assessments of their LGBT climate, but should they? *NetResults: Critical issues for student affairs practitioners.* Retrieved October 4, 2011, from www.naspa.org/membership/mem/pubs/nr/default.cfm?id=1756

Hart, J., & Lester, J. (2011). Starring students: Gender performance at a women's college. *NASPA Journal About Women in Higher Education, 4*(2), 193–217.

Hill, D.B. (2002). Genderism, transphobia, and gender bashing: A framework for interpreting anti-transgender violence. In B. Wallace & R. Carter (Eds.), *Understanding and dealing with violence: A multicultural approach* (pp. 113–136). Thousand Oaks, CA: Sage.

Hill, D.B., & Willoughby, B.L.B. (2005). The development and validation of the genderism and transphobia scale. *Sex Roles, 53,* 531–544.

Hubbard, R. (1998). Gender and genitals: Constructs of sex and gender. In D. Denny (Ed.), *Current concepts in transgender identity* (pp. 45–54). New York, NY: Garland.

Kessler, S. J. (1998). *Lessons from the intersexed*. New Brunswick, NJ: Rutgers University Press.

Kessler, S. J. & McKenna, W. (1978). *Gender: An ethnomethodological approach*. Chicago, IL: University of Chicago Press.

Lees, L. J. (1998). Transgender students on our campuses. In R. L. Sanlo (Ed.), *Working with lesbian, gay, bisexual, and transgender college students: A handbook for faculty and administrators* (pp. 37–47). Westport, CT: Greenwood Educators Reference Collection.

Lombardi, E., & Davis, S. M. (2006). Transgender health issues. In D. Morrow & L. Messinger (Eds.), *Sexual orientation & gender expression in social work practice* (pp. 343–363). New York, NY: Columbia University Press.

Marine, S. (2011a). Our college is changing: women's college student affairs administrators and transgender students. *Journal of Homosexuality, 58*(9), 1165–1186.

Marine, S. (2011b). *Stonewall's legacy: Bisexual, gay, lesbian, and transgender students in higher education.* ASHE Higher Education Report (vol. 37, no. 4). San Francisco, CA: Jossey-Bass.

Martin, J. I., & Yorkin, D. R. (2006). Transgender identity. In D. F. Morrow & L. Messinger (Eds.), *Sexual orientation and gender expression in social work practice: Working with lesbian, gay, bisexual, and transgender people* (pp. 105–128). New York, NY: Columbia University Press.

McKinney, J. S. (2005). On the margins: A study of the experiences of transgender college students. *Journal of Gay & Lesbian Issues in Education, 3*(1), 63–75.

Minter, S. P. (2006). Do transsexuals dream of gay rights? Getting real about transgender inclusion. In P. Currah, R. M. Juang, & S. P. Minter (Eds.). *Transgender rights* (pp. 141–170). Minneapolis, MN: University of Minnesota Press.

Nadal, K. L., Rivera, D. P., & Corpus, M. J. H. (2010). Sexual orientation and transgender microaggressions. In D. W. Sue (Ed.), *Microaggressions and marginality: Manifestations, dynamics, and impact* (pp. 217–240). Hoboken, NJ: Wiley

Nakamura, K. (1998). Transitioning on campus: A case studies approach. In R. L. Sanlo, (Ed.), *Working with lesbian, gay, bisexual, and transgender college students: A handbook for faculty and administrators* (pp. 179–187). Westport, CT: Greenwood Educators Reference Collection.

Pusch, R. S. (2005). Objects of curiosity: Transgender college students' perceptions of the reactions of others. *Journal of Gay & Lesbian Issues in Education, 3*(1), 45–61.

Rankin, S., Weber, G., Blumenfeld, W., & Frazer, S. (2010) *The state of higher education for lesbian, gay, bisexual, and transgender people.* Charlotte, NC: Campus Pride

Sanlo, R. L. (1998). *Working with lesbian, gay, bisexual, and transgender college students: A handbook for faculty and administrators.* Westport, CT: Greenwood Educators Reference Collection.

Sanlo, R. L., Rankin, S. R., & Schoenberg, R. (2002). *Our place on campus: Lesbian, gay, bisexual, transgender services and programs in higher education.* Westport, CT: Greenwood Press.

Schilt, K., & Westbrook. L. (2009). Doing gender, doing heteronormativity: "Gender normals," transgender people and the social maintenance of heterosexuality. *Gender & Society, 23*(4), 440–464.

Schilt, K. R., & Waszkiewicz, E. (2006, August). "I feel so much more in my body: Challenging the significance of the penis in transsexual men's bodies." Paper presented at the annual meeting of the American Sociological Association, Montreal Quebec, Canada Online.

Solorzano, D., Ceja, M., & Yosso, T. (2000). Critical race theory, racial microaggressions, and campus racial climate: The experiences of African American college students. *Journal of Negro Education, 69*(1/2), 60–73.

Spade, D. (2003). Resisting medicine, re/modeling gender. *Berkeley Women's Law Journal, 18*(15), 15–37.

Stryker, S. (2008). *Transgender history.* Berkley, CA: Seal Studies.

Sue, D. W. (2010). Microaggressions, marginality, and oppression: An introduction. In D. W. Sue (Ed.), *Microaggressions and marginality: Manifestations, dynamics, and impact* (pp. 3–22). Hoboken, NJ, Wiley.

Sue, D. W., Capodilupo, C. M., Torino, G. C., Bucceri, J. M., Holder, A. M. B., Nadal, K. L, & Esquilin, M. (2007). Racial microaggressions in everyday life: Implications for clinical practice. *American Psychologist, 62*(4), 271–286.

U.S. Census Bureau (2009). *Current population survey, school enrollment figures.* Retrieved March 1, 2011, from www.census.gov/population/www/socdemo/school.html

Valentine, D. (2007). *Imagining transgender: An ethnography of a category.* Durham, NC: Duke University Press.

Vanderburgh, R. (2009). Appropriate therapeutic care for families with pre-pubescent transgender/gender-dissonant children. *Child and Adolescent Social Work Journal, 26*(2), 135–154.

Wilchins, R.A. (2002). Queerer bodies. In J. Nestle, C. Howell, & R.A. Wilchins (Eds.), *Genderqueer: Voices from beyond the sexual binary* (pp. 33–47). Los Angeles, CA: Alyson books.

Chapter 10
Engaging Undergraduate Women and Men

Jaime Lester and Frank Harris III

The state of research on gender and student identity development expanded considerably since the first edition of this book. Concepts, such as intersectionality, critical race theory, and queer theory are being used to understand the complexity of student identity development (Torres, Jones, & Renn, 2009). In addition, as Torres et al. (2009) argue, long-held psychological and sociological theories are modified to account for more contemporary ideas that emphasize status versus stage in psychological development theories and the socially constructed nature of identity, for example. Of note in the more recent research is the attention to other populations, such as gay and lesbian students, students of different socioeconomic statuses, and underrepresented racial/ethnic minorities. Each of these identities (race/ethnicity, gender, sexuality, religion, and class) is integral to identity development among college students (Abes, Jones, & McEwen, 2007; Evans, Forney, Guido, Patton, & Renn, 2010).

There are several key areas consistent with the progressive changes in student development that need additional consideration to account for the relationship between gender and student development theory. Consistent with the two theoretical frameworks—feminist poststructuralism and social constructionism—presented in the chapter, three key areas are of note:

1. *Intersection of identity that allows for participants to define and fluidly move between identities.* While there is a burgeoning literature on intersectionality, these studies often predetermine and strictly define identities. Students are defined by the relationship between their race/ethnicity, gender, social class, and so forth.
2. *Integration of power beyond structural dynamics that limit the ability of students to express their identities.* Critical race theory places oppression as a structure that arises from the socio-historical marginalization of groups. As we will discuss, poststructualist ideas of power complicate and expand the source, presence, and use of power.

3. *Impact of conforming and performing gender norms on an individual's identity*. Much of the literature notes the impact of gender norms on individuals and shows the limiting nature of norms. However, the literature does little to explain the identity impact. How does the performing of one's gender, the doing of gender, impact one's gender identity?

These three areas are of particular importance to the examination of gender and student development theory due to the complex nature of gender social norms in the academy. Students enter higher education with 18 or more years of gender identity development that is often consistent with socio-cultural notions of gender and can have an impact on their collegiate success. Sax (2008) found in her work that women rate themselves lower in mathematical ability, intellectualism, and competitiveness as compared to men. Women are also more likely to conform to gender norms around family, service, and community while men prioritize partying, exercising, and playing video games. Students are also confronting the relationship between and among their various identities in a way that is not predetermined or prescribed. Finally, students encounter the power structures within the academy that are connected to gender norms. These can include cultural definitions of what it means to be masculine and a successful student, the majority/minority of a single gender in the classroom or academic major, and hierarchies that exist in social clubs, Greek life, and other groups on campus. Students are confronting not only their own individual identity development, but the gender norms present in their new context—a college or university. Gender intersects and interacts with other salient identity dimensions (e.g., race/ethnicity, religion, sexual orientation) and shape students' self-concept and the ways in which they experience college contexts (Abes et al., 2007; Evans et al., 2010). Moreover, there is compelling empirical evidence suggesting that students experience a range of challenges and issues (which will be discussed later in this chapter) attributable, in part, to their gender identities. Thus, our focus on gender as a salient construct in student development is warranted. The issues we consider in this chapter have significant implications for the work of college educators, notably faculty and student affairs professionals, in ensuring that students experience the gains and outcomes that are assumed to accompany participation in higher education.

For the purposes of this chapter, we conceptualize identity consistent with social constructivism. We define identity as "the interface between the individual and the world, defining as it does what the individual will stand for and be recognized as" (Josselson, 1987, p. 8). Identity is, then, constructed based on interactions with others and can change based on contexts; identity is fluid and ever changing. Identity is a central principle to the college student population as traditional-aged students enter college at a time when they are beginning the adult development process.

In this chapter, we present two theoretical frameworks to address the key areas of need in gender identity development—feminist poststructuralism and social constructionism. To begin the discussion, we first outline key issues and challenges in identity development among men and women in colleges and universities across the United States. Intricate pictures of gender in colleges and universities illustrate the complexities of the experiences of male and female students. The two theoretical frameworks and their implications for practice follow. Finally, we provide an extensive discussion of strategies for applying these perspectives to a college or university setting.

Articulation of Issues

Female Student Identity Development Issues

Female college students do not appear to suffer academically when exploring identity development during early adulthood. In fact, since the mid-1970s, the enrollment of women in college and universities across the nation has exceeded that of men. In 2005, female students received just over 62% of associate degrees, 58% bachelor's degrees, 60% of master's degrees, 50% of first-professional degrees, and 49% of doctoral degrees (National Center for Education Statistics [NCES], 2007). The largest gains are in the first-professional and doctoral degrees. Women began entering higher education in greater numbers between 1970 and 1995 making them eligible for graduate programs that require bachelor's degrees.

Disaggregating the statistics by degree completion, however, begins to show a more complex picture of gender disparities across the academy and hints at the complex nature of gender and identity development. While women are larger in number than men in undergraduate and graduate enrollment and have a slightly higher representation in community colleges, their degree completion in specific fields of study illustrates the perpetuation of male and female majority disciplines. Women account for only 18.4% of undergraduate engineers (National Science Foundation, 2003), and the number of women earning a Bachelor of Science degree in engineering has lagged in recent years (NCES, 2011). Research has noted that increasing the numbers of women in science or engineering is dependent on developing a science identity from adolescence (Brickhouse, Lowery, & Schultz, 2000). However, women in science and engineering classrooms in higher education find an overwhelmingly male dominated environment and are expected to conform to masculine ways of learning (Tonso, 1996a, 1996b). Unfortunately, the underrepresentation of women in these fields has long-term effects. Women who graduate from college are likely to earn incomes lower than their male peers with the same credentials. In 2009, the average woman with a bachelor's degree made $40,100 per year compared to $56,570 for men (NCES, 2011). The discrepancy between average salaries for men and women is attributed to the types of jobs that men and women populate after college graduation. Science and engineering graduates earn significantly higher incomes upon graduation than those with degrees in the social sciences. Aligning academic identity for men and women students alongside the particular disciplines leads to unfair long-term financial disadvantages for women.

Enrollment and degree attainment statistics, however, only provide a small picture of the overall status and experiences of women in higher education. Women may enter and complete college at greater rates than men, but the pressure to maintain femininity causes identity conflicts that are not evident in student outcome statistics. These pressures to perform and maintain socio-historical gender norms impact the experiences of female students and may deter them from specific academic majors. From the first studies that identified a "chilly" classroom climate, the experiences of women in the classroom and their interaction with peers, faculty, and the curriculum impact their success. Sax (2008) found that female students tend to react differently to interactions with faculty. Women who challenge faculty in the classroom experience heightened stress as opposed to men who have lower levels of stress from the same behaviors. The gender of the instructor also plays a role. Female students in majority female classrooms with male professors find the environment less positive and perceive less support and encouragement than all female students (Crombie, Pyke, Silverthorn, & Jones, 2003). Finally, gender norms are present in the classroom from student perceptions of how they should perform gender to their gender expectations of instructors. Bergvall (1996) found that women in engineering classrooms must confront masculine norms while addressing the expectations of femininity; female students must be masculine engineers and address the shifting expectations of what it means to be a female engineer. Research on student evaluations and gender illustrates the differing expectations for male and female instructors. Sprague and Massoni (2005) found that students perceive their best male teachers as funny and personable and best female teachers as fun and nurturing. Further research indicates that students give higher evaluation scores when they receive higher grades, but the effect is stronger for male than female instructors (Sinclair & Kunda, 2000). Gender plays a strong role in the classroom from the experiences of female students to the gender norm expectations of instructors.

Another area that has an impact of female student identity relates to participation in activities—sports, sororities, social clubs, or academic organizations—that are designed to increase students' academic and social engagement and are found to positively impact student success. Yet, female students experience identity conflicts related to these activities and exhibit psychological stress and physical symptoms (Rozin, Bauer, & Catanese, 2003). Women are more likely than men to suffer from eating disorders (Smolak & Murnen, 2001) due to media images that portray beauty alongside thinness (Levine & Smolak, 1996) and the intense relationship between body image and athletics. For women whose identity is closely related to a sport, particularly a sport that focuses on their bodies, eating disorders have emerged as a significant issue. In a meta-analysis of eating disorders and female athletes, researchers found that female athletes were more at risk for eating problems than non-athletes (Smolak, Murnen, & Ruble, 2000). Sports that emphasize thinness, such as dancing, were found to report larger numbers of students with eating disorders. Another group that has been found to be at risk for eating disorders are female students who belong to sororities (Allison & Park, 2004). In a study of university women, sorority members were more likely to strive for thinness and exhibit eating disorders than non-sorority women (Allison & Park, 2004). The pressure to maintain the ideals of femininity with a thin physique or succumbing to the norms of a group, such as some sororities, has negative effects on female students. Identity conflicts are not unique to female students; as we describe in the next section, male students also experience gender-related challenges that impact their development and outcomes.

Men's Identity Development in College

Over the past decade, a rich body of conceptual and empirical work on college men's identity development has proliferated in higher education (see Harper & Harris III, 2010; Kellom, 2004; Laker & Davis, 2011). This scholarship is primarily grounded in theories and perspectives from gender studies, psychology, sociology, and education (see Brod & Kaufman, 1994; Connell, 2005; Kimmel & Messner, 2007; Levant, 1996; and Pleck, 1981) and has been critical in making sense of the ways in which campus contexts facilitate, constrain, and complicate men's identity development in college. For example, Davis' (2002) qualitative study explored gender-related challenges and conflicts among 10 undergraduate men at a rural Midwestern university. Among Davis' key findings was the men felt constrained and overwhelmed by external pressures to behave in ways that were consistent with stereotypical notions of what it means to be a man in college. Other scholars, notably Edwards and Jones (2009), Harper, Harris III, and Mmeje (2005), and Harris III (2010), have proposed conceptual models that illuminate processes of men's identity development in college and influences with a range of contextual factors, including gender socialization prior to college, campus social norms, and campus culture. Finally, others have offered empirical and theoretical insights into the identity development and gender-related experiences of men from various subgroups, such as men of color (Guardia & Evans, 2008; Harper, 2004; Harper & Nichols, 2008; Liu, 2002), male student-athletes (Martin & Harris III, 2006), men in community colleges (Harris III & Harper, 2008), and gay men (Dilley, 2005; Holland & Holley, 2011).

At the heart of the issues concerning college men and identity development is the pressure men face to conform to narrowly-constructed and stereotypically masculine behavioral norms, which discourage or detract their engagement in behaviors and activities that lead to desirable outcomes. This phenomenon is perhaps more intensely experienced in college environments given that most traditional-aged college students are in the early phases or in periods of transition in their identity development. Moreover, the amount of time college men spend in exclusively male sub-groups (e.g., fraternities, sports teams, single-sex living arrangements) also intensify the peer pressure experienced by college men. College student development theory, which serves as the basis of student affairs practice in higher education, has traditionally assumed a genderless standpoint when it comes to men in that most of the foundational research and studies used to develop and validate these frameworks involved men as research subjects, but largely ignored gender as a construct that shapes and influences men's development in college (Evans et al., 2010; Laker & Davis, 2011). Thus, up until the recent emergence of scholarship on men and masculinities in higher education, scholars have relied almost exclusively on theories and models from other disciplines to guide their sensemaking and practice in working with men and facilitating their identity development. One widely cited model is O'Neil's (1981) Male Gender Role Conflict (MGRC) framework.

O'Neil's (1981) MGRC framework captures the negative consequences that accrue from men's inability to conform to rigid and restricted male gendered norms. O'Neil, Helms, Gable, David, and Wrightsman (1986) identified six behavioral patterns associated with MGRC: (1) restrictive emotionality; (2) homophobia; (3) socialized control, power, and competition; (4) restrictive sexual and affectional behavior; (5) obsession with achievement and success; and (6) health care problems. The consequences of MGRC have been well-documented and linked empirically to a host of behavioral problems and identity conflicts that disproportionately impact or involve college men, including alcohol and substance abuse (Capraro, 2000; Courtenay, 1998), poor help-seeking and coping strategies (Good & Wood, 1995; O'Neil et al., 1986), depression (Good & Mintz, 1990), violence and aggression (O'Neil, 1981), homophobia and fear of femininity (Davis, 2002; Edwards & Jones, 2009; Harris III, 2010; O'Neil, 1981), misbehavior (Harper et al., 2005), and sexism (Harris III, Palmer, & Struve, 2011) among college men. Similarly, Harris III and Harper (2008) discussed MGRC among four diverse community college men. To further illustrate the nexus between MGRC and the identity development of college men, we highlight several male behavioral trends occurring on college campuses. Specifically, we discuss disengagement, alcohol abuse, and misbehavior among college men.

Disengagement

Gender disparities in the level and intensity of campus engagement are of increasing concern for postsecondary educators. Several published reports indicate that college men are not as engaged in educationally purposeful activities (e.g., leadership in student organizations, study abroad, community service) as the women on their campuses. For example, in a 2003 multi-institutional survey of students involved in community service activities, Salgado reported that only 35% of the students involved in services were men, compared to 64% for women. This finding is consistent with Sax and Harper's (2007) examination of gender differences in college outcomes. Women, reportedly, have a greater orientation toward social activism (described as "helping others, influencing social values, and working in the community" p. 680), whereas college men have a "status striving orientation" and express greater concern for earning money, gaining recognition, and having authority over others (Sax & Harper, 2007). Moreover, Sax's (2008) longitudinal study revealed that college men reportedly spent more time than women engaged in activities that were typically perceived as not having an educationally-meaningful purpose, notably watching television, playing video games, and attending parties. Cuyjet (1997) conducted a College Student Experience Questionnaire (CSEQ) study of African American student engagement (2,431 men and 4,308 women). One of the most notable findings of the study was that male participants were less involved than their female counterparts in a host of student engagement activities, including searching the campus newspaper for notices about campus events and student organizations; attending a meeting, program, or event sponsored by a campus group; and serving on campus committees. Given the empirical evidence that connects purposeful campus engagement to a host of positive outcomes for all students (Astin, 1984; Kuh, 1995; Pascarella & Terenzini, 2005), disengagement among college men warrants attention and concern.

Alcohol Abuse

While alcohol consumption has been ingrained in the American collegiate experience for decades, recent reports confirm that men, particularly those who are enrolled in their first year of college, abuse alcohol disproportionately. The reasons why men abuse alcohol are perhaps infinite. However, scholars consistently link this phenomenon to college men's tendencies to embrace stereotypical expectations of masculinity (Capraro, 2000; Courtenay, 2004; McCreary, Newcomb, & Sadave, 1999; O'Neil, 1990; Sabo, 2005). Conforming to peer pressure, taking risks, and coping with stress are some of the most widely reported reasons for why men abuse alcohol. Capraro (2000) argues that the heavy drinking that characterizes college male cultures is a strategy for coping with the "paradox of masculinity." He theorizes: "My interpretation of a variety of evidence suggests that men may be drinking not only to enact male privilege but also to help them negotiate the emotional hazards of being a man in the contemporary American college" (p. 307). The privilege that comes with being a male is a source of power for men. Yet, the physical and emotional vulnerability that result from alcohol-induced conformity to traditional masculine expression render men powerless—hence the inherent paradox of masculinity suggested by Capraro.

A host of negative outcomes accrue from college men's abuse of alcohol. For example, a key finding from Wechsler, Davenport, Dowdell, Moeykens, and Castillo's (1994) national survey of 17,600 students at 140 colleges was that among the male participants who reported regularly binge drinking, 60% admitted to driving a vehicle after doing so. Furthermore, disproportionate male involvement in acts of violence, sexual assault, risky and irresponsible sex, academic problems, accidental injuries, and death have also been linked to alcohol abuse among college students (Burda, Tushup, & Hackman, 1992; Capraro, 2000; Courtenay, 1998, 2004; Doumas & Andersen, 2009). Empirical studies also confirm that environments that characterize male dominated sub-cultures, such as fraternities and sports teams, often encourage irresponsible drinking behavior (Capraro, 2000; Hill, Burch-Ragan, & Yates, 2001; Kuh & Arnold, 1993; Rhoads, 1995).

Misbehavior

The last trend we discuss is male misbehavior on college and university campuses. That men are sanctioned more often than women for acts that violate campus judicial policy (non-academic), including acts of violence, sexual assault, and sexual harassment (Foubert, Newberry, & Tatum, 2007; Hong, 2000), is consistently acknowledged in the published literature on college men and masculinities (e.g., Dannells, 1997; Harper et al., 2005; Ludeman, 2004, 2011). Dannells (1997) characterized campus judicial offenders as typically first- or second-year men who live on campus, have less positive views of the institution than students who do not violate judicial policy, and are usually under the influence of alcohol at the time of the incident. Harper et al. (2005) correlate male misbehavior with the social construction of masculinity and cultural norms related to gender. They contend that men are more prone to engage in acts that violate campus judicial policy because using violence to settle disputes, damaging property, possessing dangerous weapons (e.g., guns and knives), breaking rules, and other aggressive acts have been culturally defined as "masculine." As such, men are more likely to embrace these behaviors in their efforts to establish themselves as men and affirm their masculinities among peers. Although men who engage in these behaviors are likely to face sanctions and be held accountable in other ways (e.g., fines, arrest, suspension, expulsion), the perceived pressure to be accepted and granted status within male peer groups, and to see one's self as a man, are perhaps greater incentives to violate policy rather than to avoid punishments.

Ludeman (2011) suggests that men's misbehavior may be a consequence of being overwhelmed by the process of identity development. For example, men are socialized to be unemotional, avoid seeking help, and to hide feelings of insecurity and vulnerability. However, expressing emotions and being vulnerable, and relying on others for support, at times, are fundamental components of psychosocial development (Chickering & Reisser, 1993). Thus, if men are reluctant or refuse to seek support when they experience challenges or setbacks, the likelihood that they will rely on other, less productive, outlets to deal with these issues is perhaps greater. For example, one of the key findings in Davis' (2002) study was the participants feeling challenged and overwhelmed by the process of establishing their identities as men. Consequently, Davis' participants reportedly experienced gender role conflict manifested as stifled communication, restricted emotionality, fear of femininity, and homophobia.

Our acknowledgement of the gender-related conflicts and issues that challenge college men does not aim to devalue the realities of gender inequities in higher education. We agree that there is a system of patriarchy in higher education institutions that has historically oppressed women. However, men are also constricted by the same system that privileges patriarchy and stereotypical notions of masculinity. To address identity development among college men and women, this chapter seeks to apply new ways of considering gender identity development.

Feminist Poststructuralism: An Approach to Understanding Female Student Identity Development

Decades of research on female student identity development discuss the profound effect that social relationships have in forming and framing identity. Gilligan (1982), for example, found that women define themselves in relations to others and within the context of intimate relationships. Similarly, Belenky, Clinchy, Goldberger, and Tarule (1986) noted five epistemological perspectives—silence, received knowledge, subjective knowledge, procedural knowledge, and constructed knowledge—that are created in direct connection to patterns of family interactions during childhood. Josselson (1987) used the models of Erikson (1968) and Marcia (1960) to argue that the primary site for identity development among women occurred in relationships with family and during contact with others. This finding was dramatically different for men who have been found to develop individual identity through separation, individuation, and autonomy. The focus on relationships as the site for female student identity development presupposes a fixed and universal development for all women. The diversity of experience as well as the intersections of class, race, and sexuality and the fluidity of identity development has been largely ignored. In order to provide a different perspective of female identity development, we present a feminist poststructural approach to identity, which claims that identity is fluid, subjective, and contextually bound.

Feminist poststructuralism begins from the assumption that gender is socially constructed in a society that systematically places women in oppressive positions. The development of a gender identity is rooted in the fluid nature of social construction but is also connected to societal notions of gender. Women, for example, have multiple identities associated with race, socioeconomic class, religion, and sexuality that affect their gender development. Regardless of the differences among women, the societal norms of femininity still apply. Feminist poststructuralism explains that these social norms regarding gender are expressed in language, which in turn, constructs women's identities (Weedon, 1997). The ways in which women come to know the social norms regarding gender is through language. Furthermore, language is contextually bound. Specific contexts alter the messages of gender, thus, affecting identity development. For example, male students are twice as likely as female students to speak in the classroom environment (Sadker & Sadker, 1994), and teachers are often more likely to interrupt female students (Hall & Sandler, 1982). By silencing women in the classroom, their identities as college students are constructed alongside silence.

In feminist poststructuralism, identities are not singular. A female college student can have multiple identities. The multiplicity of identities does not infer that they are separate. Rather, identities intersect. A female student may simultaneously represent her ethnicity and sexuality. For example, a female student may be a member of an organization for gay, lesbian, bisexual, and trans* students of color. In this context, she will likely foreground her race and sexual orientation simultaneously.

Not only does a feminist poststructural perspective reconceptualize the formation and permanence of identities, the perspective also assists in connecting individual experience and social structures in new ways. According to Tisdell (2000), one of the basic tenets of feminist poststructuralism includes shifting identities within different social structures. Social settings convey meaning and place value on particular identities through both implicit and explicit messages. The college classroom is a social setting that conveys many implicit and explicit messages about gender. For example, consider a traditional, male dominated course. The desks will be organized in a row configuration. The course content will focus on so-called objective and observable facts. The passive acceptance, memorization, and subsequent regurgitation of course content on exams will be the primary mechanisms for learning. Course content will be delivered exclusively by way of lectures. Thus, students will not be co-constructors of learning as their experiences and voices will not be heard. The polar opposite of this social setting is a diverse, gender balanced course in which the desk are configured in a circle, individuals' experiences are valued and emphasized through class discussions, and multiple strategies for learning and demonstrating mastery of course content will be used. While the traditional classroom setting may value the identity of students, the non-traditional setting places meaning on a students' gender, race, and other social identities that emerge during discussions.

There are a few studies that have adopted feminist poststructural ideas regarding identity. Anderson and Hayes (1996) found that "life-ties," which are "a set of related experiences and the perceptions these experiences evoke within the lives of adults," have a meaningful impact on individual identities (p. xiii). These same researchers also found that an individual's position in the social structure (oftentimes termed positionality) also affects identity development. By evoking positionality as an important concept within identity development, ideas of the multiplicity and intersection of identities emerge. For example, a female college student from a high social class may not experience the financial difficulties of paying high tuition while another female college student from a lower social class may have to consider financial aid or finding a job to pay for college. By virtue of the identity related to social class, an individual's identity and experience positions her differently within higher education. Other researchers have applied feminist poststructuralism to women as learners (Flannery & Hayes, 2000). Although not directly related to identity development among women, Flannery and Hayes note that to examine women as learners through the lens of feminist poststructuralism "gives legitimacy to the particularity of each woman's experience, helping us recognize the complexity of our identities and our differences as well as our similarities" (p. 14).

A feminist poststructural model provides a framework for understanding college women's identity development. Starting from the premise that identities are fluid, contextual, and multiple, identity is not a fixed category, but one that is constantly constructed. In this sense, each individual has multiple identities that are available based on the particular context. A female undergraduate student, for example, may emphasize her socioeconomic class in a sorority setting, but her academic interests in the classroom. Importantly, poststructuralist assumptions about gender debunk the ways in which identity development among women have been previously conceived. This model refutes singular and monolithic categories of identity as they relate to gender; identity does not develop in one singular process or at one exacting time. To focus on the complexities of identity development as presented by feminist poststructuralism, studies examine individual experiences and refute the possibility of constructing universal theories. Tisdell (2000) explains that by looking at identity as complex and oftentimes intersecting, research can address identity development in new ways and possibly facilitate social change.

Only a handful of studies use feminist poststructuralism to examine student identity development. Of note is the work of Foor and Walden (2009) who explore the "multiple, dynamic, and competing layers of being and meaning in the construction of gender roles and identities" (p. 45). In their study of female undergraduates in industrial engineering, they found that the discourse of industrial engineering as having a less demanding curriculum and a stronger relationship to business made it more accepting of and for women. Danielsson (2011) also employed a feminist post-structural lens to gender and physics and found that female students must contend with masculine gender norms and shifting definitions of how a woman is supposed to be in a physics context. The norms included women being diligent, responsible, and unskilled in handling laboratory equipment. These few studies show that feminist poststructuralism has the potential to complicate bounded gender norms by addressing the complexity of meaning and the shifting nature of identity.

The Social Constructionist Model: An Approach to Understanding Men's Development in College

The early research on men and masculinity focused primarily on examining male "sex roles" and sought to link empirically what were believed to be essential characteristics of masculinity to men's biological and cognitive compositions (Connell, 2005; Kimmel & Messner, 2007). Researchers assumed that acts of violence, sexual aggression, athleticism, competitiveness, and other characteristics that are culturally associated with masculinity were, in fact, "natural" male behavioral traits that were inherently linked to their biology, psychology, or other physiological factors (Connell, 2005; Kimmel & Messner, 2007). A major shortcoming of the sex role paradigm is that it fails to acknowledge the "complex social meanings" associated with masculinity and the interrelated social processes by which these meanings are produced and reinforced (Kimmel & Messner, 2007, p. xvi). Consequently, this approach was effectively challenged by feminists (e.g., Chodorow, 1978; Gilligan, 1982) and gender performance (e.g., West & Zimmerman, 1987) scholars. One important outcome of this critique was a body of pro-feminist men's study scholarship that sought to make more transparent the ways in which socially prescribed gender roles privileged some groups (notably White, heterosexual, middle- and upper-class men) while oppressing and marginalizing others (women, people of color, poor, gay, and persons with disabilities). This scholarship served as the foundation of the social constructionist model, a theoretical perspective that has been advanced most notably by sociologists Kimmel and Messner (2007) for examining and deconstructing social constructions of masculinity and their corresponding sociological effects. We advocate for employing the this model to understand how masculinities are shaped and reinforced in college contexts.

Like feminist poststructuralism, the social constructionist model is grounded in the assumption that gender is not a fixed characteristic, but rather one that is produced, negotiated, and reinforced through human interactions and within social structures. Another key assumption of the model is that masculinity is not uniformly expressed and experienced by all groups of men. Race/ethnicity, socioeconomic status, religion, sexual orientation, and a range of other identity dimensions intersect gender and significantly shape men's experiences as men. For example, a Mexican man from a low-income background with an undocumented status can leverage significantly fewer social rewards from his identity as a man than would a man who is White, college-educated, and middle class. Similarly, men who are openly gay are typically afforded less status than their heterosexual male counterparts. To this point, Kimmel and Messner (2007) wrote: "In the contemporary United States, masculinity is constructed differently by class culture, by race and ethnicity, and by age" (p. xxii). An important implication follows from this assumption—a single, universal, or normative masculinity does not actually exist. Instead, masculinity is a collection of rules and norms that govern gendered behavior for men in particular contexts. Connell (2005) described these rules and norms as "hegemonic" in that the social processes by which these prevailing notions emerge and become legitimized are rarely recognized. Moreover, absent of critical reflection and examination, the destructive and consequential nature of traditional masculine ideologies is easily overlooked. Thus, the concept of "hegemonic masculinity" is central in the social constructionist model. Finally, it is important to note that men's studies scholars often refer to masculinity in the plural as "masculinities." Doing so acknowledges the range of masculine behaviors and conceptualizations that can be expressed and performed.

To further articulate the ways in which male gender identity is socially constructed, we consider some typical social processes by which this phenomenon occurs. Specifically, we highlight the influences of families, schools, sports, and the role of homophobia. While our discussion herein focuses primarily on mainstream social constructions of masculinities, scholars have also recognized culturally-specific masculine constructions and conceptualizations, particularly among African American and Latino men. For example, Majors and Billson's (1992) concept of "cool pose" describes performance of masculinities among African American men to portray calmness and resolve through unique styles of dressing, speaking, gesturing, shaking hands, and other observable behavioral patterns. Likewise, Mirande (2004) deconstructed the concept of machismo and discussed its cultural significance in the performance of masculinities among Latino men. Both Mirande and Majors and Billson argued that these, and other culturally-defined notions of masculinities, are employed by Latino and African American men to cope with racial prejudice and alienation and to "mask feelings of inferiority, powerlessness, and failure" (Mirande, 2004, p. 37) stemming from their status as minority men.

Families

As noted previously in this discussion, the social constructionist model focuses on the ways in which masculinities are developed through patterns of gender socialization and reinforced within social structures, such as schools, churches, media, sports, and other institutions. Within these institutions, clear expectations for what constitutes "appropriate" roles and behaviors for men and women are communicated, performed, and maintained. For example, in traditional American families, both men and women have clearly defined roles. Men often assume the roles of breadwinner, disciplinarian, and protector of the home whereas women are often relegated to "domestic" duties, such as preparing meals, rearing children, and cleaning the home. Children who are raised within these structures have ample opportunities to observe and practice the gendered behavior of the adults with whom they interact most frequently and to ensure the ways they perform gender are aligned with the expectations they have internalized. Moreover, when children's gendered behaviors are not performed in accordance with the expectations of their sex (male or female), they often face the consequence of scolding or punishment at the hand of adults. Conversely, when boys and girls perform gender in accordance with what is expected of men and women, respectively, they are praised and rewarded for doing so. As noted by Harper (2004), "no father wants his son to grow up being a 'pussy,' 'sissy,' 'punk,' or 'softy'—terms commonly associated with boys who fail to live up to the traditional standards of masculinity in America" (p. 92).

Schools

The aforementioned patterns of gender socialization that take place within American homes are reinforced in another prominent social institution—schools. Swain (2005) noted several aspects of school cultures that are inherently gendered, such as academic competition, testing, team games, dress codes, and patterns of authority. Swain also noted that relationships between teachers and students reinforce the "gender regime." Gilbert and Gilbert (1998) contend that teachers, like parents, interact with students according to assumptions of gender appropriate behavior. This claim is supported by Alloway's (1995) findings that teachers interacted more often with boys when they were engaged in masculine-appropriate activities, such as block construction, and more often with girls involved in stereotypically feminine activities, such as dramatic play. Moreover, the tendencies of some educators to track boys toward the sciences and mathematics while encouraging girls to master the humanities and the arts is also a well-documented phenomenon (Gilbert & Gilbert, 1998).

Male peer groups that are situated in school contexts also figure prominently in the social construction of masculinity in schools. These groups have profound influence on ensuring boys' conformity to socially-derived expectations of gendered behavior for boys. Being deemed a "nerd," a "sissy," or "unpopular" by one's male peers places boys at the margins of peer culture and puts them at risk of bullying, harassment, or social alienation (Swain, 2005). Young men who are unable to display competence in sports and other physical activities, or those who follow classroom and school rules, perform well academically, or spend time socializing with girls are especially vulnerable. As Swain noted, "one of the most urgent dimensions of school life for boys is the need to gain popularity and status. Indeed the search to achieve status is also the search to achieve an acceptable form of masculinity" (p. 218). Pollack (2001) described the phenomenon that governs gender performance among adolescent boys as the "boy code" and noted its influence on boys' dispositions toward sexism, homophobia, violence, and misbehavior in schools.

Sports

Sports and other "masculinizing" activities (e.g., Boy Scouts, martial arts) also figure prominently in the gender socialization of boys. Getting boys involved in these types of activities during their elementary school years is a practice that typically transcends race/ethnicity, socioeconomic status, and other demographic categories. According to Griffin (1998), sports serve several critical functions in the social construction of hegemonic masculinity, including (1) defining and reinforcing traditional conceptions of masculinity; (2) providing contexts for male bonding and intimacy; (3) reinforcing male privilege and female subordination; (4) establishing status among men; and (5) reinforcing heterosexuality. The hegemonic and inherently aggressive masculinities that are reinforced through sports can promote dysfunctional values among men, such as disrespect for women and intellectual success, and a reliance on physicality and violence to solve differences (Connell, 2005; Estler & Nelson, 2005).

Homophobia

Finally, homophobia and its behavioral manifestations align with socially constructed male gender identity (Herek, 1987; Kimmel, 2001; Kimmel & Messner, 2007; Messner, 2007; Plummer, 1999). Homophobia relates directly to men's fear of being viewed as gay or feminine, and their perceived need to separate their gender identities from those of women. "Gay men symbolize parts of the self that do not measure up to cultural standards [of masculinity]; directing hostility at them [gay men] is a way to externalizing the conflict" (Herek, 1987, p. 77). In learning to become men, boys are taught to avoid traits and behaviors that are typically associated with girls and women (Herek, 1987). They also discover at an early age that homophobia is one of the most accessible and socially acceptable ways to assert themselves as men (Plummer, 1999). Thus, homophobia allows boys and men to affirm their heterosexual identities while also differentiating themselves from women and their gay male peers. Heterosexual expression via homophobia is also an example of what Messner (2007) describes as "doing heterosexuality," an ongoing practice through which men avoid being stigmatized as gay or feminine by portraying themselves as "real men." Accordingly, real men are those "who are able to compete successfully with other males in sport, work, and sexual relations with women" (Messner, 2007, p. 365).

The social constructionist model is a much-needed alternative to the sex role paradigm and other frameworks that rely upon biological differences between men and women to make sense of gendered behavior. With regard to college men, this model provides insight into the extent to which the conceptualizations of masculinity that are shared among male undergraduates are both consistent with and divergent from the conceptualizations that are salient within mainstream, non-collegiate male populations.

Feminist poststructuralism and the social constructionist model are two theoretical perspectives to examine identity development among the college student population. These two perspectives are far from separate. In fact, both rely on the socially constructed nature of gender and the importance of social structures in communicating gender norms. In addition, each perspective presents the specificity of identity development as it relates to gender rather than singular monolithic categories. They also reframe the discussion of the importance of social contexts in the creation of gender identity and place significance on social institutions. Postsecondary educators are responsible for understanding how institutional practices and programmatic decisions may impact the development of students. Below is a set of recommendations or ideas to consider for student affairs professionals and faculty who are committed to assisting students in developing healthy gender identities and responding productively to gender-related challenges.

Gender-Specific Recommendations for Male and Female Student Identity

Provide Reflection Opportunities

A basic principle of feminist poststructuralism is the multiplicity of identities. Students have multiple and sometimes conflicting identities that may make identity development difficult or complicated. One suggestion is to provide structured and facilitated reflection opportunities for students, particularly in times of confusion or crisis. Reflection gives students a chance to recognize identity intersections and make sense of identity conflicts. Published literature on male gender identity suggests that men are traditionally socialized to believe in hegemonic conceptions of masculinity and to adopt sexist, homophobic, and unhealthy attitudes. Thus, providing opportunities for male students to recognize the effects of traditional male socialization is necessary and may encourage some to seek more productive ways to express their gender identities. Facilitated discussions with peers and professionals with an expertise in gender identity are first steps in this regard.

Offer Group Reflection Opportunities

Similar to the first recommendation, faculty and student affairs educators should consider group reflection opportunities. Encouraging students to talk and collaborate with others and facilitating dialogue across differences encourage reflection and self-understanding (Tierney, 1993). An exploration of the experiences of others also connects individual experiences to social structures (i.e., the college or university).

Develop Student Support Groups

Student support groups that address issues relating to gender identity development, particularly among male students, have proven effective. Intentional collaboration with men's and women's centers, faculty with expertise in gender identity and student development, counseling services, and the student health center will enhance the effectiveness of these groups. In some cases, these groups may need to be homogenous on the basis of gender, given the unique needs and challenges that characterize the identity development process for men and women. In addition, faculty and student affairs educators who advise and facilitate these groups should create strategies for reaching out to students of color, student athletes, and gay, lesbian, and bisexual students as they are typically underrepresented in student support groups.

Train Student Affairs Educators

Student affairs educators, specifically residential life staff and others serving in peer-supervisory roles, must be adequately trained to support and appropriately refer students who may need or seek assistance with gender-related issues and identity development. To this end, periodic follow-up trainings with fully credentialed college or university personnel are necessary.

Policy Change and Interventions

Offer Transition Programs

Programmatic efforts sponsored by orientation offices, residential life, campus life, and first-year programs focus primarily on assisting students in successful transitions and adjusting to college. However, rarely do these programs focus intentionally on issues directly related to gender identity. Transition programs provide timely opportunities to engage students in discussions involving their gender identities.

Examine Campus Cultural Symbols

In addition to the aforementioned programmatic recommendations, faculty and student affairs educators need to consider cultural symbols and discourses that diffuse throughout the institution. Messages that promote idealized notions of gender place students in a dichotomous paradigm. For example, on campuses with high-profile athletics programs, male students may assume that in order to be perceived as masculine, they must perform gender in ways that mirror their male student-athlete peers. However, performing gender in this way may not be a comfortable endeavor for most men on campus. Being mindful and intentional about the messages communicated about gender in campus media and other symbolic forms can help to infuse well-rounded conceptualizations of gender among students.

Devote Attention to Judicial Affairs Offices
Scholars have discussed the overrepresentation of male students as campus judicial offenders (Harper et al., 2005; Ludeman, 2004, 2011). Male students are also among those most frequently cited on multiple occasions for violating campus policies. Therefore, campus judicial officers are uniquely positioned to encourage men to explore and consider appropriate and healthy ways to express their gender identities. To the extent possible, opportunities for critical reflection should be incorporated into the sanctioning process in order to effectively engage students.

Recommendations for Curricular or Classroom-Based Support

Integrate Gender Identity Development across Curricula
Conversations about identity development are important in the context of peer groups as described above. These conversations need to also occur in the college classroom as an integrated component of curricula. We suggest that faculty and student affairs educators infuse the curricula of all courses with opportunities for students to discuss how gender impacts their lives and experiences as college students. Readings, films, guest speakers, case studies, observation assignments, and a range of other teaching and learning strategies should be used accordingly.

Offer Service-Learning Opportunities
Service-learning projects have been very effective in enhancing student learning, primarily by connecting course content outside the classroom (Markus, Howard, & King, 1993). Thus, faculty should develop projects that allow students to examine gender-related issues within and beyond the campus context. Ideally, students will gain some insight into the ways in which gender intersects everyday real-world social issues. Partnerships with local middle and high schools, family shelters, and other contexts in which gender issues are salient correspond logically with this strategy.

We recognize that most of the strategies we offer will require institutional leaders to reinvest or shift resources. While we understand that this may not be possible on some campuses, at the very least, all institutions are capable of providing opportunities for students to confidently and proactively address gender-related issues. One strategy to begin understanding the specific issues within one's college population is to inquire directly with students about their experiences. Doing so will assist in understanding how a particular campus context both hinders and facilitates gender identity development. Faculty and student affairs educators who have an interest in gender-related trends and issues can be invited to participate in the inquiry as interviewers, group facilitators, and in other important roles. Campuses have options. With thoughtful and purposeful action on the part of campus leaders, students can receive the support they need to manage the challenging, but necessary, process of gender identity development.

Conclusion

The challenges and issues that male and female students face during their undergraduate years are noticeably different. Many women are academically successful yet often exhibit eating disorders or other unhealthy habits to "fit-in" and maintain the idealized norm of beauty. Women also succumb to the pressure of traditional occupations and are deterred from math, science, and engineering fields. Men often attempt to maintain and live up to the idealized images of masculinity. As a result, some male students exhibit poor help-seeking behaviors, abuse drugs and alcohol, and perform poorly academically.

In this chapter, we presented two theoretical perspectives to consider when addressing gender identity development among college men and women. Each framework extends previous conceptualizations of gender and identity development by focusing on the fluidity of identity and the contextual meaning associated with identities. Feminist poststructuralism maintains that cultural norms regarding the appropriate behavior and identities for women are communicated within the context of higher education. These idealized norms for women and men may lead to unhealthy behaviors and work against personal and academic success. Similarly, the social constructionist model addresses hegemonic masculinity and its detrimental impact on male identity development. We suggest that postsecondary leaders consider how their institutional cultures may contribute to gender identity conflicts as well as design and implement innovative strategies to support students in their gender identity development. With a few important programmatic efforts, student affairs educators and faculty can help students successfully manage identity development conflicts.

References

Abes, E. S., Jones, S. R., & McEwen, M. K. (2007). Reconceptualizing the model of multiple dimensions of identity: The role of meaning-making capacity in the construction of multiple identities. *Journal of College Student Development, 48*(1), 1–22.

Allison, K. C., & Park, C. L. (2004). A prospective study of disordered eating among sorority and nonsorority women. *International Journal of Eating Disorders, 35*(3), 354–358.

Alloway, N. (1995). *Foundation stones: The construction of gender in early childhood.* Carlton, Australia: Curriculum Corporation.

Anderson, D. A., & Hayes, C. L. (1996). *Gender, identity, and self-esteem.* New York, NY: Springer.

Astin, A. W. (1984). Student involvement: A developmental theory for higher education. *Journal of College Student Personnel, 25,* 297–308.

Belenky, M. F., Clinchy, B. M., Goldberger, N. R., & Tarule, J. M. (1986). *Women's ways of knowing: The development of self, voice, and mind.* New York, NY: Basic Books.

Bergvall, V. L. (1996). Constructing and enacting gender through discourse: Negotiating multiple roles as female engineering students. In V. Bergvall, J. Meuller Bing, & A. Freed (Eds.), *Rethinking language and gender research: Theory and practice* (pp. 172–201). New York, NY: Longman.

Brickhouse, N. W., Lowery, P., & Schultz, K. (2000). What kind of a girl does science? The construction of school science identities. *Journal of Research in Science Teaching, 37*(5), 441–458.

Brod, H., & Kaufman, M. (Eds.). (1994). *Theorizing masculinities.* Thousand Oaks, CA: Sage.

Burda, P. C., Tushup, R. J., & Hackman, P. S. (1992). Masculinity and social support in alcoholic men. *Journal of Men's Studies, 1*(2), 187–193.

Capraro, R. L. (2000). Why college men drink: Alcohol, adventure, and the paradox of masculinity. *Journal of American College Health, 48,* 307–315.

Chickering, A.W., & Reisser, L. (1993). *Education and identity* (2nd ed.). San Francisco, CA: Jossey-Bass.

Chodorow, N. (1978). *The reproduction of mothering*. Berkeley, CA: University of California Press.

Connell, R.W. (2005). *Masculinities* (2nd ed.). Berkeley, CA: University of California Press.

Courtenay, W.H. (1998). College men's health: An overview and call to action. *Journal of American College Health, 46*(6), 279–290.

Courtenay, W.H. (2004). Best practices for improving college men's health. *New Directions for Student Services: Developing Effective Programs and Services for College Men, 107*, 59–74.

Crombie, G., Pyke, S., Silverthorn, N., & Jones, A. (2003). Students' perceptions of their classroom participation and instructor as a function of gender and context. *The Journal of Higher Education, 74*(1), 51–76.

Cuyjet, M.J. (1997). African American men on college campuses: Their needs and their perceptions. *New Directions for Student Services: Helping African American Men Succeed in College, 80*, 79–91.

Danielsson, A.T. (2011). Exploring woman university physics students' "doing gender" and "doing physics". *Gender and Education, 24*(1), 25–40.

Dannells, M. (1997). *From discipline to development: Rethinking student conduct in higher education. ASHE-ERIC Higher Education Report* (Vol. 25, No. 2). Washington, DC: The George Washington University Graduate School of Education and Human Development.

Davis, T. (2002). Voices of gender role conflict: The social construction of college men's identity. *Journal of College Student Development, 43*(4), 508–521.

Dilley, P. (2005). Which way out? A typology of non-heterosexual male collegiate identities. *The Journal of Higher Education, 76*, 56–88.

Doumas, D.M., & Andersen, L.L. (2009). Reducing alcohol use in first-year university students: Evaluation of a web-based personalized feedback program. *Journal of College Counseling, 12*, 18–32.

Edwards, K.E., & Jones, S.R. (2009). "Putting my man face on": A grounded theory of college men's gender identity development. *Journal of College Student Development, 50*(2), 210–228.

Erikson. E. (1968). *Identity, youth, and crisis*. New York, NY: Norton.

Estler, S.E., & Nelson, L.J. (2005). *Who calls the shots?: Sports and university leadership, culture, and decision making. ASHE Higher Education Report, 30*(5), 1–125.

Evans, N.J., Forney, D.S., Guido, F.M., Patton, L.D., & Renn, K.A. (2010). *Student development in college: Theory, research, and practice* (2nd ed.). San Francisco, CA: Jossey-Bass.

Flannery, D.D., & Hayes, E. (2000). Women's learning: A kaleidoscope. In E. Hayes & D.D. Flannery (Eds.), *Women as learners: The significance of gender in adult learning* (pp. 1–22). San Francisco, CA: Jossey-Bass.

Foor, C.E., & Walden, S.E. (2009). "Imaginary engineering" or "re-imagined engineering": Negotiating gendered identities in the borderland of a college of engineering. *Feminist Formations, 21*(2), 41–64.

Foubert, J.D., Newberry, J.T., & Tatum, J. (2007). Behavior differences seven months later: Effects of a rape prevention program. *NASPA Journal, 44*(4), 728–749.

Gilbert, R., & Gilbert, P. (1998). *Masculinity goes to school*. New York, NY: Routledge.

Gilligan, C. (1982). *In a different voice: Psychological theory and women's development*. Cambridge, MA: Harvard University Press.

Good, G.E., & Mintz, L.B. (1990). Gender role conflict and depression among college men: Evidence of compounded risk. *Journal of Counseling and Development, 69*(1), 17–21.

Good, G.E., & Wood, P.K. (1995). Male gender role conflict, depression, and help seeking: Do college men face double jeopardy? *Journal of Counseling & Development, 74*, 70–75.

Griffin, P. (1998). *Strong women, deep closets: Lesbians and homophobia in sports*. Champaign, IL: Human Kinetics.

Guardia, J.R., & Evans, N.J. (2008). The ethnic identity development of Latino fraternity members at a Hispanic serving institution. *Journal of College Student Development, 49*, 163–181.

Hall, R.M., & Sandler,. B.R. (1982). The *classroom climate: A chilly one for women?* Washington, DC: Association of American Colleges.

Harper, S.R. (2004). The measure of a man: Conceptualizations of masculinity among high-achieving African American male college students. *Berkeley Journal of Sociology, 48*(1), 89–107.

Harper, S.R., & Harris III, F. (2010). *College men and masculinities: Theory, research, and implications for practice*. San Francisco, CA: Jossey-Bass.

Harper, S. R., Harris III, F., & Mmeje, K. (2005). A theoretical model to explain the overrepresentation of college men among campus judicial offenders: Implications for campus administrators. *NASPA Journal, 42*(4), 565–587.

Harper, S. R., & Nichols, A. H. (2008). Are they not all the same? Racial heterogeneity among Black male undergraduates. *Journal of College Student Development, 49*(3), 199–214.

Harris III, F. (2010). College men's conceptualizations of masculinities and contextual influences: Toward a conceptual model. *Journal of College Student Development, 51*(3), 297–318.

Harris III, F., & Harper, S. R. (2008). Masculinities go to community college: Understanding male identity socialization and gender role conflict. In J. Lester (Ed.), *Gendered perspectives on community colleges: New directions for community colleges, 142* (pp. 25–35). San Francisco, CA: Jossey-Bass.

Harris III, F., Palmer, R., & Struve, L. E. (2011). "Cool posing" on campus: A qualitative study of masculinities and gender expression among Black men at private research institution. *Journal of Negro Education, 80*(1), 47–62.

Herek, G. M. (1987). On heterosexual masculinity: Some psychical consequences of the social construction of gender and sexuality. In M. Kimmel (Ed.), *Changing men: New directions in research on men and masculinity* (pp. 68–82). Newbury Park, CA: Sage.

Hill, K., Burch-Ragan, M., & Yates, D. Y. (2001). Current and future issues and trends facing student-athletes and athletic programs. *New Directions for Student Services, 93*, 65–80.

Holland, C., & Holley, K. (2011). The experiences of gay male undergraduate students at a traditional women's college. *Journal of Student Affairs Research and Practice, 48*(2), 179–194.

Hong, L. (2000). Toward a transformed approach to prevention: Breaking the link between masculinity and violence. *Journal of American College Health, 48*, 269–282.

Josselson, R. (1987). *Finding herself: Pathways to identity development in women.* San Francisco, CA: Jossey-Bass.

Kellom, G. E. (Ed.). (2004). *New directions for student services: Developing effective programs and services for college men, 107.* San Francisco, CA: Jossey-Bass.

Kimmel, M. S. (2001). Masculinity as homophobia: Fear, shame, and silence in the construction of gender identity. In S. M. Whitehead & F. J. Barrett (Eds.), *The masculinities reader* (pp. 266–287). Cambridge, UK: Polity.

Kimmel, M. S., & Messner, M. A. (Eds.). (2007). *Men's lives* (7th ed.). Boston, MA: Allyn & Bacon.

Kuh, G. D. (1995). The other curriculum: Out-of-class experiences associated with student learning and personal development. *The Journal of Higher Education, 66*(2), 123–155.

Kuh, G. D., & Arnold, J. C. (1993). Liquid bonding: A cultural analysis of the role of alcohol in fraternity pledgeship. *Journal of College Student Development, 34*, 327–334.

Laker, J., & Davis. T. (Eds.). (2011). *Masculinities in higher education: Theoretical and practical implications.* New York, NY: Routledge.

Levant, R. F. (1996). The new psychology of men. *Professional Psychology: Research and Practice, 27*(3), 259–265.

Levine, M. P., & Smolak, L. (1996). Media as a context for the development of disordered eating. In L. Smolak, M. P. Levin, & R. Striegel-Moore (Eds.), *The developmental psychopathology of eating disorders* (pp. 235–257). Mahwah, NJ: Erlbaum.

Liu, W. M. (2002). Exploring the lives of Asian American men: Racial identity, male role norms, gender role conflict, and prejudicial attitudes. *Psychology of Men and Masculinity, 3*, 107–118.

Ludeman, R. B. (2004). Arrested emotional development: Connecting college men, emotions, and misconduct. *New Directions for Student Services: Developing Effective Programs and Services for College Men, 107*, 75–86.

Ludeman, R. B. (2011). Successful judicial interventions with men. In J. Laker & T. L. Davis (Eds.), *Masculinities in Higher Education: Theoretical and Practical Implications* (pp. 193–209). New York, NY: Routledge.

Majors, R. G., & Billson, J. M. (1992). *Cool pose: The dilemmas of Black manhood in America.* New York, NY: Lexington Books.

Marcia, J. (1960). Development and validation of ego-identity status. *Journal of Personality and Social Psychology, 3*(5), 551–558.

Markus, G., Howard, J., & King, D. (1993). Integrating community service and classroom instruction enhances learning: Results from an experiment. *Educational Evaluation and Policy Analysis, 15*, 410–419.

Martin, B. E., & Harris III, F. (2006). Examining productive conceptions of masculinities: Lessons learned from academically driven African American male student-athletes. *Journal of Men's Studies, 14*(3), 359–378.

McCreary, D. R., Newcomb, M. D., & Sadave, S. (1999). The male role, alcohol use, and alcohol problems. *Journal of Counseling Psychology, 46*(1), 109–124.

Messner, M. A. (2007). Becoming 100 percent straight. In M. Kimmel & M. A. Messner (Eds.), *Men's lives* (7th ed., pp. 361–366). Boston, MA: Allyn & Bacon.

Mirande, A. (2004). "Macho": Contemporary conceptions. In M. Kimmel & M. Messner (Eds.), *Men's lives* (6th ed., pp. 28–38). Boston, MA: Allyn & Bacon.

National Center for Education Statistics (NCES). (2007). *The condition of education, 2007*. Washington, DC: NCES.

National Center for Education Statistics (NCES). (2011). *Digest of education statistics, 2010*. NCES 2011–015, Washington, D.C: U.S. Government Printing Office.

National Science Foundation (2003). *Engineering workforce commission, Engineering & technology enrollments: Fall 2002*. Washington, DC: U.S. Government Printing Office.

O'Neil, J. M. (1981). Patterns of gender role conflict and strain: Sexism and fear of femininity in men's lives. *The Personnel and Guidance Journal, 60*, 203–210.

O'Neil, J. M. (1990). Assessing men's gender role conflict. In D. Moore & F. Leafgren (Eds.), *Men in conflict: Problem solving strategies and interventions* (pp. 23–38). Alexandria, VA: American Counseling Association.

O'Neil, J. M., Helms, B. J., Gable, R. K., David, L., & Wrightsman, L. S. (1986). Gender role conflict scale: College men's fear of femininity. *Sex Roles, 14*(5/6), 335–350.

Pascarella, E. T., & Terenzini, P. (2005). *How college affects students: A third decade of research*. San Francisco, CA: Jossey-Bass.

Pleck, J. H. (1981). *The myth of masculinity*. Cambridge, MA: MIT Press.

Plummer, D. (1999). *One of the boys: Masculinity, homophobia, and modern manhood*. Binghamton, NY: Harrington Park Press.

Pollack, W. S. (2001). *Real boys' voices*. New York, NY: Random House.

Rhoads, R. A. (1995). Whales tales, dog piles, and beer goggles: An ethnographic case study of fraternity life. *Anthropology & Education Quarterly, 26*(3), 306–323.

Rozin, P., Bauer, R., & Catanese, D. (2003). Food and life, pleasure and worry, among American college students: Gender differences and regional similarities. *Journal of Personality and Social Psychology, 85*, 132–141.

Sabo, D. (2005). The study of masculinities and men's health: An overview. In M. Kimmel, J. Hearn, & R. W. Connell (Eds.), *Handbook of studies on men & masculinities* (pp. 326–352). Thousand Oaks, CA: Sage.

Sadker, M., & Sadker, D. (1994). *Failing at fairness*. New York, NY: Charles Scribner's Sons.

Salgado, D. M. (2003). *2003 Campus compact annual membership survey*. Retrieved from www.compact.org/wp-content/uploads/pdf/2003_statistics.pdf

Sax, L. (2008). *The gender gap in college: Maximizing the developmental potential of women and men*. San Francisco, CA: Jossey-Bass.

Sax, L. J., & Harper, C. E. (2007). Origins of the gender gap: Pre-college and college influences on differences between men and women. *Research in Higher Education, 48*(6), 669–694.

Sinclair, L., & Kunda, Z. (2000). Motivated stereotyping of women: She's fine if she praised me, but incompetent if she criticized me. *Personality and Social Psychology Bulletin, 26*(11), 1329–1342.

Smolak, L., & Murnen, S. K. (2001). Gender and eating problems. In R. H. Striegel-Moore & L. Smolak (Eds), *Eating disorders: Innovative directions in research and practice* (pp. 91–110). Washington, DC: American Psychological Association.

Smolak, L., Murnen, S. K., & Ruble, A. E. (2000). Female athletes and eating problems: A meta-analysis. *International Journal of Eating Disorders, 27*(4), 371–380.

Sprague, J., & Massoni, K. (2005). Student evaluations and gendered expectations: What we can't count can hurt us. *Sex Roles, 53*(11/12), 779–793.

Swain, J. (2005). Masculinities in education. In M. Kimmel, J. Hearn, & R. W. Connell (Eds.), *Handbook of studies on men & masculinities* (pp. 213–229). Thousand Oaks, CA: Sage.

Tierney, W. G. (1993). An anthropological analysis of student participation in college. *The Journal of Higher Education, 63*(6), 603–618.

Tisdell, E. J. (2000). Feminist pedagogies. In E. Hayes & D. D. Flannery (Eds.), *Women as learners: The significance of gender in adult learning* (pp. 155–184). San Francisco, CA: Jossey-Bass.

Tonso, K. L. (1996a). Student learning and gender. *Journal of Engineering Education, 85*(2), 143–150.

Tonso, K. L. (1996b). The impact of cultural norms on women. *Journal of Engineering Education, 85*(3), 217–225.

Torres, V., Jones, S., & Renn, K. A. (2009). Identity development theories in student affairs: Origins, current status, and new approaches. *Journal of College Student Development, 50*(6), 577–596.

Weedon, C. (1997). *Feminist practice and poststructuralist theory*. Malden. MA: Blackwell.

Wechsler, H., Davenport, A., Dowdell, G., Moeykens, B., & Castillo, S. (1994). Health and behavioral consequences of binge drinking in college: A national survey of students at 140 campuses. *Journal of the American Medical Association, 272*(21), 1672–1677.

West, C., & Zimmerman, D. H. (1987). Doing gender. *Gender & Society 1*(2), 125–151.

Chapter 11
Engaging Religious Minority Students

Shafiqa Ahmadi and Darnell Cole

The United States of America is the most religiously diverse nation in the world (Eck, 2009). The changes brought about from the 1965 immigration law created opportunities for an emergence of non-European immigrants. With this wave of immigrants came an array of religious traditions from Buddhists to Muslims to Sikhs. While the diversity of these non-Christian religious traditions grew, their numbers remain relatively small when compared to those who identify religiously with some form of Christianity. According to Bryant (2006) "colleges and universities provide a microcosm of American society . . . and must endeavor to create campus climates that are welcoming to students from all faith traditions" (p. 2). In an effort to create an inclusive and welcoming campus milieu for religious minority students (i.e., those who identify as non-Christian), we discuss the following in this chapter: (1) the dominant Christian context undergirding the early development of higher education institutions; (2) the continued prevalence of Christian privilege; (3) the role of religion and the experiences of religious minority students (RMS) in college; and (4) conceptual frameworks for understanding the campus climate and aspects of RMS religiousness. These theoretical perspectives are particularly useful for deconstructing students' religiousness and reconstructing individual agency and institutional responsibility toward enhancing the nature and quality of experiences for religious minority students. In the end, we offer recommendations for improving campus climate and the experiences of religious minority students.

Dominant Christian Context

Brubacher and Rudy (1997) argue that the most compelling reason for the founding of the colonial colleges was the need for "a literate, college-trained clergy" in early American society (p. 6). In fact, all of the nine colonial colleges were either founded or were substantially controlled in efforts to train clergy by an organized Christian group like the Anglicans, Lutherans, Presbyterians, Puritans, or Quakers. Consequently, Christian values and traditions lay at the foundation of American higher education. As these early colleges became today's elite institutions, they were often used as models for the development of other higher education institutions (Brubacher & Rudy, 1997; Rudolph, 1990). As the educational leadership of these early colleges slowly changed away from clergy, secularism began taking shape amid colleges and universities (Stamm, 2003; Wuthnow, 2007). While we are almost 400 years removed from the founding of Harvard in 1636, the first American university, most institutions maintain the vestiges of a Christian centric history. For instance, it is not uncommon to find a chapel on many college campuses, an extensive curriculum about Christianity, and an academic calendar where the institution is closed or classes cancelled on Christian holy days. While most of these holidays are also shared within larger society, religious holidays particular to non-Christian religious groups like Islam and Judaism are often not recognized on the academic calendars of colleges and universities (Brubacher & Rudy, 1997; Rudolph, 1990).

The secularization of American higher education has often been attributed to four historical events: (1) denominational diversity, (2) liberal and practical education, (3) access, and (4) the Carnegie Pension system. The increase of denominational diversity within the colonies and the continued desire from students for a college education prompted greater flexibility in curricular goals as institutions began catering to students' diverse religious denominations. If nothing else, institutional survival necessitated such flexibility and a general broadening of its religious obligation in students' lives. The first and second Morrill Land Grant Acts were the first federal legislation, which provided states with resources to broaden the curriculum and increase access. The first Morrill Land Grant Act of 1862 was the legislation that created, for each eligible state and its citizens, widespread access to a liberal and practical education and, in some instances, military training (Rudolph, 1990). This meant that students were not trained primarily in theology, but in agriculture, mechanics, and/or technology—a secularization of students' education and, substantively, American higher education. Hence, the inclusion of these trades in the original name of some of the oldest state-specific public institutions, such as Alabama A & M (Agricultural and Mechanical) University, Texas A & M (Agricultural and Mechanical) University, and Virginia A & M (Agricultural and Mechanical) Land College, now known as Virginia Polytechnic Institute and State University or Virginia Tech (VT). The second Morrill Act of 1890, however, extended this state-specific access to Black Americans. Primarily aimed at confederate states, where Black people were denied admissions on the basis of race, monetary resources were used to establish some 70 separate higher education institutions, which contributed to what today are federally designated as Historically Black Colleges and Universities (HBCUs)—institutions such as University of Arkansas at Pine Bluff, Alabama A & M University, and Tuskegee University.

Later in 1905, the Carnegie Foundation established a pension plan for American College professors, which specified that only non-denominational schools could partake in the program, encouraging many institutions to formally drop their religious affiliation (Kohlbrenner, 1961). The evolution of this retirement investment system is now known as Teachers Insurance and Annuity Association of America (TIAA), which later added the College Retirement Equities Fund (CREF) in the 1950s—hence TIAA-CREF. Also during the 20th century, scientific inquiry, objectivism, and modernism became more influential within college curriculum, further secularizing institutions of higher education (Eisenmann, 1999; Marsden, 1994). American colleges and universities came to embody the Western positivistic paradigm, which honored value-free inquiry (Palmer, 1993). By the last half of the 20th century, American colleges and universities began to experience the paradox that while their campuses were becoming more religiously diverse, due to the influx of a diverse student body, religion was simultaneously becoming less essential to the mission of higher education. Despite the fact that religious higher education (i.e., colleges and universities with strong faith identities) has been on the rise, religion has become further marginalized on secular college campuses (Riley, 2005).

Christian Privilege

The 2008 American Religious Identification Survey (ARIS) found that of the 228 million people polled, 76% identified as some type of Christian (Table 11.1). The Pew Forum on Religion and Public Life survey (2008a, 2008b) reported similar results with about 5% identifying as a religion other than Christian or Catholic (see Table 11.2). Subtle and overt references to Christianity can also be seen throughout American "secular" culture, such as

TABLE 11.1. Self-Described Religious Identification of Adult Population: 1990, 2001, and 2008

Religious Group	1990		2001		2008	
	Estimated Number of People	Percent of People	Estimated Number of People	Percent of People	Estimated Number of People	Percent of People
Catholic	46,004,000	26.2	50,873,000	24.5	57,199,000	25.1
Other Christian	105,221,000	60.0	108,641,000	52.2	116,203,000	50.9
Total Christian (Including Catholic)	**151,225,000**	**86.2**	**159,514,000**	**76.7**	**173,402,000**	**76.0**
Other Religions	5,853,000	3.3	7,740,000	3.7	8,796,000	3.9
Non-theist/ No Religion	14,331,000	8.2	29,481,000	14.1	34,169,000	15.0
Don't know or Declined to State	4,031,000	2.3	11,246,000	5.4	11,815,000	5.2
Total	**175,440,000**	**100**	**207,983,000**	**100**	**228,182,000**	**100**

TABLE 11.2. Statistics on Religion in America

Religious Group	Estimated Percent
Other Religions	**4.7%**
Jewish	1.7%
Muslim	0.6%
Buddhist	0.7%
Hindu	0.4%
Other World Religion	< 0.3%
Other Faith	1.2%
Unaffiliated	**16.1%**
Don't Know or Refused to State	**0.8%**
Christian	**78.4%**
Protestant	51.3%
Evangelical Churches	26.3%
Mainline Churches	18.1%
Historically Black Churches	6.9%
Catholic	23.9%
Mormon (LDS)	1.7%
Jehovah's Witness	0.7%
Orthodox	0.6%
Other Christian	0.3%

Note: Taken from the Pew Forum on Religion and Public Life (2008b) based on data obtained from the United States Census Bureau (2011).

the national celebration of Christmas, "one nation under God" in our pledge of alliance, and "in God we trust" on our currency (Clark & Brimhall-Vargas, 2003). Due to their high numbers and historical foundation, Christians typically have more power than all minority religious groups combined on campus, which can create contexts where religious minorities are vulnerable to oppression and discrimination (Clark & Brimhall-Vargas, 2003; Schlosser, 2003). The commercial proliferation of Christianity into the secular realm is often unrecognized because, like other forms of privilege, it often remains undetected by mainstream society (Clark & Brimhall-Vargas, 2003; McIntosh, 1988).

The conscious and subconscious advantages often afforded to members of the Christian faith have been identified as Christian privilege and can be seen on many colleges and universities (Clark & Brimhall-Vargas, 2003; Schlosser, 2003). The privileged majority is comprised solely of Christian denominations, which include mainline Protestant faiths—Episcopalian, Presbyterian, Methodist, Lutheran, and United Church of Christ/Congregational (Bonderud & Fleischer, 2005; Roof & McKinney, 1987). Other relatively privileged Christian groups include Roman Catholic, Baptist, Church of Christ, and other Christians (Bowman & Small, 2010). Religious minorities include those who identify as: Buddhist, Hindu, Muslim, Quaker, Jewish, and in some cases LDS (Mormon) and Unitarians (Bowman & Small, 2010) (see Table 11.3).

TABLE 11.3. Religious Self-Identification of the U.S. Adult Population 1990, 2001, 2008

Religious Group	1990 Estimated Number of People	2001 Estimated Number of People	2008 Estimated Number of People
Jewish	3,137,000	2,837,000	2,680,000
Muslim	527,000	1,104,000	1,349,000*
Buddhist	404,000	1,082,000	1,189,000
Unitarian/Universalist	502,000	629,000	586,000
Hindu	227,000	766,000	582,000
Native American	47,000	103,000	186,000
Sikh	13,000	57,000	78,000
Wiccan	8,000	134,000	342,000
Pagan	N/A	140,000	340,000
Spiritualist	N/A	116,000	426,000
Other Unclassified	991,000	774,000	1,030,000
Total	**5,853,000**	**7,740,000**	**8,796,000**

Note: Taken from data obtained from American Religious Identification Survey (ARIS) 2008.
* The number of Muslims in America has been estimated to be as much as 6 to 7 Million (Cole & Ahmadi, 2010).

In institutions of higher education, Christian students enjoy a number of daily advantages including: widely accepted positive portrayals of their faith in mainstream media, privilege in the institution's calendar, and privilege in on-campus dining options (Seifert, 2007). State and federal holidays often coincide with Christian holidays and days of religious observances, while marginalized non-Christian students must negotiate conflicts between their studies and their spiritual practices (Schlosser & Sedlacek, 2003). Christians are also unlikely to know or believe that the American college environment is oppressive because that environment has rarely, if ever, been hostile towards their faith (Schlosser, 2003). Additionally, Christian privilege has the potential to stifle non-Christian students' expression of their spiritual identity, while simultaneously forestalling or foreclosing Christian's students' critical examination of their privileged position (Seifert, 2007).

Religion in Higher Education

Most administrators and faculty within public institutions of higher education are hesitant to engage students' religious beliefs for fear of alienating students or impinging on students constitutional rights (Clark, 2003; Jablonski, 2001). Administrators often claim that issues of religion and spirituality are private matters, citing the "separation of church and state" clause as evidence that they cannot promote religion within the public realm on their campuses (Collins et al., 1987; Hamburger, 2002). Public institutions, however, are legally allowed to provide campus space (i.e., meeting room, bulletin boards), non-coercive prayer environments, opportunities to engage in religious and spiritual classroom discussions, and the right to organize—as long as the student organization pursues lawful goals, pose no significant threat of material disruption, and conform to a reasonable set of school-based policies (Lowery, 2004, 2005). Yet, public institutions must remain neutral and "cannot favor or support religion over non-religion" (Kaplin & Lee, 2007, p. 56).

Despite the fear of legal challenges, the consideration of religion in higher education has been shown to promote positive social and cognitive outcomes for students. The Fetzer institute released a report in 1999, and then a revised version in 2003, which indicates that various dimensions of religiousness and spirituality enhance students' sense of well-being (Ellison 1991), lower levels of depression and psychological distress (Idler, 1987; Williams et al., 1991), and reduces morbidity and mortality (Levin, 1996). Other scholars have also found a positive link between religiosity and mental/emotional health, which includes life satisfaction, happiness, purpose and meaning, hope, optimism, and lower numbers of depression and anxiety (Bonderud & Fleischer, 2004; Koenig, 2001; Koenig, McCullough, & Larson, 2001).

By cultivating a more conducive space for religious engagement, colleges can contribute to students' development, sense of belonging, and overall satisfaction with college, which is also significantly related to college student persistence (Astin, Astin, & Lindholm, 2011a; Hurtado & Carter, 1997; Mooney, 2005). Astin et al. (2011a) found that increased satisfaction with college was related to equanimity, or the extent to which the student feels at peace and is able to find meaning in times of hardship. While many students report that their religion provides such feelings of peace, identity development, and moments of transcendence, students who engage in spirituality-enhancing activities are also more likely to engage in a broader cross-section of collegiate activities, such as exercising, attending cultural events, and performing community service (Astin, 1993; Bryant, 2006; Kuh & Gonyea, 2005). Furthermore, religious communities can offer young adults supportive mentoring environments that allow questioning and provide challenge and support toward students' overall development in college (Parks, 2000).

Challenges Religious Minority Students Face

Although many colleges and universities have shifted away from their religious foundations, a Christian ethos continues to permeate many campus cultures, which can at times alienate non-Christian students (McEwen, 1996; Schlosser, 2003). Arguably, religious minorities are more likely to experience spiritual struggle during the college years; these struggles are often exacerbated by the lack of support and understanding from those who do not share similar beliefs. By contrast, when students have faculty support for spiritual/religious development, religious engagement, and, to a lesser extent, interactions with others who hold similar religious beliefs, they are more likely to experience positive gains in religious growth and development (Bowman & Small, 2010; Bryant & Astin, 2008). Interestingly, religious minority students are acutely aware of their marginalization and that their ways of viewing the world frequently distinguishes them from the majority of

Christian students (Small, 2008). Being surrounded by conflicting ideologies can produce cognitive disequilibrium, which, if fostered in a supportive educational environment, can enhance critical thinking skills (Gurin, Dey, Hurtado & Gurin, 2002 ; Cole & Ahmadi, 2010); yet, students can also experience behavioral barriers and psychological stressors that inhibit their religious and spiritual development (Cole & Ahmadi, 2003, 2010; Mahaffey & Smith, 2009; Schlosser & Sedlacek, 2003).

In terms of the behavioral barriers, religious holidays, dietary restrictions, access to safe spaces for spiritual expression pose significant challenges for religious minority students (Mahaffey & Smith, 2009; Mayhew & Bryant, 2013). The most obvious, as noted earlier, are religious holidays. While many institutions allow excused absences, the burden of proof and obtaining written support from one's religious community is a responsibility completely left up to the non-Christian student (Mahaffey & Smith, 2009; Schlosser & Sedlacek, 2001). For instance, Wesak, celebrated by many Buddhists, Diwali, celebrated by many Hindus, the holy days of Rosh Hashanah and Yom Kippur, celebrated by many Jewish students, and *Eid Al-Fitr* and Eid Al-Adha, celebrated by many Muslims, require similar accommodations as those taken-for-granted by many Christians celebrating Christmas during what is typically referred to simply as "winter break." Although some reports indicate an increase in vegan and vegetarian options on college campuses, students' whose religious observance requires kosher or *halal* dishes are often unable to find satisfactory dining options on campus (Mahaffey & Smith, 2009; Rifkin, 2004). As a result, dining spaces are not optimally used to facilitate natural conversations regarding the intersections of religious observance and dietary restrictions or opportunities to eat with peers who hold similar restrictions. The access to and a place for spiritual expression extends well beyond lost dining hall conversations. There needs to be prayer spaces for communal prayer for Muslim students, for example, and religious study group spaces, akin to Bible study groups.

The psychological stressors religious minority students face in large part is due to the tensions experienced by these campus barriers to religious engagement, in that students become isolated and feel alienated or marginalized through their campus experiences (Mahaffrey & Smith, 2009). World events, which inform the socio-cultural climate of college campuses, the misinformation (or lack of information) regarding different religious traditions, and religious ideology regarding "truth" provide additional stressors confronting students. Several authors, for instance, have reported on the aftermath of the September 11, 2001, terrorist attacks where Muslim college students (and those students perceived as Muslim) were threatened, attacked, and beaten (Ahmadi, 2011; Cole & Ahmadi, 2003, 2010). The recent disclosure of the New York Police Department's (NYPD) undercover surveillance operation on over a dozen college campuses throughout the northeastern United States further underscores the ongoing Islamaphobic zeitgeist that persists not only in our larger social context, but also on college campuses (Ahmadi, 2011; Hawley, 2012). The NYPD, "In one report, [had] an undercover officer . . . accompanying 18 Muslim students from the City College of New York on a whitewater rafting trip in upstate New York on April 21, 2008" (Hawley, 2012, para. 8). The perception and misinformation regarding Muslims is that anyone of them can be a terrorist. Negative stereotypes like these and others, such as all Buddhists are Asian, all Muslims are Arab, and all Jews are White, often serve to further alienate students from non-Christian mainline religious traditions. Mayhew and Bryant (2013), for example, assert that

> students' perceptions of the psychological climate around religion, spirituality, and ideology on campus create (or undermine) opportunities for curricular and co-curricular engagements and challenging experiences. (p. 65)

The psychological climates, where such stressors are pervasive for religious minority students, are likely to exaggerate students' feelings of alienation, which increases the likelihood of becoming isolated.

Theoretical Perspectives

While Fowler (1981) and Parks (2000) provide developmental models often referenced when conceptualizing and discussing faith and spiritual growth, we offer two college impact models useful for examining the effects of college on religious minority students. The first is the campus climate conceptual framework proposed by Hurtado, Milem, Clayton-Pedersen, and Allen (1998) and extended by Milem, Chang, and antonio (2005). This framework has four original dimensions, which consider both institutional responsibility and individual agency in the complex constructions of college impact on students of color. We use these dimensions and extend their application to religious minority students. The second framework is relatively new and offers conceptual measures of spirituality and religiousness. This framework, provided by Astin, Astin, and Lindholm (2011b), allows one to identify and empirically measure students' spirituality and religiousness as growth indices during one of the most important developmental contexts in the lives of young adults—college.

Campus Climate

According to Hurtado and colleagues (1998), students are educated in racial and ethnic campus climates that vary from campus to campus. While campus climate as a conceptual framework has typically been applied to the campus racial climate, we propose a similar utility for understanding the campus climate for religious minority students (Mayhew & Bryant, 2013). The racial and ethnic climate of a campus is shaped by the interaction of external and internal forces (Hurtado et al., 1998). External forces are represented in two domains: (1) governmental policy, programs, and initiatives; and (2) socio-historical forces (Hurtado et al., 1998). Examples of the former include financial aid policies and programs, court decisions on the desegregation of higher education, and state and federal policies on affirmative action (Hurtado et al., 1998). When applied to the role of religion in postsecondary education, an example of the legal view is the separation of church and state. Socio-historic forces are events or issues in the larger society that influence how people view racial and ethnic diversity in society (Hurtado et al., 1998). While external forces occur "outside" a college campus, Hurtado et al. (1998)

stress that they serve as stimuli for diversity-related discussions and/or activities that occur on campus. In the case of religion, national and world conflicts like the terrorist attacks of September 11 offer such socio-historical examples.

Internal forces are composed of four interconnected dimensions (Hurtado et al., 1998); (1) historical legacy of inclusion or exclusion; (2) structural diversity; (3) psychological climate; and (4) behavioral climate. The first dimension—an institution's historical legacy of inclusion or exclusion—refers to the institution's initial response to the admission of students of color (Hurtado et al., 1998). A college's inclusionary or exclusionary past is relevant because it can determine the prevailing climate and influence current diversity practices (Hurtado et al., 1998). Yet, in the context of religious diversity, we assert that institutional type (public vs. private) and religious affiliation (historical vs. current) are likely to impact the embedded nature in which cultural values and traditions are recognized or become implicit as the normative backdrop for which institutional policies are derived and maintained with regard to admissions practices, university holidays, and the like. Structural diversity, the second dimension, is an institution's numerical representation of various racial/ethnic groups. An institution's structural diversity is significant because it conveys whether maintaining a multicultural environment is a high institutional priority (Hurtado et al., 1998). Structural diversity in terms of ethnicity can also include the representation of different religious traditions in campus' student body. In fact, Cole and Ahmadi (2010) found that religiously diverse student groups can extend traditional definitions of diversity beyond race. They found that religious minorities, such as Muslim and Jewish students, were less likely to spend time in prayer when compared to their Christian peers; Muslim students were also more likely to interact with peers different from themselves when compared to both Christian and Jewish students.

The third dimension, psychological climate, focuses on individuals' views of group relations, institutional responses to diversity, perceptions of discrimination, and attitudes toward groups of different racial/ethnic backgrounds (Hurtado et al., 1998). Hurtado et al. (1998) indicate that *who* people are and *where* people are positioned in an institution shape the manner in which they experience and view the institution. Consequently, students' perceptions are a product of the environment and will influence future interactions as well as the outcomes gained by their interactions (Berger & Milem, 1999). These perceptions include the religious values and social dispositions students bring with them to college. The final dimension, the behavioral climate, consists of: (a) the status of social interactions; (b) the nature of interactions between individuals from different racial/ethnic backgrounds; and (c) the quality of intergroup relations (Hurtado et al., 1998). Hence, *when*, with *whom*, and *how* individuals interact serve as indicators of an institution's campus climate, which also consists of the religious activities student create and pursue during college. For instance, Cole and Ahmadi (2003) reported that Muslim women who maintained their veiling practice in the face of harsh campus-related discrimination did so because of their religious commitment and active involvement with members of their religious community on and off campus.

Milem et al. (2005), however, expand Hurtado et al.'s (1998) model and propose a fifth dimension of campus climate. Specifically, this fifth dimension represents the organizational and structural aspects of colleges, which considers among other student services, racial/ethnic community centers and racial/ethnic student organizations. The organizational aspects of college are also represented through religious-oriented student centers and student organizations that are either cultural or dogmatic in their religious affiliation; student centers, like Hillel, Chalutzim, Muslim Student Association or Muslim Student Union (MSA or MSU), offer religious minority students the structural and organizational representation to support services specific to their religious engagement on campus.

Spirituality and Religiousness

Astin and colleagues (2011b) have identified 10 interrelated measures of spirituality and religiousness; five measures for spirituality and five measures for religiousness, and offer an empirically-driven framework for examining and understanding students' spiritual sense of self. The first two measures, constructed as an inward focus of spirituality, include equanimity (i.e., feeling of peace or centering) and spiritual quest (i.e., the search for meaning and/or one's life purpose). Ecumenical worldview, charitable involvement, and ethic of caring comprise the external foci of spirituality and the extent to which students feel connected to people around them. An ecumenical worldview reflects students' interest in other religious traditions and sense of connectedness to a broad construct of humanity. Charitable involvement and ethic of caring is the extent of students' community service and value toward helping others, respectively.

Yet, within the context of this chapter, the constructs guiding students' religiousness may offer a more useful conceptual frame for understanding the role of religion in students' lives. Of the five constructs, religious commitment is considered an inward focus on the essential role of religion and how religious beliefs affect students' daily lives, whereas religious engagement is the external representation of commitment in that, religious engagement considers the type and frequency of religious-related activities such praying, attending religious services, religious singing, and reading. The other three constructs reflect students' dispositions regarding their religiousness, and include, social conservatism, skepticism, and struggle. Religious conservatism reflects students' views on social issues, "commitment to proselytize," and "God as a father figure" (Astin et al., 2011b, p. 21). Religious skepticism, however, is perhaps more agnostic in its framing and considers "beliefs such as the 'universe arose by chance' and 'in the future, science will be able to explain everything'" (p.21). Unlike religious skepticism or conservatism, religious struggle seems to be just that—the extent to which students have questions, are unsettled, or are unsure about their religious beliefs or matters concerning their religious upbringing.

While Astin et al. (2001b) identify the interrelatedness of spirituality and religiousness, there are two critical findings regarding the relationships among these constructs. First, religious commitment, engagement, and social conservatism tend to be highly correlated; students with high commitment are likely to be highly engaged and have conservative social values and dispositions. Accordingly, these students are also likely *not* to be skeptical in their religious beliefs. Students who are struggling, however, are likely ". . . not to show any substantial relationship with other religious or spiritual measures" (p. 22). These constructs provide an organizing conceptual frame for making sense of students' religious experiences while in college, but lack a specific focus on the interactions between religious minority students in a non-religious or dominant religious institutional context.

Student Engagement Strategies

America was founded on the bases of religious freedom. In fact, the establishment clause of the First Amendment states that public institutions must maintain a neutral stance regarding religious beliefs and activities (Kaplin & Lee, 2007). Institutions of higher education may permit non-coercive religious activity. Private institutions, on the other hand, have no obligation of neutrality under the Constitution. If, however, a private institution discriminates based on religion, the federal government can take action (e.g., take the private institution's tax-exempt status away), because it has a compelling interest in eradicating all forms of discrimination. Most institutions of higher education operate from a dominant Christian ideology and Christian privilege, which could be viewed as coercive religious activity. Mayhew and Bryant (2013) assert that

> Higher education administrators and faculty can strive to minimize coercion on campus by formulating non-coercive policies for recognized student religious, spiritual, and ideological organizations on campus; providing opportunities for students to engage one another with respect, compassion, and openness; and modeling the principles of constructive exchange within the classroom and co-curricular programming. (p. 81)

It is within this context of constructive curricular and co-curricular exchange that we identify a number of policy recommendations and best practices. We assert that postsecondary institutions should support underrepresented religious groups where students can have a formal mechanism for organizing themselves under a particular religious denomination or expression like RecKlez, The Harvard Klezmer Band (Ashkenazic Jewish culture), and The Hindu Student Council & Young Jains of America at University of Pennsylvania. Institutional agents, like faculty and student affairs personnel, can serve as advisors to students interested in participating in a particular religious/spiritual group (Mahaffey & Smith, 2009). Additionally, a list of recognized groups and organizations widely available could facilitate students' integration into campus life.

Institutions should consider sponsoring theme housing where students can have a residential space to live, learn, and eat together creating both intra- and intergroup engagement among students who share either the same category of religious identification or important similarities in diet, modesty, or religious/spiritual interests. Examples include the Jewish Life House at Wheaton College, the Bodhi (Buddhist) House at Earlham, or the Religious Diversity House at Union College. A seamless living-learning campus experience, when both social and academic programs are intentional, can engage the complexities of students' lived experiences and their developing religious identities.

Providing campus spaces for students' religious-related activities such as prayer rooms or programming areas display value for religious minority students and their religious needs. This can facilitate meaningful forms of institutional connectedness. Committing such institutional resources to meet the needs of religious minority students also has the capacity to communicate more than value, but a fundamental understanding of who these students are in terms of their developing religious identities. Moreover, considering the physical structure and scheduling alternatives at fitness facilities (Cole & Ahmadi, 2003; Mahaffey & Smith, 2009) can also make the campus environment inclusive. For example, fitness facilities can schedule gender-specific times for "women only swim time," which can be helpful to some Muslim and Jewish women who would not use the pool when men are present.

Institutions should sponsor multi-faith programming where students' diverse religious backgrounds offer opportunities to reflect on what it means to engage in multi-faith dialogue, awareness, and questioning in a safe environment. For example, annual inter-faith week, service-learning projects, leadership training or even a multi-faith student choir like SHANTI at the University Southern California are the types of activities common among active multi-faith organizations. Offering co-curricular opportunities for non-religious students to explore their spiritual and existential philosophies (Mayhew & Bryant, 2013) is also essential for creating a safe environment where understanding, respect, and acceptance are of utmost importance.

Initiating dialogue with students (Cole & Ahmadi, 2003; Mahaffey & Smith, 2009; Mayhew & Bryant, 2013) outside of the classroom about the nature of their religious interactions and their campus experience(s) can inform existing conversations about religion on campus. Such dialogue can alter feelings or perceptions of being marginalized, particularly if the recommendations derived from those conversations influence institutional policies and practices. These dialogues can have important institutional benefits regarding a university's mission and the quality of students' college experiences.

Providing support to religious minority students can also come in the form of mentoring. Faculty and student affairs educators who identify with these religions can mentor students not just within the context of on campus religious organizations, but also when students face issues within their academic careers or life's challenges. For instance, the University of Southern California has several positions that allow for support and mentorship, including a Dean of Religious Life, Director of Muslim Student Life, Director of Spirituality and Sexuality, and Director of Hindu Student Life. These directors assist students with religious/spiritual issues.

Understanding the intersection of identities (Cole & Ahmadi, 2010; Mahaffey & Smith, 2009) and knowing that religion is not the only identity that one possesses is important. For example, the intersection of race, gender, and religion is essential to how some students self-identify. One can be African American, Jewish, and female or Chinese, gay, and Muslim. In today's global environment, institutions of higher education should strive to celebrate and support the intersection of students' identities. These recommendations provide possibilities for religious minority students to experience a campus environment that is more attuned to their diverse needs.

References

Ahmadi, S. (2011). The erosion of civil rights: Exploring the effects of the Patriot Act on Muslims in American higher education. *Rutgers Race and the Law Review, 12*(1), 1–56.

Astin, A. W. (1993). *What matters in college? Four critical years revisited.* San Francisco, CA: Jossey-Bass.

Astin, A. W., Astin, H. S., & Lindholm, J. A. (2011a). Assessing students' spiritual and religious qualities. *Journal of College Student Development, 52*(1), 39–61.

Astin, A. W., Astin, H. S., & Lindholm, J. A. (2011b). *Cultivating the spirit: How college can enhance students' inner lives.* San Francisco, CA: Jossey-Bass.

Berger, J. B., & Milem, J. F. (1999). The role of student involvement and perceptions of integration in a causal model of student persistence. *Research in higher Education, 40*(6), 641–664.

Bonderud, K., & Fleischer, M. (2004). *New study of college students finds connection between spirituality, religiousness, and mental health.* Los Angeles, CA: University of California, Los Angeles, Higher Education Research Institute.

Bonderud, K., & Fleischer, M. (2005). *College students report high levels of spirituality and religiousness: Major study has implications for colleges, health, and politics.* Los Angeles, CA: University of California, Los Angeles, Higher Education Research Institute.

Bowman, N. A., & Small, J. L. (2010). Do college students who identify with a privilege religion experience greater spiritual development? Exploring individual and institutional dynamics. *Research in Higher Education, 51,* 595–614.

Brubacher, J. S., & Rudy, W. (1997). *Higher education in transition: A history of American colleges and universities.* Piscataway, NJ: Transaction Publishers.

Bryant, A. N. (2006). Exploring religious pluralism in higher education: Non-majority religious perspectives among entering first-year college students. *Religion & Education, 33*(1), 1–25.

Bryant, A. N., & Astin, H. S. (2008). The correlates of spiritual struggle during the college years. *Journal of Higher Education, 79*(1), 1–28.

Clark, R. T. (2003). The law and spirituality: How the law supports and limits expression of spirituality on the college campus. In M. A. Jablonski (Ed.), *The implications of student spirituality for student affairs practice. New Directions for Student Services* (No. 95, pp. 37–46). San Francisco, CA: Jossey-Bass.

Clark, C., & Brimhall-Vargas, M. (2003). Diversity initiatives in higher education: Secular aspects and international implications of Christian privilege. *Multicultural Education, 11,* 55–57.

Cole, D.G., & Ahmadi, S. (2003). Perspectives and experiences of Muslim women who veil on college campuses. *Journal of College Student Development, 44*(1), 47–66.

Cole, D.G., & Ahmadi, S. (2010). Reconsidering campus diversity: An examination of Muslim students' experience. *The Journal of Higher Education, 81*(2), 121–139.

Collins, J.R., Hurst, J.C., & Jacobsen, J.K. (1987). The blind spot extended: Spirituality. *Journal of College Student Personnel, 28*(3), 274–76.

Eck, D.L. (2009). *A new religious America: How a "Christian country" has become the world's most religiously diverse nation.* New York, NY: HarperCollins.

Eisenmann, L. (1999). Reclaiming religion: New historiographic challenges in the relationship of religion and American higher education. *History of Education Quarterly, 39*(3), 295–306.

Ellison C.G. (1991) Religious involvement and subjective well-being. *Journal of Health and Social Behavior, 32,* 80–99.

Fetzer Institute/National Institute on Aging Working Group (1999). *Multidimensional Measurement of Religiousness/Spirituality for Use in Health Research: A Report of the Fetzer Institute/National Institute on Aging Working Group* (1st ed.). Kalamazoo, MI: Fetzer Institute.

Fowler, J.W. (1981). *Stages of faith: The psychology of human development and the quest for meaning.* New York, NY: HarperCollins.

Gurin, P., Dey, E.L., Hurtado, S., & Gurin, G. (2002). Diversity and higher education: theory and impact on educational outcomes. *Harvard Educational Review, 72*(3) 330–366.

Hamburger, P. (2002). *Separation of church and state.* Cambridge, MA: Harvard University Press.

Hawley, C. (2012, February, 8). *NYPD monitored Muslim students all over the northeast.* Retrieved on April 1, 2012, from http://ap.org/Content/AP-In-The-News/2012/NYPD-monitored-Muslim-students-all-over-Northeast

Hurtado, S., & Carter, D.F. (1997). Effects of college transition and perceptions of the campus racial climate on Latino college students' sense of belonging. *Sociology of Education, 70*(4), 324–345.

Hurtado, S., Milem, J.F., Clayton-Pedersen, A.R., & Allen, W.R. (1998). Enhancing campus climates for racial/ethnic diversity: Educational policy and practice. *The Review of Higher Education, 21,* 279–302.

Idler, E.L. (1987). Religious involvement and the health of the elderly: Some hypotheses and an initial test. *Social Forces, 66,* 226–238.

Jablonski, M.A. (2001). Editor's notes. In M.A. Jablonski (Ed.), *Implications of student spirituality for student affairs practice. New Directions for Student Services* (No. 95, pp. 1–5). San Francisco, CA: Jossey-Bass.

Kaplin, W.A., & Lee, B.A. (2007). *The law of higher education.* (4th ed.) San Francisco, CA: Jossey-Bass.

Koenig, H.G. (2001). Religion and medicine II: Religion, mental health, and related behaviors. *International Journal of Psychiatry in Medicine, 31*(1), 97–109.

Koenig, H.G., McCullough, M., & Larson, D.B. (2001). *Handbook of religion and health.* New York, NY: Oxford University Press.

Kohlbrenner, B.J. (1961). Religion and higher education: An historical perspective. *History of Education Quarterly, 1*(2), 45–56.

Kuh, G.D., & Gonyea, R.M. (2005). *Exploring the relationships between spirituality, liberal learning, and college student engagement.* Bloomington, IN: Indiana University. Retrieved September 16, 2011, from, www.nsse.iub.edu/pdf/research_papers/teagle.pdf

Levin, J.S. (1996). How religion influences morbidity and health: reflections on natural history, salutogenesis and host resistance. *Social Science Medicine, 43,* 849–864.

Lowery, J.W. (2004). Understanding the legal protections and limitations upon religion and spiritual expression on campus. *College Student Affairs Journal, 23*(2), 146–157.

Lowery J.W. (2005). What higher education law says about spirituality. *New Directions for Teaching and Learning, 104,* 15–22.

Mahaffey, C.J. & Smith, S.A. (2009). "Creating welcoming campus environments for students from minority religious groups." In S.R. Harper & S.J. Quaye (Eds.), *Student engagement in higher education: Theoretical perspectives and practical approaches for diverse populations* (pp. 81–97). New York, NY: Routledge.

Marsden, G.M. (1994). *The soul of the American university: From Protestant establishment to established non-belief.* New York, NY: Oxford University Press.

Mayhew, M. J., & Bryant, A. N. (2013). Achievement or arrest? The influence of the collegiate religious and spiritual climate on students' worldview commitment. *Research in Higher Education, 54*(1), 63–84.

McEwen, M. K. (1996). New perspectives on identity development. In S. R. Komives & D. B. Woodard (Eds.), *Student services: A handbook for the profession* (3rd ed., pp. 188–217). San Francisco, CA: Jossey Bass.

McIntosh, P. (1988). *White privilege and male privilege: A personal account of coming to see correspondences through work in women's studies.* Wellesley, MA: Wellesley College Center for Research on Women.

Milem, J. F., Chang, M. J., & antonio, A. L. (2005). *Making diversity work on campus: A research-based perspective.* Washington, DC: Association of American Colleges and Universities.

Mooney, M. (2005). *Does religion influence college satisfaction of grades earned? Evidence from the National Longitudinal Survey of Freshmen (NLSF).* Manuscript submitted for publication.

National Survey of Student Engagement (2010). NSSE benchmarks of effective educational practice. Indiana Postsecondary Research and Planning. Bloomington, IN.

Palmer, P. J. (1993). To *know as we are known: Education* as *spiritual journey.* San Francisco, CA: Harper.

Parks, S. D. (2000). *Big questions, worthy dreams: Mentoring young adults in their search for meaning, purpose, and faith.* San Francisco, CA: Jossey-Bass.

Pew Forum on Religion and Public Life. (2008a). *U.S. religious landscape survey,* Chapter 1: Religious composition of the United States (pp. 10–21). November 19, 2011, from http://religions.pewforum.org/pdf/report-religious-landscape-study-chapter-1.pdf

Pew Forum on Religion and Public Life. (2008b). *U.S. religious landscape survey,* Chapter 3: Religious affiliation and demographic group (pp. 40–41). Retrieved September 16, 2011, from http://religions.pewforum.org/pdf/report-religious-landscape-study-chapter-3.pdf

Riley, N. S. (2005). *God on the quad.* New York, NY: St. Martin's Press.

Rifkin, I. (2004). *Spiritual perspectives on globalization: Making sense of economic and cultural upheaval.* Woodstock, VT: SkyLight Paths Publishing.

Roof, W. C., & McKinney, W. (1987). *American mainline religion: Its changing shape and future.* New Brunswick, NJ: Rutgers University Press.

Rudolph, F. (1990). The American college and university. Athens, GA: University of Georgia Press.

Schlosser, L. Z. (2003). Christian privilege: Breaking a sacred taboo. *Journal of Multicultural Counseling and Development, 31*(Jan.), 44–51.

Schlosser, L. Z., & Sedlacek, W. (2003). Christian privilege and respect for religious diversity: Religious holidays on campus. *About Campus, 7*(6), 28–29.

Seifert, T. (2007). Understanding Christian privilege: Managing the tensions of spiritual plurality. *About Campus, 12*(2), 10–18.

Small, J. L. (2008). *College student religious affiliation and spiritual identity: A qualitative study.* Unpublished doctoral dissertation, University of Michigan, Ann Arbor, MI.

Stamm, L. (2003). Can we bring spirituality back to campus? Higher education's re-engagement with values and spirituality. *Journal of College and Character, 4*(5). Retrieved from www.degruyter.com/view/j/jcc.2003.4.5/jcc.2003.4.5.1354/jcc.2003.4.5.1354.xml?format=INT

United States Census Bureau (2011). Statistical abstract of the United States: 2012. Retrieved November 19, 2011, from www.census.gov/compendia/statab/2012/tables/12s0075.pdf

Williams, D. R., Larson, D. B., Buckler, R. E., Heckmann, R. C., & Pyle C. M., (1991). Religion and psychological distress in a community sample. *Social Science Medicine, 32,* 1257–1262.

Wuthnow, R. (2007). Can faith be more than a slide show in the contemporary academy? In D. Jacobsen & R. H. Jacobsen (Eds.), *The American University in a postsecular Age: Religion and higher education* (pp. 31–44). New York, NY: Oxford University Press.

Chapter 12
Engaging Students with Disabilities

Kirsten Brown and Ellen M. Broido

Students with disabilities are a rapidly growing, yet historically underrepresented population in postsecondary education. Historically, underrepresented groups share a common experience: all faced unwelcoming environments when initially entering higher education (Hall & Belch, 2000). Ableism (the oppression of people with disabilities) plays a powerful role in shaping the way students with and without disabilities experience the educational environments, because "[b]y assuming one normative way to do things (move, speak, learn, and so forth), society privileges those who carry out these functions as prescribed and oppresses those who use other methods" (Evans, Forney, Guido, Patton, & Renn, 2010, p. 242). To create engaging environments for students with disabilities, we need to identify and address ways in which ableism shapes the experiences of members of our campus communities.

It is important to start by making a distinction between disability and impairment. In this chapter, we follow the definitions provided by Evans and Herriott (2009), who used *impairment* to refer to "any condition that results in a way of functioning or results in behavior that differs from the expected level of performance in any given area" (p. 29); essentially, impairments are ways in which people's bodies or minds differ from what society defines as normal. *Disability* is defined in many different ways, depending on the theoretical perspective one uses. In this chapter, we use the term to mean how society responds to people with impairments, particularly ways that exclude, discriminate against, or stigmatize people with disabilities (Sherry, 2004). Disabilities are consequences of attitudes and physical or social environments that support only putatively normal ways of doing things (Griffin, Peters, & Smith, 2007). As Riddell, Tinklin, and Wilson (2005) noted, "A key idea is that impairment does not necessarily result in disability, and in an ideal society, where all barriers were removed, disability would cease to exist" (p. 16). One way to indicate the distinction between impairment and disability is to use "person-first" language. Person-first language (e.g., student with a disability) is a way of speaking that gives precedent to the individual rather than the disability, thereby linguistically recognizing that the disability is only one facet of the individual (Hall & Belch, 2000). In summary, when conceptualizing issues of student engagement, it is important to understand that the individual may have the impairment but the environment produces the disability.

Like other marginalized groups, students with disabilities differ from each other in numerous ways. Most obvious are demographic differences, including gender, race, ethnicity, age, religion, sexual orientation, social class, nationality, and veteran status. Students with disabilities also differ from each other by their type of impairment and the extent, duration, and continuity of their impairment. Mention the term *disabled student* and many people picture a student using a wheelchair, or perhaps with a guide dog. However, most college students with disabilities have invisible forms of impairments (U.S. Government Accountability Office, 2009), such as learning disabilities, emotional disabilities, attention deficit disorder, chronic health conditions, and neurologic impairments. Some people are born with impairments, but many develop them over the course of their lifespan, including just before or while they are college students. Some impairments require medical management, but many do not. Some people's impairments are stable over the course of their lives, and others experience periods in which the impairment is or more less intrusive. Some people strongly identify as having a disability, and many others eschew this term. For all these reasons, it is important not to generalize about students with disabilities, and to instead, understand the needs and desires of the particular individuals with disabilities with whom one works.

Historical and Demographic Enrollment Trends

"No comprehensive history of people with disabilities in higher education exists . . ." (Mueller & Broido, 2012, p. 101). Notable historical examples of students with disabilities in the college or university environment include deaf students founding Gallaudet University in 1864 (Hall & Belch, 2000), Helen Keller entering Radcliffe College in 1900, and veterans with disabilities advocating for formal support programs at the University of Illinois following World War II (Dean, 2009). Despite these examples, the development of large-scale services for students with disabilities did not occur until after 1973, when Section 504 of the Rehabilitation Act became the first national civil rights legislation that provided equal access for people with disabilities to postsecondary educational institutions (Hall & Belch, 2000). In 1990, a second major piece of legislation, the Americans with Disabilities Act (ADA), extended the rights of students with disabilities to insure equal opportunities and full participation for people with disabilities (Gehring, Osfield, & Wald, 1994).

National longitudinal studies conducted by researchers at the U.S. Department of Education in 1990 and 2005 confirmed notable increases in postsecondary students with disabilities since the passage of the ADA, although their numbers still lag behind those of their peers without disabilities. Data from the National Longitudinal Transition Study (NLTS) and National Longitudinal Transition Study-2 (NLTS-2) indicated "within 4 years of leaving high school, 46% of youth with disabilities in 2005 were reported ever to have enrolled in a postsecondary school" (Newman, Wagner, Cameto, Knokey, & Shaver, 2010, p. 22). This was a significant increase over the 26% of students with disabilities who reported continuing their education in 1995 (Newman et al., 2010). In fact, between 1995 and 2005, the rate of growth of students with disabilities entering postsecondary education was greater than the general population. In 2009, 10.8% of college students reported they had a disability (Chronicle of Higher Education, 2009).

Data collected by The National Center for Education Statistics (NCES) indicated that for the 2008–09 academic year, 99% of public two-year institutions, 88% of private not-for-profit four-year institutions, and 99% of public four-year institutions enrolled students with disabilities (Raue & Lewis, 2011). While students with disabilities attend virtually all public, and most private higher education institutions, they are more likely to enroll in two-year institutions than are college students generally, with recent studies (NCES, NTLS-2) indicating between half and three-quarters of undergraduate students with disabilities enrolled in public two-year institutions (Newman, Wagner, Cameto, & Knokey, 2009; Raue & Lewis, 2011). Specifically, of the 46% of high school students with disabilities who went on to postsecondary education in 2005, 32% enrolled in two-year or community colleges whereas only 14% enrolled in four-year colleges or universities (Newman et al., 2009, p. 15). Therefore, it is important to design institution-specific interventions when engaging students with disabilities.

Postsecondary enrollment of students with disabilities also differs by demographic characteristics. Looking at students up to four years after high school graduation, Newman et al. (2009) found significant differences in postsecondary participation by income but not by gender or race and ethnicity. "Youth with disabilities from household with incomes of more than $50,000 were almost twice as likely as those with household incomes of $25,000 or less ever to have been enrolled in postsecondary education (57% vs. 30%)" (p. 19). While roughly equal numbers of women and men with disabilities enroll in college (49% women vs. 43% men), this is a notable difference from the population without disabilities, which sees significantly greater enrollment from women than from men (Newman et al., 2009).

Four years out of high school, 45% of African American students with disabilities, 39% of Hispanic students with disabilities, and 46% of White students with disabilities enrolled in a postsecondary education, rates insignificantly different from enrollment by peers without disabilities from the same racial and ethnic groups (Newman et al., 2009). It is important to note that Newman et al.'s data do not reflect all students with disabilities: disability status changes over the life course, and these data only capture students up to four years after high school graduation. Therefore, these numbers do not represent returning adult students or military veterans.

Definitions of what it means to be disabled in America have been framed primarily by "the eyes of others." (Jones, 1996, p. 347)

Existing literature outlines three theoretical perspectives on disability: the medical model (functional limitations), the minority group paradigm, and social constructivism (Jones, 1996). Historically, the conventional approach to disability was from a medical or functional limitations perspective. This perspective is cultivated from a positivistic scientific model and defines disability in the language of medicine, thereby gaining the sheen of scientific credibility (Smart & Smart, 2006). A hallmark of the medical model is the idea that disability is an individual experience (Smart & Smart, 2006). In addition, under the medical perspective, "it is the expert's job is to return the individual to 'normalcy'" (Aune, 2000, p. 55). Strange (2000) noted that this perspective implies "the need to rehabilitate the individual as the remedy to challenges of disability" (p. 19). By focusing solely on biological constraints of an individual student, the medical model ignores social and environmental components of disability. Therefore, under the medical model, students with disabilities are perceived as having deficiencies that interventions or medical services are designed to rectify. The problems is located in the student, rather than in the environment.

A second approach, the minority group paradigm, includes students with disabilities in the spectrum of diversity. This theoretical perspective moved away from assumptions regarding the biological aspects of disability. Rather, the minority paradigm focused on issues of relative social privilege, power, and oppression (Jones, 1996). Specifically, proponents of the minority model perceived prejudice and discrimination found in broader society as greater obstacles than medical impairments (Smart & Smart, 2006). "This perspective is helpful in adding to a more complex analysis of disability because it acknowledges environmental factors as well as the differential power structures, group identification . . . and discriminatory treatment" (Jones, 1996, p. 350). In addition, the minority model is useful for providing insight into the daily life of people with disabilities (Smart & Smart, 2006). Critics of the minority model point out two shortcomings. First, the minority group paradigm may continue to perpetuate a stereotype of students with disabilities as victims (Jones, 1996). Second, this theoretical framework depends on individuals with disabilities consciously identifying themselves with a minority group (Jones, 1996). In summary, the minority group lens focuses on issues of prejudice and discrimination that students with disabilities may experience as significant obstacles to engagement.

The social construction paradigm expanded the analysis to include both individuals with disabilities and those without (Jones, 1996). The foundational tenets of social construction theory consider impairment as a part of normal human variation (Denhart, 2008). This theoretical perspective views disability as a social creation rather than solely an individual attribute (Mitra, 2006). Jones (1996) explained that conceptualizing disability "as a socially constructed phenomenon shifts an analysis from one focusing primarily on the disability itself to one recognizing the intersection of individual and societal factors" (p. 349), allowing for "a more complex view of human behavior than one from a personal or environmental perspective alone" (Strange, 2000, p. 20). The social construction paradigm also allows student affairs educators to align programming with both individual and social factors (Aune, 2000; Hall & Belch, 2000). Strange (2000) wrote: "educators need to understand not only the conditions and characteristics of students with disabilities but also the conditions and characteristics of the campus environments these students inhabit" (p. 20). Under this paradigm, priority is given to academic and social engagement that requires adjustment for both students with disabilities and members of the campus community without disabilities (Aune, 2000). Therefore, through the social construction lens, both the campus community and students with disabilities are responsible for creating a receptive and integrated learning environment.

Issues Facing Students with Disabilities

To engage students with disabilities, it is imperative to consider academic and co-curricular engagement, legal issues, and barriers to engagement. Like all students, students with disabilities require both academic and co-curricular engagement to optimize their growth and success in college. We address academic engagement in the areas of retention, graduation, dealings with faculty, and the National Survey of Student Engagement (NSSE) benchmarks of Level of Academic Challenge, Active and Collaborative Learning, and Student-Faculty Interaction. In understanding co-curricular engagement, we reviewed data on the effects of on-campus living, and interactions with peers, and the NSSE benchmarks of Enriching Educational Experiences and Supportive Campus Environments. Although we present research findings in distinct subsections for the sake of clarity, it is important to understand that students' lives are integrated across their campus experiences. They rarely distinguish between academic and co-curricular engagement and experience barriers to engagement that come in multiple and overlapping forms—including physical, attitudinal, and legal barriers.

Academic Engagement

Data on graduation and retention of students with disabilities provide mixed results. In looking at the six-year graduation rates of students at public four-year, doctoral granting institution in the Midwest, Wessel, Jones, Markle, and Westfall (2009) found no overall difference in the retention and graduation rates of students with a disability and those without. However, Wessel et al. (2009) reported students with disabilities taking longer to graduate within those six years, with students without disabilities graduating in 4.44 years, students with visible disabilities graduating in 4.61 years, and students with invisible disabilities graduating in 4.67 years.

In contrast, existing research based on nationally representative longitudinal surveys conducted by the U.S. Department of Education (Newman et al., 2009) consistently found lower graduation and retention rates for students with disabilities. NLTS-2 data indicate that only 29% of students with disabilities in their sample had completed their degrees four years after leaving high school (Newman et al., 2009, p. 45). Using data collected from 1985 to 1990, Murray, Goldstein, Nourse, and Edgar (2000) found that 10 years after high school, students with learning disabilities were less likely (44% of student with disabilities vs. 55.9% of those without) to have graduated from postsecondary programs than cohort members without a disability. In reviewing these findings, it is important to note that 55% of students who are identified as having disabilities in high school (and are counted as such in the NLTS-2 data), do not identify themselves as having a disability once they enter college (Newman et al., 2009). This distinction may explain some of the divergent findings in these studies.

Unsurprisingly, academic engagement predicts retention for students with disabilities (Mamiseishvili & Koch, 2011); the authors found that students having at least minimal academic involvement were significantly more likely to be retained (77.5 % vs. 68.7%) between the first and second years of college than students with disabilities having no academic involvement. Fortunately, students with disabilities reported a higher level of student-faculty interaction than did students without disabilities, and levels of academic challenges and active and collaborative learning comparable to their peers without disabilities (Hedrick, Dizén, Collins, Evans, & Grayson, 2010). However, students did not always perceive faculty interaction as facilitating their success. In one study, only 32% of students with learning disabilities indicated they had interacted with faculty members about their learning disability, and 21% of respondents indicated they experienced obstacles to obtaining accommodations or services for their learning disability, most often from faculty unwilling to make accommodations (Cawthon & Cole, 2010).

Co-Curricular Engagement

While campuses have made significant strides toward creating accessible academic programs, co-curricular aspects of campus life have received considerably less attention and resources (Johnson, 2000), despite strong evidence of the importance of out-of-class engagement (Pascarella & Terenzini, 2005). Research indicates that co-curricular engagement benefits students with disabilities as well as those without. For example, in one study, living in a campus residence hall was a statistically significant and meaningful predictor of retention for students with disabilities between their first and second years of college (Mamiseishvili & Koch, 2011). Moreover, students with at least some level of social engagement were almost 10% more likely to persist from their first to their second year of college than their uninvolved classmates (81.1% vs. 72.6%; Mamiseishvilli & Koch, 2011). In a national study, students with disabilities reported similar levels of engagement in enriching educational experiences to classmates without disabilities, but they perceived their campus environments as significantly less supportive than did students without disabilities (Hedrick et al., 2010).

While some studies have found comparable levels of engagement between students with and without disabilities (e.g., Miller, 2001), most research indicates students with disabilities are less involved than their peers without disabilities. Alexis (2008) found that students with disabilities typically had limited forms of co-curricular involvement, usually with a single organization often related to their major or to their disability. Miller (2001) found that over half of students with disabilities were dissatisfied with their current levels of involvement. What social connection they did have required that students with disabilities be the first to initiate the friendship and help their peers become comfortable with the disability: "Participants in this study perceived that they were responsible for initiating interactions and that they had to be patient while peers without disabilities gained comfort with those interactions" (Hodges & Keller, 1999, p. 682).

Some evidence supports the notion that engagement is influenced by the kinds of impairments students have. Research by Evans and Broido (2011) found that students with visible impairments were less likely to engage in co-curricular activities than were students with invisible impairments. Students with visible impairments often face physical barriers to their engagement, such as inaccessible buildings, or poor sight-lines for wheelchair accessible spaces. A study of students with mobility and visual impairments found that students anticipated negative responses from their peers without disabilities if they were to become socially involved (Hodges & Keller, 1999). However, students with mobility and visual impairments developed social networks with other students with disabilities, with peers in the residence halls in which they lived, and within academic organizations.

In contrast to students with visible impairments, students with invisible impairments often became extensively involved in co-curricular activities (Evans & Broido, 2011; Guajardo, 2006). Guajardo found no meaningful differences in the level of involvement of first-year students with and without learning disabilities. However, this did not hold true for students with psychiatric disabilities who often faced attitudinal barriers to co-curricular involvement, felt pressure from their families to focus solely on academics, or feared the stigma that acknowledgement of their disability might bring (Evans & Broido, 2011).

Legal Issues

The law defines a minimum standard of accommodation, but best practices go beyond just making the campus accessible and actively encourage students with disabilities to access the benefits of engagement. "Access has many faces, including physical and communications access, programmatic access, and access to accommodations. The goal of access is to facilitate the increased integration of students with disabilities" (Simon, 2011, p. 98). Three major pieces of federal legislation provide guidance when considering issues of engagement for students with disabilities. Section 504 of the Rehabilitation Act of 1973 was the first national disability civil rights legislation. It stipulated that programs or activities that receive federal funding cannot deny the participation in, benefits of, or discriminate against any otherwise qualified people due to their disability (Hall & Belch, 2000).

The Americans with Disabilities Act (ADA), initially passed in 1990 and reauthorized in 2009, was intended to bring social equality for people with disabilities ("Toward Reasonable Equality," 1998). The ADA extends the protections offered in Section 504 to private employers, places of public accommodation, and programs provided by state or local governments (Wilhelm, 2003). The ADA offers a variety of recourses for students with disabilities who are dealing with discrimination, including discrimination that denies, precludes, or limits their participation in academic and co-curricular aspects of campus life. The ADA defines discrimination to include:

> (1) the use of criteria that unnecessarily screen out or tend to screen out individuals with disabilities from the use and enjoyment of goods and services, (2) the failure to make non-fundamental, reasonable modifications of policies, practices or procedures when such modification is necessary to accommodate disabled persons, and (3) the failure to take necessary steps to ensure that no individual with a disability is excluded, denied services, segregated or otherwise treated differently than other individuals. (42 U.S.C. sec 12182)

Thus, the ADA mandates that students with disabilities must have the same opportunities for engagement as students without disabilities.

The Americans with Disabilities Act Amendments Act (ADAAA), effective January 1, 2009, clarified who is considered to have a disability under the law, and effectively reduced the amount of documentation individuals must offer when establishing they have a disability (Heyward, 2011). In the Amendments Act, Congress noted that academic success did not indicate absence of a disability and made "it clear that students may be talented and gifted *and* disabled and entitled to reasonable accommodations under the ADAAA and section 504" (Simon, 2011, p. 98). The new law did not change existing requirements that applicants and students with disabilities meet the same academic and behavioral standards as students without disabilities. Because this legislation is still new, it is not yet clear how the courts will interpret ADAAA guidelines and how it will change the ways in which institutions of higher education foster the engagement of students with disabilities.

Barriers to Engagement for Students with Disabilities

While the previous part of the chapter has focused on levels of engagement of students with disabilities and legal mandates for equal access, the rest of this section calls attention to barriers to engagement for students with disabilities. A comprehensive listing is beyond the scope of this chapter; we limit our attention here to attitudinal, definitional, physical, and institutional barriers.

Attitudinal

Attitudinal barriers for students with disabilities generally fall under two assumptions. First, ableism leads to the presumption that accommodations for disabilities typically are expensive, inconvenient, hold people to lower standards, and that they have no benefit for users without disabilities (Griffin et al., 2007). Ablest attitudes, stemming from a medical model of disability, inaccurately presume that "typical" ways of doing things are the only appropriate ways, that most accommodations are expensive to the institution and/or burdensome to those providing the accommodation, and fail to perceive that everyone benefits from environments designed for universal access. These attitudes make it less likely institutions will proactively seeks ways to expand access, shifting the responsibility to students who must, therefore, ask to participate (Huger, 2011). Hence, it is important that key decision-makers in the campus community have an accurate understanding of what accommodations entail and how universal design often benefits all users.

Second, the social construction of stigma creates the assumption that students with disabilities are not capable, and therefore, need to be saved from their limitations. It is important that student affairs educators possess "the ability to empower rather than rescue students" (Brown, 1994, p. 104). The concept of empowerment applies to all students, but is particularly relevant to work with students having disabilities.

Existing research demonstrates that the attitudes of ableism and stigma extend to members of the campus community, including faculty, staff, and administrators. While some faculty are tireless advocates for and supporters of students with disabilities, many believe that accommodations lower academic standards (Kurth & Mellard, 2006). Hill (1996) reported that only 1 of 44 listed academic accommodations was willingly performed by faculty more than half the time and that for a third of the participants, this "impacted seriously on their ability to pursue an postsecondary education" (p. 22). Beilke and Yssel (1999) found multiple instances in the media in which faculty and administrators indicated they believed many students were claiming to have disabilities so that they would not have to work as hard or perform to the same standard as other students. Burgstahler and Moore (2009) examined challenges that students with disabilities face in effectively using student services. They found that students expressed difficulties in working with student support personnel. The students perceived some support personnel as insufficiently knowledgeable about disability or accommodations and as impatient or disrespectful.

Attitudes from other members of the campus community also can restrict the engagement. Administrators often relegate responsibility for enhancing the engagement of students with disabilities to whatever office provides accommodations, rather than seeing this as a shared responsibility of the campus community. Equally problematic, they often overestimate the cost of accommodations. Student affairs educators must be aware of and work to change ablest attitudes held by individuals across campus to remove barriers of engagement for students with disabilities.

Self-Report/Definitions

One barrier to engagement is that many students eligible for accommodations that would support their participation do not access those accommodations. Getzel and Thoma (2008) noted that the ability to accept one's disability and understand its effect on learning are critical to transition to and success within higher education. However, Newman et al. (2009) found that only "approximately 37% of postsecondary students who were considered by their secondary schools as having a disability disclosed a disability to their postsecondary schools" (p. 28). Students may be reluctant to self-identify because they are "anxious for a 'new beginning' in an educational setting by not having to deal with being labeled. Others decide to wait to disclose until they are experiencing academic problems" (Getzel & Thoma, 2008, p. 77). For example, most students with Type 1 diabetes did not identify themselves to their postsecondary institution because they did not view it as a disability and because they were unaware that any accommodations were available (Broido, 2006).

Physical
Physical aspects of campus environments often function as barriers to engagement for students with a variety of disabilities. Most obvious are lack of curb cuts, insufficiently wide doors, lack of elevators and automatically opening doors, insufficient and inconveniently located parking spaces, and inaccessible bathrooms that restrict the access of students with mobility impairments. Less obvious barriers are inadequate snow removal, elevator buttons and reception desks at heights that cannot be reached by people using wheel chairs, software incompatible with screen readers, computer and standard desks that cannot be raised and lowered for students who have orthopedic impairments, absence of Braille signage, and lack of software and advertising for campus events readable by those with visual impairments. All these make it difficult, frustrating, and sometimes impossible for students to fully engage with curricular and co-curricular aspects of the campus, and even when possible, often preclude the spontaneity so characteristic of traditionally-aged college students. Despite the numerous challenges in the physical environment, many campuses have begun to make their physical and on-line spaces more suited to all students, commonly making accessibility improvements during the course of new construction and substantive renovations (Raue & Lewis, 2011).

Institutional
Institutional commitment to disability is a critical component of a diverse campus. Kurth and Mellard (2006) noted that institutional support for students with disabilities occurs on a spectrum:

> Institutions that provide equal access by the letter of the law (i.e., primarily to avoid lawsuits) exhibit a philosophy that may not be verbalized on a campus but is felt and observed, and ultimately limits the success potential of a college and its students. Colleges that embrace the spirit of the law, on the other hand, are likely to invest in an accommodation process that considers the entire context of student life, individual functional needs, trade-offs between the immediate and long-term costs and benefits, and incorporates system wide universal design concepts. (p. 83)

Brown (1994) identified three important pieces in creating a welcoming and supportive campus: upper-level leadership, a community orientation and cross-campus collaboration, and supportive policies. Brown suggested one method to address institutional commitment to students with disabilities was to create a campus-wide committee composed of staff, faculty, and students to address disability issues, such as access and removal of barriers.

Barriers to engagement for students with disabilities come in a variety of overlapping and interconnected forms, including attitudinal, self-identification, physical, and institutional. Student affairs educators can create engaging campus environments by confronting ablest attitudes and encouraging students to access accommodations. Additionally, student affairs educators must address physical barriers and support an institutional commitment to disability as a component of diversity. The next section provides more strategies for better engaging students with disabilities on campus.

Student Engagement Strategies

There are many ways to enhance the engagement of students with disabilities in curricular and co-curricular aspects of colleges and universities. In the following paragraphs, we focus on six most relevant to those working in student affairs.

Universal Design

One method of engaging students, with and without disabilities, is to institute college policies that support universal design. Universal design is "the design of products and environments to be usable by all people, to the greatest extent possible, without the need for adaptation or specialized design" (Center for Universal Design, 2011, para. 1). When applied specifically to teaching and learning, it is referred to as universal instructional design (UID). UID is a pedagogical innovation that seeks to establish an accessible classroom learning environment for all students (Higbee, 2004). The concept of universal design flips the traditional campus on its head by expecting that the "environments and activities are designed in such a way that they are accessible to anyone, regardless of the person's functional limitations" (Aune, 2000, p. 57). Three fundamental principles of universal design are multiple means of representation of information, multiple means of expression of knowledge, and multiple means of engagement in the learning process (Roberts, Park, Brown, & Cook, 2011; Schelly, Davies, & Spooner, 2011). Basically, "in an ideal world, universal design would provide access to all people in advance rather than after the fact" (Kalivoda & Totty, 2004, p. 217).

Training faculty to implement universal design supports the academic engagement of students with disabilities (Schelly et al., 2011). Students reported their instructors who received universal design training made multiple changes to their teaching that supported students' academic success. However, due to inadequate staff resources, it is rare that faculty receive UID training; approximately half of faculty in two-year and four-year public institutions and only one-third of those in private four-year institutions receive training (Raue & Lewis, 2011). By advocating for training and implementation of universal design concepts, student affairs educators support an empirically demonstrated way of improving engagement for all students on their campus, including those with disabilities.

Universal design also applies to student development programs and services (Burgstahler & Moore, 2009; Higbee, 2009), institutional and departmental websites (Harper & DeWaters, 2008), residence halls (Wisbey & Kalivoda, 2008), and administrative planning (Arendale & Poch, 2008). Higbee (2009) outlined nine universal design principles of student development programs and services: create welcoming spaces; develop, implement, and evaluate pathways for communication; promote interaction among students and between staff and students; ensure equal opportunities for learning and growth; communicate clear expectations; use methods that consider diverse learning styles; provide natural supports for learning; ensure confidentiality; and define service quality.

Many of these universal design principles are similar to other guidelines for good practice in student affairs (Blimling & Whitt, 1999). These commonalities should not be surprising; however, the unique component of universal design lies in the focus on inclusion as a unifying goal (Higbee, 2004). Applying universal design principals to student affairs offers several benefits. For example, because universal design takes a proactive approach, fewer students with disabilities may need accommodations, thus increasing overall efficiency of student services (Burgstahler & Moore, 2009). Additionally, because of the focus on providing access to all students, by default universal design supports students who are aware and unaware of their disabilities, as well as the diversity of students without disabilities who benefit from multiple ways to be engaged in their campus environments (Burgstahler & Moore, 2009; Kalivoda, 2009).

Transition Programs

Transition or bridge programs can be an effective way to engage students with disabilities. Transition programs play an important role in helping students navigate the legal and social changes that occur when switching from K-12 schools to postsecondary education, which operate with major legislative and philosophical differences. In primary and secondary education, students with disabilities are covered by legislation that guarantees evaluation, remediation, and accommodation of impairments (Wolf, Brown, & Bork, 2009). Furthermore, parents and education providers are intimately involved in securing these services for the student. "As students move forward to higher education, however, the legal focus shifts from entitlement and remediation to *protection from discrimination and equal access*" (Wolf et al., 2009, p. 72, italics in original).

These legal and philosophical shifts lead to several key differences in students' experiences. First, in order to receive services, students must identify themselves to the institution as people with disabilities and become their own advocates. However, students often lack the self-advocacy skills that are crucial to success in the postsecondary setting (Camarena & Sarigiani, 2009), and many students with disabilities have trouble with the transition (Dean, 2009). Second, the student is legally an adult; hence, the Federal Educational Rights and Privacy Act (FERPA) prevents campus officials from discussing a student's personal information with parents unless the student signs a release. These changes may come as a shock both to the student who is accustomed to being provided for and to parents who are used to serving as their advocates. Therefore, programs designed to educate families about transition issues and teach students self-advocacy skills are critical to creating an engaging environment for students with disabilities.

Conceptually, self-determination and universal design offer guidance for educators committed to engaging students with disabilities in the transition to college (Korbel, McGuire, Banerjee, & Saunders, 2011, p. 35). Pragmatically, transition programs that engage students with disabilities can take several different forms. First, transition programs for all incoming students can be modified to meet the principals of universal design. Second, transition programs can be developed specifically for students with disabilities by working collaboratively with the Office of Disability Services. Third, existing transition programs can have sessions or sections (e.g., in a first-year experience course) reserved for students with disabilities. Generally, when creating effective transition programs, educators should consider three phases: preadmission, enrollment, and post-enrollment (Korbel et al., 2011). Preadmission and enrollment transition programs might occur during the summer before enrollment or during the first semester. As the majority of students with disabilities attend two-year public institutions (Newman et al., 2009; Raue & Lewis, 2011), transition programs geared at preadmission and enrollment need to consider engagement for both traditional and transfer students.

Although bridge programs generally are thought of as supporting students as they enter the college or university setting, engagement opportunities that target the transition out are equally important. "Students with disabilities face many barriers in their efforts to secure satisfying employment which have very little to do with their training since they are in fact college graduates" (Roessler, Hennessey, Hogan, & Savickas, 2009, p. 127). Hence, post-enrollment transition programs that address the move from two- to four-year institutions and from college to gainful employment and graduate education are vital (Korbel et al., 2011). Ideally, career preparation programs begin in the sophomore or junior year by exploring career options and matching individual strengths with viable career paths through engagement in career assessment, internships, co-ops, and on-campus employment opportunities. Strong examples can be found in California's WorkAbility III (for community colleges) and WorkAbility IV (for four-year institutions) programs.

Mentor Programs

Mentor programs are a way to support academic and co-curricular engagement for students with disabilities. Mentor programs have been shown to enhance general self-efficacy, learning strategies, and study skills for students with disabilities

(Zwart & Kallemeyn, 2001). As an outcome of participation in mentor programs, students with disabilities have a better understanding of skills needed to succeed, knowledge of their specific career interests, and accommodation needs (Burgstahler, 2001). Characteristics of successful mentoring programs for students with disabilities include flexibility and a system of multi-layered supports (Brown, Takahashi, & Roberts, 2010, p. 108).

Similar to transition programs, mentoring programs that engage students with disabilities can take several different forms. Existing programs can be modified to follow the principals of universal design. Topics to consider when making existing mentoring programs accessible include preparing, educating, and supporting mentors regarding disability-related issues; making the programming website accessible and screen reader friendly; designing promotional material to indicate disability inclusion; and insuring that appropriate accommodations are in place (Sword & Hill, 2003).

Alternatively, disability-specific mentoring programs can be developed. Mentor programs for students with disabilities generally are designed to target three areas: the transition to higher education, success in higher education, and career development opportunities (Brown et al., 2010). Although mentoring programs commonly conjure up the image of one-on-one in-person relationships, they also occur in small groups and via electronic communication (Axelrod, Campbell, & Holt, 2005). One-to-one models typically pair students with disabilities with an older student peer, a faculty member in area of academic interest or who has a disability, or a community member, usually in the area of the student's career interest. Group mentoring models generally pair a graduate student, faculty member, or career-related community volunteer with a small group of students. The learning outcomes of group mentoring may vary with the programs; one example is using small groups to develop social skills for students with Autism Spectrum Disorders via role playing, games, attending campus events together, and guided small-group discussion.

Web- or Internet-based mentoring uses a variety of methods for communication (e.g., e-mail, social media, and video chat) to develop relationships. Web-based mentoring programs are a successful way to address the barriers of schedule, distance, and disability (Bierma & Merriam, 2002; Burgstahler, 2001). Educators interested in creating or redesigning mentor programs designed specifically for students with disabilities are encouraged to explore the website of DO-IT, a mentoring and transition program focused on students with disabilities at the University of Washington, programs at the University of Illinois (particularly in residence life and intercollegiate athletics), and at Purdue University's Disability Resource Center.

Collaboration with Disability Service Offices

Student affairs educators can create engaging opportunities for students with disabilities by collaborating with disability resource offices on their campus. Disability service offices are as diverse as the institutions and students they serve (Harbour, 2009). They provide services and resources for students with disabilities along a continuum (Vogel, 1993) reflecting "fundamental philosophical differences, variations in allocated resources (fiscal and personnel), and/or limitations based on administrative and programmatic structure at the institution" (Wilson, Getzel, & Brown, 2000, p. 37). Staff members in the disability service offices have both ethical and legal obligations. Ethically, disability services providers' work addresses issues of stigma and creates a welcoming campus; legally, staff must insure the institution complies with federal regulations prohibiting discrimination (Cory, 2011). When seeking to collaborate with staff in an office of disability services, it is important to be aware of legal parameters as well as their financial resources and philosophical perspectives.

Student affairs educators can collaborate with the disability service offices in multiple ways. They can attend educational events sponsored by the office to gain a better understanding of students with disabilities and existing resources to support them. They can also work collaboratively with disability service offices to insure that events and programs their department sponsors are welcoming to students with disabilities. Pragmatically, this means that advertisements for events are sent out to the campus community via multiple manners, the physical space in which programs are hosted is accessible, and content provided during the program is presented in format that is varied and accessible. Moreover, educators are an integral part of developing a campus network to assist students with disabilities in negotiating the transitions into and out of higher education. Educators interact with students in a variety of settings (academic advising, student support, athletics, residence life); they are the eyes and ears of disability services, able to refer students who are struggling with academic or co-curricular engagement. Finally, when purchasing new technology (software programs and products), it is imperative that educators collaborate with both their disability service and information technology offices to ensure the technology is usable by students with and without disabilities.

Climate Assessment

Student affairs educators aspire to create learning environments that are inclusive, diverse, and affirming of human dignity and equality (Hall & Belch, 2000). These core values serve to inform all programs, individual interactions, policy decisions, and programming. "The first step in creating a supportive environment for all is to assess the needs of current and potential students at the institution" (Torres, 2003, p. 335). Climate assessments, sometimes called environmental audits, are one method of obtaining data regarding physical, attitudinal, and resource barriers to engagement for students with disabilities. Climate assessments are useful when designing interventions for students with disabilities because they provide insight into "prior experiences, needs, and preferred training formats of administrators, faculty, and students" (Izzo, Hertzfeld, Simmons-Reed, & Aaron, 2001, para. 9). In addition, climate assessment can provide evaluative information that will be used to "reveal either the efficacy and benefit of programs, or conversely, that these programs do not yet meet stated performance objectives and require more support and/or funding to achieve specific goals" (Stodden, Brown, & Roberts, 2011, p. 84).

Climate assessments may take a variety of different formats (focus groups, surveys, interviews, observations), target different levels (institutional, programmatic, or departmental), and seek information from various populations (faculty, students, administrative staff, and facilities personnel). Assessments such as those created by Wilson et al. (2000) and by Stodden et al. (2011) are good examples of disability-specific climate assessments. Stodden et al. (2011) emphasized that data collection should include assessment of "programmatic support, physical/facilities access, and instructional access" (p. 87), and that commonly multiple assessments were needed to develop a full understanding of the campus climate. An examination of their instrument also indicates the importance of assessment of attitudes toward students, staff, and faculty with disabilities.

While the design, collection, and analysis of data regarding the climate for students with disabilities can itself provide important awareness and knowledge about the climate, it is most important to act on the findings (Upcraft & Schuh, 1996) or risk losing the trust and future participation of those participating in the assessment. Data from climate assessments must be used to inform policy decisions and direct programmatic funding to create a more engaging environment for students with disabilities.

Include Disability as a Multicultural Issue

Student affairs educators can engage students by intentionally including disability in multicultural conversations, programs, and campus wide events. Most student affairs educators learned little about disability in their professional training (Evans, Herriott, & Myers, 2009), and disability is often overlooked in general discussions of diversity and multiculturalism. Pope, Reynolds, and Mueller (2004) defined multicultural competence as "the awareness, knowledge, and skills needed to work with others who are culturally different from self in meaningful, relevant, and productive ways" (p. 13), and included disability in their framework.

To most effectively engage students with disabilities, student affairs educators should be aware of their own attitudes about disability, their acceptance of socially constructed stigma associated with disability, and the extent to which they value students with disabilities as part of the campus community. They must recognize environments that are inaccessible to students with disabilities and understand their own attitudes, fears, and preconceptions about disability (Burgstahler & Moore, 2009; Evans et al., 2009).

Burgstahler and Moore (2009) found that many student affairs educators lack knowledge regarding forms of disability, available and appropriate accommodations, and their legal responsibilities to students with disabilities. Educators who desire to foster engagement must acquire knowledge about the social constructions of disability, legal parameters, universal design techniques, and accessible technology.

Multicultural skills supporting engagement include the ability to promote dignity and self-advocacy and to design programs, physical spaces, services, and curricula that are accessible to students with and without disabilities (Evans et al., 2009). Students with disabilities have reported that student affairs educators often seem unable to communicate respectfully with students with disabilities, to proactively create accessible environments and services, and to effectively advocate for inclusive practices (Burgstahler & Moore, 2009).

Conclusion

Research indicates that two of the most important components in academic success are the empowerment of students with a disability and the education of others about disability (Kurth & Mellard, 2006). In working with students with disabilities, the goal is to provide equal access in all areas of the campus. To accomplish this goal, educators must actively educate themselves on current issues and work to infuse the campus community with this knowledge. Access is not limited to classroom learning but rather, the entire campus environment should be shaped according to principals of universal design. Disability service offices are responsible for keeping accurate records, assisting students in receiving reasonable accommodations, and educating other campus members including faculty and staff about support for students with disabilities. From the institutional level, leadership must view disability as an important aspect of campus diversity and allocate funding to support educational initiatives. Finally, the values of human dignity and self-advocacy must be honored in working with students with disabilities.

References

Alexis, L. (2008). *A case study of the involvement of undergraduates with physical disabilities in campus organizations at East Tennessee State University* (Doctoral dissertation). Available from ProQuest Dissertations and Theses database. (UMI No. 3308016.)

Americans with Disabilities Act of 1990, 42 U.S.C. sec. 12102 (2010).

Arendale, D. & Poch, R. (2008). Using universal design for administrative leadership, planning, and evaluation. In J.L. Higbee & E. Goff (Eds.), *Pedagogy and student services for institutional transformation: Implementing universal design in higher education* (pp. 331–349). Minneapolis: University of Minnesota.

Aune, B. (2000). Career and academic advising. In H. A. Belch (Ed.), *Serving students with disabilities* (New Directions for Student Services, No. 91, pp. 55–67). San Francisco, CA: Jossey-Bass.

Axelrod, E., Campbell, G., & Holt, T. (2005). *Mentoring guidebook*. Partners for Youth with Disabilities. Retrieved from: www.pyd.org/storage/guidebook

Beilke, J. R., & Yssel, N. (1999). The chilly climate for students with disabilities in higher education. *College Student Journal, 33*(3), 364–371.

Bierma, L. L. & Merriam, S. B. (2002). E-mentoring: Using computer mediated communication to enhance the mentoring process. *Innovative Higher Education, 26*(3), 211–227.

Blimling, G. S., & Whitt, E. J. (1999). *Good practice in student affairs: Principles to foster student learning.* San Francisco, CA: Jossey-Bass.

Broido, E. M. (2006). *Diabetes as case study: Experiences of students with disabilities.* Presentation made at the American College Personnel Association conference, Indianapolis, IN.

Brown, J. T. (1994). Effective disability support service programs. In D. Ryan & M. McCarthy (Eds.), *A student affairs guide to the ADA & disability issues* (pp. 98–110). Washington, DC: National Association of Student Personnel Administrators.

Brown, S. E., Takahashi, K., & Roberts, K. D. (2010). Mentoring individuals with disabilities in postsecondary education: A review of the literature. *Journal of Postsecondary Education and Disability, 23*(2), 98–111.

Burgstahler, S. (2001). A collaborative model to promote career success for students with disabilities. *Journal of Vocational Rehabilitation, 16* (3–4), 209–215.

Burgstahler, S., & Moore, E. (2009). Making student services welcoming and accessible through accommodations and universal design. *Journal of Postsecondary Education and Disability, 21*(3), 151–174.

Camarena, P., & Sarigiani, P. A. (2009). Postsecondary educational aspirations of high-functioning adolescents with autism spectrum disorders and their parents. *Focus on Autism and Other Developmental Disabilities, 24,* 115–128. doi:10.1177/1088357609332675

Cawthon, S. W., & Cole, E. V. (2010). Postsecondary students who have a learning disability: Student perspectives on accommodations access and obstacles. *Journal of Postsecondary Education and Disability, 23*(2), 112–128.

Center for Universal Design. (2011). *The principles of universal design.* Retrieved from www.ncsu.edu/project/design-projects/udi/center-for-universal-design/the-principles-of-universal-design/

Cory, R. C. (2011). Disability services offices for students with disabilities: A campus resource. In W. S. Harbour & J. W. Madaus (Eds.), *Disability and campus dynamics* (New Directions for Higher Education, No. 154, pp. 27–36). San Francisco, CA: Jossey-Bass.

Dean, L. A. (Ed.) (2009). *CAS professional standards for higher education* (7th ed.). Washington, DC: Council for the Advancement of Standards in Higher Education.

Denhart, H. (2008). Deconstructing barriers: Perceptions of students labeled with learning disabilities in higher education. *Journal of Learning Disabilities, 41*(6), 483–497.

DO-IT: Disabilities, opportunities, internetworking, and technology. (n.d.). University of Washington. Available: www.washington.edu/doit/

Evans, N. J., & Broido, E. M. (2011). *Social involvement and identity development of students with disabilities.* Poster presented at the conference of the Association for the Study of Higher Education, Charlotte, NC.

Evans, N. J., Forney, D. S., Guido, F. M., Patton, L. D., & Renn, K. A. (2010). *Student development in college: Theory, research, and practice* (2nd ed.). San Francisco, CA: Jossey-Bass.

Evans, N. J., & Herriott, T. K. (2009). Philosophical and theoretical approaches to disability. In J. L. Higbee & A. A. Mitchell (Eds.), *Making good on the promise: Student affairs professionals with disabilities* (pp. 27–40). Lantham, MD: University Press of America.

Evans, N. J., Herriott, T. K., & Myers, K. A. (2009). Integrating disability into the diversity framework in the training of student affairs professionals. In J. L. Higbee & A. A. Mitchell (Eds.), *Making good on the promise: Student affairs professionals with disabilities* (pp. 111–128). Lantham, MD: University Press of America.

Gehring, D. D., Osfield, K. J., & Wald, J. (1994). Legal, ethical, and policy implications of the Americans with Disabilities Act. In D. Ryan & M. McCarthy (Eds.), *A student affairs guide to the ADA and disability issues* (pp. 1–14). Washington, DC: National Association of Student Personnel Administrators.

Getzel, E. E., & Thoma, C. A. (2008). Experiences of college students with disabilities and the importance of self-determination in higher education settings. *Career Development for Exceptional Individuals, 31*(2), 77–84.

Griffin, P., Peters, M. L., & Smith, R. M. (2007). Ableism curriculum design. In M. Adams, L. A. Bell, & P. Griffin (Eds.), *Teaching for diversity and social justice* (2nd ed., pp. 335–358). New York, NY: Routledge.

Guajardo, D. (2006). *A quantitative analysis of the student involvement and social development between first-year college students with and without a learning disability* (Doctoral dissertation). Available from ProQuest Dissertations and Theses database. (UMI No. 3211939.)

Hall, L. M., & Belch, H. A. (2000). Setting the context: Reconsidering the principles of full participation and meaningful access for students with disabilities. In H. A. Belch (Ed.), *Serving students with disabilities* (New Directions for Student Services, No. 91, pp. 4–17). San Francisco, CA: Jossey-Bass.

Harbour, W. S. (2009*). *The relationship between institutional unit and administrative features of disability services offices in higher education. *Journal of Postsecondary Education and Disability, 21*(3) 138–154. Retrieved from www.ahead.org/publications/jped

Harper, K. A. & DeWaters, J. (2008). A quest for website accessibility in higher education institutions. *Internet & Higher Education, 11*(3/4), 160–164. doi: 10.1016/j.iheduc.2008.06.007.

Hedrick, B., Dizén, M., Collins, K., Evans, J., & Grayson, T. (2010). Perceptions of college students with and without disabilities and effects of STEM and non-STEM enrollment on student engagement and institutional involvement. *Journal of Postsecondary Education and Disability, 23*(2), 129–136.

Heyward, S. (2011). Legal challenges and opportunities. In W. S. Harbour & J. W. Madaus (Eds.), *Disability and campus dynamics* (New Directions for Higher Education, No. 154, pp. 55–64). San Francisco, CA: Jossey-Bass.

Higbee, J. L. (2004). Universal design principles of student development programs and services. In J. L. Higbee & E. Goff (Eds.), *Pedagogy and student services of institutional transformation: Implementing universal design in higher education* (pp. 195–204). Minneapolis, MN: National College Learning Center Association.

Higbee, J. L. (2009). Implementing universal instructional design in postsecondary courses and curricula. *Journal of College Teaching & Learning, 6*(8), 65–77.

Hill, J. L. (1996). Speaking out: Perceptions of students with disabilities regarding adequacy of services and willingness of faculty to make accommodations. *Journal of Postsecondary Education and Disability, 12*, 22–43.

Hodges, J. S., & Keller, M. J. (1999). Perceived influences on social integration by students with physical disabilities. *Journal of College Student Development, 40*(6), 678–686.

Huger, M. S. (2011). Fostering a disability-friendly institutional climate. In M. S. Huger (Ed.), *Fostering the increased integration of students with disabilities* (New Directions for Student Services, No. 134, pp. 3–11). San Francisco, CA: Jossey-Bass.

Izzo, M. V., Hertzfeld, J., Simmons-Reed, E., & Aaron, J. (2001). Promising practices: Improving the quality of higher education for students with disabilities. *Disability Studies Quarterly, 21*(1). Retrieved from http://dsq-sds.org/issue/view/13

Jones, S. R. (1996). Toward inclusive theory: Disability as social construction. *NASPA Journal, 33*(4), 347–354.

Kalivoda, K. S. (2009). Disability realities: Community, culture, and connection on college campuses. In J. L. Higbee & A. A. Mitchell (Eds.), *Making good on the promise: Student affairs professionals with disabilities* (pp. 3–25). Lanham, MD: University Press of America.

Kalivoda, K. S., & Totty, M. C. (2004). Disability services as a resource: Advancing universal design. In J. L. Higbee & E. Goff (Eds.), *Pedagogy and student services of institutional transformation: Implementing universal design in higher education* (pp. 267–277). Minneapolis, MN: National College Learning Center Association.

Korbel, D. M., McGuire, J. M., Banerjee, M., & Saunders, S. A. (2011). Transition strategies to ensure active student engagement. In M. S. Huger (Ed.), *Fostering the increased integration of students with disabilities* (New Directions for Student Services, No. 134, pp. 35–46). San Francisco, CA: Jossey-Bass.

Kurth, N., & Mellard, D. (2006). Student perceptions of the accommodation process in postsecondary education. *Journal of Postsecondary Education and Disability, 19*(1), 71–84.

Mamiseishvili, K., & Koch, L. C. (2011). First-to-second-year persistence of students with disabilities in post-secondary institutions in the United States. *Rehabilitation Counseling Bulletin, 53*(2), 93–105.

Miller, L. (2001). *Involvement in extra-curricular activities, adjustment to college, and perceptions of campus climate among college students with disabilities.* (Doctoral dissertation.) Available from ProQuest Dissertations and Theses database. (UMI No. 302001.)

Mitra, S. (2006). The capability approach and disability. *Journal of Disability Policy Studies, 4,* 236–247.

Mueller, J., & Broido, E. M. (2012). Historical perspectives. In J. Arminio, V. Torres, & R. Pope, (Eds.), *"Why aren't we there yet?" Taking personal responsibility for creating an inclusive campus* (pp. 57–102). Washington, DC: ACPA Books and Media.

Murray, C., Goldstein, D. E., Nourse, S., & Edgar, E. (2000). The postsecondary school attendance and completion rates of high school graduates with disabilities. *Learning Disabilities Research and Practice, 15*(3), 119–127.

Newman, L., Wagner, M., Cameto, R., & Knokey, A. M. (2009). *The post-high school outcomes of youth with disabilities up to 4 years after high school. A report from the National Longitudinal transition Study-2 (NLTS-2).* Prepared for the U.S. Department of Education (NCSER2009–3017). Retrieved from www.nlts2.org/reports/2009_04/nlts2_report_2009_04_complete.pdf

Newman, L., Wagner, M., Cameto, R., Knokey, A. M., & Shaver, D. (2010). *Comparisons across time of the outcomes of youth with disabilities up to 4 years after high school. A report of findings from the National Longitudinal Transition Study (NLTS) and the National Longitudinal Transition Study-2 (NLTS-2).* Prepared for the U.S. Department of Education (NCSER2010–3008). Menlo Park, CA: SRI International. Retrieved from www.nlts2.org/reports/2010_09/nlts2_report_2010_09_complete.pdf

Pascarella, E. T., & Terenzini, P. T. (2005). *How college affects students: A third decade of research.* San Francisco, CA: Jossey-Bass.

Pope, R. L., Reynolds, A. L., & Mueller, J. A. (2004). *Multicultural competence in student affairs.* San Francisco, CA: Jossey-Bass.

Raue, K., & Lewis, L. (2011). *Students with disabilities at degree-granting postsecondary institutions* (NCES 2011–018). U.S. Department of Education, National Center for Education Statistics. Washington, DC: U.S. Government Printing Office.

Riddell, S., Tinklin, T., & Wilson, A. (2005). *Disabled students in higher education: Perspectives on widening access and changing policy.* New York, NY: Routledge.

Roberts, K. D., Park, H. J., Brown, S., & Cook, B. (2011). Universal design for instruction in postsecondary education: A systematic review of empirically based articles. *Journal of Postsecondary Education and Disability, 24*(1), 5–15.

Roessler, R. T., Hennessey, M. L., Hogan, E. M., & Savickas, S. (2009). Career assessment and planning strategies for postsecondary students with disabilities. *Journal of Postsecondary Education and Disability, 21*(3), 126–137.

Schelly, C. L., Davies, P. L., & Spooner, C. L. (2011). Student perceptions of faculty implementation of universal design for learning. *Journal of Postsecondary Education and Disability, 24*(1), 17–28.

Sherry, M. (2004). Overlaps and contradictions between queer theory and disability studies. *Disability & Society, 19,* 769–785.

Simon, J. A. (2011). Legal issues in serving students with disabilities in postsecondary education. In M. S. Huger (Ed.), *Fostering the increased integration of students with disabilities* (New Directions for Student Services, No. 134, pp. 95–107). San Francisco, CA: Jossey-Bass.

Smart, J. F., & Smart, D. W. (2006). Models of disability: Implications for the counseling profession. *Journal of Counseling & Development, 84,* 29–40.

Stodden, R. A., Brown, S. E., & Roberts, K. (2011). Disability-friendly university environments: Conducting a climate assessment. In W. S. Harbour & J. W. Madaus (Eds.), *Disability and campus dynamics* (New Directions for Higher Education, No. 154, pp. 83–92). San Francisco, CA: Jossey-Bass.

Strange, C. (2000). Creating environments of ability. In H. A. Belch (Ed.), *Serving students with disabilities* (New Directions for Student Services, No. 91, pp. 19–30). San Francisco, CA: Jossey-Bass.

Sword, C. & Hill, K. (2003). Creating mentoring opportunities for youth with disabilities: Issues and suggested strategies. *American Rehabilitation, 27*(1), 14–17.

The Chronicle of Higher Education. (2009). *Almanac of higher education: Profile of undergraduate students 2007–2008.* Retrieved from http://chronicle.com.maurice.bgus.edu/article/Profile-of-Undergraduate-St/48078/

Torres, V. (2003). Student diversity and academic services: Balancing the needs of all students. In G. L. Kramer & Associates (Eds.). *Student academic services: An integrated approach* (pp. 333–351). San Francisco, CA: Jossey-Bass.

Toward reasonable equality: Accommodating learning disabilities under the Americans with Disabilities Act. (1998). *Harvard Law Review, 111*(6), 1560–1577.

Upcraft, M. L., & Schuh, J. H. (1996). *Assessment in student affairs: A guide for practitioners.* San Francisco, CA: Jossey-Bass.

U.S. Government Accountability Office. (2009). *Higher education and disability: Education needs a coordinated approach to improve its assistance to schools in supporting students. (GAO-10–33).* Washington, DC: Author. Retrieved from www.gao.gov/new.items/d1033.pdf

Vogel, S. A. (1993). The continuum of university responses to Section 504 for students with learning disabilities. In S. A. Vogel & P. B. Adelman (Eds.), *Success for college students with learning disabilities* (pp. 83–113). New York, NY: Springer-Verlag.

Wessel, R. D., Jones, J. A., Markle, L., & Westfall, C. (2009). Retention and graduation of students with disabilities: Facilitating student success. *Journal of Postsecondary Education and Disability, 21,* 116–125.

Wilhelm, S. (2003). Accommodating mental disabilities in higher education: A practical guide to ADA requirements. *Journal of Law and Education, 32,* 217–226.

Wilson, K., Getzel, E., & Brown, T. (2000). Enhancing the post-secondary campus climate for students with disabilities. *Journal of Vocational Rehabilitation, 14,* 37–50.

Wisbey, E. W., & Kalivoda, K. S. (2008). Residential living for all: Fully accessible and "liveable" on-campus housing. In J. L. Higbee & E. Goff (Eds.), *Pedagogy and student services for institutional transformation: Implementing universal design in higher education* (pp. 255–266). Minneapolis: University of Minnesota.

Wolf, L. E., Brown, J. T., & Bork, G. R. (2009) *Students with Asperger Syndrome: A guide for college personnel.* Shawnee Mission, KS: Autism Asperger.

Zwart, L. M., & Kallemeyn, L. M. (2001). Peer based coaching for college students with ADHD and learning disabilities. *Journal of Postsecondary Education and Disability, 15*(1), 1–15.

Chapter 13
Engaging Student Athletes

Joy Gaston Gayles

Engaging student athletes in ways that have a positive impact on student learning and personal growth has become a relevant topic of concern in the literature, as well as for institutions of higher education and athletic administrators. Scholars have raised questions concerning the extent to which student athletes benefit from the college experience in ways similar to their non-athlete peers (Bowen & Levin, 2003; Clotfelter, 2011; Shulman & Bowen, 2001). Notwithstanding reform efforts to control intercollegiate athletics, concerns remain regarding the time demands required to participate in intercollegiate athletics at major higher education institutions and how such demands potentially limit the degree to which student athletes can become involved within and connected to the college environment.

Engagement can be defined as the level at which students participate in activities both inside and outside of the classroom (Astin, 1993; Kuh, Schuh, Whitt, & Associates, 2005; Pascarella & Terenzini, 1991, 2005) and is commonly used to study how college impacts various desired outcomes of undergraduate education (Pascarella & Terenzini, 1991, 2005). Interacting with faculty, participating in student groups and organizations, reading, writing, and studying for class, attending class, and other curricular and co-curricular activities are all considered to be forms of engagement. The extent to which students participate in such activities is a function of both the person and the college environment (Evans et al., 2010; Kuh et al., 2005). In other words, engagement requires student effort as well as institutional support through policies and practices that facilitate active participation in such activities.

Balancing the academic and social demands of the college experience can be challenging for all students. Attending class, completing homework, studying, and academically achieving are all aspects of the college experience that students must balance to be successful. Student athletes, however, have the added responsibility of managing athletic demands (e.g., daily practice, competitions, injuries) in addition to academic and social demands that take up a considerable amount of time (Broughton & Neyer, 2001; Jolly, 2008; Parham, 1993; Watt & Moore, 2001).

This chapter will address some of the challenges facing student athletes who participate in intercollegiate athletics within higher education institutions. In addition to discussing challenges, two theoretical frameworks will be presented that have been widely used in the research literature on college impact and have implications for engaging student athletes in their college experience. The chapter concludes with a set of recommendations for university and athletic administrators on ways to engage student athletes in the campus environment during their college years.

Challenges for Intercollegiate Athletics & Higher Education

There are many challenges facing student athletes who participate in college sports, particularly at the Division I level, that can impact the extent to which they become engaged in the college environment. All of the challenges associated with big time sports on college campuses are too numerous to cover in this chapter. Therefore, I will focus on the challenges that potentially have the greatest impact on the quality and frequency of engagement for student athletes.

Balancing Academic and Athletics

One of the major issues facing college athletes is balancing academic and athletic responsibilities in order to make good progress toward degree completion and maintain eligibility (Broughton & Neyer, 2001; Parham, 1993). In a national study of student athlete experiences in college, a little more than half of student athletes reported that they did not spend as much time on academics as they would have liked and 80% of them indicated athletic participation as the top reason (Potuto & O'Hanlon, 2006). In addition, 68% of student athletes in the same study reported that they would have liked to spend more time pursuing education opportunities such as participation in research with faculty and internships. Further, about 62% of the participants in the study reported viewing themselves as more athlete than student.

Student athletes are often considered to be a special population of college students given the unique rules and requirements that they must adhere to during their college years. Selecting a major within two years, scheduling the appropriate number of hours per semester, passing a required number of degree hours per semester, and earning a minimum grade point average are unique requirements for student athletes. Further, keeping track of the many NCAA and conference rules and regulations require support from the university to assist student athletes with balancing academic, personal, and athletic demands (Broughton & Neyer, 2001; Jolly, 2008).

Student athletes enter college with various goals and aspirations, which further complicates balancing academic and athletic tasks. Many student athletes enter college with high athletic aspirations, hoping to make it to the elite level in their sport. Some athletes come to college to succeed in their sport but also have high academic aspirations. A few scholars have examined student athletes' achievement motivation, particularly in regards to academic performance (Gaston-Gayles, 2004; Simons, Rheenen, & Covington, 1999). In order to be successful athletically, Simons et al. (1999) suggest that athletes must show dedication, put in a lot of hard work, and focus on their goal. The authors note that these same qualities, if properly transferred, can lead to success in the academic domain as well. Unfortunately, most student athletes who participate in revenue producing sports (e.g., football and men's basketball) fail to transfer the skills to their academics, whereas female student athletes and students who participate in nonrevenue sports are more apt to transfer skills from the athletic domain to the academic domain (Simons et al., 1999).

Motivation theory can be useful in understanding what drives student athletes during college and can inform policy and practice around helping students balance their academic and athletic pursuits. Not every football player who goes to college has the desire to play in the NFL, but some track and field athletes may have the goal of competing in the Olympics. Thus, understanding student athletes' academic and athletic motivation can be helpful for athletic administrators and counselors in supporting this population.

Gaston-Gayles (2005) developed a scale, the Student Athletes' Motivation toward Sports and Academics Questionnaire (SAMSAQ), using achievement motivation theory to measure student athletes' motivation toward academics and athletics. The scale consists of three sub-scales: academic, student athletic motivation, and career athletic. The academic sub-scale measures students' interest and personal beliefs regarding academic related tasks. The student athletic subscale measures the degree to which students are driven toward athletic related tasks. The career athletic sub-scale measures students' motivation toward pursuing a professional career or an elite level in their sport. Gaston-Gayles (2004) used the SAMSAQ to examine the extent to which academic and athletic motivation influenced academic performance and found that academic motivation was the only influential motivational factor associated with academic performance for student athletes in the study. This scale can be useful for understanding student athletes motivation and helping student athletes achieve a better balance between academic and athletic goals.

Academic Performance

Although student athletes as a whole graduate at higher rates than students in the general population, success in graduation rates is not consistent across gender, race/ethnicity, and sport. For instance, using the federal graduation rate, student athletes who entered college in 2004 at institutions with the largest athletic programs graduated at rates higher than students in the general population at those institutions—approximately 65% of student athletes graduated compared to 63% of students in the general student population (NCAA, 2011). The NCAA uses a different method for calculating graduation rates that does not penalize institutions for student athletes who transfer to another institution in good standing. According to the graduation success rate used by the NCAA, over 80% of student athletes who entered college between 1999 and 2003 graduated within six years.

However, 5% of Division I teams had graduation success rates lower than 50%—including three men's teams (i.e., football, men's basketball, and baseball) that have consistently held low graduation rates (Sander, 2010).

Academic performance of college athletes has been an issue of concern for quite some time. Eligibility standards came about in the 1980s as an attempt to better align the goals of intercollegiate athletics with the goals of higher education. Proposition 48 enforced a set of minimum standards for initial eligibility and continuing eligibility. Since then, other academic standards have been instituted to ensure that student athletes select a major within the first two years of college and make timely progress toward degree completion. As a result of low academic performance and increased standards for play, scholars began to examine the academic performance of college athletes to understand how student athletes were performing in the classroom relative to their peers. Many of the early studies found that student athletes were less prepared academically for college compared to their non-athlete peers (Hood, Craig, & Ferguson, 1992; Purdy, Eitzen, & Hufnagel, 1985; Stuart, 1985). More recent literature suggests that student athletes enter college less prepared than their peers, particularly those who were highly committed to their sport (Aries, McCarthy, Salovey, & Banaji, 2004; Bowen & Levin, 2003; Shulman & Bowen, 2001). However, when compared to student athletes who entered college with similar background characteristics, student athletes do not differ from their peers in academic performance while in college (Aries et al., 2004; Pascarella & Smart, 1991; Stuart, 1985).

A few studies have examined the impact of participation in intercollegiate athletics on cognitive development. These scholars were interested in how college sport participation influenced gains in critical thinking, reading comprehension, mathematical skills, and scientific reasoning (McBride & Reed, 1998; Pascarella, Bohr, Nora, & Terenzini, 1995; & Pascarella et al., 1999). Student athletes in revenue-producing sports consistently scored lower on cognitive development measures compared to their peers. However, female student athletes did not differ from their non-athlete female peers on gains in cognitive development.

Divide between Intercollegiate Athletics & Higher Education

In recent years, increased attention in the literature has focused on the extent to which student athletes are isolated from the overall campus culture and whether they are benefitting from the college experience in ways similar to their peers. Although intercollegiate athletics is deeply embedded into the culture of most higher education institutions across the country, conflict exists between the goals and functions of intercollegiate athletic programs and the mission of higher education (Bok, 2004; Bowen & Levin, 2003; Clotfelter, 2011; Duderstadt, 2003). Since the 1800s, college sports have evolved from a student-organized activity into a highly commercialized enterprise (Duderstadt, 2003). As such, many have questioned the amateur status of college sports and the proper place of intercollegiate athletics with higher education institutions (Clotfelter, 2011). The academic/athletic divide has been characterized by issues such as major clustering, social isolation, low academic performance, and low admissions standards that set student athletes apart from the larger student population (Bowen & Levin, 2003; Shulman & Bowen, 2001). Further, the divide between academics and athletics serves as the foundation of what Bowen and Levin describe as a separate athletic sub-culture operating on college campuses in which student athletes do not benefit in ways similar to their non-athlete peers from the overall college experience by not engaging in the types of activities and experiences that lead to desired student learning and personal development outcomes.

A few recent studies have examined the extent to which student athletes are engaged within the college experience. For instance, Umbach, Palmer, Kuh, and Hannah (2006), using data from the National Survey of Student Engagement (NSSE), found that, on average, student athletes were just as likely to engage in educational purposeful activities as their non-athlete peers. However, student athletes at Division III institutions were more engaged compared to student athletes at Division I & II institutions. Other studies also support that athletes at Division III institutions tend to be engaged in both their sport and campus life (Schroeder, 2000), despite the fact that it may be more difficult to participate due to athletic time constraints (Richards & Aries, 1999). A recent study examined the impact of engagement on cognitive and affective outcomes and the extent to which the impact varied in magnitude across level of sport (Gayles & Hu, 2009). The findings suggest that interaction with peers other than teammates was significant and mattered most for students in sports other than football and men's basketball. More research is needed to understand what types of involvement are most meaningful for students in high-profile sports. In addition, more research is needed to better understand the nature and types of educational experiences that matter most for various subgroups of student athletes.

Theoretical Frameworks

Two theories to inform policy and practice for engaging student athletes are Bandura's (1977) Self-efficacy Theory and Astin's (1999) Involvement Theory. Bandura's theory is rooted in the social psychology literature and has been studied extensively across a wide range of social behaviors. Astin's theory of involvement is commonly used in the college impact literature to examine how college influences student learning and personal growth. Both theories have also been useful in understanding student athletes' motivation toward sports and academics (Gaston-Gayles, 2004, 2005; Simons et al., 1999), as well as the impact of participation in intercollegiate athletics on student athletes' involvement in the college experience (Astin, 1993, 1999; Pascarella & Terenzini, 1991, 2005).

Self-Efficacy Theory

Self-efficacy is defined as an individual's belief about his or her capability to complete a task successfully (Bandura, 1977). More specifically, Bandura (1990) noted that perceived self-efficacy "is concerned with people's beliefs that they can exert control over their motivation and behavior and over their social environment" (p. 9). Bandura distinguished efficacy outcomes from expectancy outcomes in that the latter represents the belief that a behavior will lead to a desired outcome. However, efficacy outcomes represent an individual's belief about his or her ability to perform the behavior that will lead to the desired outcome. In other words, an individual might believe that studying effectively will lead to earning a good grade on an exam. However, the individual may not believe that he or she has the ability or capacity to study effectively.

An individual's belief in his or her ability to succeed at a task is rooted in his or her past experiences with success and failure. Such experiences generate a set of generalized expectations that carry over into new experiences; thus, past experiences have a strong influence on an individual's future behavior (Bandura, 1990). As such, people have a tendency to avoid and fear situations they think exceed their capabilities but engage in activities in which they feel capable of completing successfully (Bandura, 1977). Moreover, when individuals have a high sense of self-efficacy, they tend to persist and experience less stress and anxiety, particularly if difficulties arise. However, individuals with low self-efficacy do not manage difficult situations well even though they know what to do and how to do it (Bandura, 1990). In other words, people's negative beliefs about their capabilities are powerful enough to prevent them from successfully completing a task. Bandura (1990) labels such beliefs as inefficacy, which lead to vulnerability and stress.

A few studies have used Bandura's (1977) self-efficacy theory to examine student athletes' motivation; these studies have been most useful in understanding beliefs about academic-related behaviors. For example, Gaston-Gayles (2005) used Bandura's theory as a part of the theoretical framework to develop the SAMSAQ, a scale designed to measure academic and athletic motivation. The finding that academic motivation is influential in predicting academic performance has implications for increasing student athletes' self-efficacy beliefs in the academic domain. Simons et al. (1999) further suggest that student athletes experience difficulties transferring skills from the athletic domain that lead to success to the academic domain. Student athletes may possess high self-efficacy beliefs about their abilities in the athletic domain but may experience inefficacy about their abilities in the academic domain. Finding ways to engage student athletes the college experience in ways that help them boost their self-efficacy beliefs, particularly in the academic domain, is warranted.

Student Involvement Theory

Astin's (1999) theory of involvement suggests that the more students become involved in the college experience, the more likely they will experience gains in personal development and learning, as well as satisfaction with college. Involvement is defined as "the amount of physical and psychological energy that student devotes to the academic experience" (p. 518). Involvement is defined by what students do, how they behave, and the amount of effort they put forth in an activity, as opposed to what they think or feel about an activity. Thus, involvement can be characterized by any activity on a college campus that motivates and encourages students to spend time on campus. Spending time on campus increases the likelihood that students will interact in positive ways with their peers, as well as with faculty and staff.

In articulating the theory, Astin (1999) identified five principles that distinguish campus involvement activities from other types of educational experiences. First, involvement requires that students spend their time on and devote their energy to educational activities on the college campus. The second principle states that students will vary concerning the amount of time and energy invested in campus activities. In other words, involvement occurs along a continuum from high involvement to low involvement and will not be the same for all students. Further, it is unlikely that students who are involved in multiple activities will devote the same amount of time and energy across them all. The third principle further distinguishes involvement from other educational experiences by noting that involvement has both quantitative and qualitative aspects. Involvement is defined by both the frequency or amount of time spent on an activity (quantitative) and the nature or type of activity (qualitative). The quantitative and qualitative components of involvement are important to understand in order to create opportunities that are beneficial for students.

Astin (1999) warns that the last two principles are in need of more empirical support. However, there is growing evidence in the literature to support the positive association between the amount of time spent and the quality of student involvement in educational activities and growth in personal development and learning (Astin, 1993; Pascarella & Terenzini, 2005). More evidence is needed to support the notion that effective campus policies and practices are associated with increased levels of student engagement within the campus community.

Based on the definition and principles outlined above, involvement can consist of a range of educational activities on college campuses and have implications for the kinds of activities that can be beneficial for student athletes. Spending time with faculty and peers through involvement in student groups and organizations, peer study groups, and research with faculty are all types of involvement that are associated with positive student outcomes (Astin, 1993; Pascarella & Terenzini, 1991, 2005). Longitudinal student data conducted by the Higher Education Research Institute (HERI) at UCLA suggests that involvement activities, such as participation in honors programs, are associated with high self-esteem and aspirations to attend graduate school. Further, living in residence halls increases the likelihood of becoming involved and integrated into the campus environment. In addition, even working on campus has been linked to retention. Providing opportunities for student athletes to become involved in educationally purposeful activities is one way to ensure that intercollegiate athletic participation does not create a separate culture that isolates student athletes from the general population.

Unfortunately, students can become overinvolved and experience negative consequences as a result of spending too much time on activities on and off campus. There is some concern about intercollegiate athletics and the amount of time students spend in practice and competition (Bowen & Levin, 2003; Shulman & Bowen, 2001). Intense academic involvement can lead to isolation and potentially limit peer interaction (Astin, 1993). However, students who invest a heavy amount of time and energy into academics tend to be satisfied with college, particularly given the high rewards for academic excellence at higher education institutions. Any activity that pulls students' time and energy away from campus and academics can potentially have a negative impact on their college experience (Astin, 1993). For example, working more than 15–20 hours per week off campus limits the extent to which students can become involved in the campus community.

Intense athletic participation has the potential to pull students away from the campus culture, which decreases their chances of interacting with faculty and peers at the institution (Astin, 1999; Bowen & Levin, 2003; Shulman & Bowen, 2001). Because student athletes have less time for involvement due to the practice and competition demands from their sport combined with academic demands, athletic administrators must be intentional about facilitating opportunities for student athletes to engage with the campus community. Encouraging student athletes to engage with their peers has benefits for learning and personal development (Gayles & Hu, 2009; Umbach et al., 2006)

Student Engagement Strategies

Based on the challenges facing intercollegiate athletics and the theoretical perspectives discussed above, this chapter concludes with a set of recommendations for effectively engaging student athletes in the college experience.

Assess Academic and Athletic Motivation
Student athletes enter college with various aspirations and motivations toward sports and academics. Moreover, some student athletes experience more difficulties than their peers balancing academic and athletic tasks. Therefore, it is important to assess what student athletes' motivations are, as opposed to making assumptions based on sport, gender, and race/ethnicity. Further, it is important to understand what students' perceptions are about their abilities to succeed in college. The SAMSAQ developed by Gaston-Gayles (2005) is a useful tool to understand student athletes' level of motivation toward sports and academics. The SAMSAQ can assist athletic support staff with identifying student athletes who have low academic motivation and develop a plan to help them increase their academic motivation, as this type of motivation in particular was influential on academic performance (Gaston-Gayles, 2004).

Peer Interaction
Campus administrators should actively seek ways to engage student athletes with their non-athlete peers. Research supports that this type of engagement is important, particularly for student athletes, who are limited by time demands associated

with their sport. Peer interaction is one of the major ways of successfully integrating into the academic and social systems of the campus culture (Tinto, 1993). Thus, college administrators should partner to identify ways to get student athletes involved in service activities, academic clubs and organizations, and other student-based activities on campus.

Student Affairs Collaboration

Athletic department administrators who are responsible for academic support services and CHAMPS (Challenging Athletes' Minds for Personal Success) programs should collaborate with student affairs offices on campus to develop programs that facilitate greater involvement with the campus community for student athletes. Such collaborative efforts will help eliminate duplication of services and programs, and also create opportunities for increased peer interaction between athletes and non-athletes. In addition to increasing peer involvement, collaboration between student athlete support services and academic and student affairs units will also help bridge the divide between academics and athletics that has been documented in the literature.

Live on Campus

Student athletes should be encouraged to live on campus at least for the first two years of college. Given the time constraints involved with balancing academic, social, and athletic demands, living on campus will allow student athletes to spend more time on campus. Thus, spending more time on campus will increase the likelihood of student athletes engaging with their peers, faculty, and staff. Student athletes should also be encouraged to live on campus with non-athletes. NCAA rules prohibit special housing arrangements for student athletes such as residence halls occupied solely by student athletes or residential hall blocks (e.g., hall wing or floor) if such policies are not in place for students in the general population. The NCAA encourages that student athletes make up no more than 50% of a residence hall. The recommendation here is for the percentage of student athletes who make up a single residence hall to be as low as possible to increase opportunities to interact with their peers who are not student athletes.

Increase Faculty Interaction

Faculty interaction both inside and outside the classroom is an important form of engagement for student athletes and should be highly encouraged. One suggestion is to provide opportunities for faculty to learn about the athletic program at the institution by inviting them to sit in on a practice or attend a home game. Faculty perceptions of student athletes' experiences are not always favorable (Engstrom, Sedlacek, & McEwen, 1995; Howard-Hamilton & Sina, 2001; Jolly, 2008). Therefore, providing opportunities for faculty to experience a day in the life of a student athlete might help shape their perspective, facilitate a connection, and encourage increased interaction between student athletes and faculty. In addition to inviting faculty to visit the athletic department, student athletes should be encouraged to interact with faculty inside and outside the classroom.

Conclusion

Student athletes face many challenges that can potentially impact the quality and frequency of their engagement with the campus community. This chapter gave an overview of three major challenges faced by student athletes on college campuses today. Although this list is not exhaustive, the challenges such as balancing academic, athletic, and social demands, academic performance, and the student athlete subculture are all key aspects of the student athlete experience that can be detrimental to their success as students and athletes. The theoretical frameworks reviewed in this chapter have the potential to inform policy and practice for campus and athletic administrators. Finding ways to increase student athletes' self-efficacy and campus involvement can strengthen the connection between student athletes and the institution. Students who are connected to and experience successful integration into the academic and social systems of the institution are more satisfied with their college experiences and also experience gains in learning and personal development. The recommendations presented at the end of this chapter are grounded in the literature on how college impacts students and will be useful for administrators as they work to facilitate student growth and learning for the student athlete population.

References

Aries, E., McCarthy, D., Salovey, P., & Banaji, M.R. (2004). A comparison of athletes and non-athletes at highly selective colleges: Academic performance and personal development. *Research in Higher Education, 45*(6), 577–602.

Astin, A.W. (1993). *What matters in college: Four critical years revisited.* San Francisco, CA: Jossey-Bass.

Astin, A.W. (1999). Student involvement: A developmental theory for higher education. *Journal of College Student Development, 40*(5), 518–529.

Bandura, A. (1977). Self-efficacy: Toward a unifying theory of behavior change. *Psychological Review, 84,* 191–251.

Bandura, A. (1990). Perceived self-efficacy in the exercise of control over aids infection. *Evaluation and Program Planning, 13,* 9–17.

Bok, D. (2004). The benefits and costs of commercialization of the academy. In D.G. Stein (Ed.), *Buying in or selling out? The commercialization of the American research university* (pp. 32–47). New Brunswick, NJ: Rutgers University Press.

Bowen, W.G., & Levin, S.A. (2003). *Reclaiming the game: College sports educational values.* Princeton, NJ: Princeton University Press.

Broughton, E., & Neyer, M. (2001). Advising and counseling student athletes. *New Directions for Student Services, 93,* 47–53.

Clotfelter, C. (2011). *Big-time sports in American universities.* New York, NY: Cambridge University Press.

Duderstadt, J.J. (2003). *Intercollegiate athletics and the American university.* Ann Arbor: University of Michigan Press.

Engstrom, C.H., Sedlacek, W.E., & McEwen, M.L. (1995). Faculty attitudes toward male revenue and non-revenue student-athletes. *Journal of College Student Development 36*(3), 215–225.

Evans, N.J., Forney, D.S., Guido, F.M., Patton, L.D., & Renn, K.A. (2010). *Student development in college: Theory, research, and practice.* San Francisco. CA: Jossey-Bass.

Gaston-Gayles, J. (2004). Examining the academic and athletic motivation among student athletes at a Division I university. *Journal of College Student Development, 45*(1), 75–83.

Gaston-Gayles, J. (2005). The factor structure and reliability of the student athletes' motivation toward sports and academics questionnaire (SAMSAQ). *Journal of College Student Development, 46*(3), 317–327.

Gayles, J.G., & Hu. S. (2009). The influence of student engagement and sport participation on college outcomes among Division I student athletes. *The Journal of Higher Education, 80*(3), 315–333.

Hood, A.B., Craig, A.F., & Ferguson, B.W. (1992). The impact of athletics, part-time employment, and other activities on academic achievement. *Journal of College Student Development, 33*, 447–453.

Howard-Hamilton, M.F., & Sina, J.A. (2001). How college affects student athletes. In M.F. Howard-Hamilton & S.K. Watt (Eds.), *Student services for student athletes* (New Directions for Student Services, 93, pp. 35–45). San Francisco, CA: Jossey-Bass.

Jolly, J.C. (2008). Raising the Question #9: Is the student-athlete population unique? And why should we care? *Communication Education, 57*(1), 145–151.

Kuh, G.D., Schuh, J.H., Whitt, E.J., & Associates (2005). *Student success in college: Creating conditions that matter.* San Francisco, CA: Jossey-Bass.

McBride, R.E., & Reed, J. (1998). Thinking and college athletes—are they predisposed to critical thinking? *College Student Journal, 32*(3), 443–451.

NCAA (2011). *2011–12 NCAA division I manual.* Indianapolis, IN: Author.

Parham, W.D. (1993). The intercollegiate athletes: A 1990s profile. *The Counseling Psychologist, 21*(3), 411–429.

Pascarella, E.T., Bohr, L., Nora, A., & Terenzini, P.T. (1995). Intercollegiate athletic participation and freshman-year cognitive outcomes. *The Journal of Higher Education, 66*(4), 369–387.

Pascarella, E.T., & Smart, J.C. (1991). Impact of intercollegiate athletic participation for African American and Caucasian men: Some further evidence. *Journal of College Student Development, 32*(2), 123–130.

Pascarella, E.T., & Terenzini, P.T. (1991). *How college affects students.* San Francisco, CA: Jossey-Bass.

Pascarella, E.T., & Terenzini, P.T. (2005). *How college affects students: A third decade of research.* San Francisco, CA: Jossey-Bass.

Pascarella, E.T., Truckenmiller, R., Nora, A., Terenzini, P.T., Edison, M., & Hagedorn, L.S. (1999). Cognitive impacts of intercollegiate athletic participation: Some further evidence. *The Journal of Higher Education, 70*(1), 1–26.

Potuto, J.R., & O'Hanlon, J. (2006). National study of student athletes regarding their experiences as college students. Retrieved May 31, 2011, from www.ncaa.org/library/research/studentathlete_experiences/2006/2006_s-a_experience.pdf

Purdy, D.A., Eitzen, D.S., & Hufnagel, R. (1985). Are athletes also students? The educational attainment of college athletes. In D. Chu, J.O. Segrave, & G.J. Becker (Eds.), *Sport in higher education* (pp. 221–234). Champaign, IL: Human Kinetics.

Richards, S., & Aries, E. (1999). The division III student-athlete: Academic performance, campus involvement and growth. *Journal of College Student Development, 40*(3), 211–218.

Sander, L. (2010, October 27). Graduation rates for scholarship athletes hold steady at 79%, NCAA Says. *The Chronicle of Higher Education*, Retrieved June 4, 2012, from http://chronicle.com.prox.lib.ncsu.edu/article/Graduation-Rates-for/125123/

Schroeder, P.J. (2000). An assessment of student involvement among selected NCAA division III basketball players. *Journal of College Student Development, 41*(6), 616–626.

Shulman, J.L., & Bowen, W.G. (2001). *The game of life: College sports and educational values.* Princeton, NJ: Princeton University.

Simons, H.D., Rheenen, D.V., & Covington, M.V. (1999). Academic motivation and the student athlete. *Journal of College Student Development, 40*(2), 151–162.

Stuart, D. (1985). Academic preparation and subsequent performance of intercollegiate football players. *Journal of College Student Personnel 26*(2), 124–129.

Tinto, V. (1993). *Leaving college: Rethinking the causes and cures of student attrition* (2nd ed.). Chicago, IL: University of Chicago Press.

Umbach, P.D., Palmer, M.M., Kuh, G.D., & Hannah, S.J. (2006). Intercollegiate athletics and effective educational practices: Winning combination or losing effort? *Research in Higher Education, 47*(6), 709–733.

Watt, S.K., & Moore, J.L. (2001). Who are student athletes? In M.F. Howard-Hamilton & S.K. Watt (Eds.), *Student services for student athletes* (New Directions for Student Services, 93, pp. 7–18). San Francisco, CA: Jossey-Bass.

Chapter 14
Engaging Homeless Students in College

Jarrett T. Gupton

Homeless youth have received little attention in the higher education literature. One notable exception is Lauralee Summer's autobiography *Learning Joy from Dogs without Collars* (2003). The book traces Summer's life as a homeless youth, with her mother, through her graduation from Harvard in 1998. Her story demonstrates the role that resiliency and social support play in assisting homeless youth's transition through adolescence and into adulthood. Although not an academic study, Summer's autobiography reveals how one homeless student navigated her way through the various obstacles to attain a college education.

Specific to higher education, Summer discusses her experience of being an outsider at Harvard because of her low-income background. She tells of feeling awkward about not having a computer or being able to afford all the required books because of the high prices in the bookstore. Summer describes the required summer reading that included a speech on diversity issues by then Harvard President Neil Rudenstine. The speech detailed the importance that differences in race or ethnicity, physical ability, political affiliation, sexual orientation have on students' experiences. From Summer's perspective, the president's speech did not discuss "how isolated people unfamiliar with the middle-class culture like myself could feel in a university setting" (2003, p. 223). During an orientation meeting at her residence hall, students from Summer's floor were gathered to attend a discussion on their experiences with diversity. Each student was asked to introduce themselves and say a little about their experiences with diversity. Summer recalls how she felt and what she told the students in her introduction:

> Going around the circle, I was the last student to speak. My voice was shaky as I told them about my mother and my upbringing . . . I told them that I felt lost. Unlike an ethnicity, being homeless and poor didn't seem like an identity I could take pride in (not at that point). I broke down into tears. I felt alone, dirty, and ashamed, tired, and invisible. I was angry. Even in this diverse group, people couldn't identify with me as my working-class friends

from Quincy did. Afterwards, several students . . . gave me big hugs. They were glad that I had said what I did. I felt torn apart. Why did I have to be the one who was the most different, the most outside of everyone else? (p. 223)

Summers' account of feeling different and separate from her classmates expresses some of the thoughts and emotions that homeless students might experience entering college. Summer gives voice to the sense that her being homeless divided her from other students. Many students from various backgrounds may feel alienated when they enter college. Homeless students seem to represent a unique social location that crosses boundaries of race or ethnicity, gender, sexual orientation, socioeconomic status, among others all at once. In that light, how might student affairs educators best promote the success of homeless college students? This chapter is meant to assist student affairs educators in navigating the complex issue of working with homeless students in college. I offer a background on homeless youth related to demographics and definitions. I then discuss some of the pre-college educational barriers homeless students might experience. Conceptually, resiliency theory provides a useful framework for working with homeless college students. I close this chapter with several recommendations designed to improve student success and engagement.

Definitions and Demographics

In the United States, an estimated 1.7 million youth, under the age of 18, experience homelessness each year (National Coalition for the Homeless, 2008). In addition, 2.8 million youth, under the age of 18, voluntarily leave their home or are forced to leave home by their parent or guardian (Greene, Ringwalt, Kelly, Iachan, & Cohen, 1995). The harsh lifestyles of homeless adolescents often lead to low self-esteem, depression, high anxiety, and poor personal health (Robertson, 1989). In 2009, of the 19.5 million students who identified as independents on their Free Application for Federal Student Aid (FAFSA), 47,204 also identified as homeless according to the National Association for the Education of Homeless Children and Youth (Furst, 2010). Prior to 2009, the number of homeless college students was not recorded.

As Hopper and Baumohl (1996) wrote, "it seems that homelessness is at best an odd-job word, pressed into service to impose order on a hodgepodge of social dislocation, extreme poverty, seasonal or itinerant work, and unconventional ways of life" (p. 3). Homelessness is not simply the absence of residence, but rather a complex social issue. As such, clear and consistent definitions are difficult to provide (Burt, 1996; Hopper & Baumohl, 1996). The problematic issue is does homelessness refer to simply the lack of adequate housing, or the disruption of various forms of social support that are implied in what one believes to constitute a home? The issue of a definition is further complicated by the fact that the population of homeless youth is heterogeneous (Murphy & Tobin, 2011). Youth homelessness cuts across multiple lines of difference (race/ethnicity, gender, sexual orientation, ability status, documentation status, etc.). Richard Ropers (1988) noted, "Understanding who the homeless are and where they come from must be the first step in proposing strategies to help" (p. 65). How homelessness is defined shapes the approaches taken to assist homeless students.

In lieu of an all-encompassing definition of what homelessness means, most definitions offer different categories into which homeless individuals may fit. Legislative policy is helpful in setting the parameters of who is considered homeless in regards to education. The McKinney-Vento Homelessness Assistance Act (1987) defines homeless youth as individuals who meet one of four criteria (Title X, Part C, of the No Child Left Behind Act):

- Youth who lack a fixed, regular, or adequate nighttime residence (adequate residence is defined as a structure designed for human habitation);

  1 This includes children or youth who reside in a shelter, welfare hotel, transitional living program, trailer parks or camp grounds due to lack of adequate accommodations, are abandoned in hospitals, or are awaiting foster care placement;
  2 Children or youth who are doubled up or share a residence with other persons due to loss of housing or economic hardship;
  3 Children or youth who reside in parks, cars, abandoned buildings, bus or train stations;
  4 Migratory children who meet any of the three previous conditions.

While McKinney-Vento outlines general parameters on youth homelessness, the literature identifies alternative ways of thinking about homeless youth.

One way to think about homeless youth is in relationship to their family. The literature distinguishes between youth who are with their families and youth who are unaccompanied or not in the care of a parent, family member, or an adult guardian. Family homelessness is one of the fastest growing segments of the homeless population (Anooshian, 2005; National Center on Family Homelessness, 2008). Studies report that an estimated 600,000 families experience homelessness each year (Burt, Aron, Lee, & Valente, 2001). Further, homeless families account for one-third of the total homeless population.

Unaccompanied youth is a "generic term to refer to minors who are outside a family or institutional setting and who are unaccompanied by a parent or legal guardian" (Robertson, 1992, p. 288). Unaccompanied youth fit into three sub-categories: throwaway youth, service disconnected youth or street youth, and systems youth. While many homeless youth are with their families, others have left home for multiple reasons including physical and sexual abuse. Throwaway youth are those who are asked to leave home by a parent or another adult in the household. Throwaway youth are away from home overnight and prevented from returning (Hammer, Finkelhor, & Sedlak, 2002). Street youth reside in high-risk, nontraditional locations, such as under bridges or in abandoned buildings. Street youth may or may not use shelters or other homeless service agencies; however, they spend most nights sleeping outside in inadequate spaces. Systems youth are those who have been involved in government systems (e.g., juvenile justice and foster care).

A third way to think of homeless youth is provided by William Tierney and colleagues (2008). They developed a typology of homeless youth that combines the location of homeless youth along with their familial relationship.

Typology of Homeless Youth

Those who live with an adult guardian in an unstable, but secure environment (shelter or storage room).

Those who live with an adult guardian in a semi-stable, but potentially dangerous environment (hotel, motel).

Those who are unaccompanied and live in long-term group homes as a foster care placement, but have a recent history of homelessness.
Those who live, or have lived for a significant period of time, with or without a guardian on the street and may be in the care of a shelter or agency.

Those who are doubled up with a parent or guardian in another person's home for an extended period of time.

Those who couch surf without an adult in a different person's home from night to night.
(Tierney, Gupton, & Hallett, 2008, p. 8)

The typology offered by Tierney et al. (2008) provides a more nuanced understanding of homeless youth. Although the definitions presented help in understanding who may be considered homeless, they do not address how many youth are homeless or at risk of becoming homeless.

Pre-College Educational Barriers for Homeless Youth

Homelessness is characterized by constant discontinuity in life; the strain on social relationships and the worry of finding food and shelter place homeless youth in a unique social location. Homeless youth are one of the most marginalized groups in society. Not only do they experience economic hardship, but also they encounter additional negative conditions that impact their social, physical, and psychological well-being. For example, homeless youth are more susceptible to experiencing trauma, abuse, fear, neglect, and disruption in their education trajectories, which are highly correlated to poorer academic achievement (Rafferty & Shinn, 1991).

Living on the street affects homeless youth and their ability to transition into adulthood. Family instability, abuse, neglect, and lack of role models impact an adolescent's ability to build trusting relationships and establish support networks that are necessary for a successful transition into adulthood (Greenblatt & Robertson, 1993; Robertson, 1989; Yates, Mackenzie, Pennbridge, & Cohen, 1988). Homeless youth may experience a variety of challenges in becoming adults, from being taken advantage of while living on the street to participating in gang culture or in forms of prostitution. There is no single cause of homelessness in youth; however, many repeatedly cite poverty, family conflict, and mobility (school or residential) as factors (Rafferty & Shinn, 1991; Rafferty, Shinn, & Weitzman, 2004; Rumberger & Larson, 1998). I now address each of these three potential factors of homelessness. These factors work in concert to create a unique dynamic of homelessness.

Poverty

Poverty is one of the primary dimensions of homelessness (Fleming, Burns, & Haydamack, 2004). In some of the early work on homeless children, Bassuk and Rosenberg (1988) found that the experience of homelessness exacerbates the experience of poverty. As poverty makes it difficult for individuals and families to provide shelter, food, and security, becoming homeless makes providing those basic needs nearly impossible. Haber and Toro (2004) suggested that disproportionate numbers of adolescents who are homeless come from low-income or working class families and neighborhoods with family incomes under $35,000. In Los Angeles County, the 2000 Census found nearly 750,000 residents with incomes below the poverty threshold (Fleming et al., 2004). Families in poverty are impacted by the lack of affordable housing, which also adds to the homeless population. As the amount of affordable housing declines, more families will end up homeless during times of economic strife. Some families in poverty may force a child to leave home due to financial discord, thus, adding to the throwaway youth category. Further, poverty may also lead to child neglect by the parent and place the child or adolescent in the systems youth category.

Family Conflict

Homeless youth report having disrupted family histories. In a Hollywood, California, street sample of youth between the ages of 13 and 17, 16% of the adolescents had no previous contact with their biological fathers, and 9% had no prior contact with either parent (Greenblatt & Robertson, 1993). Among the parents known, almost three quarters had been divorced or were never married (Greenblatt & Robertson, 1993). Disruptive family conditions are the principal reason that young people leave home. In one study, more than half of the youth interviewed during shelter stays reported that their parents either told them to leave or knew they were leaving and did not care (Greene et al., 1995).

Abuse may precipitate separations of many youth from their homes. In the Hollywood, California, street sample described above, 37% of youth reported leaving their homes in the past due to physical abuse, and 11% reported leaving due to sexual abuse (Greenblatt & Robertson, 1993). Twenty percent had at some earlier point been removed from their homes by the authorities because of neglect or abuse (Robertson, 1989). As all families have some level of strife, this strife cannot always be reconciled for homeless youth. Homeless adolescents experience of family conflict results in their leaving home and running away. Family conflict can also result in youth becoming systems youth, if the youth are removed because neglect or abuse and placed in the care of the State.

School and Residential Mobility

Frequent moves from school to school create significant educational obstacles for homeless youth. Research indicates students who change schools due to unplanned residential mobility, such as that associated with homelessness, score lower on standardized tests and have lower overall academic achievement (Kerbow, 1996; Lash & Kirkpatrick, 1994; Rumberger & Larson, 1998). Most comparisons of these two populations have found relatively more scholastic deficits among homeless children (Rafferty, 1991; Rescorla, Parker, & Stolley, 1991; Vostanius, Grattan, Cumella, & Winchester, 1997). Mobility anywhere along the path from elementary school through high school diminishes the prospects of graduation and access to higher education (Haveman & Wolfe, 1994). However, most comparisons of academic achievement between homeless and generally impoverished youth reveal that the former group experiences more scholastic deficits than the latter (Rafferty, 1991). The effect of poverty on education compounded by frequent mobility due to homelessness hinders students' academic achievement.

Homeless children tend to experience poorer educational and cognitive outcomes than housed, impoverished children. Homelessness is more highly associated with residential mobility and other multiple risk factors that lead to grade retention and drop out (Wolff, 2000). Unstable living arrangements also contribute to adolescent homelessness. Youth who have a history of foster care placements are more likely to become homeless at an earlier age and remain homeless for longer periods (Roman & Wolfe, 1995). Other youth become homeless when they are discharged from the foster care system. While these adolescents are too old for foster care, they are also unable to support themselves independently (Robertson, 1989). Once youth become homeless, they may move multiple times between emergency shelters. The increased frequency of residential mobility in homeless youth and families may be distinct from other low-income students (Ziesemer, Marcoux, & Marwell, 1994). Residential mobility might be driven by poverty and the lack of affordable housing, forcing families to continually move to afford a place to stay. Further residential mobility also influences family conflict, by breaking social networks due to moving and thus creating more tension within the family.

Finally, school and residential mobility have negative effects on social relationships. Stable social relationships are essential if students are to grow into well-adjusted adults. Residential or school mobility can disrupt family relations especially with unaccompanied youth whose family conflicts may include abuse or neglect at home. Shelter regulations prohibiting unaccompanied youth from staying in family or adult shelters put these students at further risk. Other social relationships suffer from high mobility. Youth may face difficulties in making new friends when moving into a new school in the middle of the year. Getting accustomed to a new building, new teachers, new rules, new textbooks, and new peers can be overwhelming. When children and youth do not expect to remain in a school for an appreciable time, making friends or investing in homework can seem like a pointless endeavor (Cauce, 2000; Julianelle & Foscarinis, 2003).

Youth homelessness is not simply the lack of a home; rather, it is the confluence of multiple interrelated dimensions. Homeless youth differ from other low-income students because poverty, mobility, and family conflict work concurrently to create a complex dynamic of homelessness. Homelessness is not just one factor but consists of multiple factors that are pushing against and influencing each other. Youth who simultaneously experience multiple factors will be at a greater risk of homelessness. My intent is not to suggest that a certain amount of mobility, poverty, or family conflict leads to homelessness; rather, I wish to illustrate how multiple factors related to youth homelessness might conspire to result in becoming homeless. Understanding how the different dimensions of homelessness work in concert with each other is one way to conceptualize youth homelessness.

Postsecondary Education and Homeless Youth

Access and affordability are critical issues for potential and current homeless college students. Similar to other low-income students, homeless youth encounter obstacles in gaining access to and paying for college. While low-income youth need guidance through the financial aid process, such as having problems gaining access to college due to a lack of access to accurate and timely information, homeless youth require a greater degree of assistance. Homeless adolescents might have issues of family conflict and they may be unable to ask their parents for the necessary information to complete the FAFSA.

Despite these barriers, federal legislation has been passed to try to ease the transition from high school to college. The 2005 reauthorization of the Higher Education Act includes amendments that promote access to postsecondary education for homeless youth. For example, the amendment, "Improving Access to Education for Students Who Are Homeless or in Foster Care Act" reflects an understanding that many of the barriers, which obstruct access to K-12 education, are identical for postsecondary education. The act promotes access to and completion of higher education through: (1) early intervention to provide support in assisting and planning for a college education at the high school level; (2) independent student status, which allows the student to be considered an independent when applying for financial aid; and (3) establishing a model for improved recruitment and retention of homeless and foster care students in higher education (Improving Access to Education for Students Who Are Homeless or in Foster Care Act, 2005).

However, the act was only introduced but never voted on by the House of Representatives. In 2007, the College Cost Reduction and Access Act was signed into law. This act allows unaccompanied homeless youth to be considered independent students upon verification of their living situation by a McKinney-Vento school district liaison, a shelter director, transitional shelter, or independent living program. This improves homeless students' access to financial aid by allowing them to apply for financial aid directly without parental information or a signature. (National Association for the Education of Homeless Children and Youth, 2006). The College Cost Reduction and Access Act also allowed institutions to identify homeless students by adding questions about homelessness to the FAFSA. More recently, the McKinney-Vento Education for Homeless Children and Youth program was allocated $65 million for the 2009 fiscal year by the federal government. Furthermore, the American Recovery and Reinvestment Act of 2009 provided an additional $70 million for the Education for Homeless Children and Youth program (U.S. Department of Education, 2009). These legislative amendments and additional monies help homeless students access funding for higher education. Educational policy has helped to improve access to higher education for homeless youth and promoted awareness of homeless students in college. As more homeless students are identified, they will be able to take advantage of the vast array of supportive individuals and programs on campus.

Resiliency Theory

In recent years, the study of at-risk populations has turned from a deficit model to a resiliency model. The utilization of resiliency as a conceptual framework allows researchers to examine the strengths of at-risk students and how they cope with adversity. While prior research on homeless youth focused on problems and deficits, a new research agenda is focused on the strengths of youth to endure harsh conditions.

Resiliency is a developmental psychological theory that offers insights into why some children and youth are able to endure and persevere through traumatic experiences (Garmezy, 1991; Masten, 2001; Werner, 2000). Resiliency theory illustrates how personal factors might assist homeless youth in enduring their experiences while homeless and transitioning to a stable adult life. The premise of resiliency is that individuals with certain traits and dispositions are able to recover from various life stressors they experience. Studies of resilience support the view that human psychological development is buffered and self-correcting (Luthar, 1999; Masten, Best, & Garmezy, 1990). Resiliency theory holds promise for homeless youth, as they struggle to create positive outcomes that help them become stable and healthy adults (Hines, Merdinger, & Wyatt, 2005). Below I review the literature on resiliency theory and consider how it applies to homeless youth and higher education.

Defining Resilience

Resiliency is an umbrella term for the many instances in which an individual is able to adapt to and thrive despite adverse conditions. Specifically, "resiliency refers to a class of phenomena characterized by good outcomes in spite of serious threats to adaptation or development" (Masten, 2001, p. 228). The study of resiliency aspires to illustrate how the process of malleability operates to create pathways out of stressful and harmful conditions, such as homelessness.

The meaning of resiliency has evolved as the literature has grown. Early resiliency theorists viewed resiliency as an innate characteristic of youth (Garmezy, 1984). Resiliency was related to inherited traits, such as intelligence. To explain resiliency, researchers made an analogy to three dolls; the first doll is made of glass, the second doll is made of plastic, and the third doll is made of steel. When placed under stress, the first doll cracks, the second is permanently scarred, while the third continues to maintain its integrity due to its inherent strength. The doll analogy was used to demonstrate that certain youth have innate genetic characteristics that allow them to withstand and thrive under stressful conditions. Later research showed that resiliency is not only related to inherited genetic traits, but that it is part of the complex development of children who experienced trauma (Garmezy, 1991; Werner, 1989). As Wolff (1995) contended:

> Resilience is an enduring aspect of the person. Genetic and other constitutionally based qualities both determine and are in turn modified by life experiences. Good intelligence plays a major part, as does an easy, adaptable, sociable temperament that attract positive responses from others which in turn contribute to that inner sense of self-worth, competence and self-efficacy that has repeatedly been identified as a vital component of resilience. The sources of such positive responses are threefold: primary relationships within the family; the network of relationships with adults and children outside the family; and competence and achievement. (p. 568)

Wolff's statement details the salient features of the theoretical framework for resiliency. As such, resiliency is defined as an individual having the cognitive ability to locate and create positive and trusting relationships, having an encouraging family or family-like relationships, and possessing an external support structure.

Three Components of Resiliency

Norman Garmezy (1991) was the first to develop an articulated framework for resiliency. Based on the literature, Garmezy (1991) suggests three types of protective factors: (1) individual characteristics of the child; (2) a close relationship within the family; and (3) a certain type of social support and structure outside the family (Werner & Smith, 1992). A theoretical grounding in resilience and its underlying processes can help guide development and implementation of new and more effective practices and policies for meeting the needs of homeless children and youth.

Resiliency as a Personal Attribute

The primary factor in developing resiliency relates to the person's intelligence and disposition. A high intelligence and an easygoing disposition are frequently cited as characteristics of resilient youth (Luthar, 1993; Rutter, 1996; Wolff, 1995). Youth who possess above average cognitive abilities are able to understand their current situation. Further, intelligence allows youth to know what is within their control and what is beyond their control and decide on a coping strategy or find a more supportive environment (Block & Kremen, 1996). In a study of 132 college students, Campbell-Sills, Cohan, and Stein (2006) found that individuals who experienced childhood neglect and who scored high on resilience reported fewer current psychiatric symptoms than individuals who had not experienced childhood neglect and who scored high on resilience. The finding is consistent with the contention that resilience constitutes not just recovery but growth and strengthening from adversity. The temperament of the youth also helps them to find support. Wolff (1995) pointed out that through their behavior, individuals stimulate responses that help or hinder them. For example, an easygoing person is more likely to create a positive response in others to their request than an individual with a poor disposition.

Resiliency as Familial Support

The second factor of resiliency in youth is family support, as family members can provide validation to mediate stressful conditions. Research on stress-resilient children has shown that parents with positive parental attitudes were more involved in their children's lives (Gribble, Cowen, Wyman, Work, & Wannon, 1993). As homeless youth experience high levels of family conflict, it would appear that this factor does not apply to them. However, even when the parent–child relationship is strained, it still might serve as a source of protection if the child and the parent have a positive relationship early in the child's development (Conrad & Hammen, 1993). Many homeless youth leave home due to physical or sexual abuse, while others are forced to leave at the request of their parents. Further, some are forced to leave because their parent is unable to take care of them because of alcohol or drug abuse. Resilient youth have above-average intelligence; they are able to recognize moments and situations when a parent is out of control due to mental or physical illness. Consequently, they may ascribe the actions of their parent to the illness or medication and rely on the knowledge that when healthy, the parent cares for them. Further, because of their even temperament, resilient homeless youth may be able to reconcile with their families and ease the transition to returning home.

Resiliency as Institutional Support

The third common factor of resilient youth is external support from institutions and individuals outside the family. For example, a teacher or mentor might supplant the role of a caring parent. Further, a religious or educational institution that fosters hope, stability, and competence in youth aids the development of resiliency. Locating and gaining access to external support networks relates to the first factor of resiliency—intelligence. Research has shown that youth who recognize opportunities for support and engender trust in others are more likely to benefit from external relationships (Milgram & Palti, 1993). As many youth experience family conflict, external adults and institutions offer protection from the chaos of home. In regards to homeless youth, schools, shelters, and religious institutions provide safe havens for youth and can help them transition to independent living.

As educational institutions focus on developing competencies in youth, they are logical institutions to help in the development of resiliency (Ross, Smith, Casey, & Slavin, 1995). Schools and colleges provide relief from the stressors students may experience. Educational institutions offer more opportunities for youth to develop resiliency. Youth have the opportunity to form relationships with students, teachers, and other school staff. Further, K-12 schools and universities offer multiple extracurricular activities that might also serve as forms of external support (Consortium on the School-Based Promotion of Social Competence, 1996). When students participate in extracurricular activities (e.g., athletics or yearbook committee), they are able to form positive networks of social support.

Further, researchers have used resiliency theory to better understand student retention in higher education (Sanlo, 2004; Shield, 2004). Sanlo's (2004) article examines the survival skills that sexual minority students need to complete higher education. Sanlo points out that the higher education research and practice would benefit from an articulated model of resiliency and its effects on lesbian, gay, and bisexual students. Shield's (2004) study examines how Native American students must draw on resiliency to persist through higher education. Shield views resilience as an aspect of Native American culture; thus, most Native American students are resilient when they enter higher education. As most postsecondary institutions are hostile to Native American cultural traditions and values, having Native American student centers and student groups provides the student with an external support group on campus. The work of Sanlo (2004) and Shield (2004) highlights the importance of resiliency to marginalized students in higher education.

Based on the literature, I argue that resiliency is like a coat that people might put on to weather the tumultuous times in their life. The strength of resiliency theory is that it illustrates the characteristics needed to cope with adversity and make smooth transitions in their development toward adulthood. As such, higher education is an ideal place to continue to help homeless students develop their capacity for resiliency.

Student Engagement Strategies

Using resiliency theory as a framework, I provide several recommendations below for better engaging homeless students on campus. These strategies are grounded in the needs and challenges outlined above.

- Recognize that homeless youth are part of the campus community and create resources to meet their unique needs. While the new educational policies increase access for homeless students, postsecondary educators must also increase awareness among their colleagues regarding the experiences of homeless students on campus. Prior to the creation of new policies or programs, institutional leaders need to examine the homeless student population currently on campus. As homeless youth are a heterogeneous group, no one-size-fits-all approach will be effective. Educators should look for trends and then identify appropriate courses of action.

- Establish an access and community outreach advisory committee for low-income students, in particular homeless youth, at the institution. A committee focused on the needs of various low-income students would bring together key institutional agents and student leaders for the purpose of monitoring and improving services for low-income students. The committee would be charged with creating partnerships between the college or university and agencies that work with homeless students. Higher education institutions can implement some quick initiatives to start building linkages with homeless youth service providers. For example, colleges might create an advisory board of local youth shelters to make recommendations about how to best work with shelters and provide educational services. They might also ask shelters if any youth they serve are enrolled at the school; if so, they might speak with those students about their experiences gaining access to the college and taking courses. Further, because many homeless youth are in secondary school systems, colleges and universities should work with the local school district liaisons for homeless youth and ensure that they are aware of their college options and any programs or scholarships for homeless youth available.

- Create an economic distress student support network. The network would be a collaborative effort consisting of multiple units on campus (e.g., financial aid, student support services, and student housing). The economic distress student support network would be a repository of information and services for students experiencing financial issues. For example, University of California, Los Angeles created an Economic Crisis Response (ECR) team to help meet the needs of students facing financial distress and in danger of leaving college. The ECR assists students with both on and off campus costs (e.g., buying text books, finding scholarships, academic advisement, finding an affordable cell phone plan, privatized loans, and transitional housing programs). An ECR team helps to promote student persistence by centralizing the relevant information students need when experiencing a financial crisis. An economic distress student support network would be able to provide resources for students who become homeless during the academic year.

- Give homeless students priority in the selection of on-campus housing. Obviously, one of the best ways to help homeless students is to provide them with a stable and safe place to stay. Living in a residence hall will help homeless students acclimate to college life and have direct access to on-campus support services. Further, the institution should ensure that students have the option to stay on campus in a residence hall during extended school breaks (i.e., winter and summer break). Homeless students may not have an adequate place to go if they are forced to leave their residence hall during school breaks. In some cases, students return to a shelter or group home over the break. For homeless students who cannot find a shelter, they may need to resort to couch surfing (sleeping on a different individual's couch or floor each night). An open residence hall offers students a safe place to stay without feeling like they are burdening friends or entering a chaotic environment of a youth shelter.

- Create a higher education homeless liaison position. The McKinney Vento Act provides each school district with a homeless education liaison. The liaison works to ensure that the provisions of McKinney Vento are met. In addition, liaisons provide support and information to teachers and school administrators working with homeless students. As such, institutions of higher education should consider creating a higher education homeless liaison position. The higher education homeless liaison would be tasked with monitoring educational policy related to homeless youth at state and federal levels. The liaison would also work to bridge postsecondary institutions with shelters and community service agencies that cater to homeless youth. Finally, the liaison would update institutions regarding financial aid and scholarship opportunities for homeless students.

- Create a financial aid checklist for homeless students. Paying for college is one of the critical obstacles homeless college students experience. The creation of a financial aid checklist tailored to homeless students would help demystify the financial aid application process. As noted earlier, the College Cost Reduction and Access Act broadened the definition of who is considered an independent student to include unaccompanied homeless youth. Homeless students should have an adult guide them through the verification process. The checklist should include a list of scholarships for students who are homeless or have at some point experienced homelessness. For example the LeTendre Education Fund provides multiple scholarships each year to homeless college students. The checklist would also help students understand the jargon associated with the financial aid process. In addition, the checklist could include a section regarding on-campus jobs and work-study.

Conclusion: Homeless Youth and Higher Education

In the past, conversations regarding the educational policy and pedagogy for homeless youth focused on K-12. Yet, the recent higher education policy changes regarding homeless students and college access create new opportunities for the education of homeless youth. These polices have helped to bring the concerns of this particular student population to light. Although interest in homeless college students has picked up in the last few years, homeless students have been on college campuses for a long time. The difference is that now colleges and universities have some means of identifying homeless students and providing support.

For homeless youth, the goal of a college degree is not impossible or improbable, although it may appear to be impractical given their situation. Homelessness causes a great deal of chaos in the lives of youth, which makes long-term goals difficult to conceptualize. To be sure, the primary concerns with homeless youth are to get off the streets and into stable and safe living environments.

Attending a postsecondary institution would allow homeless youth to build their capacity for resiliency and attain their goal of a college degree. This requires a system within colleges and universities that recognizes and understands homeless youth and is willing to organize its resources to meet their needs. The opportunity to interact with other students, faculty, and staff at the institution will provide homeless students with new and positive support networks. The strategies outlined in this chapter require that postsecondary educators take into account the needs of homeless youth as an integral part of the population they are to serve.

References

Anooshian, L. (2005). Violence and aggression in the lives of homeless children: A review. *Aggression and Violent Behavior, 10*(2), 129–152.

Bassuk, E. L., & Rosenberg, L. (1988). Why does family homelessness occur? A case-control study. *American Journal of Public Health, 78*(7), 783–788.

Block, J., & Kremen, A. M. (1996). IQ and ego-resiliency: Conceptual and empirical connections and separateness. *Journal of Personality & Social Psychology, 70*(2), 349–361.

Burt, M. (1996). Homelessness: Definitions and counts. In J. Baumohl (Ed.), *Homelessness in America* (pp. 15–23). Phoenix, AZ: Oryx Press.

Burt, M., Aron, L., Lee, E., & Valente, J. (2001). *Helping America's homeless: Emergency shelter or affordable housing?* Washington, DC: The Urban Institute.

Campbell-Sills, L., Cohan, S. L., & Stein, M. B. (2006). Relationship of resilience to personality, coping and psychiatric symptoms in young adults. *Behavior Research and Therapy, 44*(4), 585–599.

Cauce, A. (2000). The characteristics and mental health of homeless adolescents: Age and gender differences. *Journal of Emotional and Behavioral Disorders, 8*(4), 230–239.

Conrad, M., & Hammen, C. (1993). Protective and resource factors in high- and low-risk children: A comparison of children with unipolar, bipolar, medically ill, and normal mothers. *Development and Psychopathology, 5*(4), 593–607.

Consortium on the School-Based Promotion of Social Competence. (1996). The school-based promotion of social competence: Theory, research, practice, and policy. In R. J. Haggerty, L. R. Sherrod, N. Garmezy, & M. Rutter (Eds.), *Stress, risk, and resilience in children and adolescents: Processes, mechanisms, and interventions* (pp. 268–316). Cambridge, UK: Cambridge University Press.

Fleming, D., Burns, P., & Haydamack, B. (2004). *Homeless in LA: Final research report for the 10-year plan to end homelessness in Los Angeles County.* Retrieved from http://www.economicrt.org/summaries/homeless_in_la_synopsis.html

Furst, R. (2010, December 28). Homeless—and going to college. *The Star Tribune.* Retrieved from www.startribune.com

Garmezy, N. (1984). The study of stress and competency in children: A building block for developmental psychopathology. *Child Development, 55*(1), 97–111.

Garmezy, N. (1991). Resilience in children's adaptation to negative life events and stressed environments. *Pediatric Annals, 20*(9), 459–466.

Greenblatt, M., & Robertson, M.J. (1993). Homeless adolescents: Lifestyle, survival strategies and sexual behaviors. *Hospital and Community Psychiatry, 44*, 1177–1180.

Greene, J., Ringwalt, C., Kelly, J., Iachan, R., & Cohen, Z. (1995). *Youth with runaway, throwaway, and homeless experiences: Prevalence, drug use, and other at-risk behaviors.* Washington, DC: U.S. Department of Health and Human Services, Administration on Children, Youth and Families.

Gribble, P.A., Cowen, E.L., Wyman, P.A., Work, W.C., & Wannon, M. (1993). Parent and child views of parent–child relationship qualities and resilient outcomes among urban children. *Journal of Child Psychology and Psychiatry, 34*(4), 507–519.

Haber, M.G., & Toro P.A. (2004). Homelessness among families, children, and adolescents: An ecological-developmental perspective. *Clinical Child and Family Psychology Review, 7*(3), 123–164.

Hammer, H., Finkelhor, D., & Sedlak, A. (2002). *Runaway/thrownaway children: National estimates and characteristics. National Incidence Studies of Missing, Abducted, Runaway and Thrownaway Children* (NISMART Bulletin Series). Washington, DC: U.S. Department of Justice, Office of Justice Programs, Office of Juvenile Justice and Delinquency Prevention. Retrieved from www.ncjrs.org/pdffiles1/ojjdp/196469.pdf

Haveman, R., & Wolfe, B. (1994). *Succeeding generations: On the effects of investments in children.* New York, NY: Russell Sage Foundation.

Hines, A.M., Merdinger, J. & Wyatt, P. (2005). Former foster youth attending college: Resilience and the transition to young adulthood. *American Journal of Orthopsychiatry, 75*(3), 381–394.

Hopper, K., & Baumohl, J. (1996). Redefining the cursed word: A historical interpretation of American homelessness. In J. Baumohl, (Ed.), *Homelessness in America* (pp. 3–14). Phoenix, AZ: Oryx Press.

Improving Access to Education for Students Who Are Homeless or in Foster Care Act. (2005). Retrieved on April, 25, from www.theorator.com/bills109/s1429.html

Julianelle, P., & Foscarinis, M. (2003). Responding to the school mobility of children and youth experiencing homelessness: The McKinney-Vento Act and beyond. *Journal of Negro Education, 72*(1), 39–54.

Kerbow, D. (1996). Patterns of urban student mobility and local school reform. *Journal Of Education for Students at Risk, 1*(2), 147–69.

Lash, A.A., & Kirkpatrick, S.L. (1994). Interrupted lessons: Teacher views of transfer students education. *American Education Research Journal, 31*(4), 813–843.

Luthar, S.S. (1993). Annotation: Methodological and conceptual issues in research on childhood resilience. *Journal of Child Psychology and Psychiatry, 34*(4), 441–453.

Luthar, S.S. (1999). *Poverty and children's adjustment. Developmental clinical psychology and psychiatry.* Thousand Oaks, CA: Sage.

Masten, A.S. (2001). Ordinary magic: Resilience processes in development. *American Psychologist, 56*(3), 227–238.

Masten, A.S., Best, K.M., & Garmezy, N. (1990). Resilience and development: Contributions from the study of children who overcome adversity. *Development and Psychopathology, 2*(4), 425–444.

McKinney-Vento Homelessness Assistance Act, Pub. L. No. 100–77, § 11301, 101 Stat. 482 (1987).

Milgram, N.A., & Palti, G. (1993). Psychosocial characteristics of resilient children. *Journal of Research in Personality, 27*(3), 207–221.

Murphy, J., & Tobin, K. (2011). *Homelessness comes to school.* Thousand Oaks, CA: Corwin Publishers.

National Association for the Education of Homeless Children and Youth. (2006). *Legislative updates* Retrieved from www.naehcy.org/legislative_update.html

National Center on Family Homelessness. (2008). *The Characteristics of and needs of families experiencing homelessness.* Retrieved from http://community.familyhomelessness.org/sites/default/files/NCFH%20Fact%20Sheet%204-08.pdf

National Coalition for the Homeless. (2008). *NCH fact sheet. Homeless Youth.* NCH Fact Sheet #13. Washington D.C. Retrieved from www.nationalhomeless.org

Rafferty, Y. (1991). Developmental and educational consequences of homelessness on children and youth. In J.H. Kryder-Coe, L.M. Salamon, & J.M. Molnar (Eds.), *Homeless children and youth: A new American dilemma,* (pp. 105–139). New Brunswick, NJ: Transaction.

Rafferty, Y., & Shinn, M. (1991). The impact of homelessness on children. *American Psychologist, 46*, 1170–1179.

Rafferty, Y., Shinn, M., & Weitzman, M. (2004). Academic achievement among formerly homeless adolescents and their continuously housed peers. *Journal of School Psychology, 42*, 179–199.

Rescorla, L., Parker, R., & Stolley P. (1991). Ability, achievement, and adjustment in homeless children. *American Journal of Orthopsychiatry, 6*(2), 210–220.

Robertson, M. J. (1989). *Homeless youth in Hollywood: Patterns of alcohol use.* Report to the National Institute on Alcohol Abuse & alcoholism. Berkley, CA: Alcohol Research Group.

Robertson, J. (1992). Homeless and runaway youth: A review of the literature. In M. Robertson & M. Greenblatt (Eds.), *Homelessness: A national perspective* (pp. 287–297). New York, NY: Plenum Press.

Roman, N. P. & Wolfe, P. (1995). *Web of failure: The relationship between foster care and homelessness.* Retrieved from www.endhomelessness.org/content/general/detail/1285

Ropers, R. (1988). *The invisible homeless: A new urban ecology.* New York, NY: Human Sciences Press.

Ross, S. M., Smith, L. J., Casey, J., & Slavin, R. E. (1995). Increasing the academic success of disadvantaged children: An examination of alternative early intervention programs. *American Educational Research Journal, 32*(4), 773–800.

Rumberger, R. W., & Larson, K. A. (1998). Student mobility and the increase risk of high school dropout. *American Journal of Education, 107*(1), 1–35.

Rutter, M. (1996). Stress research: Accomplishments and tasks ahead. In R. J. Haggerty, L. R. Sherrod, N. Garmezy, & M. Rutter (Eds.), *Stress, risk, and resilience in children and adolescents: Processes, mechanisms, and interventions* (pp. 354–386). Cambridge, UK: Cambridge University Press.

Sanlo, R. (2004). Lesbian, gay, and bisexual college students: Risk, resiliency, and retention. *Journal of College Student Retention, 6*(1), 97–110.

Shield, R. W. (2004). The retention of indigenous students in higher education: Historical issues, federal policy, and indigenous resilience. *Journal of College Student Retention Research Theory and Practice, 6*(1), 111–127.

Summer, L. (2003). *Learning joy from dogs without collars: A memoir.* New York, NY: Simon & Schuster.

Tierney, W. G., Gupton, J. T., Hallett, R. E. (2008). *Transitions to adulthood for homeless adolescents: Education and public policy.* Los Angeles, CA: Center for Higher Education Policy Analysis.

U.S. Department of Education. (2009). Guidance on McKinney-Vento Homeless Children and Youth funds made available under the American Recovery and Reinvestment Act of 2009 (U.S. Department of Education Publication No. 20202). Washington, DC: Author. Retrieved from www.serve.org/NCHE/arra/arra.php#ehcy

Vostanius, P., Grattan, E., Cumella, S., & Winchester, C. (1997). Psychosocial functioning of homeless children. *Journal of the America Academy of Child and Adolescent Psychiatry, 36*(7), 881–889.

Werner, E. E. (1989). High-risk children in young adulthood: A longitudinal study from birth to 32 years. *American Journal of Orthopsychiatry, 59*(1), 72–81.

Werner, E. E. (2000). Protective factors and individual resilience. In J. P. Shonkoff & S. J. Meisels (Eds.), *Handbook of early childhood intervention* (2nd ed., pp. 115–132). New York, NY: Cambridge University Press.

Werner, E. E., & Smith, R. S. (1992). *Overcoming the odds: High risk children from birth to adulthood.* Ithaca, NY: Cornell University Press.

Wolff, B. (2000). *Residential and academic instability: A comprehensive model linking youth homelessness to poor academics.* Retrieved from www.CTKidslink.org/pub_detail_129html-20k

Wolff, S. (1995). The concept of resilience. *Australian & New Zealand Journal of Psychiatry, 29*(4), 565–574.

Yates, G. L., Mackenzie, R., Pennbridge J., & Cohen, E. (1988). A risk profile comparison of runaway and non runaway youth. *American Journal of Public Health, 78*(7), 820–821.

Ziesemer, C., Marcoux, L., & Marwell, B. E. (1994). Homeless children: are they different from other low-income children? *Social Work, 39*(6), 658–668.

Chapter 15
Engaging Low-Income Students

Adrianna J. Kezar, MaryBeth Walpole,
and Laura W. Perna

Engagement is now commonly understood to be critical to students' success in college, whether success is defined as academic performance, persistence to degree completion, or satisfaction. But, considerably less attention has been paid to the reality that engagement is a luxury that affluent students are most able to afford. Engagement requires time, and, while people in the United States do not like to discuss class issues in our supposedly meritocratic society, time is something that is acquired through wealth. In American higher education, the wealthy students have always been more able to choose to not work, to choose to live on campus, and to choose to devote their time to their academic studies as well as co- and extra-curricular activities.

In contrast, low-income students typically do not have the time to engage in college in the same ways as wealthy students. Differences in patterns and characteristics of enrollment by family income imply the variations in time available for engagement. Data show that, compared with their higher-income peers, low-income students are more likely to work upward of 30 hours a week to pay for school, are less likely to be continuously enrolled (e.g., stopping out to work), are more often enrolled part-time, and are less likely to live on campus. While the latter may save money, it also requires time for transportation to and from school (Colyar, 2011; Walpole, 2011). Qualitative research poignantly illustrates the time and other constraints facing students who are simultaneously juggling multiple responsibilities not just of college enrollment but also employment, childcare, and other demands (Levin, Montero-Hernandez, & Cerven, 2010; Perna, 2010a; Ziskin, Torres, Hossler, & Gross, 2010). Given these patterns, it is not surprising that students from low-income families tend to be less involved in extracurricular and co-curricular activities than their peers from higher-income families (Arzy, Davies, & Harbour, 2006; Seider, 2008; Walpole, 2011).

Given the very real time constraints facing low-income students, higher education professionals must rethink how students can and should be engaged in college. Kuh, Kinzie, Bridges, and Hayek's (2006) model also stresses the importance of engagement.

This model assumes that engagement in "educationally effective practices" promotes student success, including college persistence. The five educationally-effective practices that are operationalized in the National Survey of Student Engagement (NSSE) are academic challenge, active and collaborative learning, student-faculty interaction, enriching educational experiences, and supportive campus environment. As Kuh (2001) implies, consideration of how to promote student engagement must include attention to not only how students are spending their time, but also how an institution is structuring experiences and providing opportunities for all students to participate. Yet, the institution's role in fostering engagement specific to low-income students has not been examined.

This chapter offers recommendations for ways that institutions can rethink their own operations and make "technological advances" that improve the opportunity for low-income students to be academically and socially engaged. For example, research and theory presented in this chapter underscore the need to rethink where engagement possibilities exist; constraints on low-income students' time suggest the benefits of focusing more on engagement opportunities inside rather than outside the classroom. This is just one example of the many recommendations that this chapter provides.

While some research and theory assumes that the experiences and outcomes of low-income students can be solved by simply "fixing" low-income students to behave more like higher-income students, this chapter emphasizes the value of an "anti-deficit" perspective. Such an approach conceptualizes low-income students as hard-working, strategic, responsible, creative problem-solvers who are juggling many competing demands (Walpole, 2011). Along the same lines, Colyar (2011) points out the importance of not marginalizing students by marking them as deficient or different (e.g., by designating that only low-income students participate in special programming). Engle and Lynch (2011) contend that offering to all students services that assist low-income students may reduce any stigma associated with special program participation and increase outcomes for all students.

Guided by these assumptions, in this chapter we offer information for practitioners to rethink and reframe their approach to working with low-income students. The chapter begins by describing the characteristics of low-income college students. We then discuss relevant theory and prior research for understanding the experiences and behaviors of low-income students and the role of institutions in shaping these experiences. We conclude by offering recommendations for institutional practices that will better serve low-income students. A much deeper discussion of the issues facing low-income students is offered in two books we recently authored and contributed chapters to: *Recognizing and Serving Low-Income Students in Higher Education* (Kezar, 2011), and *Understanding the Working College Student: New Research and Its Implications for Policy and Practice* (Perna, 2010a).

Characteristics of Low-Income College Students

Before understanding how to better serve low-income students, we must first identify who they are. Although low-income students are defined and categorized in several different ways (Walpole, 2007), available data and research consistently show that they are less likely than more affluent students to achieve various college-related outcomes. Low-income students across all racial groups are less likely to attend college, less likely to persist in college, and less likely to earn a degree (Bowen, Chingos, & McPherson, 2009; DesJardin, Ahlburg, & McCall, 2006; Heller & Rasmussen, 2002; Karabel, 2005; NCES, 2009; Paulsen & St. John, 2002; Perna, 2005a; Wei & Horn, 2009). This is due, in part, to current admissions and financial aid systems that favor higher income students (Heller & Rasmussen, 2002; Karabel, 2005). In 2007, the gap between the percentage of low- (55%) and high-income (78%) students who enroll in college following high school was 23 percentage points (NCES, 2009). Only 12% of low-income students obtain a bachelor's degree within six years following high school graduation compared to 73% of high-income students (Mortenson, 2007).

When they do enroll, low-income students tend to attend less selective and less costly institutions than their higher-income peers (Advisory Committee on Student Financial Assistance, 2001; Astin & Oseguera, 2004; Bailey, Jenkins, & Leinbach, 2005; Berkner, He, & Cataldi, 2002; Bowen et al., 2009; Steinburg, Piraino, & Haveman, 2009). For example, in 1995–96, 55% of community college students were from the lowest two income quartiles, compared to 38% of students attending public four-year institutions (Bailey et al., 2005). In 2008, according to data from NCES, only 15% of low-income students attended public four-year institutions, 6% attended private four-year institutions, 52% attended public two year colleges, and 19% attended private, for profit institutions (Portraits, 2011). These figures compare to: 25%, 12%, 49%, and 5% respectively for non-low-income students. Low-income students are less likely to enroll full time, enroll continuously, and live on campus (Berkner et al., 2002; Paulsen & St. John, 2002; Walpole, 2011). Moreover, low-income students work more and are less involved in extracurricular activities than their peers from higher income families (Arzy et al., 2006; Paulsen & St. John, 2002; Seider, 2008; Walpole, 2011). These factors all contribute to lower persistence and attainment rates.

Low-income students also tend to be more dependent on financial aid to pay college costs than are higher-income students. Low-income students do not receive enough information about financial aid and may believe that a college education is not financially possible (Bedsworth, Colby, & Doctor, 2006; Perna, 2010b; Swail, Redd, & Perna, 2003; Tierney & Venegas, 2007, 2009). The expectation of aid, as well as the actual award received, affect low-income students' enrollment behaviors, including the types and locations of institutions attended (DesJardins et al., 2006; Paulsen & St. John, 2002; Perna & Steele, 2011). Moreover, even when receiving aid, low-income students are more likely than their peers to have financial need that is unmet (Advisory Committee on Student Financial Assistance, 2001; Choy & Carroll, 2003; Long & Riley, 2007). Several scholars have found that the increased use of merit aid and student loans instead of grant aid has negatively affected low-income students (Advisory Committee on Student Financial Assistance, 2001; Heller & Rasmussen, 2002; Long & Riley, 2007; Mortenson, 1997).

Low-income students are more likely than higher-income students to face academic challenges to their college success and persistence (Perna, 2005b) and often need developmental courses and report more difficulty with coursework (Arzy et al., 2006; Engle & Lynch, 2011; Seider, 2008; Walpole, 2011). These students also tend to have additional demographic characteristics that influence their college experiences. Low-income students are disproportionately students of color, and Black and Hispanic students tend to attend and complete college at lower rates that Whites (Hurtado, Inkelas, Briggs, & Rhee, 1997; Perna, 2000). Moreover, within racial and ethnic communities, high-income students are more likely to attend and complete college than are their low-income peers (Hurtado et al., 1997; Perna, 2000; Teranishi, 2010; Teranishi, Ceja, Antonio, Allen, & McDonough, 2004; Walpole, 2008). Compared with higher-income students, low-income students are also more likely to be older, financially independent rather than dependent, and parents (Berkner et al., 2002; Engle & O'Brien, 2007; Perna, Fester, & Walsh, 2010), which can reduce the likelihood of living on campus, increase the amount of time spent working, and inhibit their ability to participate in co-curricular activities, all of which reduce the likelihood of persistence and attainment.

Theories and Concepts

Given the clear importance of engagement to measures of college student success, why are low-income students less likely to be engaged, and what can colleges and universities do to better support and encourage their engagement? To address these questions, we draw on four theoretical perspectives: Maslow's hierarchy of needs; the economic theory of human capital; cultural relevancy; and post-structuralism. Maslow's hierarchy of needs, human capital theory, and cultural relevancy shed light on how and why low-income students are less engaged in college (as traditionally defined by Tinto, Kuh, and others) than other students. Post-structuralism points to the need for deeply examining our institutional environments for ways they unintentionally create barriers to engagement.

Taken together, these perspectives help practitioners to better understand how to conceptualize the experience of low-income students and suggest ways to better support them.

Maslow's Hierarchy of Needs

Maslow's hierarchy of needs (1943, 1954) provides one perspective for understanding why low-income students find engagement as traditionally envisioned to be a challenge. Maslow's (1943) hierarchy of needs is typically conceptualized as a pyramid, with the most substantial and basic needs at the bottom. Only after these most basic needs are satisfied will an individual pursue other, higher-order needs. Needs progress from the most basic physiological needs (e.g., need for food, water, sleep), to safety and security needs (e.g., safe neighborhood, stable employment, shelter), to more social and psychological needs (e.g., love and friendship, self-esteem). At the top of the hierarchy is self-actualization, defined as fulfilling one's potential. Maslow assumed that individuals are motivated to act in ways that satisfy these needs.

It may be that, for low-income students, engagement is a higher-order need: low-income students can only engage in this higher-level activity after the most basic but essential needs are met. But, as described in the prior section, the basic needs of low-income students are often not met when they enter our institutions. Given the characteristics of low-income students described above, it is not surprising that low-income students often must focus first on ensuring that they have the financial resources required to pay the costs of enrollment and the academic assistance needed to make satisfactory academic progress.

Human Capital Theory

The economic theory of human capital assumes that students weigh the benefits and costs of different alternative courses of action and then select the option that maximizes their utility (Becker, 1993). Human capital theory assumes that the weighing of options reflects students' preferences, tastes, and expectations. The theory does not assume that individuals have perfect and complete information about each alternative, only that individuals act on and use the information that they have (DesJardins & Toutkoush-ian, 2005). This theory provides several potential insights for practitioners looking to increase student engagement. One insight is that increasing the availability of grant aid to help students pay college costs may increase college engagement. Studies of low-income, high-achieving students of color who received the Gates Millennium Scholarship show that this aid reduced the need for recipients to work while enrolled in college, consequently increasing their time and energy to engage in academic, social, and community activities (Trent & St. John, 2008)

A related insight pertains to the decisions that low-income students make with regard to trading-off time spent in paid employment versus time spent engaged in college-related activities. As Titus (2010) explains, labor theory assumes that, "individuals are faced with the choice of allocating time between 'renting their labor' (i.e., working) and non-market time such as leisure, or in the case of students, studying" (p. 262), or other types of student engagement. While increasing available financial resources and potentially building some types of human capital, the decision to work (especially the decision to work excessive numbers of hours while enrolled in college) is not without costs. Students who work high numbers of hours (especially when these hours are off campus) have less time and energy to become academically and socially integrated into college and may require more time to complete a degree (Titus, 2010).

Using a human capital lens also raises questions about what low-income students know about the benefits and costs of allocating their finite time to employment rather than student engagement activities. For example, do low-income students know the multiple ways that allocating time to engagement promotes learning and the likelihood of degree completion? Do they know that loans and other types of financial assistance may be available to help reduce the amount of time spent working? Do low-income students know of other institutional resources that are available to promote their college enrollment and persistence, including the possible availability of emergency loans as well as assistance with childcare and transportation?

Cultural Relevancy

Cultural relevance has been touched on in other chapters, particularly as it relates to race and ethnicity, but this concept is often ignored when it comes to issues of family income. Cultural relevancy suggests that for a program, service, or activity to be engaged by people from diverse groups, it should be modified in ways that make it understandable or accessible based on the experience or perspective of that cultural group or subgroup (e.g., male vs. female). The notion of culturally relevant engagement may be particularly useful for understanding the college-related choices made by low-income students. Even if low-income students have sufficient financial resources to pay college costs and have their other basic-level needs met, they may not find existing programs relevant to their experiences, thereby creating another barrier to engagement.

Some research suggests the role of cultural relevancy in student engagement decisions. A study by Arzy et al. (2006) found that low-income students attributed their cautious social and co-curricular involvement to their lack of comfort with their peers and the campus environment. This study also found that low-income students interacted little with faculty inside or outside the classroom, and that they did not see this lack of interaction as interfering with their academic focus. Notions of cultural relevance suggest that classrooms, services, supports, programs, and co or extra-curricular experiences should be conscious of and reflect the perspectives and characteristics of different populations (Gilbert, 2008). Low-income students are often absent from campus structures, suggesting a lack of culturally relevant programming and services (Grassi, Armon, & Barker, 2008). While many campuses offer ethnic and women's studies, few campuses offer working-class or poverty studies (Gilbert, 2008; Grassi et al., 2008). General education and curriculum reform efforts often include an effort to incorporate women and people of color in core course material (Grassi et al., 2008). However, there is not a similar effort to include individuals with a low-income background within course materials. Professors are often not sensitive to being culturally relevant in the examples they provide in class, particularly with regard to incorporating low-income students' experiences (Cunningham & Leegwater, 2011). For instance, in a math course, a professor may refer to parents' 401K accounts assuming students know what this is. Being sensitive to low-income students' experiences when presenting material may encourage their engagement and greater willingness to embrace academic challenge (Cunningham & Leegwater, 2011).

There are other ways that campuses may unintentionally offer programs that seem attractive to all students, but that represent a class bias. For instance, low-income students may not have had the opportunity to attend a play or cultural event, learn skiing, or play a sport like lacrosse prior to attending college. Campuses may not realize that these activities may be less likely to appeal to low-income students given their cost or previous inaccessibility to these populations.

Post-Structuralism

The final perspective that we employ is post-structuralism. This perspective suggests that campus leaders need to look deeply into their own campus structures and policies for biases and built in (often hidden) barriers that make it difficult for low-income students to succeed even if they get their basic needs met and are in a position to make the choice to engage with the institution. Post-structuralism assumes that low-income populations face structural and/or cultural barriers that impede their success and places the onus on institutions to change campus structures and practices rather than simply blaming students for their inability to be engaged on campus (Best & Kellner, 1991).

Post-structuralism makes visible the hidden structures and taken-for-granted assumptions about notions like engagement. This perspective also require deconstruction of who has benefited from a concept like engagement, and how various campus structures limit the opportunity for certain populations to be engaged. Post-structuralism assumes that engagement may be limited for low-income students since campus structures (just like societal structures) are often set up to promote the success of elites and consider only what has worked well for this group (Foucault, 1980). In short, this theory lays responsibility for changes on the institution and not just the individual.

Early studies of engagement (not using a post-structural lens) suggest that low-income students need to work less, drop family responsibilities, and attend a college away from home to be unencumbered by family; this perspective lays the responsibility for college success on students (Pascarella & Terenzini, 2005). But post-structuralism—through historical and current analysis—points to ways institutions have been formed to support the elite and points out that by not changing institutional structures and practices, low-income students will always be disadvantaged and the wealthy will always be advantaged. This theory challenges the meritocratic myth that anyone who works hard can achieve by suggesting that at least some individuals are constrained by institutional structures and culture. It also challenges conventional notions of engagement noted in the opening chapter of this volume Harper and Quaye quote: "The impact of college is largely determined by individual effort and involvement in the academic, interpersonal, and extracurricular offerings on a campus" (Pascarella & Terenzini, 2005, p. 602). Such definitions place primary responsibility for student success in college on the student and assume that the institution has minimal responsibility for promoting student engagement. Kuh and his colleagues (2006), as well as Harper and Quaye in their opening chapter of this volume, speak to institutional responsibilities to have intentionality and offer activities that may be perceived as engaging. Post-structuralism takes this notion a step further, to urge examination of the underlying assumptions of the institution. Intentionality alone is unlikely to cause practitioners to question the policies and structures that have been in place for years—this requires the post-structuralism processes of deconstruction and reconstruction.

When considering the ways that colleges and universities support low-income students, post-structuralism would point to the long history of colleges and universities as finishing schools for the landed gentry (Lucas, 1994). This long history has embedded traditions we sometimes do not question. As Lucas notes in his history of American colleges and universities, most institutions in the 1800s had few scholarships for low-income students, a curriculum focused on liberal education that did not necessarily prepare individuals for work, and activities focused on networking among well-to-do families. From time to time, federal and state governments created efforts that allowed low-income people opportunities to participate, including the GI Bill in the 1940s and 1950s, the federal student assistance programs established as part of the Higher Education Act of 1965 and subsequent reauthorizations, and the TRIO programs established in the 1960s and 1970s. In addition, institutional types evolved and emerged that tried out different curriculum (e.g., more vocational in emphasis and focused on job preparation) and services (e.g., open admissions, low price, and evening courses) such as land grant colleges, municipal or urban college in the late 1800s, community colleges at the turn of the last century, and the for-profit institutions that have experienced rapid rates of growth in the past decade. But these changes were often short-lived or episodic (e.g., GI Bill), reached a small number of potentially eligible individuals (e.g., TRIO programs), and were expanded to also serve middle-income students (e.g., federal student loans). As public policymakers moved on to other priorities, college and university leaders returned to traditional practices and devolved back to serve middle- and high-income students. Land-grant colleges have come to look increasingly like research universities and have lost much of their focus on supporting local communities and students. Federal policies typically did not penetrate the underlying logic and assumptions that guide many postsecondary institutions. This is not to say that federal student financial aid and TRIO programs are not important and cannot be harnessed to promote low-income students' success and engagement. However, if practitioners do not look at the underlying structures and cultures of the institution, then they may allow the persistence of barriers that make engagement difficult if not impossible for low-income students.

Post-structuralism offers a three-stage framework for critically assessing the implications for low-income students of existing institutional structures and practices: (1) *Revelation*—exposing practices that privilege one group and strain and constrain another group; (2) D*econstruction*—examining the impact of specific institutional structures, policies, and practices on low-income students; and (3) *Reconstruction*—providing ideas for new or revised institutional structures, policies, and practices. Applying this framework to understand the role of institutional structures, policies, and practices in promoting and deterring low-income students' engagement begins with revelation: describing hidden privileges that more affluent students experience. Because these privileges are not discussed actively, they remain hidden parts of the system and are "normalized." By making them visible, these practices can be examined and deconstructed so that institutional structures, practices, and policies that better serve low-income students can be developed. The following list offers examples of privileges experienced by affluent students that disadvantage low-income students.

- Affluent students do not typically have to think about working 20 or more hours a week to pay for the basics of food and shelter and/or to provide financial resources back to their families.

- Affluent students do not usually need to decide which textbooks and class materials they can afford to purchase.
- Affluent students more often choose colleges based on the quality and fit with their goals and interests regardless of sticker price, the availability of financial aid, or distance from home.
- Affluent students are more able to choose among and participate in a range of enriching educational experiences that supplement their in-class experiences such as study abroad, volunteer work, and unpaid internships.
- Affluent students typically live on or close to campus and do not have to commute long distances in order to obtain affordable housing.
- Affluent students have more money for clothes that help them fit into the campus environment and participate in social activities and schoolwide events such as commencement.
- Affluent students tend to worry less about whether needed classes are scheduled at times that conflict with their work schedule.

Deconstruction helps identify how current practices maybe changed. For example, requiring students to live on campus their first year is a common practice at many four-year residential colleges and universities. The merits of this requirement are supported by research documenting the positive relationship between on-campus residence and persistence as well as common sense: students who live on campus have greater opportunity to become academically and socially integrated. Nonetheless, colleges and universities may not realize the hardships caused by simply imposing this requirement for students from low-income students. Living on campus raises the costs of attendance; students can often live farther from campus or with multiple roommates for much less expense. If the additional costs of on-campus residence are not covered by financial aid, then students must either work longer hours or increase their loan debt. In addition, low-income students may feel socially isolated in a residence hall where there are few other students with similar social class backgrounds. Residence halls often close during holidays and other breaks with the assumption a student has a place they can go. But, low-income students who are living far from home cannot always afford to travel home. The student must negotiate alternatives or end up homeless. While the goal of engagement is admirable, the unintended consequences for low-income students of a policy that is designed to promote engagement can be severe.

Deconstruction allows us to see these problems and craft better policy to partake in reconstruction. In the example above, campus leaders might instead propose housing as optional, increase the availability of institutional financial aid to assist low-income students with paying the higher costs, create a housing unit that groups people from similar backgrounds, or link low-income students with staff or faculty mentor to help them better adjust to campus housing. An institution may also make accommodations for low-income students during breaks, such as keeping residence halls open or providing alternative locations to live, if the cost to keep an entire facility open is too costly.

Institutional leaders should involve students in the policy reconstruction process as well. Incorporating agency is critical to post-structuralism, and low-income students often have excellent problem-solving skills (Walpole, 2011).

This then completes the post-structural analysis process as a new policy is created that supports rather than creates barriers for low-income students. The institution takes responsibility and does not expect the low-income student to assimilate to structures, policies, and cultures that may be a hardship and disadvantage them.

Student Engagement Strategies

Clearly, the engagement of low-income students is shaped by multiple forces, including the extent to which students' basic financial and academic needs are met (à la Maslow's hierarchy), the availability of financial resources to reduce the need to work (à la human capital theory), and the presence of culturally relevant experiences and structures that recognize low-income students' interests and needs. Drawing on post-structuralism, a central premise of this chapter is that colleges and universities have an obligation to carefully review (even very longstanding) policies and practices to identify hidden biases that work against low-income students. Because of differences in institutional missions and other characteristics, including characteristics of the students enrolling, individual institutions need to engage in this process of revealing hidden biases. Student affairs practitioners on individual campuses should conduct an inventory of current programs, activities, and policies to consider how they may unfairly disadvantage low-income students. Using the framework offered in this chapter, practitioners can rethink existing approaches and make needed revisions leading to fewer barriers for low-income students.

Also reflecting post-structuralism, the process for identifying revisions that better support and enable greater engagement of low-income students should incorporate student agency and empowerment into programs. Low-income students have many assets that should be capitalized on as engagement opportunities are created. Low-income students may contribute important perspectives and types of expertise, drawing, for example, on their employment experience. Student affairs practitioners should consider how to obtain input from low-income students about the programs that are most interesting and relevant and the best ways to promote engagement of students from low-income families in these activities.

While "one size" will not "fit all" given variations in institutional characteristics, the various theoretical perspectives reviewed in this chapter do suggest a number of recommendations that all colleges and universities might consider for reshaping institutional practice. We begin by framing general recommendations stemming from the theories we presented. We then identify more specific recommendations to suggest ways an institution might promote students' engagement in each of the five educationally-effective practices identified by Kuh and colleagues in the NSSE.

General Recommendations for Improving Engagement

Ensure that Students' Basic Financial Needs Are Met
Both Maslow's hierarchy of needs and human capital theory indicate the importance of addressing the barriers that inadequate financial resources impose on students' ability to fully integrate and become fully engaged in college life. While working is part of many college students' identity (Kasworm, 2010), institutions need to do more to ensure that students are not working excessive numbers of hours while enrolled (Perna, 2010a).

Many campuses could do more to address the financial need for students to work while enrolled by controlling the many direct and indirect costs of attendance, as well as providing more grant aid for low-income students. While institutions are trying to meet multiple priorities with available institutional aid, these resources should be allocated to students based on financial need rather than non-need criteria (Perna, 2010a). Institutions should also consider ways to increase students' knowledge about the availability of grant aid (Perna, Lundy-Wagner, Yee, Brill, & Tadal, 2011) as well as the benefits and costs of using different mechanisms for financing college costs, including attention not only employment but also loans (Gladieux & Perna, 2005; Perna, 2010a).

Financial education is also critical to support engagement. Students who manage their money well are more likely to have time for engagement, if this management results in fewer hours worked, for example. Yet, despite the potential benefits to student engagement, financial education is not offered on most campuses (Kezar, 2011).

Focus on Engagement in the Classroom
Human capital and post-structuralism suggest that because low-income students have needs and demands that will be a priority and may divert their attention off-campus, practitioners need to rethink engagement for low-income students to focus more on the classroom. First year experience courses, learning communities, application of work to classroom material and the like are important practices. Student affairs practitioners are often not involved in classroom activities, suggesting that they need to create partnerships with faculty in order to be involved in classrooms. Student affairs practitioners on some campuses partner with faculty to offer first year experience courses, offering a model for the kind of partnerships that are desirable (Kezar, Hirsch & Burack, 2002). If activities are created for outside of the classroom, they must be created with a recognition of the conflicting demands of work and study and be offered at times that students are available (e.g., evenings or weekends, depending on the type of job students have).

Encourage and Support Students Who Work

Even with efforts to reduce the financial need to work, research suggests that many low-income students will be working (Perna, 2010a). Cultural relevancy theory suggests that work is valued not just for money, but is also a valued activity among many low-income students (Kasworm, 2010; Walpole, 2011). Therefore, student affairs professionals should consider ways to maximize the benefits and minimize the costs of working (see Perna, 2010a for more complete discussion of these issues). While the costs of working excessive numbers of hours to students' persistence are well-documented, some (see Perna, 2010a) argue the merits for reconceptualizing "student employment" as an activity that may enhance, rather than detract from students' formal educational experiences. Other research suggests the benefits of expanding the availability and attractiveness of on-campus employment opportunities (Perna, 2010a; Walpole, 2011).

Student affairs practitioners can see part of their role as helping students find work on campus, connecting low-income students to offices where they may obtain meaningful work experience, and encouraging campus offices to hire low-income students (Walpole, 2011). In addition, student affairs practitioners might offer reflection sessions or activities that help students connect their work to their learning and vice versa and may also encourage on- and off-campus employers to incorporate workplace strategies (e.g., informal training, feedback) that are positively related to student learning (Lewis, 2010). Faculty might also consider ways to incorporate work-based experiences into academic requirements and coursework and institutions might award academic credit for employment-based experiences (Perna, 2010a). Student affairs practitioners should also consider creating job banks of employers who are understanding of students' schedules (Engle & Lynch, 2011).

Create Culturally Relevant Engagement Experiences

Students will be engaged in activities, programs, and curriculum that are culturally relevant not just by race/ethnicity but also family income and social class. As the section on theory suggests, cultural relevancy encompasses all aspects of a program or activity including: timing/scheduling (e.g., whether an activity is offered when low-income students may be working); content (e.g., whether the program recognizes differences in student orientation based on family income); and cost/fees to participate (e.g., whether the cost of participation is recognized in financial aid budgets, whether fee waivers are available, whether students may participate in return for volunteer service).

Improving Engagement in Educationally-Effective Practices

In addition to the general recommendations that emerge from the four theories, these theories also have implications for policy and practice for improving engagement in the five NSEE benchmarks: academic challenge, active and collaborative learning, faculty–student interactions, enriching educational experiences, and supportive campus environment.

Enable Low-Income Students to Engage in Academically Challenging Experiences

- Promote academic readiness for college-level work. While students from all groups may face challenges to their academic preparation when first enrolling in college, research shows that academic challenges are often particularly high for low-income students (Colyar, 2011; Engle & Lynch, 2011; Walpole, 2011). Institutions may assist students with meeting academic challenges by having high quality instruction in developmental courses and first year programs that include intrusive advising and early warning systems (Engle & Lynch, 2011).
- Assist faculty with understanding and incorporating cultural relevancy. Institutions should identify ways to encourage and assist faculty with ensuring that examples provided in class are culturally relevant to all students, including low-income students (Cunningham & Leegwater, 2011).
- Eliminate policies that require particular GPA requirement for entry into specific majors that can differentially impact low-income students (Walpole, 2011). If students are unable to enroll in the major of their choice, they may become less engaged in the academic challenge of college.
- Identify ways to reduce the financial burden associated with purchasing required textbooks and other course materials. While benefiting all students, the financial burden of purchasing textbooks is particularly large for low-income students (Walpole, 2011). Institutions may address this burden by placing extra copies of required course texts in the library on reserve, so that purchase of the materials is not required.
- Monitor student progress closely through early warning systems and intrusive advising (Engle & Lynch, 2011) so that students are less likely to become overwhelmed with academic challenge. If they are contacted and offered support, they are more likely to stay engaged and not become despondent and drop out.

Enable Low-Income Students to Participate in Active and Collaborative Learning Experiences

- Encourage the use of and participation in learning communities. Because low-income students often grow up in families that emphasize interdependence, working in groups may be culturally relevant to their experience (Cunningham & Leegwater, 2001). Thus, learning communities may be a structure that fosters low-income students' active and collaborative learning

(Cabrera, Burkum, & La Nasa, 2005; Zhao & Kuh, 2004). Given that low-income students are less likely than other students to reside on campus, learning communities should identify ways to involve both residential and commuter students.

- Provide opportunities for students to engage in learning opportunities that improve their understanding of people with low income. Low-income students may enjoy working on community-based projects, as they may be connected to experiences and groups that are more known to or part of their prior experience. Because low-income students may know or be more comfortable with low-income people than their high-income peers, such community-based projects could highlight low-income students' knowledge and expertise, which could increase their comfort levels with peers (Arzy et al., 2006). For example, students in a nutrition or science course may be offered the opportunity to work with a local chapter of the national Women, Infants, and Children program. Purdue University offers a general education course on poverty where students go into the local community and learn about and document the local history around poverty. In this way, students see how social class and poverty is historically and culturally situated and experience the phenomenon by talking with and being out in the community—it is not an abstraction (Grassi et al., 2008). Student affairs staff may also show movies and documentaries about poverty to improve all students' awareness of the issue and help ease the psychic burden on low-income students, as fellow students, faculty, and staff better understand their backgrounds and experiences.

Provide a Range of Opportunities for Students to Interact with Faculty

- Educate faculty about the ways to promote student–faculty interactions. While all students benefit from interactions with faculty, low-income students may be less likely to engage in these interactions. Some research suggests that low-income students often have limited contact with faculty because of low comfort levels (Arzy et al., 2006). Campuses should consider ways to educate faculty about ways to be more approachable and less intimidating to students, and to ease low-income students' comfort levels when interacting with faculty.
- Recognize that various constraints often limit out-of-class student–faculty interactions. Low-income students may also have more limited time for engagement with faculty outside the classroom. As a result, time in the classroom may be critical for fostering students' deep engagement with material (Cunningham and Leegwater, 2001; Umbach, Padgett, & Pascarella, 2010). Faculty can maximize this interest by being available before and after class for questions, being active on email or Facebook, and being accessible for

shorter-term interactions and activities with students. For example, although low-income students may not have time to work on an undergraduate research project, they may have time to meet to discuss career goals.

- Help faculty to be more approachable to students and ease low-income student comfort level. Student affairs staff often have strategies for easing interpersonal interactions (e.g., questions that faculty may ask students) that can help with interactions.

Enable Participation in Enriching Educational Experiences

- Identify alternative types of educationally-enriching experiences. Low-income students often have limited time and money to engage in traditional, out-of-class enriching educational experiences, such as study abroad, student organizations, and community service (Kezar, 2011). Institutions may address these constraints by creating opportunities that build on students' courses, such as capstone experiences. Institutions may also allow students to be involved with projects that build on their existing employment. Faculty may also be encouraged to offer activities and/or student groups around majors and/or class times (e.g., a sociology club that meets immediately before or after a required class).
- Eliminate GPA requirements for such experiences as study abroad that can hinder low-income students' eligibility for participation (Walpole, 2011).
- Reduce the financial barriers to participating in campus activities. Individual campus activities (especially student-developed programs) often have costs that are above and beyond fees that are considered in the financial aid budget (Walpole, 2011). For instance, fraternities and sororities, and other types of social organizations, often have high initiation and participation fees that may preclude low-income students' participation. On campuses with student life cultures that are intertwined with such organizations, opportunities for low-income students' social engagement may be quite limited. By rethinking the cost of campus activities and providing scholarships or fee waivers for low-income students, engagement in activities may be facilitated. Waiver and fee reductions should be well-publicized and marketed so students are aware of their availability, as we know that students are often unaware of available aid for which they are eligible (Perna, 2010b).

Provide a Supportive Campus Environment

- Offer student support services at times and locations that are accessible to all students. Too often these services are offered only in person, on-campus, during typical business hours (Kasworm, 2010; Perna, 2010a). Ensuring that offices are open during evening hours will help students to obtain necessary tutoring, career planning and other supports (Engle & Lynch, 2011). Support services are also often spread out over campus, are hard to find, and may not allow for appointments which can minimize student wait times. All of these bureaucratic processes consume valuable time for low-income students and create unnecessary complexity. By providing services in "one-stop" areas and offering appointment times, services that can enhance student performance will be used more frequently.

- Reduce financial barriers to obtaining necessary services and participating in essential programs. Some programs (such as orientation and tutoring) charge fees, thereby creating a barrier for at least some students to accessing these important aspects of campus (Engle & Lynch, 2011; Walpole, 2011). Providing fee waivers and scholarships for such fees will encourage more student engagement.
- Provide an in-depth orientation and first year experience programs. Research suggests the importance of an institutional orientation to promoting the success of low-income students (Engle & O'Brien, 2007). Low-income students come from families in which other members have typically not attended college so information about college transition and expectations about college are critical. Engle and Lynch (2011) identified the importance of an institutional focus on first-year programming as very important to low-income student success and engagement.
- Create a task force on retention and graduation so that people across different units think about the ways that different support services help with retention and communication among units (Engle & O'Brien, 2007).
- Encourage programs to incorporate student agency. Programs should include meaningful opportunities for gathering and acting on student input, asking low-income students about the ways they want to be supported and the barriers that limit their ability to maximize available resources and opportunities (Colyar, 2011; Walpole, 2011).

Conclusion

This chapter describes the need for institutional leaders and administrators to critically consider the ways that campus structures, policies, and processes unintentionally create barriers to engagement for low-income students. While individual colleges and universities will need to determine the ways to adapt existing practices and the types of new policies and structures required to meet the particular characteristics and needs of students on their own campus, we hope that the recommendations provided here will generate institutional changes that better support and promote the engagement of low-income students.

References

Advisory Committee on Student Financial Assistance (2001). *Access denied: Restoring the nation's commitment to equal educational opportunity*. Washington, DC: Author.

Arzy, M. R., Davies, T. G., & Harbour, C. P. (2006). Low income students: Their lived university campus experiences pursuing baccalaureate degrees with private foundation scholarship assistance. *College Student Journal, 40*(4), 750–766.

Astin, A. W., & Oseguera, L. (2004). The declining "equity" of American higher education. *Review of Higher Education, 27*(3), 321–341.

Bailey, T., Jenkins, D., & Leinbach, T. (2005). *Community college low-income and minority student completion study: Descriptive statistics from the 1992 high school cohort*. New York, NY: Community College Research Center, Teachers College, Columbia University.

Becker, G. S. (1993). *Human capital: A theoretical and empirical analysis with special reference to education* (3rd ed.). Chicago, IL: University of Chicago Press.

Bedsworth, W., Colby, S., & Doctor, J. (2006). *Reclaiming the American dream*. Report prepared for the Bridgespan Group Inc. Retrieved on March 12, 2007, from www.bridgespangroup.org/kno_articles_americandream.html

Berkner, L., He, S., & Cataldi, E. F. (2002). *Descriptive summary of 1995–96 beginning postsecondary students: Six years later*. Washington, DC: National Center for Education Statistics.

Best, S., & Kellner, D. (1991). *Postmodern theory: Critical interpretations*. Basingstoke, England: Macmillan.

Bowen, W. G., Chingos, M. M., & McPherson, M. S. (2009). *Crossing the finish line: Completing college at America's public universities*. Princeton, NJ: Princeton University Press.

Cabrera, A. F., Burkum, K. R., & La Nasa, S. M. (2005). Pathways to a four-year degree: Determinants of transfer and degree completion. In A. Seidman (Ed.), *College student retention: A formula for success* (pp. 155–214). Boston, MA: Praeger.

Choy, S. P., & Carroll, C. D. (2003). *How families of low- and middle-income undergraduates pay for college: Full-time dependent students in 1999–2000*. Washington, DC: National Center for Education Statistics, U.S. Department of Education.

Colyar, J. (2011). Strangers in a strange land: Low-income students and the transition to college. In A. J. Kezar (Ed.), *Recognizing and serving low income students in higher education* (pp 121–138). New York, NY: Routledge.

Cunningham, A., & Leegwater, L. (2011). Minority serving institutions—What can we learn? In A. J. Kezar (Ed.), *Recognizing and serving low-income students in higher education* (pp. 176–191). New York, NY: Routledge.

DesJardins, S. L., Ahlburg, D. A., & McCall, B. P. (2006). An integrated model of application, admission, enrollment, and financial aid. *The Journal of Higher Education, 77*(3), 381–429.

DesJardins, S. L., & Toutkoushian, R. K. (2005). Are students really rational? The development of rational thought and its application to student choice. In J. C. Smart (Ed.), *Higher education: Handbook of theory and research*, Volume 20 (pp. 191–240). Dordrecht, The Netherlands: Kluwer.

Engle, J., & O'Brien, C. (2007). *Demography is not destiny: Increasing the graduation rates of low-income college students at large public universities*. Washington, DC: The Pell Institute for the Study of Opportunity in Higher Education.

Engle, J., & Lynch, M. (2011). Demography is not destiny: What colleges and universities can do to improve persistence among low-income students. In A. J. Kezar (Ed.), *Recognizing and serving low income students in higher education* (pp. 160–176). New York, NY: Routledge.

Foucault, M. (1980). Two lectures. In C. Gordon (Ed.), *Michel Foucault: Power/knowledge: Selected writings and other writings 1972–1977 by Michel Foucault* (pp. 78–108). Hemel Hempstead: Harvester-Wheatsheaf.

Gilbert, R. (2008). Raising awareness of class privilege among students. *Diversity Digest, 11*(3). Washington, DC: Association of American Colleges and Universities.

Gladieux, L., & Perna, L. W. (2005). *Borrowers who drop out: A neglected aspect of the college student loan trend*. San Jose, CA: National Center for Public Policy and Higher Education.

Grassi, E., Armon, J., & Barker, B. (2008). Don't lose your working-class students. *Diversity Digest, 11*(3). Washington, DC: Association of American Colleges and Universities.

Heller, D.E., & Rasmussen, C.J. (2002). Merit Scholarships and College Access: Evidence from Florida and Michigan. In D.E. Heller & P. Marin (Eds), *Who should we help? The negative social consequences of merit scholarships* (pp. 25–40). Cambridge, MA: The Civil Rights Project at Harvard University.

Hurtado, S., Inkelas, K. K., Briggs, C., & Rhee, B. (1997). Differences in college access and choice among racial/ethnic groups: Identifying continuing barriers. *Research in Higher Education, 38*(1), 43–75.

Karabel, J. (2005). *The chosen: The hidden history of admission and exclusion at Harvard, Yale, and Princeton,* NJ: Houghton-Mifflin.

Kasworm, C. (2010). Adult workers as undergraduate students: Significant challenges for higher education policy and practice. In L.W. Perna (Ed.), *Understanding the working college student: New research and its implications for policy and practice* (pp. 23–42). Sterling, VA: Stylus.

Kezar, A.J. (Ed.). (2011). *Recognizing and serving low-income students in higher education* New York, NY: Routledge.

Kezar, A.J., Hirsch, D., & Burack, K. (Eds.). (2002). *Understanding the role of academic and student affairs collaboration in creating a successful learning environment. New Directions for Higher Education* (No. 116). San Francisco, CA: Jossey-Bass.

Kuh, G.D. (2001). Assessing what really matters to student learning: Inside the National Survey of Student Engagement. *Change, 33*(3), 10–17, 66.

Kuh, G.D., Kinzie, J., Bridges, B.K., & Hayek, J.C. (2006). *What matters to student success: A review of the literature.* Washington, DC: National Postsecondary Education Cooperative.

Levin, J., Montero-Hernandez, V., & Cerven, C. (2010). Overcoming adversity: Community college students and work. In L.W. Perna (Ed.), *Understanding the working college student: New research and its implications for policy and practice* (pp. 43–66). Sterling, VA: Stylus.

Lewis, J. (2010). Job fare: Workplace experiences that help students learn. In L.W. Perna (Ed.), *Understanding the working college student: New research and its implications for policy and practice* (pp. 155–178). Sterling, VA: Stylus.

Long, B.T., & Riley, E. (2007). Financial aid: A broken bridge to college access? *Harvard Educational Review, 77*(1), 39–63.

Lucas, C. (1994). *American higher education.* New York, NY: St Martins.

Maslow, A. (1943). A theory of human motivation. *Psychological Review 50*(4), 370–396.

Maslow, A. (1954). *Motivation and personality.* New York, NY: Harper.

Mortenson, T. (1997). Georgia's HOPE scholarship program: Good intentions, strong funding, bad design. *Postsecondary Education Opportunity, 56,* 1–3.

Mortenson, T. (2007). *Bachelor's degree attainment by age 24 by family income quartiles, 1970 to 2005.* Oskaloosa, IA: Postsecondary Education Opportunity.

National Center for Education Statistics (NCES). (2009). *The condition of education.* Washington, DC: U.S. Department of Education, Institute of Education Sciences.

Pascarella, E.T., & Terenzini, P.T. (2005). *How college affects students, Volume 2: A third decade of research.* San Francisco, CA: Jossey-Bass.

Paulsen, M.B., & St. John, E.P. (2002). Social class and college costs: Examining the financial nexus between college choice and persistence. *The Journal of Higher Education, 73*(2), 189–236.

Perna, L.W. (2000). Differences in the decision to attend college among African Americans, Hispanics, and Whites. *The Journal of Higher Education, 71*(2), 117–141.

Perna, L.W. (2005a). The benefits of higher education: Sex, racial/ethnic, and socioeconomic group differences. *The Review of Higher Education, 29*(1), 23–52.

Perna, L.W. (2005b). The key to college access: A college preparatory curriculum. In W.G. Tierney, Z.B. Corwin, & J.E. Colyar (Eds.), *Preparing for college: Nine elements of effective outreach* (pp. 113–134). Albany, NY: State University of New York Press.

Perna, L.W. (Ed.). (2010a). *Understanding the working college student: New research and its implications for policy and practice.* Sterling, VA: Stylus.

Perna, L.W. (2010b). Toward a more complete understanding of the role of financial aid in promoting college enrollment: The importance of context. In J.C. Smart (Ed.), *Higher education: Handbook of theory and research, Volume XXV* (pp. 129–180). New York, NY: Springer.

Perna, L.W., Fester, R., & Walsh, E. (2010). Exploring the effects of state financial aid on the enrollment of parents: A descriptive analysis. *Journal of Student Financial Aid, 40*(1), 6–16.

Perna, L.W., Lundy-Wagner, V., Yee, A., Brill, L., & Tadal, T. (2011). Showing them the money: The role of institutional financial aid policies and communication strategies in attracting low-income students. In A. Kezar (Ed.), *Recognizing and serving low-income students in higher education: An examination of institutional policies, practices, and culture* (pp. 72–96). New York, NY: Routledge.

Perna, L.W., & Steele, P. (2011). The role of context in understanding the contributions of financial aid to college opportunity. *Teachers College Record, 113,* 895–933.

Portraits (2011). Initial College Attendance of Low-Income Young Adults. Washington, D.C.: Institute for Higher Education Policy. Retrieved from www.ihep.org/assets/files/publications/m-r/Portraits-Low-Income_Young_Adults_Attendance_Brief_FINAL_June_2011.pdf

Seider, M. (2008). The dynamics of social reproduction: How class works at a state college and elite private college. *Equity & Excellence in Education, 41*(1), 45–61.

Steinburg, M.P., Piraino, P., & Haveman, R. (2009). Access to higher education: Exploring the variation in Pell grant prevalence among U.S. colleges and universities. *The Review of Higher Education, 32*(2), 235–270.

Swail, W.S., Redd, K.E., & Perna, L.W. (2003). *Retaining minority students in higher education: A framework for success.* ASHE Higher Education Report (Vol. 30, No. 2). San Francisco, CA: Jossey-Bass.

Teranishi, R.T. (2010). *Asians in the ivory tower.* New York, NY: Teachers College Press.

Teranishi, R.T., Ceja, M., Antonio, A.L., Allen, W.R., & McDonough, P.M. (2004). The college choice process for Asian Pacific Americans: Ethnicity and socioeconomic class in context. *The Review of Higher Education, 27*(4), 527–551.

Tierney, W.G., & Venegas, K.M. (2007). The cultural ecology of financial aid. *Readings on Equal Education, 22,* 1–35.

Tierney, W.G., & Venegas, K.M. (2009). Finding money on the table: Information, financial aid, and access to college. *The Journal of Higher Education, 80*(4), 363–388.

Titus, M.A. (2010). Understanding the relationship between working while in college and future salaries. In L.W. Perna (Ed.), *Understanding the working college student: New research and its implications for policy and practice* (pp. 261–282). Sterling, VA: Stylus.

Trent, W.T., & St. John, E.P. (2008). Resources, assets, and strengths among successful diverse students: Understanding the contributions of the Gates Millennium Scholars Program, *Readings on Equal Education, Volume 23.* New York, NY: AMS Press.

Umbach, P.D., Padgett, R.D., & Pascarella, E. (2010). The impact of working on undergraduate students' interactions with faculty. In L.W. Perna (Ed.), *Understanding the working college student: New research and its implications for policy and practice* (pp. 234–259). Sterling, VA: Stylus.

Walpole, M. (2007). *Economically and educationally challenged students in higher education: Access to outcomes.* ASHE Higher Education Report (Vol. 33, No. 3). San Francisco, CA: Jossey-Bass.

Walpole, M. (2008). Emerging from the pipeline: African American students, socioeconomic status, and college experiences and outcomes. *Research in Higher Education, 49*(3), 237–255.

Walpole, M. (2011). Academics, campus administration, and social interaction: Examining campus structures using post-structural theory. In A.J. Kezar (Ed.), *Recognizing and serving low-income students in higher education* (pp. 99–120). New York, NY: Routledge.

Wei, C.C., & Horn, L. (2009). *A profile of successful Pell Grant recipients: Time to bachelor's degree and early graduate school enrollment.* Washington DC: US Dept. of Education, Institute for Education Sciences, and National Center for Education Statistics.

Zhao, C. & Kuh, G.D. (2004). Adding value: Learning communities and student engagement. *Research in Higher Education, 45*(2), 115–138.

Ziskin, M., Torres, V., Hossler, D., & Gross, J.P.K. (2010). Mobile working students: A delicate balance of college, family, and work. In L.W. Perna (Ed.), *Understanding the working college student: New research and its implications for policy and practice* (pp. 67–92). Sterling, VA: Stylus.

Chapter 16
Engaging Students in an Online Environment

Tina M. Stavredes and Tiffany M. Herder

Globalization has created an environment where learners no longer want to be place-bound and prefer flexible, online learning environments that allow them to engage in their educational goals anywhere, anytime (Dabbagh, 2007). Distance education is providing opportunities for learning anytime and anywhere. The online learning population is a heterogeneous and diverse group of learners from a variety of cultural and educational backgrounds. Noel-Levitz publishes a yearly National Online Learners Priorities Report, which includes a comprehensive examination of online learners and, according to that data (2009), the average online learner is female, around 35 years of age, working full time, and married with children. The majority are undergraduate learners taking 1–6 credits online. They are primarily White, but there is a growing population of African American, Hispanic, and Asian learners.

One of the main reasons learners engage in online learning is the flexibility it affords them to pursue their educational goals along with a number of roles and responsibilities in their life. However, there are additional challenges online learners have to overcome to be able to engage and persist to achieve their goals. Persistence refers to learners' actions, as they relate to continuing their education from the first year until degree completion. There is evidence that dropout rates among distance learners are higher than those of traditional, campus-based learners (Allen & Seaman, 2009). Therefore, in this chapter, we will look at the factors that contribute to learners dropping out to develop an understanding of how to develop effective strategies to engage learners and help them persist in learning. We also examine the impact of culture in the online environment and consider how learners engage online through the development of different types of presence. We then discuss scaffolding the learning environment to further support learners. Finally, we present a variety of strategies to support learners in the online environment.

As the number of learners who take online courses continues to increase, it is critical to understand how to support them achieve their educational goals. To develop this understanding, we draw on several theoretical and conceptual foundations, including models of persistence, conceptual foundations of cultural differences, research into the development of presence online, and, finally, research on cognitive scaffolding to support learning online. These theoretical foundations will provide deeper understanding of the variables that impact online learners' ability to persist and enable them to successfully achieve their educational goals.

Persistence of Non-Traditional/Distance Education Learners

It is important to understand the variables that impact the online learner, which can cause them to drop out instead of persisting in learning. Bean and Metzner's (1985) persistence model and the Rovai Model of Persistence (2003) are models that address persistence of distance learners. Bean and Metzner identified learners over the age of 24 as a common variable of learner attrition. Learners over the age of 24 commonly work full-time and have the responsibility of families, which can have an impact on their ability to persist in a program of study. Bean and Metzner proposed a model grounded in earlier psychological models to explain attrition of nontraditional learners. Their model predicts persistence based on student–institution "fit." Factors that affect persistence include academic variables, such as study habits and course availability, and background variables, such as age, ethnicity, educational goals, and prior GPA. Environment variables include finances, hours of employment, family responsibilities, and outside encouragement. Finally, psychological variables, such as stress, satisfaction, and commitment to a learner's educational goals, can impact her or his ability to complete a program of study online.

Alfred Rovai (2003) evaluated several persistence models relevant to non-traditional learners and developed a composite model to explain persistence of learners enrolled in online courses. He integrates Bean and Metzner's (1985) learner characteristics, including age, ethnicity, gender, intellectual development, academic performance, and preparation. In addition, he includes skills that distance learners need to acquire to navigate the online environment, including computer literacy, information literacy, time management, reading and writing skills, and online interaction skills. If learners lack these skills and do not overcome these deficiencies, it can lead to attrition. Once learners are admitted to a program of study, there are additional factors both external and internal to the institution that can affect the ability of a learner to persist. According to Rovai (2003), external factors are issues with finances, hours of employment, family responsibilities, the presence of outside encouragement, opportunity to transfer, and life crises such as sickness, divorce, and job loss.

Rovai (2003) cited internal factors affecting learners after admission, including variables researched by Tinto (1975), Bean and Metzner (1985), and Workman and Stenard (1996). According to Tinto (1975), social and academic integration as well as goal commitment, institutional commitment, and the development of a learning community are internal institutional factors that affect persistence. Workman and Stenard (1996) analyzed the needs of distance learners that influence persistence of online learners. These needs include consistency and clarity of online programs, policies, and procedures; learner's sense of self-esteem; ability to identify with the institution and not be looked at as an "outsider"; the need to develop interpersonal relationships with peers, faculty, and staff; and the ability to access academic support and services.

Online learners also expect a pedagogy that matches their learning style, which requires consideration of strategies to support adult learners' need for independence and self-direction. If learners experience problems getting answers to their questions and resolving issues, it may create incompatibility between them and the institution. If learners begin their academic work and find that they are not able to keep up with the workload due to personal issues, they may decide that this is not the right time for them to pursue their education and drop out.

Cultural Differences

The online learner population is a heterogeneous group of learners who come to the online learning environment with diverse values, beliefs, and perspectives that need to be considered. Cultural differences can have an impact on how learners engage in the online environment. Culture is the collective mind of a group of people that distinguishes it from others based on a set of values (Hofstede, 2008). Hofstede and Bond (1984) have researched the effect of culture on psychological functioning as well as its impact on sociological, political, and economic functioning of social systems. In their studies, they identified four cultural dimensions that influence social systems: power distance, uncertainty avoidance, individualism versus collectivism, and masculinity–femininity.

Power distance looks at the status position of individuals in society. It also considers the extent to which less powerful members of a society accept that power is distributed unequally and individuals of higher power exert influence on individuals or groups of lower power (Hofstede & Bond, 1984). The effect of power distance on teaching and learning is pronounced. In cultures where there are large power distances, learners tend to be dependent on the instructor to direct the learning experience and initiate all of the communications in the class. Cultures with small power distances are more learner-centered. Instructors and learners treat each other as equals, and learners initiate some of the communications in class.

Power distance differences can have an impact on learners' perceived position in the course and may result in some learners not being able to interact as equals with other learners. Bates (2001) describes how culture influences critical thinking skills, debate, and discussion. In an online environment, learners are often encouraged to critically evaluate and debate the content being presented and share their ideas and knowledge in discussion. Cultural differences may affect the degree to which individual learners interact and can interfere with their ability to challenge ideas or express opinions contrary to those of the instructor or other learners in the class (Bates & Poole, 2003).

Uncertainty avoidance relates to the degree to which certain cultures are able to tolerate unstructured or ambiguous situations and environments. Learners who come from cultures with strong uncertainty avoidance are concerned about knowing the right answers, which they believe the instructor holds, and feel pressure to conform to other students. Cultures with weak uncertainty avoidance are tolerant of individual differences. Learners enjoy good discussions, and it is acceptable for the instructor to not know all of the answers. Learners from cultures with high uncertainty avoidance may not be able to learn in an environment that is open and unstructured and where learners work at their own pace and determine the goals they want to pursue in the course (Stavredes, 2011).

Individualism versus collectivism refers to the position of a culture along a continuum. On one pole is individualism, which refers to a group of people whose concern is looking after themselves and their family. On the other pole is collectivism, which refers to a group of people that look after each other in exchange for loyalty. Individualist cultures believe the purpose of education is learning how to learn. Learners are encouraged to seek individual goals and are expected to speak up in class. They collaborate with peers who have similar interests (Hofstede, 2008). The value of education is to increase one's self-respect and economic worth. Collectivist societies believe the purpose of education is learning how to do a task. Individual goals are not encouraged, and learners speak only when asked by the group. Learners form collaborations based on popularity rather than similar interests. They believe that education will provide them entry into higher status groups. Individualism versus collectivism can affect the goals of learners and their overall motivation to collaborate with other learners. Learners from collectivist cultures may not initiate interactions with other learners (Stavredes, 2011).

Masculinity–femininity refers to how certain cultures look at differences based on gender differences and value differences. In masculine societies, men are supposed to be assertive, tough, and focused on material success. In feminine cultures, emotional roles of both genders overlap and values focus on caring for others and the quality of life. Education in masculine societies is very competitive. Instructors are admired for being experts, and failing is highly undesirable. Good students are praised, so learners tend to over-rate their own performance. Education in feminine cultures is less competitive. Instructors are liked for their friendliness, and they focus on praise of weak learners for their effort. Failing is considered a minor incident, and learners tend to under-rate their performance. Masculinity–femininity may have an impact on how learners interact with each other and how they interact with the instructor based on gender. For instance, in masculine cultures, men are more dominant and perceived as assertive and competitive, whereas women serve and care for the family. Female learners in masculine cultures might be resistant to interacting in the course, so they may benefit from encouragement to interact with their peers. Differences also exist in the competitiveness that is exhibited in male learners from masculine cultures. In feminine cultures, socially-prescribed gender roles overlap, thus, differences in competitiveness between men and women are mitigated (Stavredes, 2011).

Theoretical Framework: Developing Presence and Scaffolding in the Online Environment

Having laid the groundwork for the needs and issues faced by online learners, this section explores these needs further by discussing two theories—presence and scaffolding. Both theories place emphasis on understanding the diversity of online learners and developing strategies for engaging them in the distance learning process. In addition, these theories provide mechanisms for better supporting online learners by proposing teaching and learning practices that meet these students' needs.

Developing Presence

The development of presence in the online environment is essential for engagement and learning to occur, and the lack of it can cause learners to drop out (Tinto, 1975; Bean & Metzner, 1985; Rovai, 2003; Workman & Stenard, 1996). Research indicates that the more a student can develop relationships with other students and faculty, the greater satisfaction they will have, which can improve the likelihood of persisting in a program of study. Interaction is related to student perception of presence, which is a predictor of student satisfaction in computer-mediated environments (Picciano, 2002).

Garrison, Anderson, and Archer (1999) developed a community of inquiry model to support the achievement of educational goals in an online environment. They propose that learning is more than interactions among participants but should be embedded within a community of inquiry that develops cognitive presence, social presence, and teaching presence.

Cognitive presence is "the extent to which the participants in any particular configuration of a community of inquiry are able to construct meaning" (Garrison et al., 1999, p. 89). Cognitive presence is necessary for students to think critically, which is essential for them to meet their educational goals. It is important to recognize that cognitive presence focuses on higher-order thinking processes as opposed to specific individual learning outcomes. Critical thinking skills are a solid foundation for learners to engage in a community of inquiry to construct knowledge by providing them a skill set to help reason through concepts and ideas. High-level cognitive skills needed to think critically can be developed and integrated in asynchronous discussion questions to develop critical inquiry.

The second element, social presence, is defined as "the ability of participants in the community of inquiry to project their personal characteristics into the community, thereby presenting themselves to the other participants as 'real people'" (Garrison et al., 1999, p. 89). Social presence supports cognitive presence by facilitating critical thinking among learners and contributes to building relationships among students to develop trust and a sense of belonging. The more learners are able to establish themselves with other learners and the instructor, the more trust they will build. Trust helps learners feel comfortable with sharing their thoughts and ideas without the fear of being wrong or being criticized. As the level of interaction increases, a greater sense of community can occur where learners can share their divergent thoughts and perspectives to construct knowledge and understanding.

The third element is teaching presence, which can be performed by the instructor, a teaching assistant, or any other participant in the community. Teaching presence is critical in facilitating interactions to help learners develop social presence and cognitive presence. The role of teaching presence also includes the design of the course to help students achieve stated learning outcomes. According to Anderson, Rourke, Garrison, and Archer (2001), the instructor is responsible for facilitating effective learning with a clear purpose and focus on goals and outcomes. Garrison and Archer (2000) describe the essential responsibilities of the instructor for the design and organization of an online course, including setting the curriculum, designing instructional methods, establishing time parameters, utilizing the medium effectively, and establishing netiquette. They identified six indicators for facilitating discourse, which include identifying areas of agreement and disagreement; seeking to reach consensus and understanding; encouraging, acknowledging, and reinforcing student contributions; setting the climate for learning; drawing in participants and prompting discussion; and assessing the efficacy of the process. In addition, the instructor should provide direct instruction, which includes presenting content and questions, focusing the discussion on specific issues, summarizing the discussion, confirming understanding, diagnosing misperceptions, injecting knowledge from diverse sources, and responding to technical concerns.

The development of presence in the online environment is essential for learning to occur and the lack of it can result in learners becoming dissatisfied and eventually dropping out. Cognitive presence, social presence, and teaching presence are critical building blocks that can support online learners as they engage in the online environment to achieve their educational goals. In addition to presence, learners also need to have appropriate support to help them persist in the online environment. Cognitive scaffolding can provide the support they need to engage in the online environment, effectively learn, and persist.

Cognitive Scaffolding

Many learners enter the online environment without the requisite skills outlined by Rovai (2003), such as computer literacy, information literacy, and time management. They also lack strategies to plan, monitor, and evaluate their thinking and learning (Stavredes, 2011). Other learners may lack prior knowledge and need support in learning new content areas and competencies. Cognitive scaffolding provides a strategic way to support the diversity of needs online learners bring within a course.

Cognitive scaffolding was born out of Vygotsky's (1978) sociocultural theory and zone of proximal development. Vygotsky believed that for educators to understand development, they needed to pay attention to the social and cultural context. He studied the process by which this development might occur and developed the zone of proximal development. He defined this zone as: "The distance between the actual developmental level as determined by independent problem-solving and the level of potential development as determined through problem-solving under adult guidance or in collaboration with more capable peers" (1978, p. 86).

Cognitive scaffolding is meant to support learners in this zone—in the gap between what they are able to accomplish on their own and what they can accomplish with the assistance of an individual with more advanced knowledge and skills. The key to incorporating cognitive scaffolding strategies is to use the right amount of scaffolding to support learners in their zone of proximal development. Dabbagh (2003) wrote:

> too much scaffolding could result in dampening students' efforts to actively pursue their learning goals, causing them to lose their momentum or drive towards meaning making and self-directed learning efforts, and too little scaffolding could result in students' inability to successfully complete or perform certain tasks and instructional activities, leading to anxiety, frustration, and finally loss of motivation and attrition. (p. 40)

The use of the term *scaffolding* alludes to the nature of this strategy. Over time, cognitive scaffolding is reduced until learners can complete the task or function independently (Greenfield, 1984). This also propels them into a new zone of proximal development in which new strategies may be used to support further learning. Ultimately, if applied over time, this helps learners to become self-regulated learners able to motivate themselves, plan their learning process, assess their progress and adjust strategies, and locate and use resources to support their learning (Schunk & Zimmerman, 1994).

Hannafin, Land, and Oliver (1999) categorize scaffolding into four types—procedural, metacognitive, conceptual, and strategic. *Procedural scaffolding* guides learners about "how to utilize resources and tools." This may include orientations to a system or tool, such as an online courseroom, or just-in-time tutorials or explanations. *Metacognitive scaffolding* helps guide learners about "how to think." This may include specific strategies for working through content, such as using a critical thinking model or the scientific method. It can also include more general strategies such as prompts to reflect on goals, link concepts to prior knowledge, evaluate progress, and determine specific resource needs. *Conceptual scaffolding* guides learners about "what to consider." This means helping learners work through complex problems, correcting common misconceptions, and identifying key concepts and ideas related to the task at hand, for example, through concept maps or content trees. Finally, *strategic scaffolding* guides learners on "approaches to learning tasks or problems" especially focusing on multiple alternative approaches. This may include strategies for identifying, evaluating, and relating information to existing knowledge, providing questions to consider, and expert advice (pp. 132–134).

While Hannafin et al. (1999) focused on the application of these categories within the open learning environment (OLE), Stavredes (2011) reinterprets and adapts these categories to fit the online learning environment. She explained procedural scaffolding as supporting navigation in the online course environment and explaining how to engage in learning activities. She also divided procedural scaffolding into three types: orientation, expectation, and resource scaffolds to help learners successfully engage in the online environment. She defined metacognitive scaffolding as support for helping learners develop skills to manage their learning. She expanded metacognitive scaffolding by categorizing them into planning, monitoring, and evaluating scaffolds to support learners' thinking processes as they engage in learning activities. Stavredes explained conceptual scaffolding as focusing on supporting learners when they "encounter new information or information that is difficult to understand" (pp. 149–150). Finally, she discussed strategic scaffolding as emphasizing "alternative learning pathways that can be applied to the learning context to meet the diverse needs of learners" (pp. 149–150). She recommends using strategic scaffolding to support individual learning needs and provide just-in-time support to help learners persist.

Student Engagement Strategies

In the previous section, we discussed the theoretical and conceptual foundations of online learning to support learners to help them be fully engaged, persist, and successfully achieve their educational goals. In this section, we will elaborate on these critical theories and conceptual foundations and recommend specific strategies to use in online courses.

Strategies to Support Learners from Various Backgrounds

Being aware of cultural differences can help educators develop appropriate teaching strategies that consider the needs of diverse learners. Learners from cultures with high power distance and uncertainty avoidance may not be able to learn in an environment that is open and unstructured and where learners work at their own pace and determine the goals they want to pursue in the course (Stavredes, 2011). Consider using a variety of teacher-directed and student-directed learning strategies that support learners along a path that gradually moves them to become more self-directed and in control of their learning. Structure learning activities in ways where the educator directs the activities at the beginning and then slowly moves learners toward more student-directed activities where the learner makes more of the decisions. For students who are already self-directed, providing them with choices will facilitate greater independence.

Cultural differences can also affect learners who consider the instructor to have more power. Instructors should take on the role of the facilitator of the discussion rather than a participant in the discussion. Cultural differences may also affect the degree to which individual learners interact and can interfere with their ability to challenge ideas or express opinions contrary to those of the instructor or other learners in the class (Bates & Poole, 2003). Therefore, it is important to provide specific instructions to help learners understand the expectations of the activities as well as the expected level of interaction. Masculinity–femininity may have an impact on how learners interact with each other and how they interact with the instructor based on gender. Instructors may find female learners from masculine cultures resistant to interacting in the course, so these students may benefit from encouragement to interact with their peers. Instructors may also see differences in the competitiveness that is exhibited in male learners from masculine cultures, so it is important to monitor the online environment to ensure that all learners have an equal opportunity to interact and engage in activities. Finally, it is important to continuously monitor the learning environment and reach out to learners who are not participating to ensure that they are not having difficulties based on their own cultural norms. Understanding that this can be an issue can help resolve issues early on and help the learner become more fully engaged.

Strategies to Develop Presence in the Online Environment

Instructors should consider how to create a community in the online learning environment to reduce transactional distance and provide opportunities for high dialogue. Social presence should be established at the beginning of the course through the use of introduction discussions and individual emails to learners, welcoming them to the course and encouraging them to dialogue with the instructor frequently. Discussions and team activities can also encourage social presence and provide opportunities for learners to develop relationships with each other. Instructors may also want to provide a general discussion thread and call it the "cyber café" or some other name to communicate that it is a place to have casual conversations. This café can encourage learners to share favorite places they like to vacation, thoughts on interesting movies, or other topics that provide them with opportunities to engage in social interactions to establish themselves socially with their peers to foster trust.

Cognitive presence can be established by implementing a critical thinking model in online courses. The Elder–Paul Model of Critical Thinking (Elder & Paul, 2010) is a model that focuses on everyday thinking skills that learners can develop to help them develop strong thinking skills inside and outside class. Instructors should encourage learners to take a stand on an issue and express a personal opinion on the topic, develop arguments to support their opinion, bring in concepts and evidence to support their arguments, and discuss the implications of their line of reasoning. This will provide a foundation for sustaining cognitive presence in the online environment.

Teaching presence is also important in helping students persist online, so instructors should conceive of a number of ways to interact with learners on a regular basis. Some examples include providing a written introduction each week to the unit of study and activities as well as pointing out areas where learners have had difficulty in the past. Equally important is demonstrating one's presence in discussions. Instructors can do this by providing prompts to encourage the discussion and asking for learners to elaborate on their posts or clarify what they have written. Instructors can then post a summary of the discussion to date and weave together the multiple perspectives as well as challenge the learners to think more broadly or deeply.

Learners want frequent feedback, so it is important to communicate regularly with online learners and provide specific and actionable feedback on their discussions and assignments. Begin with addressing the learner by name and letting her or him know where he or she has excelled in the assignment. Next, provide feedback on improvement with specific and actionable ways to improve performance. It is important to end the communication with a positive comment of encouragement that shows appreciation for learners' challenges and efforts.

Finally, incorporate a variety of communication tools into online courses, such as email, private discussion journals, instant messaging, and web conferencing. Utilizing an array of communication channels establishes greater presence with learners.

Strategies to Scaffold the Online Environment

Sharma and Hannafin (2005) define three main activities for implementing scaffolding in practice: (1) establishing the goal of the activity at the beginning; (2) continuing to refine the goal throughout the activity; and (3) leveraging appropriate support and communication strategies to enable the achievement of the goal. These activities help to situate the learning activity within a goal and help learners to internalize, adapt, and achieve the goal. Within an online course, instructors may implement cognitive scaffolding as either static or dynamic. Static scaffolding focuses on anticipating needs in advance and designing the instruction to support all learners. This may include thinking about common misconceptions, anticipating difficult subject matter, or reflecting on previous experiences teaching specific concepts. Dynamic, collaborative scaffolding, on the other hand, are implemented in facilitation and may be used for individual learners or the group.

Stavredes (2011) describes procedural scaffolding as guiding learners as they learn how to navigate the online course environment and engage in learning activities. She explains that learners may have difficulty understanding where to start in an online course especially given the diversity in how content may be delivered online, the variety of resources available, and new expectations for participating in a course. She describes three types of procedural scaffolds that can help the leaner persist—orientation, expectation, and resource scaffolds. An orientation is a basic way to engage learners in the course. Palloff and Pratt (2003) suggest the inclusion of internet basics, basic computer skills, time management skills, an explanation of the role of interaction, skills in providing feedback, and netiquette rules. These suggestions incorporate many of the student skills that Rovai (2003) includes in his persistence model that learners need to be successful in the online environment. Instructors should also develop a Faculty Expectations Statement to ensure learners are aware of one's personal teaching style, the organization and pace of the course, important due dates, and specific policies as they apply in the online setting. Finally, if instructors are integrating the use of any specific processes such as a critical thinking or writing model, developing resource scaffolds to outline how to use the processes and templates to guide learners' thinking will support learners.

Metacognitive scaffolding that supports learners' development of thinking skills is especially important for online learners given their diverse previous experiences with education, their potential gaps in education, as well as their potential new exposure to the new forms of learning online. Stavredes (2011) offers many metacognitive scaffolding strategies to support learners' planning, monitoring, and evaluating skills. An important step in planning is to help learners establish goals throughout the course and plan for the achievement of those goals. Course overviews and roadmaps that outline the most important activities, due dates, and resources can help learners develop an overall plan for the course and manage any conflicts in their schedule early on to ensure engagement throughout and timely completion of the course. For each unit or module, unit introductions and checklists can help learners plan their learning activities and focus their efforts from week to week. Checklists can also help learners monitor their learning activities to make sure they are focusing on the correct activities. Integrating a space for learners to track their time can help them further focus their time and may illustrate when learners need to approach the instructor for assistance. Finally, grading rubrics, evaluation strategies, and opportunities for self-reflection at the end of activities can help learners evaluate their learning efforts.

Conceptual scaffolding guides learners about "what to consider" during learning especially in the case of complex concepts (Hannafin et al., 1999). Advance organizers, study guides or questions, definitions, graphical organizers, outlines, and hints are examples of conceptual scaffolding strategies instructors may implement to support learners' development of new knowledge (Stavredes, 2011). Knowledge maps are another effective type of conceptual scaffolding. O'Donnell, Dansereau, and Hall (2002) explain that knowledge maps scaffold learning by reducing cognitive load, facilitating the representation of relationships, providing many paths for knowledge retrieval, supporting learners with low verbal skills, and supporting the communication of knowledge. Knowledge maps can help support a wide range of learning activities, including helping learners to frame their integration of prior knowledge with new knowledge, to illustrate relationships that may be difficult to understand from the reading and activities alone, or to provide a high level overview of the content. Knowledge maps can also help learners illustrate their key understandings and for instructors to provide feedback on any potential misunderstandings.

Strategic scaffolding supports learners in completing learning tasks or problems specifically focused on multiple alternative approaches (Hannafin et al., 1999). Stavredes (2011) uses strategic scaffolding as a just-in-time strategy for supporting individual learner performance. In the online classroom, this just-in-time approach requires frequent dialogue, that Palincsar (1986) argues "has a critical role to play in scaffolded instruction, facilitating the collaboration necessary between the novice and expert for the novice to acquire the cognitive strategy or strategies" (p. 95). Palincsar discusses the importance of supporting learners' contributions, linking learners' ideas to new ideas, providing focus and direction, making instruction explicit, and moving learners' responses from negative statements to more constructive statements. Stavredes (2011) also suggests using examples, expert advice, and alternative explanations to help learners delve deeper into the learning tasks at hand.

Conclusion

In order to support engagement for online learners, it is important to understand factors that contribute to them dropping out and the cultural diversity that contributes to their participation in online modalities and develop effective strategies to support learners achieving their educational goals. Reducing the transactional distance between the learner and the online environment and structuring activities to help them develop social and cognitive presence are critical to engagement. The role of the instructor in supporting teaching presence is also vital in supporting the development of an effective online course, facilitating interaction and engagement, and providing feedback to help learners persist. Using cognitive scaffolding to help learners navigate the online environment; plan, monitor, and evaluate their learning; develop an understanding of concepts; and strategically support learners just-in-time can reduce stress, help them develop effective academic skills to support their learning, and stay engaged throughout a course to completion. Together, these strategies assist online instructors in addressing many variables that affect persistence and learner engagement and provide them with valuable tools to support learners in achieving their educational goals and completing their program of study.

References

Allen, I. E., & Seaman, J. (2009). *Learning on demand: Online education in the United States.* Babson Survey Research Group, Needham, MA: Sloan-C. Retrieved from www.sloanconsortium.org/publications/survey/pdf/learningondemand.pdf

Anderson, T., Rourke, L., Garrison, D. R., & Archer, W. (2001). Assessing teaching presence in a computer conferencing context. *Journal of Asynchronous Learning Networks, 5*(2), 1–17.

Bates, T. (2001). International distance education: Cultural and ethical issues. *Distance Education, 22*(1), 122–136.

Bates, A.W., & Poole, G. (2003). *Effective teaching with technology in higher education. Foundations for success.* San Francisco, CA: Jossey-Bass.

Bean J.R., & Metzner, B. (1985). A conceptual model of nontraditional undergraduate student attrition, *Review of Educational Research, 55*, 485–650.

Dabbagh, N. (2003). Scaffolding: An important teacher competency in online teaching. *TechTrends, 47*(2), 39–44.

Dabbagh, N. (2007). The online learner: Characteristics and pedagogical implications. *Contemporary Issues in Technology and Teacher Education [Online serial], 7*(3). Retrieved September 30, 2011, from *www. citejournal.org/vol7/iss3/general/article1.cfm*

Elder, L., & Paul, R. (2010). *The thinker's guide to analytic thinking.* Tomales, CA: The Foundation for Critical Thinking.

Garrison, D.R., Anderson, T., & Archer, W. (1999). Critical inquiry in a text-based environment: Computer conferencing in higher education. *The Internet and Higher Education, 2*(2–3), 87–105.

Garrison, D.R., Anderson, T., & Archer, W. (2001). Critical thinking, cognitive presence, and computer conferencing in distance education. *The American Journal of Distance Education, 15*(1), 7–23.

Garrison, D.R., & Archer, W. (2000). *A transactional perspective on teaching and learning: A framework for adult and higher education.* Oxford, UK: Pergamon.

Greenfield, P.M. (1984). A theory of the teaching in the learning activities of everyday life. In B. Rogoff & J. Lave (Eds.), *Everyday cognition* (pp. 117–139). Cambridge, MA: Harvard University Press.

Hannafin, M., Land, S., & Oliver, K. (1999). Open learning environments: Foundations, methods and models. In C.M. Reigeluth (Ed.), *Instructional-design theories and models: A new paradigm of instructional theory* (Vol. 2, pp. 115–140). Mahwah, NJ: Erlbaum.

Hofstede, G. (2008, May 8). *Cultural differences in teaching and learning.* FUHU conference on Education and Training in the Multicultural Classroom, Copenhagen, Denmark.

Hofstede, G., & Bond, M.H. (1984). Hofstede's culture dimensions: An independent validation using Rokeach's value survey. *Journal of Cross-Cultural Psychology, 15*, 417–433.

Noel-Levitz, Inc. (2009). The 2009 national online learners priorities report. Iowa City, IA: Noel-Levitz, Inc. Retrieved December 4, 2011, from www.noellevitz.com/upload/Papers_and_Research/2009/NatSatisfac tionReportOnlineLearners09.pdf

O'Donnell, A.M., Dansereau, D.F., & Hall, R.H. (2002). Knowledge maps as scaffolds for cognitive processing. *Educational Psychology Review, 14*(1), 71–86.

Palincsar, A.S. (1986). The role of dialogue in providing scaffolded instruction. *Educational Psychologist, 21*(1 & 2), 73–98.

Palloff, R.M., & Pratt, K. (2003). *The virtual student: A profile and guide to working with online learners.* San Francisco, CA: Jossey-Bass.

Picciano, A.G. (2002). Beyond student perceptions: Issues of interaction, presence and performance in an online course. *Journal of Asynchronous Learning Networks, 6*(1), 21–40.

Rovai, A.P. (2003). In search of higher persistence rates in distance education online programs. *Internet and Higher Education, 6*, 1–16.

Schunk, D.H., & Zimmerman, B.J. (1994). *Self-regulation of learning and performance: Issues and educational applications.* Hillsdale, NJ: Erlbaum.

Sharma, P., & Hannafin, M. (2005). Learner perceptions of scaffolding in supporting critical thinking. *Journal of Computing in Higher Education, 17*(1), 17–42.

Stavredes, T.M. (2011). *Effective online teaching: Foundations and strategies for student success.* San Francisco, CA: Jossey-Bass.

Tinto, V. (1975). Dropout from higher education: A theoretical synthesis of recent research. *Review of Educational Research, 45*, 89–125.

Vygotsky, L. (1978). *Mind in society.* Cambridge, MA: Harvard University Press.

Workman, J.J., & Stenard, R.A. (1996). Student support services for distance learners, DEOSNEWS, 6, 3. Retrieved September 30, 2011, from the Distance Education Online Symposium Website: www.ed.psu. edu/acsde/deos/deosnews/deosnews6_3.asp

Chapter 17
Engaging Community College College Transfer Students

J. Luke Wood and Carl S. Moore

At 25 years of age, Robert enrolled in community college. Having a wife and young child while working full-time made focusing on school difficult; however, Robert was ready for the challenge. He had been working for five years as a licensed vocational nurse after attending Job Corps (a vocational training program). His primary goal while at community college was to make a career change and enter a profession about which he was more passionate. To a lesser degree, he was also motivated to attend college for financial aid, particularly loans, which had the short-term benefit of providing his family with a greater quality of life.

Robert excelled academically, often earning "A's" and on occasion a few "B's." He felt supported by the institution. In particular, one counselor, Ms. Delgado, took Robert under her wing; she looked after him, checking in frequently in person and via phone to see how he was doing. Delgado came to know Robert personally, his family, his line of work, and his aspirations. She helped him better define his goals and make plans for the future. When Robert had problems in class, she stepped in, serving as an intermediary between him and his instructors. Delgado's office was a safe haven for Robert, fostering an atmosphere of support, which attracted regular student visitors. Often, these visitors became friends.

After several years of coursework, Delgado encouraged Robert to transfer and pursue a bachelor's degree in political science from a local four years university. Feeling confident in his academic abilities and eager for the next step in his educational journey, he transferred. The transition to the university was more difficult than Robert expected. He struggled in acclimating to the social environment of the university. He felt that "cliques" and bonds were already formed between students, and he was the outsider peering in. For instance, in his upper division coursework in political science, students already knew each other, having already had several courses together. These students had developed a culture derived from shared academic experiences, a culture of which Robert was not a part. Robert also felt isolated outside of class. While he wanted to participate in a student organization, he was self-conscious about being too old for this kind of personal exploration. To exacerbate his feelings of estrangement and isolation, he only knew a handful of students who had also transferred, but he rarely saw them on campus. Simply put, he felt completely alone.

Academically, Robert was overwhelmed. He was studying hard but falling short. The writing expectations, for example, were significantly greater at the university, both in volume and in quality. Feelings of academic inferiority were complicated by the fact that Robert was older than other students who seemed to struggle less, study less, but perform better. Robert's grades dipped and he considered quitting college. Whereas at the community college, Robert could go talk with Ms. Delgado and receive encouragement, his relationships with counselors at the university were different. They focused less on getting to know and counsel Robert, concerned more with the technical aspects of academic planning. Robert's interactions with instructors weren't much better; faculty interactions with students were less personal at the university. Robert felt like they assumed everything was okay, but for him, it wasn't. He was struggling, trying to balance a new educational environment, enhanced academic expectations, a marriage, family, and full-time employment.

However, each semester following his initial transition led to an enhanced sense of belonging at the university. Robert began establishing friendships with students and faculty alike. While he continued to struggle academically, particularly with writing, his confidence increased. He slowly established bonds with peers in his major, moving from the "out-group" to the "in-group." Feeling as though he had to make up for lost time, Robert became intensively involved in campus life, running for student government, leading several clubs and organizations, engaging in public service, pledging a fraternity, attending campus activities and sporting events, and even creating a student-led retention program for incoming students. He wanted to have "the college experience," and he did. Robert's time dedicated to studying quickly shifted toward exhaustive social involvement, detracting from his studies and his school-life-family balance. Robert's grade point average dropped precipitously.

After a couple years, Robert stopped out (a short-term departure) from school. Returning several years later, per the advice of family and college friends, Robert avoided social participation altogether and focused his efforts on academic matters. He completed a couple of courses that still remained in his plan of study and retook some classes, which he had previously failed. Ten years after his journey began at community college, Robert graduated with a bachelor's degree, the first to do so in both his immediate and extended family.

Currently, Robert is an administrator for a political marketing organization and has plans to further his education. His story presents many thematic elements aligning with literature on transfer students. These elements include: differences in community college and university culture, challenges in academic and social adjustment, feelings of academic inadequacy, and the effect of external pressures on university success.

In this chapter, we discuss research on transfer students, focusing on their academic and social experiences at four-year institutions. To provide a context for understanding this student population, we begin by discussing some general characteristics of transfer students. Then, we discuss challenges faced by these students and describe a theoretical framework that can aid in conceptualizing factors affecting their experience. This chapter concludes with recommendations for college administrators and faculty on fostering academic climates conducive to transfer student success.

The Transfer Student

Community colleges are an integral sector in the American higher education system. These institutions are well-known for their low-cost enrollment and open-access mission committed to providing postsecondary educational opportunities for all prospective students (Cohen & Brawer, 2003). As a result, community colleges enroll a wide array of students. In general, these students are more likely than four-year collegians to be low-income, commuter students, part-time enrollees, students of color, and/or first-generation college-goers. Further, they are also more likely to have delayed their enrollment into higher education. As such, many community college students are older, more likely to be independent, work full-time, and have dependents (Rhine, Milligan & Nelson, 2000). While many of the aforementioned characteristics are at-risk identifiers, they situate the community college with the potential to make an important impact (e.g., academic, economic, political) on the local communities which they serve. In line with Jain, Herrera, Bernal, and Solórzano (2011), we employ an anti-deficit perspective, seeing community college students as "at-potential" not "at-risk."

Another unique element of community colleges is their varied academic functions. Students can enroll in community college for a multiplicity of reasons: to update their job skills, to engage in personal enrichment, to pursue a certificate degree in a vocational-technical field, to earn an associate's degree in an applied or traditional arts and science discipline, or to complete coursework that positions them for transfer (Nevarez & Wood, 2010). Our focus here is on the latter. The community college transfer function has been a core operation since the institution began in 1901 (Townsend, 2001). As historically conceptualized, transfer is modeled after the German educational system whereby students complete their general education coursework (the U.S. equivalent of grade 14) before moving to the university (Kane & Rouse, 1999). Informed by this ideal, students complete their first two years of collegiate coursework at the community college before transferring to a four-year institution where they can pursue a baccalaureate degree (Townsend & Wilson, 2006).

A large contingent of community college students (41.3%) enter with the goal of transferring to a four year university. These data differ by racial/ethnic affiliation, with Asian-Americans most likely, at 54.3%, to indicate transfer as a primary goal. The breakdown for other racial/ethnic groups is as follows: Whites, 40.5%, Hispanic/Latino, 40.2%, and African-American, 39.5% (BPS, 2009a; the sample size issues prevent the presentation of data for Native Americans). Despite a large percentage of students entering community colleges with the goal of transferring, the majority (77.6%) will not. In a six-year time frame, only 22.4% will transfer to a four-year institution. As with intent to transfer, outcomes differ by racial/ethnic affiliation. Hispanic/Latino students have the highest transfer rates, at 38.3%, with declining rates as such: White, 20.4%, African-American, 18.8%, and Asian-American, 18.0% (BPS, 2009b).

Given differential outcomes, several studies have examined predictors of predisposition to transfer and actual transfer. With regard to the prior, Nora and Rendón (1990) examined indicators of students' predisposition to transfer to four-year institutions. Using variables relevant to students' academic and social integration into the campus setting, they found that students with greater levels of integration at the community college were more likely to transfer. Wood, Nevarez, and Hilton (2011) investigated background factors indicative of student transfer. They found that younger students, non-minorities, students without disabilities, students from higher socio-economic ranks, and full-time students were significantly more likely to transfer than their counterparts. Extending upon this work, and guided by Nora and Rendón's (1990) notion that academic and social integration are important considerations in transfer, Wood, Nevarez, and Hilton (2012) examined background, integration, and environmental factors predictive of actual transfer. In terms of background variables, they found that female students, students with higher GPAs from high school, and non-first-generation students were more likely to transfer. Interestingly, social integration (participation in campus activities), academic involvement with faculty and participation in study groups had no impact on transfer. However, participation in school clubs and school sports were both positive predictors of transfer. Finally, increasing hours worked per week and having children were negative predictors of transfer.

Regardless of transfer predictors, transfer students, like other community college students, are more likely than their four-year counterparts to come from diverse backgrounds. For example, nearly 40% of transfer students are students of color (BPS, 2009c). As such, for four-year colleges and universities, transfer students present an opportunity to diversify. This serves as an added benefit to those students who began their postsecondary careers at the four-year university level (i.e., native) and transfer students who gain exposure to demographically diverse student populations. Moreover, transfer students have a proven record of success, having completed all or most of their general education coursework with sufficient grades for four-year university admittance. As such, Jain and her colleagues (2011) suggest that institutions of higher education should be guided by the belief that these "students will be successful *because* they are transfer students" (p. 253).

The Transfer Student Experience

Despite their potential for success, many four-year institutions are leery of admitting transfer students. In the past, some scholars have noted perceptions of transfer students as "risky ventures" (Diaz, 1992) or "academically suspect" (Cejda, 1997). This paradox of a proven potential for success yet apprehension for enrollment is difficult to negotiate. Some scholars suggest that university apprehension is a result of limited resources available to orient transfers to campus life and culture as well as perceptions of inadequate preparation for university success (Berger & Malaney, 2003; Laanan, 1996). The latter is likely a result of elitist notions held by university officials about community colleges and, to some degree, the students they serve. This is not to say that transfer students do not face barriers to success; all students do. Transfer students do encounter challenges as they enter and progress through four-year institutions. The primary challenges addressed here include: transfer shock, college adjustment, student persistence and attainment, credit acceptance and articulation issues, and work-life-school balance concerns.

Transfer Shock

When making the transition from community college to a four-year institution, many students experience an initial period of poor academic success. Scholars refer to this difficult encounter as "transfer shock" (Berger & Malaney, 2003). Traditionally, transfer shock "refers to the decrease in grade point average (GPA) that often occurs when a student transfers to a 4-year institution" (Rhine et al., 2000, p. 443). Usually, this temporary lull in grades occurs during students' first semester after transferring. For example, Pennington (2006) examined pre- and post-transfer grades among students in Missouri, finding a mean GPA decrease of -0.28 in the first semester after transfer. This mean grade dip is in line with prior research on transfer shock (e.g., Carlan & Byxbe, 2000; Diaz, 1992). Whether in comparison to their grades at the community college or to the grades of native four-year collegians, research has continuously confirmed the existence of transfer shock.

While some scholars have attempted to connect transfer shock to other student outcomes (e.g., attrition, attainment; see Rhine et al., 2000), predominantly, the phenomenon is conceptualized as solely inclusive of grades. It has been postulated that transfer shock is an outcome of social and psychological stress. This stress comes as a result of adjusting to a new and markedly different collegiate environment and culture (Laanan, 2004). Some research has noted differential transfer shock experiences. For example, Cejda (1997) found that business, science, and math majors experienced the greatest levels of transfer shock, while students in the social sciences, education, humanities, and fine arts experienced an increase in GPA (referred to as transfer ecstasy). Further, scholars have also noted that transfer shock may be greater at more academically competitive four-year institutions (Pennington, 2006; Preston, 1993).

College Adjustment

There are countless differences between community colleges and four-year institutions, all of which exacerbate the difficulty of transition. In terms of academics, community colleges are more likely to have institutional climates that foster students' academic development. In part, this is attributed to institutional characteristics such as smaller campuses and lower course enrollments. Smaller class sizes provide greater opportunities for students to gain individual attention from faculty. This opportunity for faculty–student interaction is enhanced by institutional commitments to a teaching and learning mission as opposed to research productivity (Piland, 1995). For example, Townsend and Wilson (2006) found that transfer students felt like "a number" in a course at four-year institutions, noting differences in personal interaction with faculty. This notion of feeling like "a number" is recurrent in transfer literature (Laanan, 1996). Furthermore, research has noted that transfer students perceive four-year courses as more academically rigorous, having higher writing expectations and moving at a faster pace (Townsend, 1995). Unfortunately, such perceptions reinforce elitist notions about four-year institutions in relation to community colleges.

Transition experiences are intensified by new social environments (Laanan, 2004) with new students, who (as already noted) are demographically distinct. In particular, transfer students are usually in their 30s while native students are in their early 20s (Piland, 1995). This difference complicates transfer students' level of comfort with engaging in campus activities, establishing relationships with other students, and their general integration into the social milieu of university life. Integration into campus social life can be particularly challenging for transfer students, given that native students are more likely to have previously established social bonds. Therefore, some transfers have found that native students have little interest in expanding their existing social groups. This can have a negative academic impact when transfer students attempt to form study groups with native students (Townsend & Wilson, 2006).

After experiencing transfer shock, most students have partial or full GPA recoveries. In general, it is assumed that this occurs after student adjustment to the new campus environment has run its course. While it is expected that transfer students will have difficulties in adjusting to the new collegiate environment, four-year institutions do very little to ease this process. For instance, transfer programming is usually limited to a welcome and one-day orientation. These events fail to provide the support needed for transfer success. Furthermore, transfer students desire greater support in learning more about campus resources, extracurricular activities, and facilitating interactions with other students (Townsend & Wilson, 2006).

Persistence and Attainment

Transfer shock has been found to be a significant predictor of student attrition and lower graduation rates at four-year institutions (Gao, Hughes, O'Rear, & Fendley, 2002). As such, research has shown that transfer students are less likely to persist or earn a bachelor's degree than native students (Pascarella, Smart, & Ethington, 1986). This phenomenon has been shown to exist even when taking into account demographic and academic characteristics for both populations (Christie & Hutcheson, 2003; Glass & Harrington, 2002; Porter, 2002). As noted by Cejda, Kaylor, and Rewey (1998), approximately 20% of transfer students will drop out after their first semester. Wang (2009) illustrates several key predictors of persistence and baccalaureate attainment among transfer students.

With respect to persistence, Wang (2009) found that an internal locus of control (students' perceived control over their environment and future) and community college grades serve as integral predictors of persistence. Community college grades also served as significant predictors of attainment. In addition, other predictors of attainment include gender (being female), lack of mathematics remediation, baccalaureate aspirations, taking a rigorous high school curriculum, and higher socio-economic status. Bearing Wang's findings in mind, persistence and attainment after transfer seems to be a confluence of personal, aspirational, and psychological factors. That being said, earlier studies have noted that persistence after the initial transition period (first or second semester) is a function of traditional academic and social integration factors (Anglin, Davis, & Mooradian, 1995; Best & Gehring, 1993; Pennington, 2006).

Credit Acceptance and Articulation Issues

Pascarella (1999) has suggested that difficulties in transfer are a result of structural factors existing within and among institutions. He noted that difficulties in gaining admittance, navigating the financial aid process, and transferability of credits are primary deterrents of transfer. The transferability of credit from community colleges to four-year institutions is a persistent problem facing transfer students (Donovan, Schaler-Peleg, & Forer, 1987). Some four-year institutions will only accept a portion of credits towards students' academic degree. This increases the time to graduation for transfer students and has a negative effect on their likelihood of degree attainment (Eimers & Mullen, 1997).

Problems in course credit transfer can result from several areas. At the community college, minimal advising resources may lead to students' unintentional enrollment into coursework that is not transferrable. Depending upon the checks and balances in place and students' usage of academic and transfer services, non-transferable coursework may not be identified until a student has completed the necessary credits for transfer. Townsend and Wilson (2006) interviewed nineteen transfer students and found that only six received transfer assistance from their respective community college. Participants remarked that they felt frustrated due to the lack of support received from their respective community college. Some students were even told to contact the institutions they intended to transfer to on their own, rather than receiving support from the community college in this process.

Culpability for lack of acceptance of transfer credit can also result from academic policies at the four-year university. Students could have completed transferable units; however, some university departments add additional prerequisites and requirements, which are major-specific. In such cases, students may be required to take additional general education coursework (Rhine et al., 2000). Sometimes, this can limit transfer students to searching for majors that will accept the most credits toward the baccalaureate. Further, credit acceptance issues can also result from a lack of articulation between community colleges and four-year institutions (Hagedorn, Cypers, & Lester, 2008). The quality of articulation is often a function of personal relationships among college and university officials, placing students at the whim of inter-institutional social networks (Turner, 1990, 1992).

Work-Life-School Balance

Transfer students often experience challenges in working while attending college. Community college academic scheduling allows students to work while in school (Rhine et al., 2000). Mostly, this is due to academic programming geared toward working adults, which feature numerous online, hybrid, weekend, evening, and other convenient course models (e.g., television). In contrast, undergraduate courses at the four-year university are concentrated during work hours, making it difficult for students to work full-time while attending college. Further, student services (e.g., financial aid, academic advising, counseling, registrar) and academic affairs (e.g., academic departments) offices typically operate during traditional business hours (8:00 a.m.–5:00 p.m.). Thus, these operations are not easily accessible for working adults, especially those with children or who commute to campus.

Research from Berger and Malaney (2003) illustrates that transfer students had to reduce external commitments to be successful at the University of Massachusetts. For instance, while attending community college, the average transfer student worked 18.07 hours per week; however, at the four-year institution, this dropped to 10.53 hours per week. Additionally, students' time spent with family dropped after transfer. While at the community college, transfer students spent 12.17 hours per week with family; this dropped to 8.74 per week at the university. In exchange, time commitments for studying increased from 13.61 hours per week to 18.10 at the university. Finally, time spent socializing increased from 10.31 hours per week at the community college to 14.96 hours per week at the university. In all, findings from this research suggest that to be successful at the university-level, transfer students may need to reduce external commitments and increase campus commitments.

However, reduction in external commitments (particularly work) may not be realistic for all transfer students, especially for those supporting others (e.g., children, family) or those with full-time jobs. Cameron (2005) provides some insight as to how external commitments are balanced with school-related concerns. She found that nursing transfer students with dependents (especially single mothers) reduced their time spent in social activities to balance academic and external concerns (e.g., caring for dependents, financial pressure). This resulted in dismal social lives, limiting college relationships to in-class interactions. As such, students reported feeling unsatisfied, citing acute loneliness.

As made clear by the identification of barriers facing transfer students, the challenges these students encounter are a combination of factors emanating from community colleges, universities, and the students themselves. The next section offers a framework that can aid in conceptualizing and addressing these barriers.

Theoretical Framework

We identified one primary framework that can facilitate understanding of the transfer student experience in postsecondary education. The strength of this framework for scholars and practitioners alike is that the burden of transfer success is directed toward institutions as opposed to students. Further, this framework takes an anti-deficit perspective, viewing transfer students as valued additions to university settings.

Transfer Receptive Culture

As noted throughout this chapter, transfer student challenges are often attributable to the sending (community college) and receiving (four-year) institutions themselves. This notion is grounded in earlier community college studies that surmised that social networks between student affairs professionals at two and four-year institutions affected the propensity of inter-institutional transition as well as clarity in articulation (Turner, 1988, 1990, 1992). Following this logic, discrepant linkages between these college professionals could result in more challenging transitory experiences. Extending upon this notion and guided by the tenets of critical race theory (see Solórzano, 1998), Jain et al. (2011) offered the notion of a transfer-receptive culture. This framework articulates five elements that are essential for sending and receiving institutions to employ in supporting the successful transition, expeditious progress, and baccalaureate attainment of transfer students. Of the five elements presented, two are specific to pre-transfer success while three focus on post-transfer success.

The first element is placing "a high institutional priority" on transfer (Jain et al., 2011, p. 258). Community colleges and four-year institutions must perceive transfer as vital to their success. For community colleges, transfer is one of several core functions (e.g., terminal degrees, remediation, continuing education). However, low transfer outcomes are indicative of low institutional commitment to transfer. At four-year institutions, this necessitates that accessibility for transfer students be considered separate from first-year student admission counts. Jain et al. argue that in placing a high priority on transfer, four-year institutions should view transfer students' diverse demographic characteristics and experiences as an asset.

The second element is providing *"information and resources focused on the specific needs of transfer students"* (p. 259; italics are added to emphasize transfer-receptive elements). Institutions should work collaboratively to inform students about the transfer process and to help them learn about the receiving institution. Jain et al. postulate that doing so will foster a greater sense of belonging among transfers with four-year institutions. Information on transfer should be accessible in multiple mediums (e.g., web, print) and from several sources (e.g., outreach personnel, counselors, transfer officers). Once students enter the four-year institution, adjustment programming should be in place to facilitate ease of transition.

The third element is to "*offer financial and academic support*" for transfer students (Jain et al., 2011, p. 258). Given that funding can serve as a deterrent to transfer, Jain and her colleagues suggest that scholarship monies be dedicated for transfer students. Further, academic support programs should be in place to provide students with counseling, tutoring, and training (e.g., learning strategies) while also affirming their academic abilities.

The fourth element is to "*acknowledge the lived experiences that students bring to campus*" (Jain et al., p. 260). This element is guided by the notion that each student has unique experiences, perceptions, and knowledge that are of value. In particular, Jain and her colleagues discuss the importance of family and culture, arguing that institutions must foster environments where transfer students and their families are welcomed and honored.

The final element of a transfer-receptive culture is that transfer programming should be subject to "*a reflective and analytical process*" (Jain et al., p. 261). As such, benchmarks and outcomes coupled with assessment and evaluation should be implemented to ensure that community college and university resources are maximized for the benefit of transfer students.

In all, the five elements of Jain et al.'s (2011) framework require community colleges and four-year institutions to *prioritize, inform, support*, and *affirm* transfer students and to *assess* the effectiveness of the institutions' efforts. Researchers using this framework can focus on how these five elements affect transfer student success. This framework can facilitate a necessary shift in the transfer literature from a focus on student-level predictors (e.g., demographics, prior academic performance, psychology) to institutional predictors (e.g., faculty–student interactions, support services, policies) of university success. The next section illustrates this transition, offering strategies that institutions can employ to best engage transfer students from community colleges to four-year institutions.

Student Engagement Strategies

The previous blend of research and theory alludes to the importance of supporting and engaging community college transfer students as they transition to four-year institutions. Clearly, there are a number of inherent barriers that are best addressed proactively through institutionalized efforts. Therefore, there is no single solution to addressing these issues. Increased awareness of these potential issues can undoubtedly assist colleges in creating a seamless transition for transfer students. In doing so, four-year institutions must understand that engagement is key. In this section, we offer recommendations for engaging transfer students. It must be noted that the strategies extended in this chapter require collaboration and participation from a range of stakeholders (e.g., faculty, administration, counselors, community members, students).

Educational Goals
Inform students of educational options available at the four-year institution and assist them in establishing academic goals. This is perhaps the most important, but often missed, opportunity for all students (e.g., native, transfer, returnees). Students with a clear sense of direction are more motivated and focused than those who do not have a planned trajectory. Goal setting can serve as a motivational tool for

students as they progress toward degree completion. Educational goals established should be strictly based on an understanding of educational offerings at the four-year institution. Students should be able to identify why they are pursuing a specific major, what opportunities this major will afford them, which goals they seek to pursue out of the potential options, and what steps need to be taken to reach the goal.

In order to help students clearly define their educational goals, academic advising and counseling, career services, faculty, and other key resource offices must work collaboratively. Career services can help students find career paths that match their degree goals, personal interests, natural skillsets, and professional interests. Career centers offer a variety of tools such as Strengths Quest, Myers Briggs Type Indicator (MBTI), and the Self-Directed Search (SDS), all of which can be utilized to connect students to careers according to their skills and abilities. Career centers should also have "What Can I Do With This Major?" sheets that inventory the common careers according to major.

Academic advisors can help students clearly understand the academic path (e.g., carousel of courses, institutional policies) needed to complete the degree they seek to earn. These advisors should also help students strategize what courses to take, when to take them, what prerequisites they need to be aware of, and relevant policies. Lastly, faculty teaching in students' major areas should be utilized to bring texture and clear understanding of current trends in the field. They can offer career information and recommend classes that are ideal to take for the students' goals.

Intensive Orientation

Develop and implement mandatory transfer orientations that are as thorough in connecting transfer students to the institution as freshman orientations. Schools cannot assume that transfer students have the information they need to succeed. Therefore, orientations must be mandatory. Additionally, all information provided to first-year students should also be provided to incoming transfer students. Topics should include general institution information (i.e., the location and hours of key campus offices and resources), financial aid, parking, transportation (including discounts on public services), food services, counseling and/or advising, childcare, student organizations, and tutoring. If time does not permit for a full orientation, the information can be condensed and captured through video or web recording and turned into interactive web-based presentations or modules. Students should be required to complete web modules before they visit campus for an in-person transfer orientation. If this route is taken key information presented online can be reinforced by the presenters.

Web-based orientation tools will allow students to engage with vital orientation information at their convenience; it also assures that information presented is consistent across experiences. Academic and student affairs professionals should work together to determine the key information to be presented. To accommodate the range of schedules usually associated with transfer students, the in-person orientation should be offered at various times during the day, evenings, and weekends. With the understanding that transfer students have varying needs, transfer orientations should have a series of themed sessions that address differential student needs. The specialized sections of the orientation can also be captured and turned into interactive web-based modules. Modules should be engaging and concise, in order to increase the likelihood that students utilize them.

Transfer Equivalencies Website

Create a web tool that allows students to run fictitious audits of course equivalencies for courses they have taken at the community college. Such a tool could allow for transfer students to both plan ahead (so they do not take unnecessary courses at their primary institution), and manage their expectations of progress toward completion. The creation and implementation of this technology would require close communication between the four-year institutions and community colleges. It would also require academic departments at both institutions to work with information technologists to establish an accurate, user-friendly web tool. In the initial stages of development, the transfer equivalencies could be limited to community colleges and four-year institutions that have pre-existing articulation agreements. In addition, academic departments at both four-year institutions and community college will have to keep course numbers and equivalencies updated on an ongoing bases to assure that students are receiving accurate information.

Predictive Modeling

Develop a predictive modeling system that allows the institution to identify transfer students with characteristics (e.g., demographic, academic history) that place them at a greater potential for attrition. Predictive modeling can identify the risks associated with these students so that they can be intensively targeted with efforts to connect students to particular campus resources and services that would alleviate potential barriers. A system of predictive modeling can also assess student outcomes for transfer students and yield data that can inform future program offerings. As a starting point, institutions should employ the Laanan-Transfer Students' Questionnaire, which is useful for assessing transfer student adjustment into four-year institutions. Researchers have affirmed that at-risk and other predetermining factors are indicative of a student's success. However, what transfer institutions do once students arrive has an even greater impact and potential for prediction. As such, predictive modeling should also employ institutional variables that may be predictive of transfer student barriers.

Early Alert Systems

Early alert systems can be implemented to assist in the ongoing assessment of student performance. An early alert system would allow faculty members to report on students' academic performance. This system could report defined risk performance indicators (RPIs) that put students in danger of failing a class. These RPIs could be factors such as low test scores, tardiness, missed assignments, disengagement, and absenteeism. The system should allow faculty to report the RPIs of students at any point during the semester. Many early alert systems wait until 20% and 50% of semester or quarter completion before challenges are identified; this may be too late to have an effect on student performance.

Faculty would have to be educated intensely and encouraged to participate in the system. This is a particularly important consideration given the large number of adjunct faculty at the university level. As an intervention, transfer students could be required to meet with academic advisors, utilize writing centers, and/or tutoring when they receive the alert. The intervention would correspond to the type of alert they receive. Registration privileges of these students could be held to ensure students seek the appropriate service or action. Given the current economic downturn, which has strained resources at public universities, implementing an early alert system for all students may be cost prohibitive. In such cases, the authors suggest limiting the scope of the system to transfer students, especially those in majors that tend to have lower persistence and attainment rates.

Transfer Seminar

Offer a for-credit transfer seminar course. This course would introduce students to opportunities and resources at their new institution as well as assist in preparing them for their future educational/career plans. In addition, this seminar could provide opportunities for students to work on professional planning and development. The topics covered in this course could address the following: exploring individual strengths, academic majors, potential careers, internships, research opportunities, getting involved on campus, and graduate school preparation. Academic advisors or faculty from any academic unit could teach this course. Transfer students can be placed into this class according to risk factors and/or encouraged to register during orientation. The promotion of this course would have to take place prior to orientation, during orientation, and during advising sessions.

Student Involvement

Connect transfer students with student organizations. This connection can take place during orientation and via electronic means prior to orientation. Questionnaires that gauge academic and social interests can be sent out to transfer students after they commit to transferring. This assessment can be used to connect students with organizations that correspond to their preferences. Students can also be connected to clubs or organizations through social media. For example, if a student is interested in being an accountant, she or he can be contacted by the accounting club's president and provided with links to Facebook, Twitter, and club websites. In addition, during orientation, student activities staff can discuss campus involvement, and student representatives from key campus organizations (including the transfer students club, if any) can present related information to transfer students.

Campus or Academic Buddy

Establish an academic buddy program that connects transfer students to peers at the transfer institution. Mentor students should have completed at least one academic year at the four-year institution and be in good academic standing. Academic buddies should also be working towards degrees in the same department, or school, as their transfer buddy. This program could be a paid position that encourages peer interaction and promotes academic success. Academic buddies should be encouraged to study together and attend social and academic events. Both academic buddies and the students they mentor should receive support from the university. This will ensure that both remain academically motivated and ultimately graduate.

Academic Plan

Establish a policy that would require transfer students to complete an academic plan upon entrance to the four-year transfer institution. Commonly, transfer students "lose credits" in the transfer process and, as a result, do not graduate in a timely manner. Although graduating in four years is based upon an antiquated concept of a four-year model, students still need to move through college in a timely fashion. Students rarely meet the likelihood of graduating in four years when they have transferred. The academic plan would encourage students to establish clear goals relative to their academic situation. It would also promote an enhanced understanding of the course requirements at their institution. This academic plan can serve as a way of verifying where students are in their program.

Institutions should have a standardized academic plan form. The critical elements of the form would detail a semester grid that lists the student's name, student identification number (four-year institution specific), matriculating term, degree being sought, and academic year. This would be fractioned into sections that allow students to list a specific semester (e.g., fall 2017) and the name/number of the courses they will take each semester. Some institutions may benefit from having suggested sequence sheets for transfer students in two-, three-, and four-year increments. These academic planning sheets will supplement preexisting technologies that inform students and advisors of the remaining degree requirements. In many cases, these electronic tools can be used in conjunction so that students are encouraged to be active participants in their academic planning.

Conclusion

The recommendations offered in this chapter are not an exhaustive list of strategies; yet, they offer promising practices that address common issues facing transfer students. The fact that transfer students come from a range of backgrounds and experiences makes the barriers they face just as dynamic as the population itself. For this reason, there is not a one-size-fits-all approach to engaging transfer students. A breadth of institutional policies, practices, and interventions must be employed to engage different populations. Postsecondary faculty, staff, and administrators should implement these interventions. All interventions must be integrated into a systematic and institutionalized approach. Further, in line with Jain et al.'s (2011) articulation of transfer receptive culture, appropriate assessment and evaluation must be employed. The strategies used to enhance transfer student success should be proactive and comprehensive and take place prior to enrollment as well as upon entry into the university. The interventions should be intentional and connected seamlessly to outcomes that not only seek to retain transfer students but to support them in matriculating through the institution.

References

Anglin, L.W., Davis, J.W., & Mooradian, P.W. (1995). Do transfer students graduate? A comparative study of transfer students and native university students. *Community College Journal of Research and Practice, 28*(19), 321–330.

Berger, J.B., & Malaney, G.D. (2003). Assessing the transition of transfer students from community colleges to a university. *NASPA Journal, 40*(4), 1–23.

Best, G.A., & Gehring, D. (1993). The academic performance of community college transfer students at a major state university in Kentucky. *Community College Review, 21*(2), 32–41.

BPS (2009a). *Reason enrolled 2004 to transfer to four year college (yes) by community college student 6-year retention and attainment 2009, for race/ethnicity. Beginning Postsecondary Students Longitudinal Study.* Washington, DC: National Center for Education Statistics.

BPS (2009b). *Community college student 6-year retention and attainment 2009 by race/ethnicity, for reason enrolled 2004: Transfer to a 4-year college. Beginning Postsecondary Students Longitudinal Study.* Washington, DC: National Center for Education Statistics.

BPS (2009c). *Race/ethnicity by community college student 6-year retention and attainment 2009, for reason enrolled 2004: Transfer to a 4-year college. Beginning Postsecondary Students Longitudinal Study.* Washington, DC: National Center for Education Statistics.

Cameron, C. (2005). Experiences of transfer students in a collaborative baccalaureate nursing program. *Community College Review, 33*(2), 23–44.

Carlan, P.E., & Byxbe, F. (2000). Community colleges under the microscope: An analysis of performance predictors for native and transfer students. *Community College Review, 28*(2), 27–42.

Cejda, B.D. (1997). An examination of transfer shock in academic disciplines. *Community College Journal of Research and Practice, 21,* 279–288.

Cejda, B.D., Kaylor, A.J., & Rewey, K.L. (1998). Transfer shock in an academic discipline: The relationship between student's majors and their academic performance. *Community College Review, 26,* 1–13.

Christie, R.L., & Hutcheson, P. (2003). Net effects of institutional type on baccalaureate degree attainment of 'traditional' students. *Community College Review, 32*(2), 1–20.

Cohen, A.M., & Brawer, F.B. (2003). *The American community college* (4th ed.). San Francisco, CA: Jossey-Bass.

Diaz, P.E. (1992). Effects of transfer on academic performance of community college students at the four-year institution. *Community/Junior College Quarterly of Research and Practice, 16*(3), 279–291.

Donovan, R.A., Schaler-Peleg, B., & Forer, B. (Eds.). (1987). *Transfer: Making it work*. Washington, DC: American Association of Community and Junior Colleges.

Eimers, M., & Mullen, R. (1997). Transfer students: Who are they and how successful are they at the University of Missouri? *College and University, 72*, 9–20.

Gao, H., Hughes, W., O'Rear, M., & Fendley, W. (2002, June). *Developing structural equation Models to determine factors contributing to student graduation and retention. Are there differences for native students and transfers?* Paper presented at the Association for Institutional Research Forum, Toronto, Quebec, Canada.

Glass, J.C., & Harrington, A. (2002). Academic performance of community college transfer students and 'native' students at a large state university. *Community College Journal of Research and Practice, 26*(5), 415–430.

Hagedorn, L.S., Cypers, S., & Lester, J. (2008). Looking in the review mirror: Factors affecting transfer for urban community college students. *Community College Journal of Research and Practice, 32*, 643–664.

Jain, D., Herrera, A., Bernal, S., & Solórzano, D. (2011). Critical race theory and the transfer function: Introducing a transfer receptive culture. *Community College Journal of Research and Practice, 35*(3), 252–266.

Kane, T.J., & Rouse, C.E. (1999). The community college: Educating students at the margin between college and work. *The Journal of Economic Perspectives, 13*(1), 63–84.

Laanan, F.S. (1996). Making the transition: Understanding the process of community college transfer students. *Community College Review, 23*(4), 69–84.

Laanan, F.S. (2004). Studying transfer students: Part I: Instrument design and implications. *Community College Journal of Research and Practice, 28*, 331–351.

Nevarez, C., & Wood, J.L. (2010). *Community college leadership and administration: Theory, practice, and change*. New York, NY: Peter Lang.

Nora, A., & Rendón, L.I. (1990). Determinants of predisposition to transfer among community college students: A structural model. *Research in Higher Education, 31*(3), 235–255.

Pascarella, E.T. (1999). New studies track community college effect on students. *Community College Journal, 69*(6), 8–14.

Pascarella, E.T., Smart, J., & Ethington, C. (1986). Long-term persistence of two-year college students. *Research in Higher Education, 24*, 47–71.

Pennington, R. (2006). Rethinking grade transfer shock: Examining its importance in the community college transfer process. *Journal of Applied Research in the Community College, 14*(1), 19–33.

Piland, W. (1995). Community college transfer students who earn bachelor's degrees. *Community College Review, 23*, 35–44.

Porter, S.R. (2002). Assessing transfer and first-time freshmen student performance. *Journal of Applied Research in the Community College, 10*(1), 41–56.

Preston, D.L. (1993, May). *Interfacing two-year and four-year transcripts for transfer students*. Paper presented at the Association for Institutional Research Annual Forum, Evanston, IL.

Rhine, T.J., Milligan, D.M., & Nelson, L.R. (2000). Alleviating transfer shock: Creating an environment for more successful transfer students. *Community College Journal of Research and Practice, 24*(6), 443–453.

Solórzano, D.G. (1998). Critical Race Theory, race and gender microaggressions, and the experience of Chicana and Chicano scholars. *Qualitative Studies in Education, 11*(1), 121–136.

Townsend, B.K. (1995). Community college transfer students: A case study of survival. *The Review of Higher Education, 18*(2), 175–193.

Townsend, B.K. (2001). Redefining the community college transfer mission. *Community College Review, 29*(2), 29–42.

Townsend, B.K., & Wilson, K.B. (2006). A hand hold for a little bit: Factors facilitating the success of community college transfer students at a large research university. *Journal of College Student Development, 47*(4), 439–456.

Turner, C.S. (1988). *Organizational determinants of the transfer of Hispanic students from two-to four-year colleges*. Unpublished Doctoral Dissertation, Stanford, CA: Stanford University.

Turner, C.S. (1990). A California case study: Organizational determinants of the transfer of Hispanic students from two- to four-year colleges in the bay area. *Metropolitan Education, 6*, 1–24.

Turner, C.S. (1992). It takes two to transfer: Relational networks and educational outcomes. *Community College Review, 19*(4), 27–33.

Wang, X. (2009). Baccalaureate attainment and college persistence of community college transfer students at four-year institutions. *Research in Higher Education, 50,* 570–588.

Wood, J.L., Nevarez, C., & Hilton, A.A. (2011). Creating a culture of transfer in the community college. *Making Connections: Interdisciplinary Approaches to Cultural Diversity, 13*(1), 54–61.

Wood, J.L., Nevarez, C., & Hilton, A.A. (2012). Determinants of transfer among community college students. *Journal of Applied Research in the Community College, 19*(2), 64–69.

Chapter 18
Engaging Commuter and Part-Time Students

Barbara Jacoby

Although approximately 85% of today's college students live off campus and more than 60% attend part time or part of the academic school year, little is known about their engagement patterns and college experiences (Jacoby & Garland, 2004; National Center for Education Statistics, 2009). Even less is known about differences that exist within this diverse student population, because much of the existing research treats commuter students as homogenous and ignores the need to examine within-group differences (Jacoby, 1989; Jacoby & Garland, 2004). One result of this dearth of knowledge is the application of what Pascarella (2006) refers to as "rational myths," or the adoption of programs and policies that lack empirical evidence of effectiveness but that seem to make logical or intuitive sense (p. 513). Rational myths include the continued utilization of programs and interventions designed for full-time resident students to serve commuter and part-time students assuming that the effect on learning will be equivalent. Another result is that the programs and interventions that are most likely to promote student engagement may not be offered at all to commuter or part-time students.

Without doubt, the topic of enhancing the success of commuter and part-time students is exceedingly complex. Astin (2001) reports that commuting is negatively associated with attainment of the bachelor's degree and enrollment in postgraduate education. Commuting has negative effects on self-assessment of emotional health, and "substantial commuting seems to raise the level of stress experienced by undergraduate students" (pp. 390–391). Data reported from the National Survey of Student Engagement (Kuh, Gonyea, & Palmer, 2001) and the Cooperative Institutional Research Program point to the need to focus attention on commuter and part-time students but offer little in the way of specific implementation strategies to increase the likelihood of their persistence to graduation (Astin, 2001).

Part of the complexity surrounds the definition of commuter students. Because part-time students are rarely interested in, able to, or eligible to live on campus, they are, by definition, commuter students. No matter how commuter students are defined, they account for a majority of today's college students (Jacoby, 2000). Despite their numbers, the residential traditions dominant in American higher education have impeded institutional response to their presence. The unique needs of commuter students have been neither adequately understood nor appropriately incorporated into policies, programs, and practices (Jacoby, 1989).

This chapter describes how to use what we know about commuter and part-time students to design and implement strategies that enhance their success. It begins with a snapshot of the extraordinary diversity of this population and their common needs and concerns. It then offers several theoretical frameworks that are useful in understanding commuter and part-time students, institutional environments, and the nature of interactions between them. It finally presents an organizing model together with specific strategies that promote student success. It should be noted that the term "commuter students" is used interchangeably with "commuter and part-time students" occasionally for simplicity and to avoid repetition.

Who are Commuter and Part-Time Students?

The National Clearinghouse for Commuter Programs (NCCP) and the Council for the Advancement of Standards in Higher Education (CAS) define commuter students as those who do not live in institution-owned housing on campus (Jacoby, 1989). Over the last several years, the traditional distinction between resident students (those who live in institution-owned housing on campus) and commuter students (those who do not) has become considerably blurred. Many colleges and universities have responded to increased student demand for on-campus residence by working with private developers to build housing on or close to the campus. In addition, some institutions are seeking to extend their sphere of influence by creating university districts that extend campus services and programming to students who live in rental housing near the campus. Regardless of how commuter students are defined, they are different from resident students in that, for them, home and campus are not synonymous (Likins, 1988).

According to the NCCP and CAS definitions, commuter students represent more than 85% of U.S. college students today (National Center for Educational Statistics, 2009). Commuter students include full-time students of traditional age who live with their parents, part-time students who live in rental housing near the campus, adults with full-time careers, and parents whose lives intersect with one or more of the previous characteristics. While this is a broad definition of commuter students, the NCCP finds it useful in drawing attention, both nationally and on individual campuses, to this generally underserved population. As mentioned earlier, commuter students and their needs are diverse. Traditional and non-traditional age, full- and part-time attendance, and commuting distance to campus are just a few descriptors used to understand the commuter student experience. The National Survey of Student Engagement makes the distinction between "walking" vs. "driving" commuters. However, there is a powerful reality that emerges above and beyond any differences: No matter where commuter students live or what type of institution they attend, the fact that they commute to the college campus profoundly influences the nature of their educational experience (Likins, 1988).

Another characteristic of commuter students that strongly affects their college experience is attendance status. More and more students attend part time, alternate semesters of full and part-time attendance, and "stop out" of college to focus their time and energy on family or work issues. In addition, a majority of college students attend more than one institution of higher education. This phenomenon, known as "swirling," is becoming more prevalent. A report by the U.S. Department of Education revealed that 59% of undergraduates had attended at least two institutions, and more than 20% had attended three or more. The report also associated "swirling" with significantly reduced likelihood of attaining a degree. Seventy-two percent of students who attended only one college had obtained a bachelor's degree within six years as compared to 46% who attended more than one. Only 34% who attended more than three colleges had obtained a bachelor's degree within six years (Peter & Forrest-Cataldi, 2005).

Commuter and part-time students attend practically every institution of higher education and may represent a small percentage of students at a private residential liberal arts college or the entire population of a community college or urban institution. More than 40% of all undergraduates are 24 years old or older (National Center for Educational Statistics, 2009), and virtually all of these students are commuters. Part-time students, likewise virtually all of whom are commuters, make up approximately 60% of undergraduate enrollment (National Center for Education Statistics, 2009). The number of commuter students will continue to increase and to become more diverse as the numbers of part-time and adult students continue gaining access to higher education. Many more adults will have to enroll in college for the United States to meet President Obama's goal of having the world's largest proportion of college graduates by 2020 (Pell Institute for the Study of Opportunity in Higher Education, 2011).

Although commuter students are the majority of college students, common misperceptions and myths about them persist and reflect outdated or inaccurate perspectives. Commuter students of both traditional and non-traditional age continue to be thought of as disinterested in student activities or other aspects of campus life. Another persistent myth is that what works for traditional on-campus residential students would work equally well for commuter students if they would just be a little more serious about their education (Jacoby, 1989, 2000).

In reality, the educational goals of commuter and part-time students are more likely than not to be similar to those of residential students. They are just as likely to seek to be involved in their learning and in the campus community; however, their lives consist of balancing many competing commitments, including work, family, and other responsibilities. The National Center for Educational Statistics reports that 80% of undergraduates work, with 48% doing so to defray college expenses (2002). Over 46% of full-time students work 25 or more hours per week to make ends meet. Commuter students are more likely to work, to work more hours, and to work off campus than resident students

(Jacoby, 2000). As a result, they may appear to be less committed to, and engaged in, their education. There are certainly both commuter and residential students who seek minimal engagement while earning a degree. The critical point is not to assume that this is more likely true of commuter and part-time students. Despite their commitment, many commuter students simply cannot always make campus life, or, for some, even their college education, their primary focus.

There is, however, ample evidence that attending college part time puts students at greater risk of not attaining their educational goals. Research indicates that students who attend college part time are at a disadvantage relative to their full-time peers. Compared with their full-time counterparts, part-time students tend to be older, financially independent, and first in their families to attend college. Most part-time students attend two-year colleges, as compared with 25% of full-time students. Eighty-three percent work while enrolled in courses. Of those, half work full time. Forty-seven percent consider themselves employees first and students second. Part-time enrollment correlates negatively with achievement of academic outcomes (National Center for Education Statistics, 2006). Additionally, it is not surprising that part-time students report lower levels of engagement than their counterparts (Community College Survey of Student Engagement, 2011).

In sum, Keeling describes commuter students as "reinvented students." He explains: "Students' lives, like those of their parents and caregivers, are absolutely more complicated today (by jobs, debt, and transportation, for example) and the ranking of college . . . or of studying, or classes, among their immediate priorities have clearly changed . . . 'Student' is no longer every student's primary identity . . . 'Student' is only one identity for people who are also employees, wage workers, opinion leaders or followers, artists, friends, children . . . parents, partners, or spouses" (1999, p. 4).

Common Needs and Concerns of Commuter Students

Although commuter students are extraordinarily diverse, a common core of needs and concerns can be identified (Jacoby, 1989). The following set of core needs has been used by the NCCP and many institutions as a basis for the design of services, programs, and needs assessment instruments for commuter students. Since virtually all part-time students commute, these needs and concerns are applicable to that population.

Transportation

The most obvious concerns shared by commuter students are those related to transportation: parking, traffic, fixed transportation schedules, inclement weather, vehicle maintenance, transportation costs, and locating alternative means of transportation when their primary means fails. No matter the mode, commuting to and from campus places demands on students' time and energy. As a result, they frequently concentrate their classes into blocks, take some classes online, and have little free time to spend on campus. The convenience of classes, services, and programs is of paramount importance (Wilmes & Quade, 1986).

Multiple Life Roles

For most commuter students, being a student is only one of several important and time-consuming roles. As mentioned earlier, most commuter students work to defray the costs associated with higher education. Many work the equivalent of full time and at more than one job. In addition, many have responsibilities for managing households including children, siblings, and relatives. Commuter students' time is a critical and finite resource that directly impacts their ability to engage in academic and out-of-class activities. By necessity, they select their campus involvements carefully. The relative value of a campus activity when compared with other priorities is a major factor in their decision to participate (Wilmes & Quade, 1986).

Integrating Support Networks

Commuter students often lack the supportive campus environment that has been identified by the National Survey of Student Engagement as one of the benchmarks of effective educational practice (Kuh et al., 2001). As a result, the support networks for commuter students generally exist off, rather than on, campus including: partners, parents, children, siblings, employers, coworkers, and friends. Although these individuals can be supportive, students must negotiate with family, employers, and others to establish priorities, responsibilities, and time commitments. These negotiations are more difficult if significant others do not understand both the challenges and opportunities of higher education, as do campus-based advisors, counselors, and others who generally provide support to students.

Sense of Belonging

Students who commute often lack a sense of belonging to, or of feeling wanted by, the institution. Some institutions fail to provide even the most basic facilities, such as lockers and lounges, which allow students to feel physically connected to campus. In many cases, there are inadequate opportunities for commuter students to develop relationships with faculty, staff, and peers. Individuals rarely feel connected to a place where they have no significant relationships. Students who do not have a sense of belonging may complain that their college experience is like "stopping at the mall" to get what they need on the way to somewhere else (Wilmes & Quade, 1986; Jacoby, 2000).

In recognition of the realities of commuter and part-time students' busy lives, Astin (1985) summarizes the challenges that higher education institutions face in increasing engagement in learning: "Educators are in reality competing with other forces in the student's life for a share of that finite time and energy. The student's investment in matters relating to family, friends, job and other outside activities represents a reduction in the time and energy the student has to devote" to his or her education (p. 143). Astin further asserts that, as a result, colleges and universities must recognize that almost every institutional policy and practice can affect how students spend their time and how much effort they devote to their education.

Theories and Concepts

Although theories and models cannot capture the complexity of human beings or environments, they can serve as lenses that bring relationships and situations into sharper focus. Several theoretical frameworks have direct application to commuter student success. Maslow's (1982) hierarchy of needs is not one of the frameworks covered in this chapter, but it is helpful in thinking about the experience of commuter and part-time students both on and off the campus. Because of their various life situations, commuter and part-time students are often preoccupied with satisfying their most fundamental needs. As a result, it is essential for institutions to provide services to help meet students' basic needs for housing, transportation, food, security, health care, and child care. On the next level, students need to feel a sense of membership in and acceptance by the campus community. Before students can take full advantage of the institution to achieve self-actualization, their need for esteem must be met.

Mattering and Marginality

The concept of mattering (Rosenberg & McCullough, 1981) is related to the needs for belonging and esteem described by Maslow (1982). Mattering is "the feeling that others depend on us, are interested in us, [and] are concerned with our fate" (Rosenberg & McCullough, p. 165). Schlossberg, Lynch, and Chickering (1989) applied this concept to colleges by developing a mattering scale for use in determining to what extent policies, practices, and classroom activities are geared toward making adult students feel that they matter. The NCCP has broadened this application to include all types of commuter students.

Schlossberg (1985) identified the construct of marginality as the polar opposite of mattering. Commuter and part-time students have been, and have felt, marginal in colleges and universities since first participating in higher education. Although feeling marginal during a period of transition into a new environment is to be expected, institutions should employ policies and practices that make all students feel that they matter—that they are central rather than marginal.

Theories of Student Engagement

Research indicates that the more time and effort students invest in their learning and the more intensely they engage in their own education, the greater will be their achievement, growth, and satisfaction with the college experience. Investment in learning also increases the likelihood of persistence toward attainment of educational goals (Study Group on the Conditions of Excellence in American Higher Education, 1984). The concept of student engagement includes activities that are traditionally associated with learning, such as reading and writing, preparing for class, and other key activities that more recently have emerged as being important, such as collaborating with peers on projects and community service.

Kuh et al. (2001), in an analysis of data from the National Survey of Student Engagement, compare three categories of students: on-campus residents, walking commuters, and driving commuters. They found that both first-year students and seniors who lived on campus had higher scores on all the benchmarks of effective educational practice, although many of the differences were relatively small. Some of the largest differences were found in the benchmarks of interactions with faculty members and enriching educational experiences. The latter benchmark includes complementary learning experiences inside and outside the classroom; experiencing diversity; using technology; and opportunities to synthesize and apply knowledge. Results also indicated that, although many commuter students' time is constrained by work and family matters, they put forth just as much effort as resident students in areas that relate directly to the classroom.

Astin (1985) explicitly states that the effectiveness of all educational policies and practices is directly related to their capacity to increase student engagement. However, many commuter and part-time students cannot become involved in the same ways that traditional-age, residential students can. Nevertheless, by using what we know about commuter students, we can create opportunities to enhance their involvement in learning in ways that meet their needs. Rather than expecting commuter and part-time students to adjust their lifestyles and schedules, it is the responsibility of colleges and universities to design curricular and cocurricular mechanisms specifically and intentionally to involve students deeply and intentionally in learning.

Transition Theory

Schlossberg (1989) defines a transition as any event or non-event that changes relationships, routines, assumptions, and roles. For some students, their transitions are obvious, traditional, and well-marked, such as when a first-time college student leaves home and moves into a residence hall to begin a new life on campus. For commuter and part-time students and those close to them, their transitions are often perceived as "non-events," such as when a fully employed adult begins taking courses at the local community college on a part-time basis while keeping most other aspects of her life intact. Many students returning to school after a break in their education do so because of some sort of life transition. Such transitions include employed or unemployed individuals trying to keep up with an increasingly competitive job market, homemakers whose children have grown up, or spouses and partners who suddenly find themselves single parents. Students transferring from community colleges to four-year institutions and those who alternate between semesters of full- and part-time enrollment also may perceive these transitions as "non-events." First-time, full-time commuter students may feel that going to college while continuing to work at the job they had in high school, eating dinner and participating in social activities with their family, living in the same house, and hanging out with their high-school friends is not much of a transition. Regardless of whether students realize that they are in transition, transitions that are both "events" and "non-events" are challenging. Colleges need to recognize these transitions and provide appropriate supports.

Ackell's Stages of Institutional Integration

If an institution really wanted to provide an optimum educational environment for commuter and part-time student success, what would it look like? Considerable change would be necessary to create such an environment. Ackell (1986) describes the process of institutional adaptation to the presence of adult students in three developmental stages. These developmental stages apply equally well to the process of institutional adaptation to the presence and success of the broader commuter and part-time student population (Jacoby, 1989).

Stage 1: The "Laissez-Faire" Stage

Institutions in the "laissez-faire" stage simply remove obvious barriers or constraints and permit students to do the best they can within a system that works neither for nor against them. Students are allowed to be as entrepreneurial and aggressive as they choose in dealing with the institution, but no organized or official administrative intervention is offered on their behalf. The operating assumption is that variables like age, residence, and attendance status are not significant. It is unknown whether some students leave the institution at a higher rate than others or whether some are less successful or satisfied with their experiences (Ackell, 1986; Jacoby, 1989).

Stage 2: The "Separatist" Stage

In this stage, certain groups of students (e.g., commuters on a residential campus, part-time students when most attend full time) are essentially separate from the majority of the student body. Some separate, specific programs and services are offered for them, but these programs and services have lower institutional priority and status than traditional ones. In this stage, commuter and part-time students are clearly marginal. It could even be argued that they are subject to a subtle form of economic exploitation, as the institution expects them to manage with substantially less support than is appropriated for programs and services for mainstream students. Marginalized student populations are consistently less satisfied and successful and leave the institution at a higher rate (Ackell, 1986; Jacoby, 1989).

Stage 3: The "Equity" Stage

According to Ackell, equity means an "active use of the principles of justice and fairness to correct inequities in a system that de facto discriminates against one group in favor of another" (1986, p. 3). An institution that has begun to evolve toward the final or equity stage, takes concrete steps toward treating all students fairly and providing the same quality experience for all. It is probable that no institution at the fully developed equity stage exists today, but some institutions have moved sufficiently beyond the separatist stage that some of the characteristics of a full equity institution can be discerned. There would be few differences among student groups regarding degree attainment and satisfaction with the college experience (Ackell, 1986; Jacoby, 1989).

Student Engagement Strategies

Schlossberg et al. (1989) propose a comprehensive, integrated approach to creating an educational environment that supports adult learners. Putting their transition theory into practice, Schlossberg and colleagues describe students' transitions in terms of "moving in, moving through, and moving on" as a model for enhancing the college experience (Evans, Forney, & Guido-DiBrito, 1998, p. 112). This approach works equally well as a model for organizing success strategies for commuter and part-time students.

Moving In

As far as moving in, Schlossberg et al. (1989) emphasize the need to recognize that, from the commuter or part-time student's viewpoint, finding one's way into (or back into) college, understanding its plentiful opportunities, figuring out how things work, and then making the college experience part of one's life require a new set of complex learnings. Whether they enter college after a period of full-time work homemaking, a community college, or high school, most commuter and part-time students must make the transition from a world in which they felt comfortable and in control to a new world in which they feel like strangers. They are faced with opportunities, along with uncertainties and risks. They may lack confidence in their ability to handle the academic work at the new institution and may have doubts about whether they can meet their professors' expectations. If the campus environment is not intentionally designed to make commuter and part-time students feel that they matter and that they are full members of the community, they will feel marginal. And, as Schlossberg (1989) reminds us, students who feel marginal are less likely to engage in the kinds of college experiences that lead to educational success and satisfaction.

Acknowledging that the first semester is particularly challenging for new commuter and part-time students, Schlossberg and her colleagues (1989) believe that a comprehensive institutional strategy is ideal. They recommend that institutions consider establishing an "entry center" that brings together all functions related to entry: recruitment, pre-admission counseling and admission functions, assessment of prior learning, academic advising, financial aid, orientation, and registration. Although most of these services can and should be offered electronically, one should not assume that this alleviates the need for personal interaction. In fact, Schlossberg, Lynch, and Chickering suggest that a single staff member be assigned to work with each new student from pre-admission through the first semester (1989).

Recruitment and Admission

Although it is attractive, this comprehensive strategy would require massive reorganization on most campuses. There are nonetheless other interventions that are easier to implement. As early as the recruitment and pre-admission stage, much can and should be done. Students' early impressions of the degree to which they will "fit" at an institution are influenced by the ways in which the institution chooses to portray itself in its publications and on its web site. In this vein, print and on-line text and photographs should represent all types of students and a variety of lifestyles.

Educational success depends on a sound match between students' educational goals and needs and an institution's ability to provide the appropriate opportunities, environment, and support. Therefore, it is incumbent upon recruitment and admissions personnel to work with each student to determine, to the best of their abilities, whether this fundamental congruence exists. Because commuter and part-time students may have more limitations (often those of location and/or finances) on their choice of institution, it is particularly critical to help them ascertain before admission that there is a good fit between what they seek and what the institution offers. In addition, recruitment and admissions officers should be able to provide prospective commuter students with thorough and accurate information about housing, transportation, child care, and other services as well as how commuter students are involved in campus life (Jacoby, 1989).

Financial Aid and Employment

Financial aid and employment opportunities that allow students to connect their academics with experience are major factors contributing to student success. Financial aid officers should ensure that expense budgets used to determine the amount of financial need realistically reflect costs, including transportation, rent, child care, and food. Scholarships specifically for adult learners and part-time students should be established, and eligible students should be strongly encouraged to apply. Information, programs, and individual assistance regarding managing personal finances should be offered. In addition, commuter students who must work should be strongly encouraged to work on, rather than off, campus. They should be informed about the advantages of on-campus employment: avoiding the "three-point" commute between home, campus, and work; flexible scheduling around and between classes; supervisors' willingness to reduce work hours at times of heavy academic work; and the work setting as a place to learn about the campus, meet people, and find a "home away from home" on campus.

New Student Orientation

Orientation programs should make all students—commuters on a predominantly residential campus, adult learners, part-time students, and transfers—feel equally welcome to the campus community. If a "one program for all" is the institution's approach, activities should be appropriate for all students and should enable them to interact with both new and experienced students who are similar to them. Adult learners returning to school, for example, should not be expected to view skits about alcohol abuse or date rape or to participate in physical activities that may make them feel uncomfortable. Various orientation program formats should be considered, including, but not limited to, weekday evening, weekend, overnight, and online options.

For all students, an essential element of orientation is the opportunity to work with an advisor or mentor to carefully think about and articulate their educational goals. While most commuter and part-time students are serious about and committed to achieving their educational goals, they are less likely to have the opportunity to make college their only or sometimes even their top priority. For example, if a 30-year-old entering student who has been working full time since graduating from high school sets as her goals to complete her bachelor's degree and take time off to have a child and be a "stay-at-home mom" in the next ten years, her advisor should be prepared to work with her to develop a plan to achieve them. Advisors should also refer students to the institutional opportunities and resources that can help them achieve their goals. Well-trained peer advisors can also serve to ease the transition of new students by informally providing information, guidance, companionship, and introductions to others who have experienced similar issues and concerns.

Family Orientation

For many commuter and part-time students, whether they are of traditional age living with their parents or living independently with a spouse or partner, the first people they turn to for support and guidance are most likely to be family members. This is particularly true for students who lack an on-campus support system. As a result, orientation programs for family members are important and should be designed to address a wide variety of family situations. For example, first-generation college students often find that their parents and other relatives do not understand why students are strongly encouraged to spend large amounts of time on campus and to become involved in activities that do not seem to relate directly to their classes. Similarly, family members may expect the student to continue to be involved in family life to the same extent as before entering college and may be resentful when the student is unable to be at the family dinner table or finds it difficult to be home by the family curfew hour. Spouses, partners, or siblings who find themselves suddenly left with more child care and household responsibilities because the student is otherwise engaged would likely be more supportive if they better understood the challenges and opportunities they face. Orientation programs that address these issues up front can also provide language and tools for families to use to work through them. Children who find that their student-parents have less time and energy for their concerns would also benefit from programs designed to help them deal with this transition.

In addition, programs can be created for students' parents and partners to enable them to offer immediate support to the student in times of need. While parents and partners should not be expected to substitute for on-campus advisors and mentors, they can complement and supplement them. On-line or on-campus workshops could be offered to parents and partners, together with training on how to access information and resources to address their students' concerns.

Campus Environments

The manner in which campus facilities are designed and the ways in which services are delivered can create either a welcoming or a chilling climate for commuter and part-time students. For example, older students are unlikely to feel comfortable in a student cafeteria where there is very loud music and bean-bag chairs that are difficult for them to get in and out of. Campus health centers that offer workshops on sexually transmitted diseases and "date-rape drugs" should also offer information on menopause, osteoporosis, and low-back pain, for example. If services are not open during hours when commuter and part-time students need them, such as early mornings and evenings, students may feel frustrated and disenfranchised. Conversely, commuter lounges with lockers, microwaves, eating areas, and computers go a long way to making students feel that they matter and that they have a "place to be" on campus.

Moving Through

The issues, concerns and challenges for commuter and part-time students moving through college are both similar to and different from those when moving in. They include balancing competing demands, dealing with multiple stressors, feeling marginal, mastering skills, maintaining self-esteem, and handling the academic and life transitions that occur along the way (Schlossberg et al., 1989). Work and family issues are sure to arise, ranging from job loss to promotion, from new babies to elder care needs, from unanticipated academic challenges to unexpected opportunities. A reality of "moving through" is that no matter how dedicated a student may be to earning a degree, he or she may need to stop out to attend to family or work priorities. The extent to which a commuter or part-time student feels engaged in the institution, both intellectually and socially, can make a tremendous difference in whether the student overcomes these challenges and persists to graduation or leaves the institution.

Learning Communities

Without doubt, one of the most powerful means of engaging students in learning and enabling them to develop academic and social connections with peers and faculty is through learning communities. Among the many well-documented benefits of learning communities are that they organize students and faculty into smaller groups, encourage curricular integration, help students become socialized to the expectations of college or specific disciplines, and offer community-based delivery of academic support programs (Shapiro & Levine, 1999). Unfortunately, at many institutions, learning communities are in fact living-learning communities that are designed for students who live in residence halls on campus or are only available to first-time, full-time freshmen.

However, there are excellent models of curricular learning communities that can be designed intentionally for commuter and part-time students. Classroom-based learning communities enroll a common cohort of students in clustered or linked courses to create an environment that promotes greater academic and social engagement. In the clustered-course model, a group of 20 to 30 students enrolls in two or more courses, often including an integrative seminar. Another model involves first-year students and is commonly referred to as freshman interest groups (FIGS). To be welcoming to commuter and part-time students, curricular learning communities can be arranged to meet two to three days rather than five with classes held back to back rather than spread throughout the day. Upper-level students who have participated in these learning communities can be engaged on an ongoing basis as teaching assistants or as peer teachers, advisers, or tutors (Jacoby, 2000).

Individual Courses

In addition to learning communities, individual courses can be designed to engage different types of commuter students. In one simple but innovative example, a freshman seminar that meets twice weekly could be set for Mondays and Wednesdays at 11 a.m. Students selecting this section would be advised not to schedule a class during the noon hour so that they would be able to have lunch, study, and relax together. Two enhancements to this scenario would further increase its benefits: the professor could regularly or occasionally join the students for lunch and the classroom could be reserved on Fridays for the students who so desired to meet for study groups.

Aware that inside the classroom is the one opportunity that all students have for educationally meaningful interaction with peers, more and more faculty are shifting from the lecture mode to an active learning mode in the classroom. For example, an effective approach for commuter and part-time students would be to assign group projects during class and to deliver the lectures online outside of class time.

Class Scheduling

Class scheduling policies for both individual courses and learning communities that are intentionally designed to fit into the lifestyles of commuter and part-time students are essential. In addition to traditional day and evening classes, institutions should consider "twilight" classes (4:00 to 6:00 p.m.), "dawn" classes (6:00 to 8:00 a.m.), and classes that meet once or twice a week rather than three or four times. All types of courses—including upper-level, laboratory, and language—should be offered in alternative formats. Without doubt, distance learning enables commuter and part-time students to take courses when and where it is convenient for them. However, it is important to realize that not all commuter students prefer distance learning, and that distance learning does not meet all their curricular needs. To provide opportunities for prolonged interaction and, at the same time, to schedule a course that is easy to work into the lifestyle of a student employed full time or with family-care responsibilities, it is possible, for example, to organize the approximately 48 semester hours for a three-credit course into six full-day Saturday sessions and two extended Friday evening sessions at the beginning and end of the semester.

Cocurricular Programs

The realities of commuter and part-time students' lives may impede or limit their ability to participate as fully as they would like in campus life outside the classroom. While some students are more interested than others in being actively involved in cocurricular activities and organizations, it is critical not to assume that this is more true of traditional-age students who live on campus. Rather, it is incumbent upon administrators to carefully examine policies and practices related to cocurricular programming and to ensure that there are no institutional barriers, however inadvertent, to commuter and part-time students' involvement. Likewise, they should be intentionally and explicitly invited to engage. Merely stating "all are welcome" is not enough. A range of social, cultural, educational, and recreational sports program that includes activities appropriate for all students should be offered. Programs should also be scheduled at a variety of times to accommodate students' varied schedules, including lunch time, late afternoon, and early evenings. Information about activities and meetings should be disseminated sufficiently in advance of the event so that commuter and part-time students have time to rearrange their family, work, and transportation schedules to attend.

All types of students should be encouraged to participate in student government and in campus governance organizations. Too often, the "typical" student leaders are the ones we solicit and nominate for key leadership positions. However, at many institutions, adult learners, part-time students, and long-distance commuters have been successful campus leaders. It is also important to design criteria for campus awards that recognize student leadership accomplishments off campus (e.g., Parent-Teacher-Student Association president, church choir member) to the same extent that on-campus involvement and leadership are recognized.

Programs that encourage the involvement of commuter students' families should be offered in addition to traditional programming. Family days or evenings at the campus recreation center are popular at many institutions, as are family movies and live performances. For students with children, simultaneous programming is an innovative way to provide opportunities for their engagement. As one of many examples, a lecture or performance could be held simultaneously with a children's art class or puppet show next door.

Using Information Technology
Information technology offers multiple opportunities for affiliation and community development for commuter and part-time students. Virtual communities by neighborhood or zip code of residence, for instance, can be established and nurtured via Facebook or Twitter, as are floor and building communities for students living in residence halls. Smaller, more focused communities based on specific majors or interests can readily splinter off (e.g., government majors or martial arts enthusiasts living in a particular town). Portal technology enables students to personalize their relationship to the institution to build affiliation, increase access to information, and encourage engagement in campus life. Portals permit students to set up their own entry screen that provides them immediate or one-click access to personal calendars, reminders, course schedule and bill information, academic records, information about upcoming events that address their specific interests, and real-time weather and traffic on their route to campus.

Charting Progress
Finally, students who are "moving through" should have an advisor or mentor who regularly reviews with them their progress towards their academic and other life goals. It is important to define success in terms that are appropriate for students with non-traditional paths. As students and advisors assess progress, students should be encouraged to revise their educational plans as appropriate. In this way, students who have not progressed as far as they would have liked would not feel that they have

failed but, rather, that they are empowered to make modifications as a result of life circumstances or changes in their academic program. To revisit the example of the 30-year-old woman who plans to complete her degree and to raise a child by the time she is 40, a revised educational plan would be required if she had another child along the way. E-mail mentoring programs have tremendous potential for engaging commuter students in regular, albeit asynchronous, communication that may be difficult or impossible in person. Again, the important thing is not to assume that traditional students prefer traditional, in-person mentoring and that commuter and part-time students prefer online contact.

Moving On

As essential as it is to support commuter students as they enter and move through college, it is equally critical to help them move on and out. A multitude of issues arise as students approach the transition out of college: "Did I choose the right major after all?," "Will my degree really enable me to get the promotion or the job I've been working towards?" and "What did I really learn and how can I make meaning of it?" We must make students aware that moving on is an important and normal transition that is often filled with conflicting feelings and doubts and help them as they work through their complex personal and career issues.

Capstone Experiences

Many institutions offer senior capstone courses that enable students to tie the various aspects of their learning together and to bring coherence to their collegiate experience. Although they often include integrative papers, capstone courses can take many forms. Among these are internships, research projects, service-learning, and forms of artistic expression such as films, poetry, or performance. In designing capstone courses, it is important to ascertain that they are developmentally appropriate for all students, not just for traditional-age students finishing college in four years. For example, an internship may be just the right bridge to the world of work for a twenty-two year old who has held only student jobs on campus. However, requiring an adult who has worked for a number of years to do the same type of internship may not be useful. A creative project that ties the curriculum to prior life experiences in a meaningful way may be more appropriate.

Career Guidance

Career counseling and searching are essential for most students as they transition out of college. It is important that career counselors are prepared to assist students who have significant work experience, who are changing careers mid-life, and who are dealing with being laid off in addition to those seeking their first career position. Students whose path through college has not been traditional may need assistance in putting together a resume or portfolio that fully and accurately represents the knowledge, experience, and skills they have acquired, including school, work, off-campus leadership positions, and community service.

Celebrating Success

Celebration of academic success and achievement of students' other educational and personal goals is another critical aspect of transition out of college. Commencement ceremonies should be designed and speakers chosen to celebrate the achievements of all students and not to marginalize those who did not graduate in the traditional four years. In addition to recognizing the parents of traditional-age graduates, the family members, work colleagues, and friends of non-traditional students should be specifically recognized.

A final aspect of "moving on" is the transition to alumni status. There are multiple benefits to encouraging the continued involvement of soon-to-be and new alumni. Reaching out to students who are still enrolled as they near degree completion reinforces the message that they are important members of the institutional community and enhances their sense of belonging at a time when they may be anxious about their future. Students who feel that they are valued community members are likely to be goodwill ambassadors for the institution. This is another reason why activities to recognize seniors and to celebrate graduation should be appropriate for all students, no matter their age, family status, or length of time to degree.

Conclusion

As commuter and part-time students continue to become more diverse and attend an increasingly wider variety of institutions, educators must develop a thorough understanding of their needs, useful theoretical frameworks, and strategies that increase success and retention. While the frameworks and strategies described in this article are general, they are readily adaptable to institutions and their particular populations of commuter and part-time students. In the current climate in which institutions of higher education are held accountable for translating policies, practices, and programs into degree completion and success, these frameworks and strategies will enable institutions to comprehensively and effectively enhance the educational experience of all students.

References

Ackell, E. F. (1986). Adapting the institution to adult students: A developmental perspective. In W. H. Warren (Ed.), *Improving institutional services to adult learners*. Washington, DC: American Council on Education.

Astin, A. W. (1985). *Achieving educational excellence*. San Francisco, CA: Jossey-Bass.

Astin, A. W. (2001). *What matters in college: Four critical years revisited*. San Francisco, CA: Jossey-Bass.

Community College Survey of Student Engagement. (2011). *National student characteristics 2009, 2010, 2011*. Retrieved October 14, 2011, from www.ccsse.org/survey/national3.cfm

Evans, N. J., Forney, D. S., & Guido-DiBrito, F. (1998). *Student development in college: Theory, research, and practice*. San Francisco, CA: Jossey-Bass.

Jacoby, B. (1989). *The student as commuter: Developing a comprehensive institutional response*. ASHE-ERIC Higher Education Report no.7. Washington, DC: School of Education and Human Development, The George Washington University.

Jacoby, B. (2000). *Involving commuter students in learning.* New Directions for Higher Education, no. 109. San Francisco, CA: Jossey-Bass.

Jacoby, B., & Garland, J. (2004). Strategies for enhancing commuter student success. *Journal of College Student Retention: Research, Theory and Practice, 6*(1), 61–79.

Keeling, R. P. (1999). A new definition of college emerges: Everything that happens to . . . a (newly defined) student, in the context of a noisy visual "datascape". *NASPA Forum, 20*(5), 4–5.

Kuh, G. D., Gonyea, R. M., & Palmer, M. (2001). The disengaged commuter student: Fact or fiction. *Commuter Perspectives, 27*(1), 2–5.

Likins, J. M. (1988). *Knowing our students: A descriptive profile of commuter students at a large, public, Midwestern university.* Unpublished manuscript.

Maslow, A. H. (1982). *Toward a psychology of being (2nd ed.).* New York, NY: Van Nostrand Reinhold.

National Center for Education Statistics. (2002). *Profile of undergraduates in U.S. postsecondary institutions: 1999–2000.* Washington, DC: U.S. Department of Education.

National Center for Education Statistics. (2006). *2003–2004 Part-time undergraduates in postsecondary education.* Washington, DC: U.S. Department of Education.

National Center for Education Statistics. (2009). *2003–2004 and 2007–2008 National Postsecondary Student Aid Study.* Washington, DC: U.S. Department of Education.

Pascarella, E. T. (2006). How college affects students: Ten directions for future research. *Journal of College Student Development, 47*(5), 508–520.

Pell Institute for the Study of Opportunity in Higher Education. (2011). *Developing 20/20 vision on the 2020 degree attainment goal.* Washington, DC: Author.

Peter, K., & Forrest-Cataldi, E. (2005). *The road less traveled? Students who enroll in multiple institutions.* Washington, DC: U.S. Department of Education, National Center for Education Statistics.

Rosenberg, M., & McCullough, B. C. (1981). Mattering: Inferred significance and mental health among adolescents. In R. Simmons (Ed.), *Research in community and mental health* (Vol. 2; pp. 163–182). Greenwich, CT: JAI Press.

Schlossberg, N. K. (1985, April). *Marginality and mattering: A life span approach.* Paper presented at the annual meeting of the American Psychological Association, Los Angeles, CA.

Schlossberg, N. K. (1989). *Overwhelmed: Coping with life's ups and downs.* New York, NY: Lexington.

Schlossberg, N. K., Lynch, A. Q., & Chickering, A. W. (1989). *Improving higher education environments for adults.* San Francisco, CA: Jossey-Bass.

Shapiro, N. S., & Levine, J. H. (1999). *Creating learning communities: A practical guide to winning support, organizing for change, and implementing programs.* San Francisco, CA: Jossey-Bass.

Study Group on the Conditions of Excellence in American Higher Education. (1984). *Involvement in learning: Realizing the potential of American higher education.* Washington DC: U.S. Department of Education.

Wilmes, M. B., & Quade, S. L. (1986). Perspectives on programming for commuters: Examples of good practice. *NASPA Journal, 24*(1), 25–35.

Chapter 19
Engaging Returning Adult Learners in Community Colleges

Linda Serra Hagedorn

An experience common to all of us is the desire for a second chance. Be it in a game, sport, an important test, or even in a personal relationship, an occasional "do-over" would be a welcomed opportunity to learn from past experiences and a chance to reverse actions that have not worked in our best interest. Typically, life offers few "do-overs," but America's community colleges are a rare exception, permitting a revisit to education choices to adults who have either never attended college or who began the process did not earn degrees. Community colleges also provide a second chance to degree holders who are in search of a new educational journey. It is for that reason that community colleges are frequently called "second-chance institutions." Offering open-door admissions practices, community colleges provide the opportunity to "do-over" earlier postsecondary education choices to a wide array of adults. Today, "going back to school" is an accepted American practice, but prior to World War II the idea of an adult attending college to pursue a degree often seemed implausible (Bound & Turner, 2002). Former social norms promoted a tri-partitioned life cycle of education, followed by work, followed by leisure in old age. In fact, among many countries, formal education continues to remain reserved only for the young leaving no second chances to "do-over" formal education decisions, regrets, or deficits.

College students over the age of 25 years are commonplace on most community college campuses. Although less prevalent, the number of older students on university campuses is also growing. Between 2000 and 2009 general postsecondary enrollments of older students increased 43% (National Center for Education Statistics [NCES], 2011). Surprisingly, adult students comprise more than 42% of all degree-granting institution enrollments (NCES, 2011) with a strong concentration in community colleges and for-profit institutions (American Council on Education, 2008). Despite their growing numbers, the literature specific to older college students remains sparse (Pusser et al., 2007). A somewhat troubling development for those interested in the education of adult students is the current spotlight cast on delivering younger and younger students to the college curriculum. Colleges and universities are building their early college programs with increased dual credit programs and encouraging advanced placement credits. According to the National Center for Education Statistics (2009), more than 800,000 high school students participated in dual credit in the 2002–2003 school year. Obviously, there is a limit to how many students the colleges can serve. If attention is diverted to the untraditionally young, there is simply less attention and resources for those on the other end of the untraditional age spectrum.

Following the decision to attend or to return to college, adult students are much more likely to choose a community college due to their lower tuitions, convenient locations, flexible scheduling, as well as the availability of vocational and other short-term degrees, certificates, and diplomas (Hagedorn, 2005; Laanan, 2003). These factors are especially poignant to adults because the majority will maintain employment responsibilities and/ or have family obligations while enrolled (Silva, Calahan, & Lacireno-Paquet, 1998). Also significant is a finding reported by Levin (2007), that the majority of adult students are in the lower income quartiles. Older students present a paradox in that while they are more likely to earn higher grades and be academically successful than their younger counterparts, the evidence indicates they are also more likely to encounter difficulties and obstacles on their postsecondary paths. Clearly, despite growing numbers, older students are understudied and misunderstood.

In a longitudinal study of the Los Angeles Community College District, I presented clear evidence that older students were more likely to be successful than their younger counterparts when success was measured as higher grades (Hagedorn, 2005). In addition to comparing older students to those younger, I also took advantage of a somewhat common pattern of "stop-out and return" that many adults take while co-mingling work, family, and study. I was able to compare transcript grades of students as they progressed through life-stages. For example, some students first enrolled as a traditional student (21 years of age or less), stopped-out, and returned as a young adult (22 to 30 years of age). Other students first enrolled as a young adult, stopped-out, and returned later as what I labeled a "prime-timer" between the ages of 31 and 45. When I examined these students' transcripts, I identified a clear pattern of statistically significant increased GPA as they aged. In other words, a student going back to college at a later age is more likely to earn higher grades than she/he earned when younger.

Of course, GPA does not present the full story. A simple comparison of lifestyle with traditional, full time, university students shows some of the stark difference. Traditional students are college students first and foremost. If living on campus or in Greek facilities, the traditional students' life is engulfed by campus life; athletics, friends, the student union, clubs, and other college related activities. Although they have other non-university related aspects of their lives such as family and church or temple and some hold part-time jobs; their main focus in life is college and university life embraces them. Typically, older students bring a more complex set of life circumstances (Kasworm, 2008). Many must see themselves as workers first due to financial responsibilities for themselves and others.

Many adult students cast themselves as parents first. So, while college is important to adult students it doesn't fully define them (Horsman, 1999, Kasworm, 2008; Kasworm, Poison, & Fishback, 2002; Maehl, 2000; Pappas & Jerman, 2004). In this chapter, I proceed to utilize and more fully elaborate a conceptual framework for understanding adult learners and the obstacles they meet. I also present recommendations for both community colleges and the learners themselves.

Defining Adult Learners

Frequently, adult learners are cast into the diverse and heterogeneous category of "non-traditional students." Indeed, adult students aptly fit the definition of non-traditional by virtue of their membership in more than one of the descriptors of the category. For example, the majority of the adult students fit into at least one of the "non-traditional descriptors" of enrolling part-time, working off-campus, have dependents, are financially self-supporting and/or are first-generation-college students (Kasworm & Pike, 1994; Kuh, 1993, 1995; McKinney, 2005; McMillion, Barone, & Webster, 2004; Metzner & Bean, 1987; Vogel & Adelman, 1992). Adult students also are more likely to be female and to be people of color (NCES, 2011). Of course, they are just as likely as their younger counterparts to deal with heath or mobility issues, learning disabilities, or be battling issues such as depression or addiction. Ignoring the diversity of aspirations, older students have often been viewed as predominantly displaced workers or as former homemakers seeking short-term training (Pusser et al., 2007). Compton, Cox, and Laanan (2006) posit that whatever other categories define specific students, adult students are unique and deserve to be studied in isolation. In addition, historically the extant research has emphasized the deficits of older adults while giving short shrift to the benefits they provide to their institutions (Marshall & Nicolson 1991; Richardson & King, 1998).

There are misunderstandings and confusion in the very definition of older students. Since most higher education research is limited to the more traditional university students, much of the work under the heading of "older students" has followed the classification provided by Wolfgang and Dowling (1981) as students who are 23 years of age or older. Kasworm (2008, 2010), who studies adult students intently, defined adult learners as those aged 25 years of age or older. In my own studies of community colleges I noted that it is not uncommon to see students in their forties, fifties, and even older taking advantage of the "second chance." Noting, for example, the vast differences between a 25-year-old and a 45-year-old student, I felt the need to do more than provide a starting age for adult students. In contrast, I portioned adult students into three categories. I feel that this delineation is more essential today than it was when I first presented it in 2005 because with the advent of dual enrollment and other programs bringing younger students to the community college classroom, even the "younger group of adult students" may feel some pangs of "older age." Figure 19.1 provides my hierarchy of community college students (young adults, prime-timers, and last-chancers) as classified by age. The

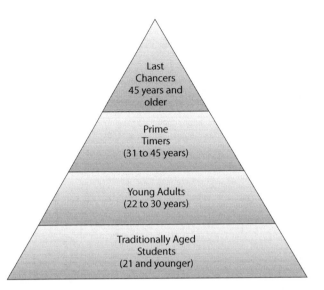

FIGURE 19.1. Adult Students as Defined by Age

pyramid shape of the figure is purposeful showing the numbers of students decreases as student age increases (NCES, 2011).

In this chapter, I interchangeably use the descriptors "adult students" and "older students." I further develop the conceptual framework first presented in 2005 to describe the interaction between adult students and community colleges.

Theories and Concepts

Adult Success

Simply put, in the era of the current knowledge economy and global interaction, it is crucial that the United States has access to a trained and educated workforce that includes the effective utilization and continued development of adults, many of whom were educated in an earlier less technological environment (Pusser et al, 2007). With the rapid integration of technology and change (Zahra & Nielsen, 2002), it is likely for many workers to face the need for additional education and, in some cases, new degrees within their working lifespan. This need is being increasingly understood in the European Union where policies and plans have been developed to meet the needs of both continuing education and degrees for returning adults (Commission of the European Communities, 1991; Davies, 2003). The earlier literature that assumed older students were less capable of being academically successful due to assumed decreased cognitive ability have been successfully challenged (Kasworm, 1990; Kasworm & Blowers, 1994; Merriam & Caffarella, 1991). While there is evidence that significantly older learners may need more time to learn new material (Cross, 1981; Tentori, Osherson, Hasher, & May, 2001), adult intelligence appears to remain stable "at least until the sixth or seventh decade. If a decline in functioning does exist, it appears to apply primarily to the maximum versus average levels of functioning" (Merriam & Caffarella, 1991, p. 158).

Institutional Response

Relying on the earlier literature (Ackell, Epps, Sharp, & Sparks, 1982; Apps, 1988; Hall, 1991), Kasworm and Blowers (1994) described four distinct types of institutions based on their response to adult students. As seen in Figure 19.2, Kasworm and Blowers used the labels of Institutions A through D, I have provided sub-headings that are more descriptive of the distinct typology; adult accommodating, adult-oriented, adult-ignored, and adult-added.

Each college and campus should be judged individually for its welcome and accommodation of adult students. Although as a general rule, the nation's community colleges have been more inviting to adult students than the typical four-year university, there are examples of each of the institutional types represented among them. Moreover, programs and services within a specific college may vary across the types. I argue, therefore, that the Kasworm and Blowers (1994) framework may be more valid and useful at a micro level as measured at the program, department, or even the classroom level rather than at the institutional level.

To examine how community colleges, their programs, and services interact with adult students, I provide the enhanced conceptual framework used in my earlier study titled, *Square Pegs: Adult Students and Their "Fit" in Postsecondary Institutions* (Hagedorn,

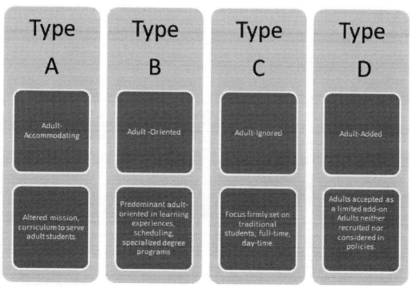

Adapted from Kasworm and Blowers (1994)

FIGURE 19.2. Institution Types for Adult Learners

2005). The Square Pegs analogy likened the integration of older students into an environment designed for traditional students as similar to the fitting of a square peg into a round hole. The misalignment produces four corners of friction that I labeled: access, success, retention, and institutional receptivity (see Figure 19.3). The first corner, access, is the availability of admission and includes such issues as convenient scheduling and services that allow and support enrollment. The second corner, success, is typically measured by positive academic performance (typically GPA). Certainly achieving high grades indicates a success, but success should not be solely defined by grades but rather more broadly inclusive of a progression along a program of studies leading to goal completion. The third corner is retention or continuous enrollment leading to the acquisition of a degree, diploma, certificate or transfer. While it can be argued that retention is another measure of success, it should be noted that success can occur without retention. Take for example the older student who enters the college with the goal to acquire a certain skill or knowledge. This student may not complete a program or in some cases may not even complete a college course; but if the skill was acquired the student was successful in the fulfillment of the goal. While I accept this level of success, I also argue that degrees, certificates, and diplomas matter. On the simple matter of income, people with a college degree are less likely to be unemployed and much more likely to be paid more than those without one (Carnevale, Cheah, & Strohl, 2011). Interestingly, the improved salary effect for college degree holders is not only due to employment in higher paying positions, but also has been found to bring higher pay even in fields that do not specifically require a degree. For example Carnevale et al (2011) report that dishwashers without a college degree earn on average $19,000/year but those with a college degree average $34,000.

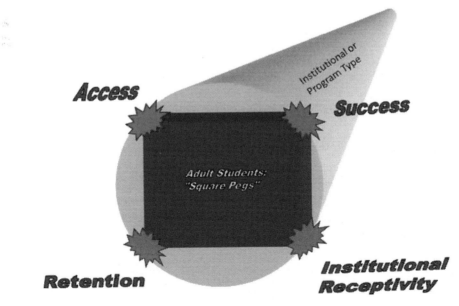

FIGURE 19.3. Square Pegs Conceptual Framework

Similarly childcare workers, dental hygienists, and hairdressers with college degrees on average earn 80%, 76%, and 69% more, respectively, than their counterparts without a degree.

The fourth area of friction, institutional receptivity, deals directly with the level of recognition and accommodation for older students within environments originally designed to develop traditional aged students (Evans et al., 2010). Often the friction can consist of a series of micro-irritations or offenses that may build to a crescendo of dissatisfaction and resentment that leads to further friction in the areas of success and retention.

Figure 19.3 has been modified from the 2005 framework through the integration of the Kasworm and Blowers (1994) institutional type structure that now defines the round tube (or hole) that represents the institution. The framework indicates that the extent and nature of the friction at each of the corners is dependent on the institutional type.

Friction Points

Within the typography of types, it is important to understand that rarely is a type so pervasive as to permeate every program, office, or classroom. Moreover, the institutional type within the institution may change due to the time of day (day versus evening courses), the program (transfer versus vocational), and the specific faculty and staff providing the instructional or other services. With the caveats in place I describe the friction points for each of the institutional types.

Adult-Ignored

I choose to begin with the adult-ignored, or Type C institutions or programs, as they are the most adult-caustic. Type C institutions have developed their missions and goals with disregard for students over the traditional college age. The programs operate under the assumption that IF adults choose to attend, it is their sole responsibility to adapt. Schedules are created for students who have little to no life interference. Adult students in this environment likely feel alienated and less likely to continue enrollment. Some community colleges take on the "adult-ignored" role in the day time when most students are full-time and traditional but may switch to another type in the evening classes when more adults are assumed to be able to be on campus.

In the adult-ignored institutions, access is limited because adults are not sought or recruited. The recruitment efforts are in high schools probably with a large dose of dual enrollment students. Because classes are conducted for the convenience of full-time traditionally aged students, there may be few available courses offered at times that working adults can enroll. Moreover, adult-ignored institutions are more likely to focus exclusively on the transfer-program and not include vocational or work-force development offerings that are attractive to many older students.

When adult students are successful in adult-ignored institutions, it is in spite of the institution. Hence, only those adult students who are determined and focused will be likely to find success. The successful adults accommodated to the institution and ignored those instances when they appeared invisible. Similarly, retention will be difficult because of the predominant part-time status of adult students, who will often find that courses are not offered, or they are closed prior to their opportunity to enroll. Of course, in terms of institutional receptivity, this institutional type registers dead last. The institution is not going to bend to accommodate the adult student, but rather expects the student to be totally receptive to the institution. There are likely no day care facilities, no veteran's support facility, no food on campus in the evening to assist the weary student who rushed to class directly from work. In essence, there is no give and take. Essentially, the message is, "sorry, adult student . . . if you enroll here, it is your journey and yours alone—good luck."

Adult-Added

Adult-added, or Type D institutions, are significantly more adult friendly than the adult-ignored variety but still have issues in their service of older students. While not considered in recruitment or policymaking, in this institutional type, adults may be discussed AFTER the policy is made to see IF they can also be included and then how. Just like the Type C Adult-Ignored institutions, the adult-added variety do not specifically recruit adults in their major recruitment endeavors. However, they may seek some adults in a specific program if a contract or other issue develops where it may be especially lucrative or bring in funds that are very much needed. Success interventions and programs such as learning communities, tutoring services, or special developmental course supports are designed with the traditional student in mind with the encouragement to faculty to adjust their curriculum for the enrolled non-traditional students. A typical response to an adult-added institution may be to add a section of tutoring in the evening when adults are more likely to be on campus. Of course, this section may have less tutors available and will likely not be managed by faculty, but rather by the students themselves. Type D institutions may have day care or veteran's affairs support but they likely exist as separate entities and not well intermeshed within the institution. Student success and retention is compromised and older students may not feel welcome or a part of the college. In this variety, the institution is receptive to adults but does not see them as part of their main mission. The motto here may be "traditional students first and what is left over can be cast to adults."

Adult-Oriented

The third institutional type, labeled Type B by Kasworm and Blowers (1994), is focused solely on the adult learner. In its purest form, this very unique type of institution solely targets and markets to older students providing a learning environment that is ostensibly and specifically fashioned for the needs of adults. Upon initial inspection this type of institution sounds ideal for adults, however it must be noted that there are virtually no public community colleges of this ilk. Perhaps due to their historical roots of originating as an extension of high school (AACC, 2012), the American public community college mission has always included a deep interest in recent high school graduates. However, many community colleges do have specific programs or divisions that are adult-oriented.

It is not surprising that for-profit colleges have recognized a void in the adult market and have utilized it to their advantage. For example, the proprietary University of Phoenix, the country's largest university, clearly states on its website that the university is specifically designed for working adults (University of Phoenix, n.d.). Many other proprietary postsecondary institutions have taken the adult-oriented path. Aggressively targeting military students and veterans, the for-profit sector has recently come under scrutiny with questions of value to this unique set of adults versus the federal aid that they bring to their college (Blumenstyk, 2011) and high default rates (U.S. Department of Education, 2012). Federal aid aside, access to this sector may be limited by the high cost of tuition. For example, the tuition at Full Sail University, a for-profit adult-oriented institution, may be as much as $48,300 a year (Fain, 2012).

A recent and extensive study of for-profits (Deming, Goldin, & Katz, 2011) found that proprietary adult-oriented institutions may enjoy greater success in the retention of first-year students and even boast of higher completion of certificates and associate degrees; but compared to students from the non-profit sector, the students are more likely to be unemployed or earning lower salaries six years later and have accrued higher student debt.

The predominant instructional mode for most adult-oriented institutions is online. Kerr, Rynearson, and Kerr (2006) reported that online learning success is dependent on "reading and writing skills, independent learning, motivation, and computer literacy" (p. 101). While online may offer convenience for some students, it is not always the ideal learning mode for all adult students, who may be more anxious and less comfortable with technology (Dyck, Gee, & Smither, 1998; Laguna & Babcock, 1997). The message to students from this type of institution is "thank you customers for your business."

Adult-Accommodating

The last institutional type in the typography, adult accommodating or Type A, is arguably the goal for the better integration of adult students. These institutions recognize the diversity of their student bodies and appropriately accept their responsibility to serve all adult age groups in their community. Unlike the adult-oriented variety, the adult-accommodating embraces the diversity of all those eligible to receive services without specifically favoring one to the disregard of another.

Adult-accommodating institutions offer a wide variety of programs including short-term training that is aligned with workforce development and the needs of local industry. In terms of services, the adult-accommodating institutions will offer adult-friendly services and accommodations such as:

- Day care facilities including sick-child care
- Adult-centered orientation sessions
- Adult support networks
- Adult reentry counseling
- Veteran/military support services
- Career advising

- Assessment and provisions for credit for prior learning
- Accelerated course options
- Extended hours of operation for facilities such as the library, labs, the student union, and the bookstore
- Flexible time-frames for enrollment, registration, and financial aid counseling

Of course, adult-accommodating institutions cannot completely eliminate the friction points, but extending the analogy, through the use of adult-friendly programs and services coupled with the responsibility of serving adults, the corners have an added lubricant that helps ease the way. In adult-accommodating institutions, access is more inviting, success is more possible, and retention is more likely. The message is "welcome."

Student Engagement Strategies

It is safe to assume that the number of adults turning to the community colleges for an educational "do-over" will continue to rise. Over 54 million adults in the United States do not hold a college degree; and over half of them (63%) have had no postsecondary training (Pusser et al., 2007). In addition, many degree-holders will turn to the community college sector to upgrade their skills and/or seek additional credentials. Despite the growing need, unless institutions prioritize their role in the service of adult students, the friction points will continue to chafe and irritate thus limiting success. I now turn to some recommendations to figuratively "lubricate" the way. I proffer that the key to increasing the number of adult students who meet success is through creating greater institutional receptivity through practices that impact the other three corners.

Access

It is simple: If enrollment procedures do not include adult-friendly practices, older students will not feel welcome and will likely not enroll. There are two contemporary growing practices that may add friction to the adult access corner; dependency on technology and the green movement. It is easy to forget that many older (and younger) students may not have ready access to a computer, Internet access, or have the technological training to navigate their way through online admission processes. In fact, a recent study (November, 2011) prepared jointly with the U.S. Department of Commerce reports 30% of American households do not subscribe to broadband services. Moreover, there is a strong correlation between Internet access and socio-economic factors such as income and education as well as gaps by racial and ethnic lines. Therefore, it is likely that older adults lacking a college degree are likely to be overrepresented among those without technology access or training.

Colleges should not assume that their communities are following in lock step to the nation's increasing dependency on technology. Not everyone has an iPad, a Twitter account, or knows how to "like us" on Facebook. Many adults will turn to the telephone when they are interested in applying for admission and will appreciate a "real person" who can answer questions and not meet with what appears to be an interminable loop of "press 1 for this" and "press 2 for that." Moreover, the institution must be willing to follow the call with the appropriate information sent in hard copy via traditional mail. Yes, this practice may not be in alignment with the green paperless movement, but accommodating institutions understand that there are still students in their service areas who do not have technology access, and/or are comforted by written materials that can be touched, shared, and filed.

Access also includes financial aid counseling. Many adults mistakenly believe that they are ineligible for any aid. Intrusive counseling may be necessary to inform adults that neither federal student financial aid nor most scholarships have age restrictions. Of course, those adults that are enrolling at less than half-time will not qualify for most forms of aid. Future development of Lifelong Learning Accounts (LiLAs) and Career Advancement Accounts (CAAs) that provide employer-matched educational accounts for workers will greatly enhance adult student access.

Finally, many adults taking advantage of the second chance will have some prior college credits. Some may bring credits from other parts of the country or from multiple institutions. Acknowledgement of prior study and credits when possible is likely to be positively accepted by adult students.

Success

An important impediment to success is the elapsed time between adult students' classroom experiences and the present. Many adults may need an academic refresher prior to taking the college's placement exams to prevent inappropriate placement in deep developmental courses. Low scores on placement exams may be more related to forgotten material and rustiness in test-taking than to actual ability. Of course, when adults merit developmental placements, they must be offered during times and in modes that make the enrollments possible.

Adult students want to complete their goals in a timely fashion. Perhaps it is feelings of being older, but students are more likely to enroll, be successful, and persist if there is an accelerated program. Of course, the proprietary online institutions have recognized this desire, incorporated it, and can attribute this to their success (Pusser et al, 2007; Wlodkowski, Mauldin, & Gahn, 2001).

An area of importance to adults contemplating college enrollment is prior learning assessment (PLA) and its acknowledgement. According to the Council for Adult and Experiential Learning (CAEL), "PLA is the process by which many colleges evaluate for academic credit the college-level knowledge and skills an individual has gained outside of the classroom (or from non-college instructional programs), including employment, military training/service, travel, hobbies, civic activities and volunteer service" (2010, p. 6). The extant research on PLA is in general agreement that PLA students are more likely to be successful across a wide array of outcomes such as participating in a degree program (Peruniak & Powell, 2007), earning a bachelor's degree (Freers, 1994), and in achieving a higher GPA (Pearson, 2001) as compared to non-PLA students. A recent study across 48 institutions verified that PLA students are not only more likely to achieve higher success rates in the aforementioned categories but was also more likely to persist and have a shortened time to degree (CAEL, 2010). PLA can be assessed a number of ways including standardized exams (the most popular being CLEP), portfolio assessment, or through American Council on Education (ACE) evaluated corporate or military training.

Retention

Retention for adult students may take a different form than that of their younger counterparts. Since many are returning to college for the second-chance, they are the former non-retained students of earlier years. Since the list of evidence linking engagement and retention is long and respected (Astin, 1984, 1993; Endo & Harpel, 1982; Mallette & Cabrera, 1991; Pascarella & Terenzini, 1980, 1991, 2005; Tinto 1997), it may be assumed that engagement is equally important for adult students. However, engagement for these non-traditionals may take a different form such as intermeshing education with adult support services.

A common adult service that has shown to predict retention for adult women students is the provision of day care. Providing day care does not directly lead to academic or social engagement but does allow the parent-student to become active on campus. Adult women students whose children are cared for in campus-based child care centers, display greater persistence, higher grade point averages, and graduate in fewer years (AAUW, 2009).

Finally, integrating an Office of Adult Services equipped to handle adult needs may be an important link to keeping adults on campus. Adult services may include many of the topics already discussed but also include support of students attending college under special circumstances such as the Workforce Investment Act (WIA) and the Trade Adjustment Act (TAA). The office of Adult Services can also assist students in noncredit programs and bridge experiences from non-credit to credit.

Conclusion

Community colleges and their provision for a "do-over" for adult students come at an opportune time. With projected declines in the numbers of high school graduates (Hussar & Bailey, 2011), the future student roles of community colleges are likely to include more non-traditional students on both sides of the age spectrum. While dual enrollment will supply increases in the number of untraditionally younger students, the technology and globalization needs of the 21st century also predict that adults will seek the services of community colleges sporadically throughout the work-lifespan. In addition, education will grow stale, meaning that what is learned today may become obsolete in a very short time requiring update and even new degrees and certificates. The conclusion is that adults will need not only a second-chance, but perhaps even a third and a fourth opportunity. Many adults will call upon community colleges for a "do-over."

References

Ackell, E., Epps, R., Sharp, N., & Sparks, H. (1982, January). Adapting the university to adult students: A developmental perspective. *Continuum, 46*(2), 30–35.

American Association of Community Colleges (AACC). (2012). *Historical information.* Retrieved from www.aacc.nche.edu/AboutCC/history/Pages/default.aspx

American Association of University Women (AAUW). (2009 November). *Improve access to higher education. AAUW Public Policy and Government Relation* (pp. 1–12). Retrieved from www.aauw.org/act/issue_advocacy/actionpages/upload/111_050310.pdf

American Council on Education (ACE). (2008). *Mapping new directions: Higher education for older adults.* Second Report on Reinvesting in the Third Age: Older Adults and Higher Education. Washington DC. Retrieved from www.acenet.edu/Content/NavigationMenu/ProgramsServices/CLLL/Reinvesting/MapDirections.pdf

Apps, J.W. (1988). *Higher education in a learning society.* San Francisco, CA: Jossey-Bass.

Astin, A.W. (1984). Student involvement: A developmental theory for higher education. *Journal of College Student Personnel, 25,* 297–308.

Astin, A.W. (1993). *What matters in college? Four critical years revisited.* San Francisco, CA: Jossey Bass.

Blumenstyk, G. (2011, April 2). Colleges scramble to avoid violating federal-aid limit: For-profits' tactics to comply with 90/10 rule raise questions. *The Chronicle for Higher Education.* Retrieved from http://chronicle.com/article/Colleges-Scramble-to-Avoid/126986/

Bound, J., & Turner, S. (2002). Going to war and going to college: Did World War II and the G.I Bill increase educational attainment for returning veterans? *Journal of Labor Economics, 20*(4), 784–815.

Carnevale, A.P., Cheah, B., & Strohl, J. (2011). *Hard times. College majors, unemployment and earnings. Not all college degrees are created equal.* Report from the Center on Education and the Workforce. Georgetown University. Retrieved from www9.georgetown.edu/grad/gppi/hpi/cew/pdfs/Unemployment.Final.update1.pdf

Commission of the European Communities. (1991). *Memorandum on higher education in the European community.* Brussels, Belgium: Task Force on Human Resources, Education, Training, Youth.

Compton, J.I., Cox, E., & Laanan, F.S. (2006). Adult learners in transition. *New Directions for Student Services, 114,* 73–80.

Council for Adult & Experiential Learning (CAEL). (2010). *Fueling the race to postsecondary success: A 48 institution study of prior learning assessment and adult student outcomes.* Retrieved from www.cael.org/pdfs/PLA_Fueling-the-Race.pdf

Cross, P. (1981). *Adults as learners.* San Francisco, CA: Jossey-Bass.

Davies, P. (2003). Widening participation and the European Union: Direct action—indirect policy? *European Journal of Education, 38*(1), 99–116.

Deming, D.J., Goldin, C., & Katz, L.F. (2011). *The for-profit postsecondary school sector: Nimble critters or agile predators.* NBER Working Paper 17710 (National Bureau of Economic Research. Cambridge, MA. Retrieved from www.nber.org/papers/w17710.pdf

Dyck, J.L., Gee, N.R., & Smither, J.A. (1998). The changing construct of computer anxiety for younger and older adults. *Computers in Human Behavior, 14*(1), 61–77.

Endo, J.J., & Harpel, R.L. (1982). The effect of student faculty interaction on students' educational outcomes. *Research in Higher Education, 16*(2), 115–136.

Evans, N.J., Forney, D.S., Guido, F.M., Patton, L.D., & Renn, K.A. (2010). *Student development in college: Theory, research, and practice* (2nd ed.). San Francisco, CA: Jossey-Bass.

Fain, P. (January 24, 2012). Full said in the spotlight. *Inside HigherEd*. Retrieved from: www.insidehighered.com/news/2012/01/24/romney-right-about-full-sail-university# ixzz1kNokLWlj

Freers, S. (1994). *An evaluation of adult learners' perceptions of a community college's assessment of prior-learning program*. Digital Dissertations online, 56–01A, 59.

Hagedorn, L.S. (2005). Square pegs: Adult students and their "fit" in postsecondary institutions. *Change*, 37(1), 22–29.

Hall, J. (1991). *Access through innovation: New colleges for new students*. New York, NY: National University Continuing Education Association, American Council on Education, and Macmillan.

Horsman, J. (1999). *Too scared to learn: Women, violence, and education*. Toronto, Canada: McGilligan.

Hussar, W.J., & Bailey, T.M. (2011). *Projections of education statistics to 2020*. NCES 2011–026. Retrieved from http://nces.ed.gov/pubs2011/2011026.pdf

Kasworm, C. (1990, Fall). Adult undergraduates in higher education: A review of past research perspectives. *Review of Educational Research*, 60(3), 345–372.

Kasworm, C.E. (2008). Emotional challenges of adult learners in higher education. *New Directions for Adult and Continuing Education*, 120, 27–34.

Kasworm, C.E. (2010). Adult learners in a research university: Negotiating undergraduate student identity. *Adult Education Quarterly*, 60(2), 143–160.

Kasworm, C.E., & Blowers, S.S. (1994). *Adult undergraduate students: Patterns of learning involvement*. Final project report. ERIC Education Resources Information Services. ED376321.

Kasworm, C.E., & Pike, G.R. (1994). Adult undergraduate students: Evaluating the appropriateness of a traditional model of academic performance. *Research in Higher Education*, 35(6), 689–710.

Kasworm, C., Poison, C., & Fishback, S. (2002). *Responding to adult learners in higher education*. Malabar, FL: Krieger.

Kerr, M.S., Rynearson, K., & Kerr, M.C. (2006). Student characteristics for online learning success. *Internet and Higher Education*, 9, 91–105.

Kuh, G.D. (1993). In their own words: What students learn outside the classroom. *American Educational Research Journal*, 30, 277–304.

Kuh, G.D. (1995). The other curriculum: Out-of-class experiences associated with student learning and personal development. *The Journal of Higher Education*, 66, 123–155.

Laanan, S.F. (2003). Older adults in community colleges: Choices, attitudes, and goals. *Educational Gerontology*, 29, 757–776.

Laguna, K., & Babcock, R.L. (1997). Computer anxiety in young and older adults: Implications for human-computer interactions in older populations. *Computers in Human Behavior*, 13(3), 317–326.

Levin, J. (2007). *Nontraditional students and community college: the conflict of justice and neoliberalism*. New York, NY: Palgrave Macmillan.

Maehl, W.H. (2000). *Lifelong learning at its best*. San Francisco, CA: Jossey-Bass.

Mallette, B.I., & Cabrera, A.F. (1991). Determinants of withdrawal behavior. *Research in Higher Education*, 32(2) 179–194

Marshall, H., & Nicolson, P. (1991). Why choose psychology? Mature and other students' accounts at graduation. In J. Radford (Ed.), *The choice of psychology* (Group of Teachers of Psychology, Occasional Paper No. 12) (pp. 22–29). Leicester, U.K.: British Psychological Society.

McKinney, J.S. (2005). On the margins: A study of the experiences of transgender college students. *Journal of Gay & Lesbian Issues in Education*, 6(3), 63–76.

McMillion, T.C., Barone, S., & Webster, J. (2004). *First-generation college students: A literature review*. Retrieved from www.tgslc.org/pdf/first-generation.pdf

Merriam, S. & Caffarella, R. (1991). *Learning in Adulthood*. San Francisco: Jossey-Bass, 159–180.

Metzner, B.S., & Bean, J.P. (1987). The estimation of a conceptual model of nontraditional undergraduate student attrition. *Research in Higher Education*, 27(1), 15–38.

National Center for Education Statistics (NCES). (2009). *Dual credit in U.S. public high schools: Prevalence of courses for dual credit in regular public high schools*. Washington DC. The Whitehouse Social Statistics Briefing Room. Retrieved from http://nces.ed.gov/ssbr/pages/dualcredit.asp?IndID=25

National Center for Education Statistics (NCES). (2011). *Digest of Education Statistics, 2010* (NCES 2011–015). Retrieved from http://nces.ed.gov/programs/digest/d10/

Pappas, J., & Jerman, J. (2004). Developing and delivering adult degree programs. *New Directions for Adult and Continuing Education, 103*. San Francisco, CA: Jossey-Bass.

Pascarella, E. T., & Terenzini, P. T. (1980). Predicting freshman persistence and voluntary dropout decisions from a theoretical model. *The Journal of Higher Education, 51*, 60–75.

Pascarella, E. T., & Terenzini, P. T. (1991). *How college affects students: Findings from twenty years of research.* San Francisco, CA: Jossey-Bass.

Pascarella, E. T., & Terenzini, P. T. (2005). *How college affects students: A third decade of research* (vol. 2). San Francisco, CA: Jossey-Bass.

Pearson, W. (2001). Prior learning assessment corner: The arguments for prior learning assessment. *The Journal of Continuing Education, 49*(3), 47–50.

Peruniak, G., & Powell, R. (2007). Back eddies of learning in the recognition of prior learning: A case study. *Canadian Journal of University Continuing Education, 33*(1), 83–106.

Pusser, B., Breneman, D. W, Gansneder, B. M., Kohl, K. J., Levin, J. S., Milam, J. H., & Turner, S. E. (2007). *Returning to learning: Adults' success in college is key to America's future.* Retrieved from www.luminafoundation.org/publications/ReturntolearningApril2007.pdf

Richardson, J. T. E., & King, E. (1998). Adult students in higher education: Burden or boon? *The Journal of Higher Education, 69*(1), 65–88.

Silva, T., Calahan, M., & Lacireno-Paquet, N. (1998). Adult education participation decisions and barriers. *Review of Conceptual Frameworks and Empirical Studies.* Washington, DC: U.S. Department of Education, National Center for Education Statistics.

Tentori, K., Osherson, D., Hasher, L., & May, C. (2001). Wisdom and aging: Irrational preferences in college students but not older adults. *Cognition, 81.* B87–B96.

Tinto, V. (1997). Colleges as communities: Exploring the education character of student persistence. *The Journal of Higher Education, 68*(6), 599–623.

University of Phoenix. (n.d.). www.phoenix.edu/

U.S. Department of Commerce. (November, 2011). *Exploring the digital nation: Computer and internet use at home.* Prepared by the Economics and Statistics Administration and the National Telecommunications and Information Administration. Retrieved from www.ntia.doc.gov/files/ntia/publications/exploring_the_digital_nation_computer_and_internet_use_at_home_11092011.pdf

U.S. Department of Education. (2012). *Direct Loan and Federal Family Education Loan Programs: Institutional default rate comparison of FY 2007, 2008, and 2009 cohort default rates.* Retrieved from www2.ed.gov/offices/OSFAP/defaultmanagement/instrates.html

Vogel, S. A., & Adelman, P. B. (1992). The success of college students with learning disabilities: Factors related to educational attainment. *Journal of Learning Disabilities, 25*(7), 430–441.

Wlodkowski, R. J., Mauldin, J. E., & Gahn, S. W. (2001). Learning in the fast lane: Adult learners' persistence and success in accelerated college programs. *New Agenda Series[TM]. 4*(1). Retrieved from www.eric.ed.gov/PDFS/ED459317.pdf

Wolfgang, M. E., & Dowling, W. D. (1981). Differences in motivation of adult and younger undergraduates. *The Journal of Higher Education, 52*(6), 640–648.

Zahra, S. A., & Nielsen, A. P. (2002). Sources of capabilities, integration and technology commercialization. *Strategic Management Journal, 23*, 377–398.

Chapter 20
Engaging Student Veterans Inside and Outside the Classroom

Corey B. Rumann and Stephanie Bondi

Veterans are an increasing student population in higher education. With the wars in Iraq and Afghanistan coming to a close, the number of enrolled veterans at institutions of higher education is expected to continue to increase as more and more of them use their GI Bill funding to attend college and pursue college degrees (Cook & Kim, 2009; Sander, 2012). While the focus on student veterans in higher education is gaining increased attention, there is still some question as to how best serve this population (NSSE, 2010). This chapter addresses student veteran engagement in higher education by first providing a snapshot of these students from recent demographic data. In addition, Abes, Jones, and McEwen's (2007) reconceptualized model of multiple identities will help readers understand the complex nature of student veterans' identities and how multiple social identities must be considered in our work with this population. The chapter includes a brief discussion of current research on student veterans, most of which focuses on their transition experiences. Using Rendón's (1994) Validation Theory as a guiding framework, the chapter concludes with recommendations for increasing veteran student engagement.

Who Are Student Veterans?

Veterans and military servicemembers (on active duty and reserve) make up approximately 4% of undergraduates at institutions of higher education (Radford & Wun, 2009). When comparing the 2007–08 demographics of student veterans to traditional college students, who are likely to be dependents of their parents, the veterans are more likely to be older, married, have dependents, and attend college part-time (Radford & Wun, 2009; see Tables 20.1 & 20.2). For the purposes of this chapter, student veterans are considered to be any student who is currently serving or has served in the United States military and who may or may not have been deployed. This includes students who are serving

TABLE 20.1. Demographics of Military Undergraduates by Race, Gender, and Family Status Compared to Non-Military Independent and Dependent Undergraduates

	Undergraduate Veterans	Non-Military Independent	Non-Military Dependent
Race			
White	60%	57%	66%
Black/African American	18%	18%	10%
Hispanic/Latino	13%	15%	14%
Asian	3%	6%	6%
Native American/Native Alaskan/ Native Hawaiian			
Pacific Islander/Multiracial/Not Listed	6%	4%	4%
Gender			
Male	73%	35%	47%
Female	27%	65%	53%
Family Status			
Married with dependent(s)	33%	25%	—
Married without dependents	15%	12%	—
Single with dependent(s)	15%	30%	—

Source: Radford and Wun (2009). U.S. Department of Education, National Center for Education Statistics, *Issue Tables: A Profile of Military Servicemembers and Veterans Enrolled in Postsecondary Education in 2007—08.*

TABLE 20.2. Types of Institutions Student Veterans Attend and FT/PT Status of Student Veterans

	Undergraduate Student Veterans
Type of Institution	
Public 2-year	43.3%
Public 4-year	21.4%
Private, non-profit 4-year	13.5%
Private, for-profit 4-year	12.4%
Other or multiple institutions	9.4%
Enrollment Status of Veterans	
Full-time	40%
Part-time	60%

in the military reserves or National Guard. Student veterans possess many similar characteristics to other non-traditional, independent students such as those described above (part-time, older, with dependents). The most significant difference is that 73% of student veterans are male while closer to 50% of traditional (non-military dependent) students are male (Table 20.1). These demographics are important to understand because they should inform how faculty and staff encourage student veteran engagement.

Current Research on Student Veteran Transitions

Much of the current research on contemporary student veterans has focused on their transition experiences to the higher education environment (see, for example, Bauman, 2009; Livingston, 2009; DiRamio, Ackerman, & Mitchell, 2008; Rumann, 2010; Rumann & Hamrick, 2010). Some common themes of these studies help explain student veterans' experiences (Livingston & Bauman, 2013). For example, student veterans tend to feel more mature and report a more focused approach to their academic and career goals than their non-military peers (DiRamio et al., 2008; Rumann & Hamrick, 2010). This increased level of maturity can help student veterans be more successful in college, but it can also lead them to feel more alienated from their non-military college student peers (Livingston, 2009; Rumann, 2010).

Regarding the transition process itself student veterans are navigating an environment (i.e., the college environment) that is very different from the military environment. The military environment tends to be much more structured than college, and student veterans have reported challenges adjusting or re-adjusting to the academic experience (Bauman, 2009; Livingston, 2009). Further complicating this process is the disconnect student veterans may feel from their non-military student peers as well as faculty and staff at the institution (DiRamio et al., 2008). As they navigate the collegiate environment, student veterans tend to seek each other out for support and understanding in hopes of finding someone who understands their experiences (Rumann, 2010; Rumann & Hamrick, 2010). Simultaneously, many student veterans are learning what being a veteran means to them in relationship to their other social identities. This negotiation and meaning making process will be discussed in a future section.

The research to date on student veterans helps faculty and staff understand how policies, practices, and initiatives can help ease the transition of student veterans at institutions of higher education, but it does not necessarily tell us how to engage student veterans in college, which is the purpose of this chapter.

Student Veteran Engagement Data

Currently, there is little known about student veterans' engagement or their retention and persistence rates in college. The National Survey of Student Engagement (NSSE, 2010) data indicate student veterans are in many areas less engaged than their non-veteran peers suggesting student veteran engagement should be considered an area of concern. NSSE (2010) data reported for first-year students and seniors indicate the following comparisons with non-veteran peers:

- Veterans spent as much time studying but more time working and caring for dependents;

- First-year student veterans were less engaged in reflective learning;
- First-year noncombat veterans were less engaged with faculty;
- First-year combat veterans perceived less campus support; and
- Senior veterans were less engaged in every category and perceived less campus support.

These findings suggest that in some areas, such as reflective learning and connections with faculty, student veterans are less engaged than their non-veteran peers. Focused effort in student veteran engagement in these areas is warranted.

Theories and Concepts

Theories on intersecting identities among college students and the outcomes that accrue when undergraduates are appropriately validated in campus environments are useful for determining how to effectively engage student veterans in higher education.

Multiple Identities and/or Intersectionality

At times student veterans may be viewed as a homogenous group which is not accurate (Iverson & Anderson, 2013). Each veteran is unique and brings with him or her a different set of experiences and social identities. People often assume student veterans in college are White, heterosexual, 25-year-old men. In reality, student veterans include women, students of color, gay/lesbian/bi-sexual people, and/or students with disabilities. Abes, Jones, and McEwen (2007) described how students negotiate and make sense of multiple intersecting identities through a meaning-making filter acknowledging the "changing contexts and relative salience" of their lives (p. 3). Their model illustrates multiple identities as intersecting circles surrounding a core or inner self.

Student veterans possess multiple identities simultaneously and tensions among them may plague student veterans (Iverson & Anderson, 2013). Educators who want to connect with and support student veterans must understand they are more than their military experiences. It is also important to know that many student veterans returning from wartime deployment are trying to make meaning of their newly acquired veteran status and how that influences their other social identities (Rumann, 2010; Rumann & Hamrick, 2010). The salience of these identities follows Abes et al.'s (2007) model indicating students work to make meaning of salient identities through a meaning making filter influenced by the context (e.g., college, military). This meaning making process can be a factor in student veterans' transition to the college environment and their level of engagement with in-class and out-of-class activities. For example, some student veterans may try to conceal their veteran identity on campus because they are not sure how others on campus perceive veterans, and they have had negative experiences with stereotypes about military experience (DiRamio et al., 2008). Other student veterans may have difficulty seeing themselves as successful in higher education because they have had different experiences than traditional college students. In other words, their identity as student is in tension with one of their other identities such as veteran, racially minoritized person, student with a disability, or first-generation student. Negotiating these various identities may pose challenges to student veterans and impact their ability to engage in higher education.

Validation Theory

In order to offer recommendations for engaging student veterans, we turn to a theory of supporting non-traditional college students—Validation Theory (Rendón, 1994; Rendón & Muñoz, 2011). Rendón advocates this theory for any non-traditional students who are unsure about their ability to be successful in college or are unfamiliar with college values (L. Rendón, personal communication, March 19, 2012). Since student veterans are often older than traditional students and have taken time away from college to serve military duty, many student veterans fit within the non-traditional student classification. Additionally as discussed earlier, student veterans have multiple identities and may identify with other social identity groups associated with non-traditional students. Although student veterans as a group may not be marginalized in society and on campus in the same ways as other non-traditional student populations such as low-income, religious minority students, or lesbian, gay, bisexual, trans*, or queer (LGBTQ) students (and veterans may receive substantial admiration and benefits), they, as a group, still need support to engage in college (Rumann, Rivera, & Hernandez, 2011).

Validation Theory was developed from results of a larger study of the factors contributing to student learning and retention in higher education (Rendón, 1994). During the study, non-traditional students reported validation allayed doubts about their ability to learn and was important to their academic success. Rendón (1994) found the opposite of the prevailing belief that college students will take advantage of opportunities provided for them. She found many non-traditional students would not engage in opportunities without validation. Non-traditional students require validation to overcome existing anxieties, fears, and prior invalidations. Validation serves as an important foundation for involvement, academic success, and development in college (Rendón, 2002; Rendón & Muñoz, 2011).

Validation Theory suggests non-traditional students experience incongruence between their experiences and those of peers. For student veterans as mentioned earlier, the incongruence may arise from being more serious about their academics, having more life experiences outside of college than peers, and/or raising a family. The incongruence may also be related to one of their other social identities such as socioeconomic status or race. Additionally, many non-traditional students have experienced prior academic invalidation and need support in order to believe they can be successful learners (Rendón, 1994). Veterans may have received invalidation specifically related to their veteran status (e.g., messages such as "you probably rely on your brawn instead of your brain"), and/or, they may have received invalidation related to other identities.

Rendón suggests validation is the support non-traditional students need. It takes the form of someone actively encouraging them. Validation counters the notion that college students must navigate the college system relying primarily on self-responsibility where faculty and staff serve primarily to hold students accountable. Validation should be reframed from unnecessary coddling to necessary support for non-traditional students.

Validation is grouped into two categories: interpersonal and academic (Rendón, 1994; Rendón & Muñoz, 2011). In the classroom, faculty can provide interpersonal validation through personal connections with students and through genuine concern for them (Rendón & Muñoz, 2011). This means developing opportunities for student veterans to connect with faculty, staff, and each other is vital to their engagement on campus. Faculty and staff must take initiative to nurture connections with student veterans. Instructors and staff who practice academic validation create therapeutic learning environments (Ezeonu, 2011) and opportunities for students to experience success (Rendón, 1994). They also provide valuable feedback (Rendón, 2002). Another tactic used to validate students is to provide opportunities for students to connect their life experiences with the academic experiences (Rendón, 1994). These connections can be made through discussion, activities, or assignments.

The timing of validation should be early within the academic experience and continue as a part of ongoing student development (Rendón & Muñoz, 2011). Since engagement has been shown to be an important factor in student development and retention, a lack of validation for non-traditional students like student veterans indicates a potential barrier to engagement. This suggests validation is an important prerequisite for many non-traditional students' engagement and success in college. There are many possibilities for validating non-traditional students interpersonally and academically. In this chapter we have named just a few. We use these elements of validation to offer strategies to increase student veteran engagement.

Student Engagement Strategies

Elements of validation (Rendón, 1994) are used in this section to offer a set of recommendations for more effectively engaging student veterans on college and university campuses, inside and outside of classrooms. First, validation is a supportive, enabling process fostered by in- and out-of-class validation agents. Second, validated students feel capable of academic success and that their life experiences are valued. Finally, validation is part of an ongoing process that is most critical early in students' academic careers. The following strategies address these elements of validation.

Build Genuine, Reciprocal Relationships

Based on these elements of validation, faculty and staff should invest energy in building genuine, reciprocal relationships with students (see, for example, Nora, Urick, & Quijada Cerecer, 2011). Staff and faculty must go beyond limited interactions with student veterans; Veterans Day celebrations, socials, and orientation programs are not likely to foster the types of interactions to build the genuine relationships necessary for promoting engagement through validation. Educators will need to find ways to make genuine connections with student veterans.

Some initial connections may be built during typical student veteran focused major events such as orientation. These initial connections contribute to validation if they are personal, continue on a regular basis, and/or build meaningful relationships where faculty and staff help student veterans to feel valued and capable. The challenge is that genuine connections are often difficult to make at an event like an orientation with a large group of students and a limited time frame. Faculty and staff interested in validating student veterans should find ways to continue contact with students they meet after the event. Contact after the event could be in the form of phone calls, individualized emails, personalized invitations to smaller events like a brown bag lunch gathering or small social events where a few people can connect.

Utilize Individual Advising, Small Seminars, and Learning Communities to Connect

Individual advising, small seminars, and learning communities may be ideal spaces for building relationships because of the increased opportunities for student and faculty/staff interaction over time (Minnis, Bondi, & Rumann, 2013). For instance, a student veteran's advisor may make a point to learn about the student veteran's experiences inside and outside of school. If the student veteran's advisor learns that since starting classes she misses the time spent with military peers, the advisor should encourage her to join a group with other military servicemembers such as the student veteran organization (SVO). Without encouragement, the student veteran may not have the academic self-confidence to get involved or the social capital to understand the benefits of involvement, utilizing campus resources, and networking with peers and mentors. Environments such as individual advising, small seminars, and learning communities lend themselves to interpersonal interaction over time where faculty and staff can get to know the needs of individual student veterans and encourage them to engage in academic and co-curricular activities.

Connecting Off-Campus Validation Agents with the Institution

In addition to all the on-campus agents like faculty and staff, parents, siblings, children, and community members are prime candidates to validate student veterans. Family and community members may already be validating student veterans regardless of institutional efforts to validate. Family and community members may promote feelings of connectedness, competence, and self-worth through their personal, genuine relationships with student veterans. The institution should consider how to promote connections with these out-of-class agents to strengthen the impact of validation on academic pursuits. For example, the institution could provide a newsletter, website, Facebook page, Twitter feed, or listserv of opportunities on campus to student veteran family members because these validating agents may be able to encourage student veterans to engage in these activities. These groups may be especially important agents for validation since research suggests student veterans rely more heavily on family members and other veterans during their transitions to college (Rumann, 2010).

Develop a Mentoring Program in Spaces Where Student Veterans Are

Validation must begin in places where student veterans already are present. Assess your institution to identify where student veterans can be found. This may be a cafeteria, required courses, advising in the student veterans' office, or a space on campus like a veteran's lounge. Go to these spaces and offer mentoring in the form of ongoing regular contact with faculty, staff, and/or more advanced student veterans. The mentors should be trained about student veterans' concerns, campus climate issues related to student veterans, academic and other resources available for support on campus and in the community, and validation practices. Goals of the mentoring program should be to support students personally and academically. Mentors can help by showing student veterans their life experiences have prepared them for academic success and acknowledging and celebrating successes throughout their academic journey. For instance, a mentor can help a student veteran see how successfully applying for and obtaining financial aid demonstrated knowledge of the academic system and a persistence and determination to obtain a college degree. Mentors can help student veterans build and maintain a strong sense of academic self-confidence and interpersonal connection.

Acknowledge the Complex Multiple Identities of Student Veterans

When getting to know student veterans, it is important that staff and faculty not only understand their experiences directly related to being students and veterans, but their other life experiences as well (e.g., as a family member, community member, member of a minoritized group). Focusing only on student veterans' experiences as military servicemembers essentializes their experiences and is likely to ignore salient aspects of student veterans' life skills. Faculty and staff should provide opportunities for student veterans to explore how their identities intersect. For example, educators can provide opportunities for them to pursue questions such as (a) What does it mean to be a Latina student veteran? or (b) How does being gay inform how people perceive your veteran experience? or (c) How are student veterans who are parents successful in college? Students who are able to explore their multiple intersecting identities are more likely to feel a sense of wholeness contributing to a sense of self-confidence.

Empowerment to Get Involved

Validation Theory indicates that non-traditional students, such as student veterans, are likely not to take advantage of resources without validation (Rendón & Muñoz, 2011) meaning many student veterans are unlikely to participate in optional activities without encouragement by someone they trust. Faculty and staff must take an active role to get students involved in academic and co-curricular opportunities. It is not enough to create or offer an opportunity. Institutions must find ways to assist student veterans in believing they are worthy of these opportunities and foster the confidence for student veterans to fully participate in them. When faculty and staff have built genuine relationships with student veterans, they will have more information about the student veteran to ascertain what kinds of activities and opportunities will match her/his interests, experiences, and needs. Also, the student veteran will be more likely to trust the faculty or staff member's recommendation to participate after they have established a genuine relationship.

Ensure In-class and Out-of-Class Opportunities Reflect Student Veterans' Experiences

Validating student veterans' experiences requires acknowledging the ways they may differ from traditional students. Student veteran demographics indicate they are more likely to have dependents and work more hours than traditional students. Educators should consider these lifestyle characteristics when planning academic and co-curricular opportunities. Faculty may assign a project to be due the next day assuming that students would be able to complete it within a day but student veterans who are more likely to have dependents and work more hours than traditional students may not be able to complete assignments within this time frame. When activities and assignments are planned with only traditional students in mind, it invalidates the experiences of non-traditional students like student veterans. Creating more opportunities for non-traditional students (e.g., family picnics, brown bags lunch speakers, flexible support service hours, assignments with flexibility, etc.) can show support for their experiences and provide validation non-traditional students are expected and belong in college.

Since student veterans, like other non-traditional students, are more likely to question their academic capabilities based on their prior invalidating experiences and perceived differences from traditional students (Rendón, 1994), their life experiences must be recognized by staff and faculty as valuable and contributing to their preparedness for college and academic success. Students should have the opportunity to connect their experiences within and outside the military with classroom discussion, projects, and/or co-curricular activities. Incorporating student experiences in the classroom may require some faculty to reform their pedagogies since many rely on lecturing and assignments that ask students to focus on evaluating experts' experiences. Instructors need to create opportunities for students to connect the course concepts to their own experiences. Instructors can accomplish this by making time for discussion in the classroom or by asking students to relate classroom concepts or problems to their own lives. For instance, in a math course, students may be asked to find examples of how they could use the math concepts to help them address problems they face in their daily lives.

While discussion in class can be a useful tool, educators are cautioned that calling on student veterans in group settings may put them on the spot or make them feel like they are expected to be experts on the military experience. Faculty and staff may invite students to share their personal experiences to the extent they feel comfortable while remembering they cannot speak to the experiences of all student veterans. Educators should ask students in private how comfortable they are sharing their experiences in groups or make general solicitations for sharing (e.g., "Does anyone have personal experiences being in the military they would like to share with the group?"). Remember to solicit contributions from student veterans about their experiences outside the military as much as experiences within the military because student veterans are more than their military experience.

Create Opportunities to Validate through Academic Success

Another way to validate student veterans so that they feel capable of success is by affording opportunities to experience success in the classroom (Rendón, 2002). One method for helping students experience success is to have students complete tasks while in the presence of supportive faculty and staff. Faculty and staff should demonstrate to students their abilities to complete college tasks and provide useful feedback (Rendón, 2002). When the in-class and out-of-class agents at the college or university have validated student veterans, these students are more likely to have increased confidence in their academic abilities. In a course, validation could be accomplished by providing a writing task in the classroom showing students that they can write prior to expecting a larger writing project to be completed. In a lab course, teaching assistants or a lab technician could review students' lab notes and give positive feedback in areas where students are on the right track. They could provide encouragement that students have the tools, including support people to answer questions, to be successful in the course. Student veterans are more likely to imagine themselves succeeding in college and persisting to graduation once they have been able to see their own academic success—even in a small task.

Create a Comprehensive Institutional Plan and Curriculum

Institutions must take a comprehensive approach towards validating student veterans (see, for example, Ekal, Hurley, & Padilla, 2011). The support of student veterans cannot be relegated to the veterans' affairs office, or any other single office, but must be the responsibility of educators across the institution. A comprehensive campus effort to support student veterans is more likely to touch a significant number of student veterans and provide them with validation throughout the process of their development in college. The institution should bring together a group of stakeholders from different departments—academic and co-curricular—plus student veteran representatives to devise an institutional plan the administration and other significant leaders will implement and support. The plan should have support from top leaders at the institution who will devote time and resources to encouraging its implementation widely across campus.

Part of the plan should be a validation curriculum addressing how students will be validated throughout their college experience. While early validation is crucial to the success of non-traditional students, it is only part of a developmental process rather than an end within itself (Rendón, 1994). Therefore, validation throughout the college experience fosters ongoing validation. It should be addressed at various times during student veterans' collegiate experience. For example, a first-year or transfer seminar for student veterans would an appropriate place to demonstrate student veterans' experiences are valued on campus. After an initial validation experience, a writing seminar where student veterans commit their experiences to paper might be the next point of validation. Then, academic advising focused on career development services related to their interests, experiences, and goals could follow. This is just one scenario of how to create validating experiences over a period of time. Communicate the institutional plan and curriculum to all stakeholders. Finally, implement follow-up through assessment at the institutional level.

Recognize and Reward Faculty and Staff for Validating Students

Faculty and staff are often rewarded for creation of well-attended programs, for generating a high number of publications, and serving on a multiple of campus initiatives, but they are rarely recognized and compensated to the same extent for validating students. Institutions committed to supporting engagement of student veterans and other non-traditional students should devote resources to recognizing and rewarding faculty and staff in ways that will promote more relationship building, student experiences, and opportunities to experience success. If faculty and staff are not recognized for validation efforts, institutions are severely limiting the validation student veterans will be able to receive through campus agents.

Train Faculty and Staff to Validate Student Veterans

In order to have validation agents across campus, faculty and staff need to be trained to validate students (Rendón, 1994). Faculty and staff need to understand how student veterans mirror other non-traditional student populations. Further, training should provide demographics and unique concerns of student veterans. Educators also need information about issues specific to student veterans such as access to GI-Bill benefits, structured military culture, deployments and active duty interruptions, and veterans' disabilities such as PTSD, mobility constraints, and traumatic brain injuries. A key piece of this training should include helping faculty and staff understand military culture (see resource list for military culture training offered by the Department of Defense). Educators should be cautioned during training that military servicemembers have experiences, abilities, and concerns going beyond their military affiliation related to their other identities and responsibilities. Essentializing student veterans to servicemembers could be as harmful as ignoring their student veteran experiences.

In addition to learning about student veteran demographics and common concerns, faculty and staff need training on validation. Faculty and staff need to learn how to initiate and build genuine interpersonal connections with student veterans. They may need tips on how to build and maintain relationships when other obligations for instruction, research, and service monopolize their time. Instructors may need examples of how to incorporate student experiences in the classroom. They may also need ideas of how to create a caring, supporting environment where students are more likely to feel capable of and experience academic success.

Discuss the importance of validation and the role of Validation Theory in education and success of non-traditional students such as student veterans during staff development and higher education and student affairs preparation programs. Validation Theory should be included as part of the curriculum for new professionals and those enhancing their professional education. Retention theories like Tinto's based on traditional students' experiences are included in the canon. Educators should add Validation Theory to address non-traditional student experiences in the academy.

Train Faculty and Staff to Incorporate Multiple Perspectives in the Classroom

Institutions need to train faculty and staff how to include multiple perspectives in the classroom (Rendón, 1994). Traditional lecture formats often result in one perspective being centered in the classroom—the professor's. Faculty need to learn how they can bring multiple perspectives in the classroom through using a diverse array of worldviews or ways of being and types of sources in the classroom to broaden the perspectives. Also, faculty need demonstrations of how to solicit participation of students to share their perspectives and experiences in the classroom in order to have multiple perspectives voiced. Students should be able to talk about and incorporate into their coursework cultural values important to them.

Initiate Statewide or Institution-wide Policies for Recognizing Military Service

Since student veterans have had a variety of training experiences through the military, they have gained skills that may mirror learning outcomes of college courses. Institutions should work to establish and communicate standards for granting credit to student veterans for military experience. Granting credit for military experience would serve to reduce the number of courses required of student veterans, but more specific to validation, it would be a meaningful way to recognize the skills and experiences of student veterans. Failing to recognize their experience by not awarding credits to student veterans signals to them their military experience is different from college experiences and contributes to questions about their academic readiness. The American Council on Education (ACE) and Servicemembers Opportunity Colleges (SOC) provide resources to assist institutions in implementing policies to award credit for military service. A list of related resources is included at the end of this chapter.

Confront Tensions Among Validation, Accountability, and Responsibility

One of the tensions of implementing validation in the academy is the perception validation is counter to prevailing attitudes about accountability and responsibility. Educational leaders must confront these tensions and reframe validation as positively contributing to students' potential for academic success. Some may fear that providing support to students coddles them and interferes with their development of independence. However, Rendón and Muñoz (2011) argue:

> It is not about pampering students or making them weaker. In fact, it is about the opposite; it is about making students stronger in terms of assisting them to believe in their ability to learn, acquire self-worth, and increase their motivation to succeed. (pp. 17–18)

Validation is a critical element for supporting non-traditional students and can be provided while simultaneously holding high expectations of students. Leaders of the institution must convey this message in order to successfully implement validation.

Conclusion

Student veterans are an increasing population in higher education who share many characteristics with other non-traditional students. They come to college with rich personal histories and salient life experiences that institutions should utilize to engage them. Validation in the form of creating supportive environments, building genuine interpersonal connections, and offering opportunities to incorporate personal experiences within classroom and co-curricular activities will help student veterans engage in college. Validating agents across campus and in the community should be trained and practice validation early in the student veterans' college experience and at various time throughout, encouraging them to get involved and reinforcing their capability for success in college.

Resources

American Council on Education—Military Programs: www.acenet.edu/AM/Template.cfm?Section=Military_
Programs

Department of Defense—Understanding Military Culture: www.ptsd.va.gov/professional/ptsd101/course-
modules/military_culture.asp

Iraq and Afghanistan Veterans of America: http://iava.org

National Association of Veterans Upward Bound: www.navub.org

National Center for Veterans Studies at the University of Utah: http://ncvs.utah.edu

Servicemembers Opportunity Colleges: www.soc.aascu.org

Student Veterans of America: www.studentveterans.org

References

Abes, E.S., Jones, S.R., & McEwen, M.K. (2007). Reconceptualizing the model of multiple dimensions of identity: The role of meaning-making capacity in the construction of multiple identities. *Journal of College Student Development, 27*(1), 1–22. doi org/10.1353/csd.2007.0000

Bauman, M. (2009). *Called to serve: The military mobilization of undergraduates.* (Doctoral dissertation.) The Pennsylvania State University, State College. Available from ProQuest Digital Dissertations. (AAT 3380873)

Cook, B.J., & Kim, Y. (2009). *From soldier to student: Easing the transition of service members on campus.* Retrieved from the American Council on Education website: www.acenet.edu/AM/Template.cfm?Section=HENA&Template=/CM/ContentDisplay.cfm&6;ContentID=33233

DiRamio, D., Ackerman, R., & Mitchell, R.L. (2008). From combat to campus: Voices of student-veterans. *NASPA Journal, 45*(1), 73–102.

Ekal, D.E., Hurley, S.R., & Padilla, R. (2011). Validation theory and student success: The UTEP way. *Enrollment Management Journal, Summer 2011*, 138–147.

Ezeonu, R.F. (2011). Fostering a therapeutic learning environment: Highline Community College. *Enrollment Management Journal, Summer 2011*, 148–156.

Iverson, S.V., & Anderson, R. (2013). The complexity of veteran identity: Understanding the role of gender, race and sexuality. In F.A. Hamrick & C.B. Rumann (Eds.), *Called to serve: A handbook on student veterans and higher education* (pp. 89–115). San Francisco, CA: Jossey-Bass.

Livingston, W.G. (2009). *Discovering the academic and social transitions of re-enrolling student veterans at one institution: A grounded theory.* (Doctoral dissertation.) Clemson University, Clemson, South Carolina. Available from ProQuest Digital Dissertations. (AAT 3355150)

Livingston, W.G., & Bauman, M. (2013). Activations, deployments, and returns. In F.A. Hamrick & C.B. Rumann (Eds.), *Called to serve: A handbook on student veterans and higher education* (pp. 41–70). San Francisco, CA: Jossey-Bass.

Minnis, S., Bondi, S., & Rumann, C. (2013). Focused learning environments for student veterans. In F.A. Hamrick & C.B. Rumann (Eds.), *Called to serve: A handbook on student veterans and higher education* (pp. 201–220). San Francisco, CA: Jossey-Bass.

National Survey of Student Engagement. (2010). *Major differences: Examining student engagement by field of study—annual results 2010.* Bloomington, IN: Indiana University Center for Postsecondary Research.

Nora, A., Urick, A., & Quijada Cerecer, P.D. (2011). Validating students: A conceptualization and overview of its impact on student experiences and outcomes. *Enrollment Management Journal, Summer 2011*, 34–52.

Radford, A.W., & Wun, J. (2009). *Issue tables: A profile of military servicemembers and veterans enrolled in postsecondary education in 2007–08.* Alexandria, VA: National Center for Education Statistics (NCES).

Rendón, L.I. (1994). Validating culturally diverse students: Towards a new model of learning and student development. *Innovative Higher Education, 19*(1), 33–51. doi:org/10.1007/BF01191156.

Rendón, L.I. (2002). Community College Puente: A validating model of education. *Educational Policy, 16*(4), 642–667. doi:org/10.1177/0895904802016004010.

Rendón, L., & Muñoz, S. (2011). Revisiting Validation Theory: Theoretical foundations, applications, and extensions. *Enrollment Management Journal* (Summer), 12–33.

Rumann, C.B. (2010). *Student veterans returning to a community college: Understanding their transitions.* (Doctoral dissertation). Iowa State University, Ames. Available from ProQuest Digital Dissertations. (AAT 3403830)

Rumann, C.B., & Hamrick, F.A. (2010). Student veterans in transition: Re-enrolling after war zone deployments. *Journal of Higher Education, 81*(4), 431–458. doi:org/10.1353/jhe.0.0103.

Rumann, C., Rivera, M., & Hernandez, I. (2011). Student veterans and community colleges. *New Directions for Community Colleges, 155,* 51–58. doi:10.1002/cc.457.

Sander, L. (2012, March 11). Out of uniform: At half a million and counting, veterans cash in on Post-9/11 GI Bill. *The Chronicle of Higher Education.* Retrieved from http://chronicle.com/article/Out-of-Uniform/131112

Chapter 21
Engaging Graduate and Professional Students

Susan K. Gardner and Marco J. Barker

Despite representing over 14% of the total student enrollment in higher education in the United States (U.S. Department of Education, 2008), relatively little is known about graduate and professional students when compared to undergraduate students and their engagement. We define graduate students as those students seeking post-baccalaureate degrees, including academic master's degrees and research doctoral degrees, and professional students as those pursuing post-baccalaureate degrees in professional areas such as medicine and law (Council of Graduate Schools, 2004). These individuals represent a significant proportion of the student population on many university campuses and present higher education professionals with many opportunities for engagement. In this chapter, we discuss this diverse population of students, the issues they face in higher education institutions, theoretical perspectives for working with them, and practical strategies for engaging them on our campuses.

Defining Graduate and Professional Education

The goals, scope, and aims of graduate and professional education are quite different from undergraduate education and merit some explanation. Unlike undergraduate education, which serves to provide students with a wide range of subjects of study and the opportunity to gain skills such as effective reading, writing, and argument skills, graduate education is "focused on a specific area of interest and acquiring specialized skills to practice a profession or do advanced research" (Kidwell & Flagg, 2004, p. 2). More specifically, two kinds of graduate degrees exist: (1) professional degrees, and (2) research degrees at the two levels of degrees (master's and doctoral). In addition, post-baccalaureate certificate programs exist that are short-term and specialized, often to meet career needs and require two or three semesters to complete (Kidwell & Flagg, 2004).

At the master's level, students pursuing a professional degree find a program focused on "a specific set of skills needed to practice a particular profession" (Kidwell & Flagg,

2004, p. 2). These are typically final or terminal degrees. Many professional master's degrees are found in areas such as education, business, engineering, fine arts, social work, or other professional areas. The research master's degree, on the other hand, provides experience in research and scholarship and may be either a final degree or a step toward a doctorate (p. 2). In either type of master's degree, study usually lasts one or two years of full-time enrollment.

The doctoral level also features research and professional degrees. Most commonly, we think of professional doctorates as those including the M.D. for medicine and J.D. for legal practice. Research doctoral degrees, such as the Ph.D., generally include both coursework and a major research project, which encompass five to seven years of full-time study (Kidwell & Flagg, 2004). Additionally, the research doctorate involves a close academic relationship between the student and a faculty research advisor (Lovitts, 2001).

As such, the focus of the graduate and professional student in higher education will be much more centered upon professional and career goals than the undergraduate student may be. What this means is that the home of the graduate and professional student is generally found in the program or department, rather than the larger university like the undergraduate student. The implications for this differing focus will be discussed later in this chapter.

Who Are Graduate and Professional Students?

Graduate and professional students represent a significant portion of the higher education student population. A recent report from the U.S. Department of Education (Choy & Cataldi, 2011) documents that enrollment of graduate and professional students has risen over 57% in the past two decades; even more, this enrollment growth is not predicted to dwindle. When compared to the 45% growth among undergraduate enrollment in the same time period, it is important for those working in higher education to become more aware of the graduate and professional student population on their campuses. In fact, about 40% of those graduating with a bachelor's degree will go on to pursue a graduate or professional degree at some point in their lives (Choy & Cataldi, 2011).

One thing is certain, graduate and professional students encompass as many different subpopulations of students as those discussed in the remainder of this book. Whether speaking of age, gender, race, nationality, ability, religious affiliation, socioeconomic status, or enrollment status, graduate and professional students represent a wide array of diversity in U.S. higher education. For example, while the average age of graduate and professional students is obviously older than the typical undergraduate, a great diversity of age range exists among these students. As presented in Table 21.1, students 25 years of age and older tend to enroll part-time in their programs; however, there still exists significant variation in ages among degree programs and concentrations. Another such example is in business master's degree programs (e.g., MBA), wherein the majority of students will delay their enrollment for seven or more years after receiving their bachelor's degrees and will continue to work full-time while pursuing the degree (Choy & Cataldi, 2011). In contrast, the majority of students pursuing professional degree programs in medicine or dentistry enroll in these programs less than two years after receiving the bachelor's degree and will enroll full-time (Choy & Cataldi, 2011). Due to the frequent part-time status of many graduate and professional students, it is often difficult to determine exact numbers in terms of enrollment but a recent snapshot of earned degrees by sex, race, and nationality demonstrates some of the other diverse elements of this population in comparison to the undergraduate population.

As shown in Table 21.2, much like undergraduate enrollment, more women than men are currently pursuing and receiving graduate degrees and in almost equal numbers

TABLE 21.1. Graduate Student Enrollment by Age and Status, 2008

Age	Full-Time	Part-Time
20–24	37.4%	9.9%
25–34	45.6%	40.4%
35+	15.9%	49.7%
Total enrollment	1,867,000	1,810,000

TABLE 21.2. Degrees Conferred by Sex, Race, and Ethnic Group, 2007–2008

	Total	% American Indian	% Asian American	% Black	% Latino	% White	% International
Associate's							
Men	282,542	0.99	5.24	9.84	11.12	63.80	2.00
Women	467,741	1.17	4.58	13.09	11.49	61.39	1.87
Total	750,283	1.10	4.83	11.87	11.35	62.30	1.92
Bachelor's							
Men	667,930	0.63	6.92	7.29	6.68	68.81	3.24
Women	895,145	0.73	6.23	10.47	7.86	66.09	2.53
Total	1,563,075	0.69	6.52	9.11	7.36	67.25	2.84
Master's							
Men	247,472	0.45	6.07	6.48	4.61	54.92	16.81
Women	378,925	0.58	4.71	10.93	5.56	59.71	8.23
Total	626,397	0.53	5.25	9.17	5.19	57.82	11.62
Doctorate							
Men	41,780	0.46	6.08	3.90	3.36	52.67	26.86
Women	43,180	0.56	7.74	7.26	4.15	58.45	14.98
Total	84,960	0.51	6.93	5.61	3.77	55.61	20.82
Professional							
Men	34,370	0.66	10.58	4.93	4.47	68.64	2.50
Women	34,317	0.62	13.73	8.45	5.02	62.58	2.23
Total	68,687	0.64	12.15	6.69	4.75	65.61	2.37

among professional degrees. For some racial and ethnic groups, however, a larger proportion of degrees are conferred at the graduate and professional levels than at the undergraduate level, including international students and Asian Americans.

Issues Among Graduate and Professional Students

Across all graduate and professional student populations, however, one concern is prevalent: retention. Many higher education professionals may believe retention issues are less prevalent among graduate and professional students. Surprisingly, doctoral students' national completion rates hover only around 50% (Council of Graduate Schools, 2008). While the reasons for student departure at the graduate level are multi-faceted, research has found a number of general issues. The Council of Graduate Schools summarizes these influences upon graduate student retention in Figure 21.1. Viewing the attrition-completion kaleidoscope, there are certain issues over which educators and administrators will have control while others will be in the control or experience of the student. Funding, for example, is a common issue for graduate and professional students. Since the majority of financial support to graduate students is often ear-marked for full-time students (Nora & Snyder, 2007; Syverson, 1999), part-time students must often find their own resources to subsidize their graduate work. Further, the debt burden for graduate students is often much higher than for undergraduates given the lack of federal grants and subsidies to assist these students (Choy & Cataldi, 2011). Graduate students also rely

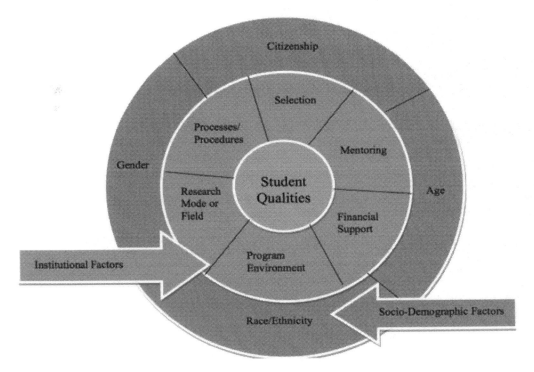

FIGURE 21.1. The Attrition-Completion Kaleidoscope

on assistantships, which present the additional challenge of maintaining a healthy working relationship where the student is not exploited (Bargar & Mayo-Chamberlain, 1983).

Because of their older age and often part-time enrollment status, many graduate and professional students will face issues related to balancing their studies with family responsibilities as well as professional obligations (Choy & Cataldi, 2006; Curran, 1987; Davis & McCuen, 1995; Smith, 2000; Watts, 2008). Gardner and Gopaul (2012) found that part-time doctoral students, in particular, had difficulty balancing the many responsibilities in their lives. Further, the students in their study expressed concern at the lack of services available to them on campus that took into consideration their varied hours and these other responsibilities in their lives.

Another issue among graduate and professional students is the resulting stress that accompanies these distinct concerns in their lives. For example, graduate students have been found to have more negative life events, greater depression, and higher anxiety than their undergraduate peers (Mallinckrodt & Leong, 1992) but also do not tend to take care of themselves as well, given their many stressors (Caple, 1995; Kidwell & Flagg, 2004). At the same time, graduate students will wait longer before seeking help than undergraduates (Caple, 1995). Nevertheless, one study found 67% of the graduate students at the University of California-Berkeley reported feeling hopeless at least once in the past year and 54% reported feeling so depressed that they had a hard time functioning. In fact, nearly 10% said that they had considered suicide. At the same time, nearly 25% of those same students said they were unaware of mental-health services on their campus (Fogg, 2009). According to Baird (1990), when compared to undergraduate study, "graduate study is much less structured, much more individualized, and consequently often much more unclear and ambiguous in its demands on students. These demands call for unusual coping strategies and are met at an emotional cost" (p. 371). Furthermore, the graduate experience may be made further stressful for students from underrepresented populations (Patton, 2009; Patton & Harper; 2003; Pontius & Harper, 2006).

To summarize, graduate and professional students are a distinct and yet diverse population in higher education. Their reasons for pursuing an advanced degree are often quite different from undergraduate students and thus require a different focus and understanding by higher education professionals and educators. In the next section, we provide a few theoretical lenses that assist professionals in better serving and engaging this student population.

Theories and Concepts

Given the distinct needs of graduate and professional students, their advanced age while in graduate and professional school, and their educational goals, different theoretical perspectives are also warranted. Here we present three such theoretical lenses: (1) adult learning theory, or andragogy; (2) socialization theory; and (3) graduate student development.

Adult Learning Theory

One appropriate theory for working with this student population is adult learning theory. Also known as andragogy, adult learning theory focuses on the different needs of adult learners. Adult learning is built upon five assumptions, according to Merriam (2001, p. 5). First, an adult learner is someone who has an independent self-concept and who can direct his or her own learning. Second, the adult learner has accumulated a reservoir of learning experiences that is a rich resource for learning. Third, the adult learner has learning needs closely related to changing social roles. Fourth, the adult learner is problem-centered and interested in immediate application of knowledge. And, fifth, the adult learner is motivated to learn by internal rather than external forces.

This theory is particularly helpful when considering designing programming for graduate and professional students, such as orientation programs. For example, the first assumption of adult learning would be encompassed in such a program by providing a cafeteria-style approach to an orientation, allowing the student to pick and choose from multiple programs and topics that suit his or her needs (Barker, Felstehausen, Couch, & Henry, 1997). The second assumption would be included in an orientation program that allows students themselves to share their knowledge in a panel. The third assumption might be incorporated through a peer-mentoring program that allows for more advanced students to share their expertise with others. Similarly, assumption four might be included in an orientation program that allows for immediate application of concepts and knowledge that students may need in their first few days and weeks of graduate school. Finally, it is important to realize that adult learners may attend an orientation program for their own benefit and may not be as motivated by contests, give-aways, and external motivators that may compel younger undergraduates, for example.

Socialization Theory

Given the career and professional focus of graduate students, a second fitting theoretical lens to understand this population is socialization theory. Socialization in the graduate education context is described by Golde (1998) as a process "in which a newcomer is made a member of a community—in the case of graduate students, the community of an academic department in a particular discipline" (p. 56). She continues, "The socialization of graduate students is an unusual double socialization. New students are simultaneously directly socialized into the role of graduate student and are given preparatory socialization into graduate student life and the future career common to most doctoral students" (p. 56). This socialization tends to occur in stages or developmental phases throughout the education of the graduate student (Baird, 1993). Therefore, much like other models of undergraduate student development, socialization for graduate students is also developmental as students change their roles and relationships to their discipline and to their future profession (Bragg, 1976; Weidman, Twale, & Stein, 2001).

One such model of socialization in graduate school is that of Weidman, Twale, and Stein (2001) who described graduate student socialization as "the processes through which individuals gain the knowledge, skills, and values necessary for successful entry into a professional career requiring an advanced level of specialized knowledge and skills" (p. iii). According to these theorists, socialization for graduate students occurs in four developmental stages: Anticipatory, Formal, Informal, and Personal.

The Anticipatory Stage occurs primarily as students enter the program, and need to learn new roles, procedures, and agendas to be followed. These students will tend to seek information and listen carefully to directions. This stage can be described as the student becoming "aware of the behavioral, attitudinal, and cognitive expectations held for a role incumbent" (Weidman et al., 2001, p.12).

The Formal Stage is characterized by the graduate student observing roles of incumbents and older students, while learning about role expectations and how they are carried out. Students in this stage are primarily concerned about task issues, and communication at this stage is informative through course material, regulative through embracing normative expectations, and integrative through faculty and student interactions (Weidman et al., 2001).

The Informal Stage is described as the stage in which "the novice learns of the informal role expectations transmitted by interactions with others who are current role incumbents" (Weidman et al., 2001, p. 14). At this stage, the graduate student receives behavioral cues, observes acceptable behavior, and subsequently responds and reacts accordingly. Many of these cues will be received from the students' cohort, those with whom most interaction occurs at this stage. Through the lessons learned in the Informal Stage, the student will then begin feeling less "student-like" and more professional.

Finally, the Personal Stage is the time in which the students' "individual and social roles, personalities and social structures become fused and the role is internalized" (Weidman et al., 2001, p. 14). During this final stage, the graduate student accepts a value orientation and relinquishes his or her former ways. The conflict impeding the total role transformation is resolved, and the graduate student will be able to separate from the department in search of his or her own identity.

Such a theory is useful in understanding how graduate and professional students will have changing needs and concerns as they progress through their degree programs. Again, the focus on the professional skills and knowledge will be emphasized for these students rather than a broad experience that might interest undergraduate populations. In this way, providing social opportunities that emphasize career and professional development may be more opportune for this population, including existing co-curricular involvement opportunities (Gardner & Barnes, 2007).

Graduate Student Development Theory

A large focus of the literature on undergraduate students reflects their development (Evans, Forney, & Guido-DiBrito, 1998) and does not extend beyond graduation. Naturally, graduate and professional students will continue to have developmental experiences through their educational experiences (Gardner, 2009). Gardner's theory of graduate student development encompasses many of the theoretical perspectives above, including adult learning and socialization, as well as the distinct concerns and issues facing graduate students at different turning points in their educational experience.

As illustrated in Figure 21.2, graduate student development occurs in three phases. The three phases of the model incorporate what is described as Phase I, or Entry; Phase II, or Integration; and, Phase III, or Candidacy, with overarching identity development or possible program departure occurring throughout these phases (Gardner, 2009).

Phase I is described as the time leading up to admission into the graduate program until the period when coursework begins. This phase generally only lasts a few months, but according to many students (Gardner, 2007; Gardner, 2008, 2010), impresses greatly upon the rest of their program, solidifies their decision to attend one institution over another, and even influences their decision to persist to doctoral education altogether. Phase I presents multiple sources of challenge to the new student, including applying to prospective programs and institutions, submitting requisite materials to programs, visiting campuses, meeting and talking with faculty members, staff, and graduate students in these prospective programs, making a final decision in regard to the program of choice, moving to the new location, beginning course work, learning to balance the demands of life and graduate school, and understanding the changing expectations of the graduate

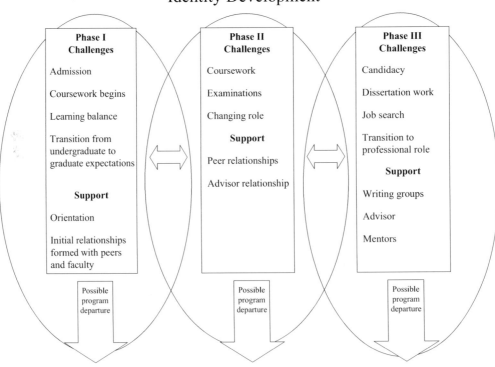

Identity Development

Phase I Challenges	Phase II Challenges	Phase III Challenges
Admission	Coursework	Candidacy
Coursework begins	Examinations	Dissertation work
Learning balance	Changing role	Job search
Transition from undergraduate to graduate expectations	**Support**	Transition to professional role
	Peer relationships	**Support**
Support	Advisor relationship	Writing groups
Orientation		Advisor
Initial relationships formed with peers and faculty		Mentors

Possible program departure

Possible program departure

Possible program departure

FIGURE 21.2. Gardner's (2009) Model of Graduate Student Development

student role. To mitigate these challenges, however, are several sources of support for new graduate students, including students they will meet during orientation, the faculty with whom they will connect and have in their initial courses, and the staff who provide support and direction through the beginning months (Gardner, 2009).

Phase II generally encompasses time in coursework, but also represents much of the social and academic integration that the students will experience as they progress toward candidacy. The challenges facing students in Phase II include demonstrating competency and skills; this challenge occurs first in their coursework and then through the examination process. During this phase, students are transitioning from being a knowledge consumer to a knowledge producer through demonstrating skills in the research process. Students face additional challenges of forming deeper relationships with both peers and faculty. Supportive relationships with these individuals are therefore imperative to student success and development in this phase (Gardner, 2009).

After moving through the challenges of Phase II, students move into the final phase of their graduate experience. Phase III marks the period after which students have passed their examinations or candidacy status. At this phase, students encounter the challenge of completing independent research in the thesis or dissertation experience or may also begin seeking professional positions. During this phase in the process, students may have less accessible support, whether through close peer relationships in coursework or daily interaction with faculty, intensifying any challenges associated with the research process (Gardner, 2009).

As students progress through the three phases, they also experience personal identity development in response to potential challenges and support mechanisms. As seen in Figure 21.2, the identity development that occurs is as fluid as the phases, wherein the student may confront developmental challenges or issues directly related to the experiences within the three phases or may be simply experiencing overarching developmental issues external to the graduate student experience. For example, a student might enroll in a course that emphasizes issues related to social justice, thereby facilitating racial identity development or intercultural sensitivity. At the same time, a student may experience issues external to the graduate program, such as a changing recognition of sexuality, that might facilitate sexual identity development. Whether enrolled in graduate education or not, of course, identity development continues throughout adulthood (Merriam & Clark, 2006).

Such an understanding of graduate student development may be helpful to higher education professionals designing programming for this population. For example, professionals will benefit from understanding that students in early phases may be more interested in connecting with peers in similar circumstances through professional associations or in campus student organizations; contrastingly, more advanced graduate students in Phase III may require more career development assistance or job seeking assistance through a career center.

In this section, we utilize the theoretical perspectives introduced above to address the unique needs of graduate and professional student populations. It is important to reiterate that there is varying diversity among graduate and professional students and each student represents a unique experience. We do not recommend here a "one size fits all" approach; rather, we highlight overarching strategies to engage these students on campus and beyond.

Services

Professionals should keep in mind that graduate and professional students are often very degree program-focused and in some cases, may rarely leave their departments or programs. Moreover, the many part-time students among this population may rarely visit the campus altogether. The types of services utilized by these students must be easily accessible, available beyond typical working hours, and cognizant of these students' often hectic schedules and conflicting responsibilities (e.g., balancing family and school). For example, graduate and professional students who utilize financial aid may require assistance after typical working hours. User-friendly websites and chat-enabled technologies may be beneficial to these students in this regard. Beyond these types of services, these students will also be focused on using the library and related technologies. Universities should consider the accessibility of these services by off-campus students and what services exist to orient students to these services if they cannot make it to campus.

Out-of-Class Engagement

There is often a misconception that graduate and professional students do not want to become involved on their campuses. While not all students will be able to engage in co-curricular organizations and activities, some students will actively seek involvement opportunities. In particular, students from underrepresented populations may seek out connections with others on campus, such as students with children, students of color, or students with disabilities. Moreover, graduate and professional students tend to be driven by more professional development activities than leadership development activities. Hence, providing career development and professional networking opportunities may be the one method for engaging these students (Gardner & Barnes, 2007). Finally, graduate student affairs professionals should consider the spectrum of students, including students with families, and design family-oriented programs and events that occur outside a typical 9 to 5 work schedule.

Counseling and Support

The graduate and professional student population has distinct stressors that result in mental health needs. Being purposeful in advertising free or low-cost counseling and therapy services available on campus provides another support system for students and may positively impact this population. In addition, initiating support groups for these students at different developmental phases may be helpful. For example, providing dissertation support groups for students in Phase III or comprehensive or qualifying exam support groups for students in Phase II. Much like other services, universities must consider how to provide remote (i.e., online) counseling support outside of typical business hours to reach this unique population.

Orientation

While many graduate and professional students will receive specific orientations in their respective degree program, campus-wide orientation sessions, and opportunities are also warranted. Often, these types of sessions focus on bureaucratic policies and procedures rather student services and development. Developing orientation sessions using a cafeteria-style approach (Barker et al., 1997) maximizes students' time and allows for intentional interactions, including opportunities for existing students to share their expertise with incoming students. This approach incorporates adult learning strategies and creates meaningful experiences for graduate and professional students and adult learners.

Peer Mentoring Programs

Similarly, institutions can offer these diverse students a myriad of peer mentoring programs suited to specific needs. Some examples include peer mentoring programs for graduate students of color on a predominately White campus, a program for graduate student parents, or a program for working professionals. Particularly as many graduate students will rely on their peers for advice in the early stages of their programs (Gardner, 2009), these structured programs may go a long way in providing support to these students.

Financial Aid

The recent elimination of subsidized federal loans for graduate students is just one of many financial barriers this student population may face (Nelson, 2011). These students often carry a high debt burden (Choy, 2000; Choy & Cataldi, 2011) and very little need-based aid exists for these students. For part-time students, the cost of pursuing an advanced degree can be astronomical, particularly if their place of employment does not subsidize these costs. Institutions should consider more need-based aid for graduate and professional students, including the expansion of grants and scholarships for part-time and full-time students. However, such opportunities must be well advertised, accessible after traditional working hours, and visible (e.g., in orientation programs or websites) in order to reach graduate and professional students and prove reliable.

Faculty Development

Institutions, and particularly faculty, tend to assume that graduate and professional students begin programs with a full knowledge of how to navigate the degree program (Golde, 2005). However, these students sometimes struggle with navigating the institution and the department and attempting to understand their new roles as graduate and professional students. Additionally, these students undergo both personal and professional developmental challenges, ultimately facing identity development issues. It is essential that faculty and specifically advisors participate in professional development opportunities that focus on graduate student development and responding to the diverse demographic of graduate and professional students. These professional development seminars should provide faculty and departmental staff with recommendations for creating positive developmental environments for this population. Aforementioned strategies may serve us a starting point, but strategies and programs should account for the unique culture and context of the student, department, institution, and geography.

Holistic Assessment

In this chapter, we highlighted the diversity of graduate and professional students. While universities may capture graduate student enrollment and completion, including demographic data, institutional research should also capture the day-to-day experiences of these students. Institutional assessments should provide opportunities for students to report their overall experiences on campus to gain greater insight into issues that may be specific to the institution. For example, students may report that they prefer weekend courses versus weekly courses, due to work or family obligations.

Institutional Culture

Overall, there is a need to incorporate graduate and professional students in campus life. Considering the recommendations in this chapter, institutions should assess how institutionalized practices or campus-wide programs either neglect or discount the participation of graduate and professional students. Additional consideration should be given to subpopulations (e.g., women, ethnic minorities, persons with disabilities, etc.) that experience the campus through multiple lenses reflective of their identity. Graduate schools also have a tremendous responsibility to advocate for these students and make the needs of this population salient to other campus constituencies.

Conclusion

In conversations of student development and campus life on our campuses, the lives of graduate and professional students tend to go ignored or are rarely considered in decision-making processes. When, in fact, this population comprises a significant percentage of the student body whose enrollment is steadily increasing. While under-graduate enrollment constitutes the larger demographic on college campuses, it is important to note that 40% of undergraduate completers enroll in graduate or profes-sional degree programs (Choy & Cataldi, 2011). In this chapter, we sought to first define and distinguish graduate and professional students and then, to bring greater attention to the diversity and dynamics of graduate and professional students while providing theoretical and practical considerations for practitioners and scholars. Additionally, we include Gardner's (2009) theory of graduate student development to further explore the relationship between student identity and the mechanics of graduate education.

Graduate and professional education includes a series of milestones or benchmarks in conjunction with a socialization process where students must not only successfully complete steps prior to moving forward in their education, but also orient themselves to better understand and become immersed in their chosen profession. This hybrid devel-opmental relationship is further complicated when we consider the unique background of those enrolled in graduate and professional programs. This unique population repre-sents full-time and part-time students, where over 45% of students attending full-time are 25–34 years of age and 49.7% of students attending part-time are 35 year of age and older (U.S. Department of Education, 2008); multiple disciplines and programs; family dynamics (e.g., parents); and a myriad of ages, genders, ethnicities, and nationalities.

Issues facing graduate and professional students represent institutional and socio-demographic factors related to the institution, the department, and the individual. Depending on the department and the background of the student, some issues for this population may include budgeting the financial costs of their education, balancing work, family, and school, managing stress, and dealing with day-to-day experiences. We presented three theoretical frameworks that provide lenses for understanding this pop-ulation: adult learning theory, socialization, and graduate student development. Adult learning theory is a useful tool in understanding the ways in which adults make sense of the world and form knowledge. This theory aids in forming a sense of self, drawing from lived experiences, changing one's social role, developing and applying knowledge to real-world and immediate situations, and being intrinsically motivated to learn. Socialization is the belief that and the process by which students learn the norms, culture, and tradi-tions within their chosen profession or discipline. This process may occur through stages or phases, but remains organic in the sense that the individual is learning their new role as a member in the academic or professional community.

Similarly, Gardner's (2009) theory of graduate student development explains the dual journey that students take during their graduate and professional programs. Once a stu-dent commits to beginning her program, she begins a process of completing the major phases of her program (i.e., coursework, general examinations, and defense) and simul-taneously begins the process of acclimating to the profession. During these processes, students encounter both internal and external factors and continuously reconcile their identity as individuals, students, and professionals in their field. Although the pro-cess of navigating graduate and professional studies and negotiating one's identity may be challenging for some students, there are clear, intentional strategies that may assist students transition and successful completion. Providing support services, peer-mentoring, counseling, and student involvement opportunities for this population may assist students in forming connections to the campus and in establishing a support network. However, these services and opportunities must consider the unique demographics of most students, offering after-hours contact or remote access, and address the special needs of subgroups within the population. Additionally, student- and activity-centered orientations provide opportunities for students to learn more about the psychosocial support mechanisms on campus and stimulate the learning process of adult learners.

This chapter ended with institutional initiatives and campus environment strategies that can have a positive effect on graduate and professional students. We proposed that institutions establish financial aid policies that increase need-based aid funding sources, promote professional development for faculty who work with this population, conduct more holistic-student outcome assessments beyond retention and completion data, and incorporate graduate and professional students in institutional conversations on student development, persistence, and success (i.e., completion). Graduate and professional education dates back to the late 1800s with the adoption of the German research university. This model of education and professional training is responsible for shaping the modern day research university. However, in its formation, the research university has often failed to adequately address the personal identity and experiences of students in these programs. Consequently, this population may be at risk, and it hinges on universities and colleges to develop effective strategies to support and develop the social and academic lives of graduate and professional students.

References

Baird, L.L. (1990). The melancholy of anatomy: The personal and professional development of graduate and professional school students. In J.C. Smart (Ed.), *Higher education: Handbook of theory and research Vol. 6* (pp. 361–392). New York, NY: Agathon Press.

Baird, L.L. (1993). Using research and theoretical models of graduate student progress. In L.L. Baird (Ed.), *Increasing graduate student retention and degree attainment* (pp. 3–12). San Francisco, CA: Jossey-Bass.

Bargar, R.R., & Mayo-Chamberlain, J. (1983). Advisor and advisee issues in doctoral education. *The Journal of Higher Education, 54*(4), 407–432.

Barker, S., Felstehausen, G., Couch, S., & Henry, J. (1997). Orientation programs for older and delayed-entry graduate students. *NASPA Journal, 35,* 57–68.

Bragg, A.K. (1976). *The socialization process in higher education.* Washington, DC: The George Washington University.

Caple, R.B. (1995). Counseling graduate students. In A.S. Pruitt-Logan & P.D. Isaac (Eds.), *Student services for the changing graduate student population* (pp. 43–50). San Francisco, CA: Jossey-Bass.

Choy, S. (2000). *Debt burden four years after college.* Washington, DC: U.S. Department of Education, Office of Educational Research and Improvement, National Center for Education Statistics.

Choy, S.P., & Cataldi, E.F. (2006). *Student financing of graduate and first-professional education, 2003–04* (NCES 2006–185). Washington, DC: National Center for Education Statistics.

Choy, S.P., & Cataldi, E.F. (2011). *Graduate and first-professional students: 2007–08.* Washington, DC: U.S. Department of Education.

Council of Graduate Schools. (2004). *Organization and administration of graduate education.* Washington, DC: Author.

Council of Graduate Schools. (2008). *Ph.D. completion and attrition: Analysis of baseline program data from the Ph.D. completion project.* Washington, DC: Author.

Curran, C. C. (1987). Dealing with the distant learner as part-time learner. *Journal of Education for Library and Information Science, 27,* 240–246.

Davis, A. P., & McCuen, R. H. (1995). Part-time graduate education: Obstacles, conflicts, and suggestions. *Journal of Professional Issues in Engineering Education and Practice, 121*(2), 108–113.

Evans, N. J., Forney, D. S., & Guido-DiBrito, F. (1998). *Student development in college: Theory, research, and practice.* San Francisco, CA: Jossey-Bass.

Fogg, P. (2009, February 20). Grad-school blues. *The Chronicle Review,* B13–B14.

Gardner, S. K. (2007). "I heard it through the grapevine": Doctoral student socialization in chemistry and history. *Higher Education, 54,* 723–740.

Gardner, S. K. (2008). "What's too much and what's too little?": The process of becoming an independent researcher in doctoral education. *The Journal of Higher Education, 79,* 326–350.

Gardner, S. K. (2009). *Doctoral student development: Phases of challenge and support.* San Francisco, CA: Jossey-Bass.

Gardner, S. K. (2010). *Contrasting the socialization experiences of doctoral students in high- and low-completing departments: A qualitative analysis of disciplinary and institutional contexts. The Journal of Higher Education, 81,* 658–679.

Gardner, S. K., & Barnes, B. J. (2007). Graduate student involvement: Socialization for the professional role. *The Journal of College Student Development, 48,* 369–387.

Gardner, S. K., & Gopaul, B. (2012). *The part-time doctoral student experience. The International Journal of Doctoral Studies, 7,* 63–78.

Golde, C. M. (1998). Beginning graduate school: Explaining first-year doctoral attrition. In M. S. Anderson (Ed.), *The experience of being in graduate school: An exploration* (pp. 55–64). San Francisco, CA: Jossey-Bass.

Golde, C. M. (2005). The role of the department and discipline in doctoral student attrition: Lessons from four departments. *The Journal of Higher Education, 76*(6), 669.

Kidwell, C. S., & Flagg, C. A. (2004). Graduate school and you: A guide for prospective graduate students. Washington, DC: Council of Graduate Schools.

Lovitts, B. E. (2001). *Leaving the ivory tower. The causes and consequences of departure from doctoral study.* Lanham, MD: Rowman & Littlefield.

Mallinckrodt, B., & Leong, F. T. L. (1992). International graduate students, stress, and social support. *Journal of College Student Development, 33,* 71–78.

Merriam, S. B. (2001). Andragogy and self-directed learning: Pillars of adult learning theory. *New Directions for Adult and Continuing Education, 89,* 3–13.

Merriam, S. B., & Clark, M. C. (2006). Learning and development: The connection in adulthood. In C. Hoare (Ed.), *Handbook of adult development and learning* (pp. 27–51). Oxford, England: Oxford University Press.

Nelson, L. A. (2011, August 17). *A graduate student burden.* Retrieved from Inside Higher Ed website: www.insidehighered.com/news/2011/08/17/students_will_bear_brunt_of_changes_to_graduate_financial_aid

Nora, A., & Snyder, B. P. (2007, April). *Structural differences in scholarly engagement among full- and part-time doctoral students.* Paper presented at the annual meeting of the American Educational Research Association, Chicago, IL.

Patton, L. D. (2009). My sister's keeper: A qualitative examination of significant mentoring relationships among African American women in graduate and professional schools. *The Journal of Higher Education, 80*(5), 510–537.

Patton, L. D., & Harper, S. R. (2003). Mentoring relationships among African American women in graduate and professional schools. In M. F. Howard-Hamilton (Ed.), *Meeting the needs of African American women. New Directions for Student Services* (No. 104, pp. 67–78). San Francisco: Jossey-Bass.

Pontius, J. L., & Harper, S. R. (2006). Principles for good practice in graduate and professional student engagement. In M. Guentzel & B. Elkins Nesheim (Eds.), *Supporting graduate and professional students: The role of student affairs.* New Directions for Student Services (No. 115, pp. 47–58). San Francisco, CA: Jossey-Bass.

Smith, P.R. (2000). A meeting of cultures: Part-time students in an Ed.D. program. *International Journal of Leadership in Education, 3*, 359–380.

Syverson, P.D. (1999). Part-time study plus full-time employment: The new way to go to graduate school. *Education Statistics Quarterly, 1*(3), 13–15.

U.S. Department of Education. (2008). NCES Fast Facts. Retrieved August 15, 2011, from www.nces.ed.gov

Watts, J.H. (2008). Challenges of supervising part-time PhD students: Towards student-centered practice. *Teaching in Higher Education, 13*, 369–373.

Weidman, J.C., Twale, D.J., & Stein, E.L. (2001). *Socialization of graduate and professional students in higher education: A perilous passage?* San Francisco, CA: Jossey-Bass.

About the Editors

Stephen John Quaye is a faculty member in the Student Affairs in Higher Education Program in the College of Education, Health, and Society at Miami University. He is a 2009 ACPA Emerging Scholar and was awarded the 2009 Melvene D. Hardee Dissertation of the Year Award from NASPA. Quaye's research and teaching broadly focus on understanding how to enable undergraduate and graduate students to engage difficult issues (e.g., privilege, oppression, power) civilly and honestly, as well as how storytelling is used as an educational tool to foster reflection and learning across differences. He also is interested in the strategies educators use to facilitate these dialogues and what they learn about themselves in the process. Quaye convened the inaugural ACPA Think Tank on Civil Discourse in 2012 in which he and three of his colleagues proposed challenging questions and possible solutions for student affairs educators in fostering civility and relationship-building on their campuses and was one of three HEd Talk Theorists at the 2014 ACPA Convention. His work is published in different venues, including *The Review of Higher Education*, *Teachers College Record*, *Journal of College Student Development*, and *Equity & Excellence in Education*. He holds degrees from The Pennsylvania State University (Ph.D., Higher Education), Miami University (M.S., College Student Personnel), and James Madison University (B.S., Psychology).

Shaun R. Harper is on the faculty in the Graduate School of Education, Africana Studies, and Gender Studies at the University of Pennsylvania, where he also serves as executive director of the Center for the Study of Race and Equity in Education. Harper's research examines race and gender in higher education and social contexts, college access and achievement among undergraduate men of color, and college student engagement. He is author of over 80 peer-reviewed journal articles and other academic publications. *The Journal of Higher Education*, *Review of Research in Education*, *Journal of College Student Development*, *The Review of Higher Education*, and *Teachers College Record* are among the journals in which his research is published. His 12 books include *College Men and Masculinities*, *Advancing Black Male Student Success from Preschool through Ph.D.*, and the 5th edition of *Student Services: A Handbook for the Profession*. Several associations have praised Harper's scholarship, including the Association for the Study of Higher Education (2008 Early Career Award), the American Educational Research Association (2014 Relating Research to Practice Award), and the National Association of Student Personnel Administrators (2012 Robert H. Shaffer Award for Faculty Excellence). Harper earned his bachelor's degree in education from Albany State, a historically Black university in Georgia, and his Ph.D. in higher education from Indiana University.

Contributors

Shafiqa Ahmadi is Assistant Professor of Clinical Education at the Rossier School of Education at the University of Southern California.

Marco J. Barker is a Senior Director for Diversity and Multicultural Affairs at the University of North Carolina at Chapel Hill.

Jonathan Berhanu is a doctoral candidate in the School of Education at the University of Wisconsin, Madison.

Stephanie Bondi is an Assistant Professor of Practice in the Department of Educational Administration at the University of Nebraska—Lincoln.

Ellen M. Broido is an Associate Professor of Higher Education and Student Affairs at Bowling Green State University.

Kirsten Brown is an Academic and Career Advisor at the University of Wisconsin-Madison.

D. Chase J. Catalano is the director of the LGBT Resource Center at Syracuse University.

Darnell Cole is an Associate Professor of Higher Education at the Rossier School of Education at the University of Southern California.

Charles H.F. Davis III is director of Higher Education Research and Initiatives in the Center for the Study of Race and Equity in Education at the University of Pennsylvania.

Lori D. Patton is an Associate Professor in the School of Education at Indiana University.

Susan K. Gardner is Associate Professor of Higher Education and Director of the NSF ADVANCE Rising Tide Center at the University of Maine.

Joy Gaston Gayles is an Associate Professor in the Department of Leadership, Policy and Adult and Higher Education at North Carolina State University.

Kimberly A. Griffin is an Associate Professor in the Higher Education, Student Affairs, and International Education Policy Program at the University of Maryland.

Jarrett T. Gupton is an Assistant Professor in the College of Education and Human Development at the University of Minnesota.

Linda Serra Hagedorn is Associate Dean of Undergraduate Programs in the College of Human Sciences and Professor in the School of Education at Iowa State University.

Shaun R. Harper is Executive Director of the Center for the Study of Race and Equity in Education, and a faculty member in the Graduate School of Education, Africana Studies, and Gender Studies at the University of Pennsylvania.

Frank Harris III is an Associate Professor in the College of Education at San Diego State University.

Jessica C. Harris is a doctoral student in Higher Education and Student Affairs at Indiana University.

Tiffany M. Herder is Director of Curriculum and Instructional Design at Corinthian Colleges, Inc.

Mary F. Howard-Hamilton is the Raleigh Holmstedt Distinguished Professor of Education and Coordinator of the Higher Education Program in the Department of Educational Leadership at Indiana State University.

Barbara Jacoby is Faculty Associate for Leadership & Community Service-Learning and Associate Affiliate Professor of Higher Education and Student Affairs at the University of Maryland—College Park.

Adrianna J. Kezar is a Professor and Co-Director of the Pullias Center for Higher Education at the University of Southern California.

George D. Kuh is Chancellor's Professor Emeritus of Higher Education at Indiana University.

Jenny J. Lee is an Associate Professor in the Center for the Study of Higher Education at the University of Arizona.

Jaime Lester is an Associate Professor in the Higher Education Program at George Mason University.

Joyce Lui is a Research Associate for the César E. Chávez Institute of the College of Ethnic Studies at San Francisco State University.

Susan B. Marine is Assistant Professor of Higher Education at Merrimack College.

Keon M. McGuire is Assistant Professor of Higher Education at Arizona State University.

Carl S. Moore is Associate Professor in the Research Academy of Integrated Learning at the University of the District of Columbia.

Samuel D. Museus is Associate Professor of Higher Education in the Morgridge College of Education at the University of Denver.

C. Casey Ozaki is an Assistant Professor in the Department of Teaching and Learning at the University of North Dakota.

Laura W. Perna is Professor in the Graduate School of Education at the University of Pennsylvania, Executive Director of the Alliance for Higher Education and Democracy (AHEAD), and 2014–2015 President of the Association for the Study of Higher Education.

Stephen John Quaye is a faculty member in the College of Education, Health, and Society at Miami University.

Jessica Ranero-Ramirez is the Coordinator of the Transition Center at Del Mar College.

Robert D. Reason is Professor of Student Affairs and Higher Education at Iowa State University.

Kristen A. Renn is Professor of Higher, Adult, and Lifelong Education and Associate Dean of Undergraduate Studies/Director for Student Success Initiatives at Michigan State University.

Corey B. Rumann is an Assistant Professor of Practice in the Department of Educational Administration at the University of Nebraska—Lincoln.

Tina M. Stavredes is Chief Academic Officer for Online Services at Corinthian Colleges, Inc.

Dafina-Lazarus Stewart is an Associate Professor of higher education and student affairs at Bowling Green State University.

Isabella Villacampa is Program Administrator in the Student Resource Center at New York University.

MaryBeth Walpole is a Professor in higher education at Rowan University.

J. Luke Wood is an Associate Professor in the doctoral program in community college leadership at San Diego State University and Co-Director of the Minority Male Community College Collaborative (M2C3).

Index

Americans with Disabilities Amendments Act (ADAAA) 194
Anderson, D.A. 158
Anderson, T. 261–2
andragogy 344
anticipatory stage of socialization 345
anti-deficit achievement framework 64–5
anti-deficit perspective: low-income students 238; transfer students 273, 278–80
antonio, a.l. 6, 7, 22, 123–4, 178
Anzaldua, G. 46
appearance 94
Arab students 8
Archer, W. 261–2
Argyris, C. 61
articulation 277
Arzy, M.R. 242
Asian American and Pacific Islander (AAPI) students 40; women 40, 42, 43–4, 45
Asian students 38, 109, 110, 113
assignments 331
Association of American Colleges and Universities xii
Astin, A.W. 4, 176, 178, 180–1, 213, 214–16, 289, 293–4, 295
Astin, H.S. 178
at risk students 11
athletes 209–20; challenges for 210–13; female 151; student engagement strategies 216–18; theoretical frameworks 213–16
athletic subculture 213
athletics teams 124
attendance status 291
attitudes: barriers for students with disabilities 194–5; traditional White racial identity models 79–81
attrition-completion kaleidoscope 342–3
audit of campus policies and procedures x, 99
Australia 105, 106, 111
awareness, knowledge and skills framework 85–6

Baird, L.L. 62
Balibar, E. 113–14
Bandura, A. 213–14
Banning, J.H. 7, 8–9, 62
Barnett, M.A. 44
Bassuk, E.L. 225
Bates, T. 259
Bauer, K.W. 21
Baumohl, J. 222
Baxter Magolda, M.B. 7, 76–7
Bean, J.P. 4
Bean, J.R. 258
behavioral climate 22–3, 179
Beilke, J.R. 195
belonging, sense of 293–4
Benjamin, L. 46
Bensimon, E.M. 61, 67
Berger, J.B. 278

Bergvall, V.L. 152
beta presses 62
Billson, J.M. 160
Bilodeau, B. 126, 141–2
biological perspective 38
bio-medical transition services 139
bisexual students see lesbian, gay and bisexual (LGB) students
Black cultural centers 20
Black matriarch 46
Black men 55–7, 58–60, 126; Harper's anti-deficit achievement framework 64–5
Black/White binary 40
Black/White biracial women 98
Black women 41, 42, 44, 46–7, 58–9
Blowers, S.S. 311
Bornstein, K. 143
boundary-crossing 101–2
Branscombe, N.R. 109
bridge programs see transition programs
Bridges, B.K. 2–3, 58, 237–8
Bronfenbrenner, U. 95–6
Brown, J.T. 196
Bryant, A.N. 178, 181
Bucceri, J. 40
Buchmann, C. 37
Buckley, J.A. 2–3
buddy program 284
building design 8–9
Burgstahler, S. 195, 203
buzzwords 11

cafeteria-style approach to orientation 344, 349
California State University-Northridge xii
Cameron, C. 278
campus climate 21, 123–4; assessments of 26–7, 201–2; campus racial climate 21–3, 26–7; religious minority students 178–80
campus culture 21–2; audits of 26–7; boundary-crossing 101–2; campus racial culture 23–5; graduate and professional students 350; intercollegiate athletics and 212–13; symbols and gender identity 164
campus ecology ix-x, 95–7, 99
campus environments 5, 192; commuter and part-time students 299–300; environmental presses 62; LGB students and 123–4; physical barriers for students with disabilities 196; supportive 5, 238, 251–2; transfer students' adjustment to 275–6
campus organizations: culturally-based 19–20, 20–1, 26; women of color 51; see also student organizations
campus racial climate 21–3; assessments 26–7
campus racial culture 23–5
candidacy phase 346, 347
Capraro, R.L. 155
capstone courses 303

career advancement accounts (CAAs) 317
career planning 125
career preparation programs 199
career services 281, 303
caring, ethic of 180
Carini, R.M. 58
Carnegie Foundation 172
Carnevale, A.P. 312–13
Cejda, B.D. 275
celebration of success 304
Chang, J.C. 6
Chang, M.J. 6, 7, 22, 123–4, 178
charitable involvement 180
Cheah, B. 312–13
Chesler, M. 84
Chickering, A.W. 294
child abuse 225
child care provision 318
Christianity 171; Christian privilege 173–5, 181;
    dominant Christian context 171–3, 176, 181
class, social 126
class bias 242
class scheduling 301
classroom activities: discussions 30; low-income
    students 247; student veterans 331–2
classroom environments 16–20
Clayton-Pedersen, A.R. 178
climate assessments 26–7, 201–2
co-curricular activities 182; commuter and part-time
    students 301–2; graduate and professional stu-
    dents 348; rates of engagement 18–19; students of
    color 18–21; students with disabilities 191, 192–3
cognitive development: athletes 212; White
    students 76–7
cognitive presence 261, 265
cognitive scaffolding 261, 262–4, 266–8
collaboration: with athletic department
    administrators 217; with disability service
    offices 201; among stakeholders 66–7;
    partnerships across the campus 67–9
collectivist cultures 24, 109, 260
College Cost Reduction and Access Act (2007)
    227–8, 233
College Retirement Equities Fund (CREF) 173
colonial colleges 171–2
coming out 123
committees and task forces: access and community
    outreach advisory committee 232; disability
    issues 196; improving academic status of male
    students of color 68–9; retention and gradua-
    tion 252; trans students 144
communication channels, online 266
communities of inquiry 261–2
community-based projects 250
Community College Survey of Student Engagement
    (CCSSE) 58–9
community colleges 273–4; returning adult
    learners see adult learners; transfer students

see transfer students; varied academic
    functions 273
community members 329–30
commuter and part-time students 289–305;
    characteristics 290–4; common needs and
    concerns 292–4; student engagement strategies
    297–304; theories and concepts 294–6
complicated Whiteness 78–9
compositional diversity 22–3, 123–4, 179
comprehensive approach 332–3
conceptual scaffolding 263–4, 267
connections: connecting students of color 20–1;
    with international students 115–16; multiracial
    students 100; with veterans 328–9
Connell, R.W. 160
consensual beta press 62
Constantine, M.G. 113
cool pose 160
costs: campus activities 251; international students
    110–11
Council for Adult and Experiential Learning
    (CAEL) 317–18
Council for the Advancement of Standards in
    Higher Education (CAS) 290
Council of Graduate Schools 342
counseling 348–9
counter-narratives 130
credit transferability 277
Crenshaw, K. 47, 48
critical race theory (CRT) 149; men of color 63–4;
    and Whiteness 79, 82–3
critical thinking model 265
cross-dressers 136
cultural audits 26–7
cultural centers 20, 118
cultural differences, and online learners 259–60,
    264–5
cultural dissonance 24, 76
cultural incongruence 24, 43–5
cultural integration 24–5
cultural loneliness 108
cultural norms 109–10
cultural relevancy 240, 242, 249; creating culturally
    relevant engagement experiences 248
cultural symbols 164
culturally-based organizations 19–20, 20–1, 26
culturally responsive curricular content 17–18
curricular learning communities 300
curriculum: commuter and part-time students
    300–1; diverse content 30; Eurocentric and
    culturally responsive content 17–18; integration
    of gender identity development across curricula
    165; LGB students 131; multiracial issues 101;
    race relations and Whiteness 84–5; sensitivity to
    low-income students 242; studies on women of
    color 49–50; validation of student veterans 332–3
Cuyjet, M.J. 59, 154
Cytron-Walker, A. 84

rewards 29–30; incorporating multiple perspectives in the classroom 334; multiracial 100; professional development 29, 143–4, 333–4, 350; recruitment and hiring 29, 100; and students with disabilities 195, 197; universal design training 197; validating student veterans 333–4; women of color 51–2

Faculty Expectations Statement 266–7

faculty interaction 5, 238; athletes 217–18; low-income students 250–1; students with disabilities 192

familismo 43

family: graduate and professional students and 343; homelessness 223, 224; involvement for commuter and part-time students 302; male identity development 160–1; resiliency as familial support 229, 230; transfer students and work-life balance 278; validation of student veterans 329–30; women of color and 43–5, 51

family conflict 225–6, 227

family orientation programs 299

Fassinger, R.E. 123

Federal Educational Rights and Privacy Act (FERPA) 199

federal student financial aid 244

feedback 266

fees for student services 252

female identity development *see* women

feminine cultures 260

feminist poststructuralism 156–9, 163–4, 166

Fetzer Institute 176

financial aid 145; checklist for homeless students 233; commuter and part-time students 298; counseling for adult learners 317; federal 244; graduate and professional students 349; homeless students 227–8; low-income students 239, 241, 244, 247; transfer students 279

financial contributions, international students' 106

financial education 247

financial needs, meeting 247

financial support 116, 279

First Amendment 181

fitness facilities 182

Flannery, D.D. 158

Fleming, J. 46

food 177

Foor, C.E. 158–9

for-profit community colleges 315

formal stage of socialization 345

Forrest-Cataldi, E. 291

Forshee, A.S. 140

foster care 226, 227

fourteen-stage model of transsexual identity development 140–1

France 105, 113–14

Frankenberg, R. 83

fraternities 60, 124, 251

Freire, P. 9

freshman interest groups (FIGs) 300

Frey, W.H. 93

friction points 312, 313–16

Fries-Britt, S.L. 16

functional limitations perspective 190

funding for graduate and professional students 342–3

Gable, R.K. 154

Gardner, S.K. 345–7, 351

Garmezy, N. 229

Garrison, D.R. 261–2

Gaston Gayles, J. 211, 214, 216

Gates Millennium Scholarship 241

gay students *see* lesbian, gay and bisexual (LGB) students

gender: and degree attainment 37, 55–6; degrees conferred 341; disengagement and 154–5; engagement of students of color and 58–60; intersection with race and religion 183; intersection with race and sexuality 126–7; intersectionality and multiracial students 98–9; sex and 135–6; student veterans 324–5; students with disabilities 189; trans students *see* trans students

gender expression 125

gender gap reversal 37

gender identity development 149–70; articulation of issues 151–6; feminist poststructuralism 156–9, 163–4, 166; men 153–6, 159–62; social constructionist model 159–62, 163–4, 166; student engagement strategies 163–5; women 151–3, 156–9

gender norms 150

gender radicals 136

gender-reflection work 142–3

gender roles, male 159, 160–1

genderism 137

genderqueers 136

general discussion thread 265

Germany 105, 273, 352

Getzel, E.E. 195

Gilbert, P. 161

Gilbert, R. 161

Giroux, H.A. 79, 82

giving back 20

globalization 106–7, 257

goals: educational 280–1, 298–9; realization of x–xi

Golde, C.M. 344

Goldstein, D.E. 192

grade point average (GPA) 275, 308

graduate and professional students 339–54; characteristics 340–2; defining graduate and professional education 339–40; issues 342–3; student engagement strategies 348–50; theories and concepts 343–7

graduate student development theory 345–7, 351

graduation rates: athletes 211–12; students with disabilities 191–2; women of color 41; *see also* degree attainment

grant aid 239, 241, 247

Greenblatt, M. 225

Griffin, P. 162

group mentoring 200

group reflection opportunities 163

group work 109; student veterans and sharing experiences 332

Gupton, J.T. 224

Haber, M.G. 225

Hagedorn, L.S. 308, 311–12

Hall, R.H. 267

Hallett, R.E. 224

Hanassab, S. 113

Hannafin, M. 263, 266

Hannah, S.J. 213

Harper, C.E. 154

Harper, S.R. 6, 7, 55, 58, 59–60, 155–6, 161; anti-deficit achievement framework 64–5

Harrington, W.P. 75

Harvard 172, 221–2

Harvey, W. 16

hate crimes 19, 111–12

Hayek, J.C. 2–3, 58, 237–8

Hayes, C.L. 158

Hayes, E. 158

hegemonic masculinity 160, 162

Heggins, W.J. 110

Helms, B.J. 154

Helms, J. 79, 80

help-seeking 45–7

Herek, G.M. 162

heritage seeking 20

heterogeneity 130

heteronormativity, combating 130

hierarchy of needs 240–1, 294

Higbee, J.L. 197

high-impact practices xi–xii, 5

high schools 77–8

higher education homeless liaison position 233

higher-order cognitive skills 76

Hill, J.L. 195

Hill Collins, P. 41

Hilton, A.A. 274

historical legacy 22, 123–4, 179

Historically Black Colleges and Universities (HBCUs) 59–60, 172

Hmong American women 44

Hofstede, G. 259

holidays, religious 172, 177

holistic assessment 350

holistic learning environment 10–11

homeless education liaison 233

homeless students 221–36; definitions and demographics 222–4; postsecondary education

227–8; pre-college educational barriers 224–7; resiliency theory 228–31; student engagement strategies 231–3; typology of homeless youth 224

homophobia 162

hooks, b. 15

Hopper, K. 222

human capital theory 240, 241–2

human rights 128, 130

Humes, K.R. 93

Hune, S. 45

Hurtado, S. 20, 22, 178–9

identity 92; defining 150; gender identity development *see* gender identity development; graduate student development theory 346–7; intersectionality *see* intersectionality; LGB students 122; multiple identities *see* multiple identities; problematic White identities 78; queer theory and 129; racial *see* racial identity; trans 136–7, 137–8, 139, 141–2; transsexual identity development model 140–1

impairment 187–8; *see also* students with disabilities

Improving Access to Education for Students Who Are Homeless or in Foster Care Act (2005) 227

incentives 29–30

incongruence: cultural 24, 43–5; validation theory 327

individual advising 329

individual courses 301

individualistic cultures 24, 260

informal stage of socialization 345

information provision 279

information technology: commuter and part-time students 302; dependency on 316–17; *see also* online learners

Institute of International Education (IIE) 105, 106, 110–11, 113

institution types, and adult learners 311–16

institutional adaptation, stages of 296

institutional apprehension 274–5

institutional assessments 350

institutional commitment 4; to disability 196–7; to transfer 279

institutional legacy 22, 123–4, 179

institutional mission 25

institutional plan 332–3

institutional policies and practices ix–x, 5–11; audit of policies and procedures x, 99; interventions in gender identity development 164–5; inventory of 246; poststructuralism and 243–6; and programs for homeless students 231–3; recognition of military service 334–5; shifting the onus for engagement 5–10; trans students 144–5; using theory to guide practice 9–11

institutional quality 5–6

institutional receptivity 312–16

Obama, B. 93, 291
O'Donnell, A.M. 267
office of adult services 318
Oliver, K. 263
on-campus employment 248, 298
one of few 16
one-to-one mentoring 200
O'Neil, J.M. 153–4
online learners 257–69; adult learners 315; needs and issues 258–60; student engagement strategies 264–8; theoretical framework 261–4
online mentoring 200, 303
onus for engagement, shifting 5–9
Opio, T. 114
Organisation for Economic Cooperation and Development (OECD) 105–6
organizational learning theory 61–2
organizational structure 22–3, 123–4, 180
orientation programs 328–9; adult learning theory and 344; commuter and part-time students 298–9; graduate and professional students 344, 349; low-income students 252; transfer students 281–2
orientation scaffolds 266
outreach 117
Overberg, P. 93

paid work *see* work/employment
Palincsar, A.S. 268
Palloff, R.M. 266
Palmer, M.M. 213
parental involvement 51
part-time students *see* commuter and part-time students
participation: in decision making 8–9; encouraging in student veterans 331
partnerships, collaborative 67–9
Pascarella, E.T. ix, 5–6, 277, 289
patriarchy 47, 156
Patton, L.D. 20, 42, 46, 126
Pedersen, P. 85–6
peer groups, male 161
peer interactions: athletes 216–17; students with disabilities 192–3
peer mentoring programs 49, 349
peer networks 27
peer-reviewed journals 55–6, 57
peers, learning with 5
Pennington, R. 275
perceived discrimination 109
perceptions of climate 123–4
Perry, P. 77–8
persistence 3–4; online learners 257, 258–9; transfer students 276–7
Person, D.S. 46
person-first language 187–8
personal attributes 229–30
personal loneliness 108

personal stage of socialization 345
Peter, K. 291
Pew Forum on Religion and Public Life survey 173–4
physical barriers 196
physics 159
placement exams 317
Pollack, W.S. 161–2
Pope, R.L. 202
portal technology 302
positionality 158
post-enrollment transition programs 199
poststructuralism: feminist 156–9, 163–4, 166; low-income students 240, 243–6
poverty 225, 226, 227, 250; *see also* low-income students
power 83, 149
power distance 259
practical assistance 116–17
practice, guided by theory 9–11
Pratt, K. 266
praxis 9
preadmission transition programs 199
predictive modeling 282
predisposition to transfer 274
prejudice 19
presence: development of in the online environment 261–2; strategies to develop 265–6
presses, environmental 62
prime timers 309–10
prior college credits 317
prior learning assessment (PLA) 317–18
prioritization: men of color 66; transfer students 279
private beta press 62
privilege: affluent students 244–5; Christian 173–5, 181; White 83
problematic White identities 78
procedural scaffolding 263, 266–7
professional degrees 339–40, 341–2
professional development: faculty 29, 143–4, 333–4, 350; for student leaders 28–9; on trans issues 143–4; validation of veterans 333–4
professional students *see* graduate and professional students
programmatic missions 25
progress, charting 302–3
'proving process' 16
psychological climate 22–3; religious minority students 177–8, 179
public policies 22, 178; historical perspective and low-income students 243–4; racial categories 92–3, 94
Purdue University 250
Pusch, R.S. 137–8
pushing through barriers 45–7

Quaye, S.J. 6
queer theory 129, 130–1

self-identification of disability 195–6, 198
self-reflection 7
self-segregation 28
'separatist' stage 296
September 11 2001 terrorist attacks 111, 177
service disconnected youth 223
service-learning projects 165
Servicemembers Opportunity Colleges (SOCs) 335
sex, and gender 135–6
sex roles 159, 160–1
sexual orientation: disclosure of 123; intersection with multiracial identity 98–9; LGB *see* lesbian, gay and bisexual (LGB) students
Sharma, P. 266
Shield, R.W. 231
Simmons, S.L. 126
Simons, H.D. 211, 214
Sims, S. 75
single-loop learning 61
situational identity 96
small seminars 329
Smith, D. 17
social class 126
social conservatism 180–1
social constructionism 150; students with disabilities 190–1
Social Constructionist Model 159–62, 163–4, 166
social integration 274, 276
social interactions 192–3
social isolation 19, 108–9
social loneliness 108
social presence 261, 265
social relationships *see* relationships
social structures 157–8
socialization theory 344–5, 351
societal context 92–3
sociocultural theory 262–3
socio-historical forces 22, 178
sororities 60, 124, 152, 251
Spears, R. 109
spiritual quest 180
spirituality 46, 126–7, 180–1
sports: engaging student athletes *see* athletes; gender identity development 152, 162
Square Pegs conceptual framework 311–16
staff: incorporating multiple perspectives 334; multiracial 100; validating student veterans 333–4; *see also* faculty, student affairs educators
stakeholder collaboration 66–7
static scaffolding 266
Statistical Directive 15 82, 83
status levels 80
Stavredes, T.M. 263–4, 266, 267, 268
Stefancic, J. 63
Stein, E.L. 344–5
STEM areas 106
Stenard, R.A. 259

stereotype threat 16–17
stereotypes: racial 16–17, 41–3, 46–7; religious 177–8; women of color 41–3, 46–7
stigma 195
Stodden, R.A. 202
Strange, C.C. 7, 8–9, 62, 191
strategic planning 66
strategic scaffolding 263–4, 268
street youth 223, 224
stress 343
Strohl, J. 312–13
structural (compositional) diversity 22–3, 123–4, 179
Stryker, S. 135–6
student advisory committees 28
student affairs educators 10–11; collaboration with athletic department administrators 217; collaboration with disability service offices 201; outreach among 117; and students with disabilities 195, 201, 202–3; training in identity development 164
student affairs offices, multicultural 86–7
student agency 246, 252
student athletes *see* athletes
Student Athletes' Motivation toward Sports and Academics Questionnaire (SAMSAQ) 211, 214, 216
student development programs 198
student-directed learning strategies 264
student engagement strategies: adult learners 316–18; athletes 216–18; commuter and part-time students 297–304; gender identity development 163–5; graduate and professional students 348–50; homeless students 231–3; international students 114–18; LGB students 129–31; low-income students 246–52; men of color 67–9; multiracial students 99–102; online learners 264–8; religious minority students 181–3; student veterans 328–35; students of color 25–30; students with disabilities 197–203; trans students 142–5; transfer students 280–4; White students 83–7; women of color 48–51
Student Exchange Visitor Information System (SEVIS) 111
student leaders: commuter and part-time students 302; men of color 59–60; multiracial students 101; professional development for 28–9; women of color 49
student organizations: connecting transfer students with 283–4; culturally-focused 19–20, 20–1, 26; equal treatment of 100–1; low-income students and 251; multiracial 94–5, 100–1; race/ethnicity-based 26, 94–5; religious minorities 180, 181
student outcomes 3
student services *see* support services
student support groups 164, 349
student veterans *see* veterans

students of color 7–8, 15–35; campus racial climate and culture 21–5; classroom environments 16–18; co-curricular environments 18–21; low-income students 240; men of color *see* men of color; student engagement strategies 25–30; women of color *see* women of color

students with disabilities 187–207; barriers to engagement 194–7; disability and impairment 187–8; historical and demographical enrollment trends 188–9; issues facing 191–7; student engagement strategies 197–203; theoretical perspectives 190–1

success *see* academic success

Sue, D.W. 40, 45

Summer, L. 221–2

summer bridge programs 27–8

support: external 229, 230–1; familial 229, 230; financial 116, 279; LGB students 131; strategies to support students from various backgrounds 264–5; students who work 248; transfer students 279

support groups 164, 349

support networks 293

support services: collaboration between athletics services and student affairs 217; graduate and professional students 348–9; international students and 110; LGBT 144–5; low-income students 251–2; religious minority students 180; trans students 138; universal design 198

supportive campus environment 5, 238; low-income students 251–2

Swain, J. 161

swirling 291

symbols, cultural 164

Syracuse University Multicultural Living-Learning Community 87

systems youth 223, 225

Talburt, S. 129

task forces *see* committees and task forces

teacher-directed learning strategies 264

Teachers Insurance and Annuity Association of America (TIAA) 173

teaching presence 261, 262, 265–6

technology 106; access to and dependence on 316–17; *see also* information technology, online learners

Terenzini, P.T. ix

terrorist attacks of September 11 2001 111, 177

textbooks 249

themed communities/housing 50, 182

theory: adult learners 310–16; athletes 213–16; commuter and part-time students 294–6; gender identity development 156–62; graduate and professional students 343–7; international students 112–14; LGB students 127–9; low-income students 240–6; men of color 60–5; multiracial students 95–9; online learners

261–4; practice guided by 9–11; religious minority students 178–81; resiliency and homeless students 228–31; students of color 21–5; students with disabilities 190–1; trans students 139–42; transfer students 278–80; veterans 326–8; White students 79–83; women of color 47–8

Thoma, C.A. 195

Thomas, D.M. 46

Thompson, B. 81, 82

throwaway youth 223

Tidwell, R. 113

Tierney, W. 224

time allocation/management 115, 241, 278, 343

time constraints 237, 250–1

Tinto, V. 4, 258–9

Tisdell, E.J. 157, 158

Titus, M.A. 241

Torino, G.C. 40

Toro, P.A. 225

Torres, V. 149

Townsend, B.K. 277

Trade Adjustment Act (TAA) 318

traditional White racial identity models 79–81

training: diversity 100; validation of veterans 333–4; *see also* professional development

trans college student identity development framework 141–2

trans oppression 135, 137

trans students 135–48; defining terms 135–7; issues 137–9; student engagement strategies 142–5; theories and concepts 139–42

transfer equivalencies website 282

transfer-receptive culture 279–80

transfer seminar course 283

transfer shock 275

transfer students 271–87; challenges 274–8; characteristics 273–4; student engagement strategies 280–4; theoretical framework 278–80

transition programs: and gender identity 164; students with disabilities 198–9; summer bridge programs for students of color 27–8

transition theory 295–6

transitioning (trans students) 139

transitions of student veterans 325

transportation 292–3

transsexuals 136; 14-stage model of identity development 140–1

Turner, B. 16

Twale, D.J. 344–5

typology of homeless youth 224

Umbach, P.D. 213

unaccompanied youth 223, 224

unachieved attitudes 80

uncertainty avoidance 260

understanding before acting 7–9

unexpected maltreatment 117

40118333R00218

Made in the USA
Middletown, DE
03 February 2017